Which? Way to
Save & Invest

Which? Way to
Save & Invest

CONSUMERS' ASSOCIATION

Which? Books are commissioned and researched by
Consumers' Association and published by
Which? Ltd, 2 Marylebone Road, London NW1 4DF
Email address: *books@which.net*

Distributed by the Penguin Group:
Penguin Books Ltd, 80 Strand, London WC2R 0RL

Chief contributor: Mick McAteer
Other contributors: Anthony Bailey, Jonquil Lowe, Mike Naylor and
Virginia Wallis

First edition 1982
Second edition 1983
Third edition 1988
Fourth edition August 1989
Fifth edition January 1991
Sixth edition January 1993
Seventh edition April 1994
Eighth edition April 1995
Ninth edition April 1997, reprinted October 1997
Tenth edition September 1998
Eleventh edition September 1999
Twelfth edition September 2000
Thirteenth edition September 2001

British Library Cataloguing-in-Publication Data
A catalogue record for this book is available from the British Library

ISBN 0 85202 876 8

For a full list of Which? books, please write to Which? Books,
Castlemead, Gascoyne Way, Hertford X, SG14 1LH
or access our web site at *www.which.net*

Editorial and production by Vicky Fisher and Robert Gray
Typographic design by Lee Riches
Cover design by Sarah Watson
Cover photograph by gettyone Stone
Typeset by SetSystems, Saffron Walden, Essex
Printed in England by Clays Ltd, St Ives plc

Contents

* An asterisk next to the name of an organisation or a publication in the text indicates that the address can be found in this section.

Introduction

It has been another turbulent year on the world's stock markets. All the major markets suffered significant falls to the end of June 2001 – UK shares (including dividend payments) fell by 8 per cent, US shares by 9 per cent in sterling terms, European shares by 17 per cent, and Japanese shares by 24 per cent. The rout in the dotcom and technology shares continued – the FTSE techMARK 100 index fell by a massive 47 per cent. In contrast, investors in government bonds achieved a positive return of 2.5 per cent.

It's at times such as these that consumers need to know how to develop a strategy that helps them to set long-term financial goals, how to choose the sort of investments that are right for their personal circumstances, how to manage the risks involved, and how to shop around to get the best deal available so that hard-earned cash is put to work. *Which? Way to Save & Invest* can help to formulate that strategy and offer independent, unbiased advice.

Many financial and economic experts think that the UK has entered a sustained period of low inflation and low interest rates. Moreover, many of them believe that, even with the large fall in share prices, some of the major stock markets remain overvalued, with the result that some analysts have now revised downwards their forecasts for future investment growth. In the past, the general consensus was that if you were thinking about investing in the stock market you should invest for at least five years. Now many are saying that you should be prepared to invest for up to ten years to make sure that the returns from share-based investments significantly outstrip safer investments such as government bonds and cash.

Mortgage endowment policies

The financial services industry has been hit by yet another major scandal since the last edition of this book. The general reduction in forecast investment growth has caused particular concerns for the millions of consumers who took out a mortgage endowment policy in the late 1980s and early 1990s to repay their mortgage. A recent survey by the Financial Services Authority (FSA) showed that fewer than ten per cent of people interviewed said they had been informed that there was a risk that the endowment might not grow enough to repay the mortgage. The majority of those surveyed said that they were told that the endowment would be 'guaranteed to' or would 'definitely' pay off the mortgage. However, because of the high up-front charges imposed by the life-insurance industry on mortgage endowments, and the reduction in forecasts for future investment growth, a huge number of these policies are no longer on track to repay the mortgage. Indeed, the latest research indicates that 45 per cent of policyholders have recently received a letter from their mortgage endowment provider showing that a shortfall on the mortgage is likely or possible. The latest FSA survey revealed that many policyholders are not taking action to make up the shortfall in their mortgage payments. They may have good reason not to, for example if they no longer need the policy to repay the mortgage. But it is also clear that many need to do so or else they could end up being unable to pay off their mortgage. As Chapter 1 stresses: before you start to worry about your investment needs you must ensure that you have covered the basics – and making sure you have something in place to pay off your mortgage is one of those basics. The FSA has produced a fact sheet, 'Your Endowment Mortgage – Time to Decide', which can be obtained from the FSA Consumer Helpline on (0845) 606 1234.

More financial reviews

Two major reviews of the financial services industry were announced by the regulator and the government in early 2001. First, the FSA has set up a review of with-profits funds following a sustained campaign from Consumers' Association (CA). About ten million people have a stake in a with-profits fund, through their mortgage endowment policy, a with-profits bond, annuity or pension fund. Such investments are hugely important in people's lives, yet the way in which the funds are operated and the lack of protection for policyholders are sources of major concern. These funds are sold as a less risky way for consumers to get access to the stock market compared to direct investments such as unit trusts. The providers claim that these funds smooth out the inherent fluctuations in stock markets. However, CA's research found that while this smoothing may happen behind the scenes, in practice many consumers do not reap the benefit of it and actually lose out (see Chapter 23).

The findings of the with-profits review will feed into the influential Sandler review. This was instigated by the Chancellor Gordon Brown in March 2001 and will take a wide-ranging look at the long-term savings and investment market. The review will concentrate on issues such as the information provided to consumers, financial advice, the role of commission payments in the sales process, and the suitability of products. It is hoped that the outcome of the Sandler review will result in financial services companies designing flexible, value-for-money products that meet the changing needs of the consumers rather than the commercial needs of the companies.

On the issue of regulation, the Treasury announced in July 2001 that, after many delays, 'N2' will finally happen at midnight on 30 November 2001. N2 is the date when the FSA will officially become the single statutory financial regulator for the UK, and will put into force the legal provisions of the Financial Services and Markets Act. Given the litany of financial scandals consumers have suffered at the hands of the financial services industry over the years, much is expected of the FSA to ensure that the industry has cleaned up its act. And given the powers that it will soon have, the FSA will have no excuse for not protecting consumers.

Finally, an indication that ethical investment has at last become established came with the launch of a new stock-market index, FTSE4Good. This tracks the performance of the shares in listed companies which meet certain criteria. This index will help ethical investors to track and compare how well their own investments are performing against a similar basket of shares.

1 Your investment strategy for life

Whether you are a small-scale investor, or whether you are looking for a home for many thousands of pounds, your problem will not be lack of choice. Two years ago *Which?* estimated that there were around 30,000 financial products on the market. That number is bound to have increased, so the big challenge is to put yourself into a position to make a sensible and informed choice.

Everyone has different needs but, whatever your circumstances, it pays to plan ahead for the future. You need to work out a strategy which suits your requirements. A strategy allows you to set realistic objectives and, importantly, helps you to discipline yourself to use your finances efficiently and make your money work as hard as it can for you. A good investment strategy is a set of long-term plans that help you set and reach your financial goals.

This book tells you how to develop a successful strategy, based on a six-point plan, which will help you stay on course.

A six-point plan
1 Sort out the basics first
Before you start to worry about your investment needs, you must ensure you have covered the basics: your home, your pension, your dependants and funds for emergencies (see the 'Investment priorities checklist', page 12). Then you can work out how much you can afford to invest. One of the golden rules is 'Only invest what you can afford to lose.'

2 Know your objectives
Before you start to save and invest, be clear about your objectives. You should know why you are investing. Are you looking to boost your income now? Or are you planning to invest for long-term growth, for example to boost your income in retirement or to provide for your children? Take into account your personal circumstances – your health, your family situation, how long you can invest for – and decide how much risk you are willing to take. Once you know what you are looking for, you can narrow down your search for suitable products. See page 13 for an 'Investment strategy checklist' and page 16, 'Your aims in investing'.

3 Make the most of your hard-earned money

Use suitable tax-efficient investments where you can. Your personal circumstances will affect your tax position (see Chapters 10 and 11). Similarly, try to get a good deal when you save and invest. Remember, cheapest is not always best as the cheapest product might not be exactly right for your personal circumstances; but there is no point in paying unnecessarily high charges. High charges simply eat into your money. Also be careful of hidden charges. Many investment-based products will appear to be good value if you hold on to them long-term. But, if you want to switch to a new provider or cannot keep up payments, then you may incur severe penalties. It is critical that the charging structure of the product you choose suits your circumstances. These pitfalls apply particularly to investment-based life-insurance products (see Chapter 23).

4 Manage the risk involved

Almost every savings and investment product carries some element of risk, some more than others. Generally speaking, the higher the long-term return you need, the higher the risk you have to take, but there is no point taking more risk than is necessary. Equally, do not let the element of risk put you off – it is part of the process. There are simple steps you can take to manage some of the risk out of your plan. Chapter 4 – *Risk and how to live with it* – helps you identify your attitude to risk, covers the different types of risk and provides advice for minimising the chances of things going wrong.

5 Monitor your savings and investments regularly

If you want your investment strategy to be effective, you must monitor your savings and investment portfolio regularly to make sure your plans are still on course to meet your objectives. Bear in mind that your needs change as your circumstances and lifestyle change: the objectives you have during each different stage of your life are unlikely to be the same as the ones you had on starting out. But also, at a more basic level, you need to check your savings and investments regularly to make sure you are getting the best rates available and that your investments are performing well. You want to make your money work hard for you and keeping an eye on the rates and making the most of your savings makes a big difference over time.

Chapter 5 – *Monitoring your investments* – helps you keep track of your investments, shows you how to work out what is right for you at different stages of your life and gives advice on how to get the best from your savings and investments.

6 Protect yourself

There is another golden rule in the world of savings and investments: do not believe the hype – if it sounds too good to be true, then it probably is. The entire regulatory framework has been reformed and watchdogs such as Consumers' Association and *Which?* magazine will be watching closely to see if the Financial Services Authority (FSA)* does a better job than its predecessors in preventing scandals and improving the quality of financial services products in the UK. However, it is not all down to the regulators: consumers need to take responsibility for their decisions and you can protect yourself by not walking blindfold into your investment transactions.

The three chapters you need to read in order to protect yourself are grouped together. 'Forewarned is forearmed' is an important principle and Chapter 6 deals with the basics of protection. It tells you what rules and regulations are there to protect you, who to complain to and how to seek compensation if things go wrong. This is becoming more important now that the Internet is changing the way financial products are bought and sold. (There is a separate chapter on what the Internet means for savers and investors – see Chapter 9.)

If you are not confident about going it alone, it is worth considering getting advice (see Chapter 7). For some investments, if you go it alone, you can lose much of the protection that comes with advice and the money you spend on advice can repay itself in the long run. But this depends on how confident and experienced you are and how complex the products are: you probably do not need advice for simple products such as savings accounts but we would suggest, for example, that everyone except the most experienced and confident should get advice when buying a pension plan.

One of the most important things to remember is to shop around for the best deal. But recent research from the FSA suggests that prospective customers are requesting details from one provider only on the back of seeing an advertisement for the product. Consumers are not comparing the features of a number of products. Advertisements can be persuasive and influential, so it is important that you do not take them at face value. It may be time consuming and you may have more pressing priorities to deal with, but make sure you request details from around six providers so you can compare products and choose the best deal.

A new sense of realism

One thing that has changed over the past two years is that a new sense of realism has crept into the investment markets.

It has become accepted wisdom that investors in equities can no longer expect the same fantastic growth rates seen over the past 20 years or so. Investors' expectations are being revised downwards and lower investment returns are expected to be the norm.

This has happened for two main reasons. First, as the general consensus is that the UK has entered an era of sustained low inflation, the regulators revised downwards their projections for investment growth rates. Second, as returns from the stockmarket have been so good over the past 20 years or so there are doubts that this momentum can be maintained.

A period of turmoil

The past year or so has certainly not been easy for investors, with markets fluctuating wildly on the back of fears over the USA economy and further bad news for the technology and dotcom shares. At the time of writing, the FTSE 100 index was around 15 per cent off its previous all-time high. Just a couple of weeks earlier the index had fallen to a point where it was 25 per cent below the peak but then staged a 10 per cent recovery.

Expert opinion is divided as to which way the market will go next. Many experts believe the market remains overvalued and shares have still some way to fall. Others take the view that, while markets had risen too high and had to fall, share prices have now gone too far the other way. This group thinks that the markets have fallen to a level that represents reasonable value and shares are worth buying again.

Truth is, no one can ever predict how the market will behave. To judge by the experience of history, equity investments remain the best way to deliver real long-term growth. But, by comparison with the past 25 years, investors may have to accept that nominal returns may not be as high in future.

One of the basic rules of saving and investing is that unless you can afford to keep invested for at least five years you should not choose equity-based products. Now experts are saying that investors might have to be prepared to invest over a ten-year period to ensure that the return on investment from equities is substantially greater than from safer assets.

For most people fortunes are not made overnight on the stockmarket. Investing with a long-term view in mind, and taking steps to minimise the risks involved, is the best approach to investment.

Chapter 8 deals with financial advertisements. Successful saving and investing is all about making informed choices and decisions. This chapter helps you to spot the tricks of the advertising pages and work out whether something is as good as it claims.

Investment priorities checklist

Whatever your personal circumstances, there are some basics that you need to consider *before* you start thinking about investments in detail.

Are you buying your own home?

Owning property has been less financially attractive following the boom years of the late 1980s, as the graph in Chapter 28 shows, but over the long term investing in property still tends to produce a real investment return over inflation.

Your home, if you buy it, is probably the biggest financial commitment you will ever make and managing your mortgage to your best advantage must be one of your first considerations.

If you have got money to invest, repaying part of your mortgage can make financial sense, depending on how big your mortgage is, how interest rates on borrowing and investing compare and how much flexibility you have if your financial circumstances change.

Are you planning for your retirement?

Most experts are convinced that, in years to come, state pensions will be worth little. It is likely that we will all have to take more responsibility for providing financially for our old age. So, although you cannot predict the future, the sooner you start to make some provision for what it could bring, the easier it is to cope when the time comes. In Chapters 16 and 17, we give details of pension schemes, both from the state and from employers, and in Chapter 18 we tell you about the stakeholder pensions introduced in April of this year. Try to work out how well off the state pension, together with any employer's pension and income from your savings, will leave you – see Chapter 14, *A comfortable retirement*. If you are self-employed, or not in an employer's pension scheme, consider taking out a stakeholder pension or a personal pension plan (see Chapter 18 for details).

Are your dependants protected?
What would happen if you died tomorrow? Would your mortgage be paid off? Would your spouse have to go back to work earlier than planned? Would he or she have enough income to pay someone to look after the children?

For most people, the solution to this protection problem is life insurance, not saving and investing. A cheap type of life insurance is *term insurance* – see Chapter 23.

Have you put some money aside for emergencies?
Could you cope with an unexpected disaster (major car repairs or damage to your home, say)? If not, build up an emergency fund from which you will be able to withdraw the money at short notice (within about a week). See 'Investing your emergency fund', on page 16, and Chapters 2 and 3 for investments to consider.

Investment strategy checklist
Once you have sorted out the basics, your next step is to choose the investments that are best for you, taking your own personal circumstances and aims into account.

Some investments make sense only for people of a certain age (e.g. annuities for the over-70s); others (e.g. school fees policies) are obviously aimed only at those with children to educate. These are extreme examples of how personal circumstances shape investment strategy. Even so, like most people, you will probably find that there is an overall purpose to your saving and investing. You may be saving for something in particular – a new car or a holiday, for example – or simply to accumulate cash.

Different investments may be suitable for each purpose, so most people are likely to end up putting their money into a variety of investments. It is worth thinking about the points below and reading the section on 'Keeping up with inflation' in this chapter and Chapter 4, *Risk and how to live with it,* before you decide on a particular investment. When comparing interest rates on different investments, see 'Keep an eye on interest rates' on page 54.

Your age
The world isn't as predictable as it was and our lives do not always follow a pattern; but your age remains one of the most important factors. If you are 50, for example, you are more likely to be concerned with saving for retirement and how to invest any lump sum you receive than with building up a deposit for your first home. Your children may be off your hands too, leaving you with spare cash to save.

Your health
If you have a weak heart, for example, you may find it difficult (or expensive) to get the right kind or amount of life insurance. You may want to supplement your life cover with additional savings. Investing through a life-insurance policy is likely to be less worthwhile for you than for someone in good health.

Your family
You may want to save up (or invest a lump sum) for your children's education. And you need to think about how your assets will be passed on when you die. You may want to build up a capital sum for your heirs to inherit.

Your expectations

If you expect your income to drop at some point (when you start a family, perhaps, or when you retire), you may want to build up savings to draw on when you are less well-off. On the other hand, if you expect a big rise in salary (when you get an additional qualification, say, or finish training), you may feel you can run down your savings, since you expect to be better off later. Alternatively, you may be coming into a large inheritance and need to find a suitable home for it.

Your tax position

You should always consider the effect of your tax position before making an investment decision. Some investments are particularly suitable for non-taxpayers, while others may be especially good for higher-rate taxpayers. We cover tax in Chapters 10 and 11. People aged over 64 should look out for the effect of losing age-related allowances.

What you want from your investments

If you want to build up a fund for next year's holiday, you probably need to consider a different range of investments from those of someone saving up for retirement or passing on a capital sum to his or her heirs. Similarly, if you are looking for a high income from your investments, the ones you select will differ from those chosen by someone prepared to accept a mixture of income and capital growth. For more details, see Chapter 3.

How much you can invest

How much money can you afford to invest? Some investments are open to you only if you have a sufficiently large lump sum, whereas other investments are open only to those who can save a regular sum each month. Others are more flexible and can take your savings as and when you want to increase your investment.

How long you can invest for

The length of time you can invest for is important, too, because it affects how much risk you can take. Experts advise that you should consider stocks and shares only if you plan to invest for, at the minimum, five years. Anything less and you would be at risk from the volatile nature of stock markets.

You also need to think carefully before you commit yourself to saving a definite amount each month for a long time (25 years, for example) or locking up a lump sum for a lengthy period. All sorts of changes could happen over the period of the investment that might make it hard or inappropriate to continue with them, and most long-term savings plans penalise you if you cash in early.

The range of investments you are prepared to consider

When you save or invest your money, it will be put to work – for instance, a unit trust company may well use your money to buy shares in a company that the unit trust managers think will provide them with a good return. But you may want to restrict the uses to which your money is put: for example, you may not want it invested in companies making military weapons. Alternatively you might want to see your money going to help causes you support. These days, there is a range of *ethical investments* designed to make this easier – see Chapter 29.

Keeping up with inflation

With some savings, the amount of the capital you invest stays the same; but, of course, this does not allow for the effects of inflation. If inflation averages 2.5 per cent a year, and you invest £1,000 now, spend the income (i.e. any interest) from the investment and get your £1,000 back in five years' time, it will be worth only around £884 in terms of today's buying power – and, if you got your money back in 20 years' time, it would be worth only £610.

Looked at another way, an inflation rate of 5 per cent means that you have to see the total value of your investments (after allowing for tax) rise by at least 5 per cent a year on average, just to be able to spend that money in the future in the same way as you can today. That is before you draw an income from your investment.

The diagram below shows the devastating effect of long-term inflation, even at the current low levels. Bear this in mind when considering how much your investments (or the income from them) will be worth in the future.

One strategy you could consider for long-term investing is to go for index-linked investments, which keep pace with inflation (and perhaps give a little extra interest too). Alternatively, you could go for riskier investments like unit trusts, shares or alternative investments (see Chapter 30), which might do better than keep up with inflation (but could do a lot worse or even end up worth less than at the start).

In the diagram on page 17, we compare the rates of return you might have achieved over different periods of time for various lump-sum investments. You can see that over the longer period the riskier investments, such as shares, have made a better job of keeping up with inflation than have safer ones, such as deposits with building societies. On the other hand, some of the more conservative homes for your money, such as building society ordinary shares, have produced a more

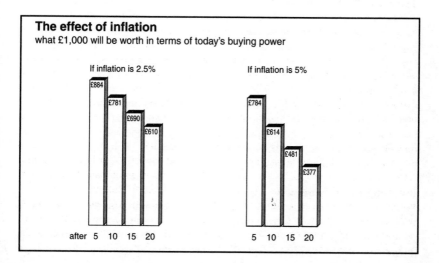

The effect of inflation
what £1,000 will be worth in terms of today's buying power

If inflation is 2.5%

£884
£781
£690
£610

after 5   10   15   20

If inflation is 5%

£784
£614
£481
£377

5   10   15   20

constant and reliable return. (Note that over different periods the results have been very different, so do not use this diagram in isolation to draw conclusions about where to invest your money.)

You may be prepared to put up with a drop in purchasing power for some of your money because, for example, you are looking for a particularly 'safe' investment or you want to be able to withdraw your money at short notice (e.g. for your emergency fund).

Investing your emergency fund

When deciding on a home for this part of your capital, you need to look for three things:

- safety – no risk that, when you cash in, you will get fewer pounds back than you put in
- instant accessibility – you do not usually get even two weeks' notice of an emergency, so you want to be able to get the money back on the spot or in a couple of days at most
- highest possible return – though you have to be prepared to take less than you get for an investment that ties your money up for longer. But do not forget to shop around. This is crucial in today's low interest-rate environment. In some cases you will find you can get a better interest rate from an instant-access account than from a notice account.

See the route maps in Chapter 2 for some suggestions. Remember to update regularly the amount of money you keep in reserve for emergencies. Inflation erodes its buying power unless you reinvest the interest you get.

Your aims in investing

Many people want their investments to produce an income now. Others invest for capital growth to provide an income later (on retirement, say), to pass capital on to their heirs or to buy something (a house or car, for example). Below, we outline some factors to consider in each case. You might in fact want a combination of income and growth.

Of course you can always cash in some investments from time to time to give you an income to live on. Equally, if you reinvest income from your investments, the value of your capital should go up over time. However, there can be considerable tax differences between receiving income or capital gain (see the box on 'Building capital by reinvesting income' on page 19).

Investing for income now
You need to consider how long you are likely to go on needing the income from your investments. If it is for more than a couple of years, you cannot afford to ignore the effect of inflation on the purchasing power of any income your investments produce. You will need a rising income. To achieve this, you are

Table 1: Investments compared: This table shows you how much you got back 'in the first quarter of 2001' on £1,000 invested 5, 10, 15 and 20 years before

	first quarter 1996	first quarter 1991	first quarter 1986	first quarter 1981
UK shares (1)	1,678	3,071	5,356	16,536
UK Government Bonds (Gilts) (2)	1,520	2,332	3,140	5,786
Houses (3)	1,635	1,540	2,356	3,539
Typical savings account (4)	1,084	1,312	1,889	2,717
What you needed to keep pace with inflation (5)	1,140	1,314	1,781	2,425

(1) Based on the FTSE All Share Index, net income reinvested; source Hindsight REUTERS
(2) Based on the FTSE Actuaries British Government All Stocks Index, net income reinvested; source Hindsight REUTERS
(3) Source Nationwide Building Society
(4) Based on Money£acts average of £1,000 deposit accounts; source Hindsight REUTERS
(5) Retail price index (income not applicable)

17

likely to have to put some of your capital at risk or buy an index-linked investment. It may be sensible to invest some of your money for capital growth, with a view to cashing in part of it on a regular basis to provide income.

You have to make your own choice about how much of your capital to risk. Put the remainder in a place where the income from it is assured – see the route maps in Chapter 3 for suggestions.

If you do not anticipate having to rely on your extra investment income for longer than a year or two, you may well decide there is no point taking risks to get an income that will keep up with inflation.

If you do not pay tax and if the interest is paid without deduction of tax, some investments may be particularly attractive. These are marked • in the route maps. Other investments, also paid tax-free, look more attractive the higher your rate of tax. These are marked ★ in the route maps. Check in the route maps (and with current rates of return) that your investments are giving you the best possible after-tax return.

Investing to provide income later

If you are going to need your capital to give you an income later, you cannot afford to risk all of it. But you do need to try to make up for the effects of inflation on its buying power over the years between now and the time you plan to draw the income.

You could consider investing part of your money in index-linked National Savings Certificates. With this investment, the value of what you invest is adjusted each month in line with inflation (provided you hold the certificate for at least a year). You can invest up to £10,000 per person or £20,000 jointly as a married couple. You could also consider index-linked gilts – see Chapter 24.

If you have capital left over, it makes sense to put some of it into investments which may give a return high enough to make up for inflation. To minimise the chances of all your risky investments doing a nose-dive at once, follow the advice on risk given in Chapter 4.

Investing to pass on more for your heirs

You may feel you can take risks with more of your capital for longer if the main aim is to pass money on to your heirs.

What you need to be particularly aware of is the impact of inheritance tax on what your heirs will get when you die – though it will not bite unless what you leave (together with taxable gifts made in the seven years before your death) tops £234,000 (in the 2001–2 tax year). This tax-free limit means that many people do not need to worry about potential inheritance tax. However, if you have life insurance, or a mortgage that is covered by a life-insurance policy, these could be included in your total assets, pushing them close to or beyond the limit. To minimise the effect of inheritance tax, consider:

- giving away each year as much as is allowed without incurring any liability to inheritance tax
- taking out life insurance, with the proceeds going straight to your children
- leaving your possessions directly to the youngest generation (your grand-

children, rather than your children) if you want the possessions to go to them eventually.

For more details on inheritance tax, see Chapter 10.[1]

Investing to build up a fund to buy something

If you are investing in order to buy something in the future, bear in mind that the value of some investments (e.g. shares, property or alternative investments) tends to fluctuate, so you may find that when you want to cash in your investments the return is not very good. It makes sense to steer clear of these investments if you are likely to want to use the money in the near future.

If, on the other hand, you need the money in, say, five to ten years' time, you could still go for investments that fluctuate in value. Always be prepared to cash in the investments *before* you need the money (preferably when they are doing well) and transfer the cash to a safer place such as a building society account. It would be a pity if you had to cash in your investment when its value was depressed – for example, by a slump in the share or property markets.

Cashing in investments to give income

With certain lump-sum investments (e.g. single-premium bonds), it is possible to cash in part of the investment each year to give yourself an income. However, you should note that with, for example, single-premium bonds or unit trusts which run a withdrawal scheme the value of your investment fluctuates, so you may have to cash in a higher proportion of your investment from time to time or else face a drop in income. And, if you cash in more than the growth of your bond, you are eating into your capital. This makes it even harder for your capital to meet your income requirements the following year, so you risk reducing your capital even more in future years.

With other investments (e.g. shares and alternative investments) there are no special schemes. You may get a poor price at the time you want to cash part of the investment if you want to sell small parts of your investments to provide an income, and the cost of selling may be high.

Building capital by reinvesting income

As the tax system stands, if you invest for income with a view to reinvesting it to build up capital, you may pay more tax than if you had achieved an equivalent rise in value through a straight capital gain. Most investment income is taxed at either 10 per cent or 32.5 per cent for the 2001–2 tax year, depending on your taxable income. Capital gains are taxed at the same rate but the first £7,200 of capital gains you make by disposing of assets in the 2001–2 tax year is tax-free. If you have not used up all of this tax-free allowance, it may be sensible to invest for capital gains rather than income.

---

[1] See also *The Which? Guide to Giving and Inheriting,* Which? Books

Ethical investment

More and more people are taking an interest in how investment managers use their money. If you are concerned that you may be investing indirectly in companies you do not approve of, see Chapter 29.

The Internet

By changing the way financial products are bought and sold, the Internet has had a huge impact on the savings and investment world. Chapter 9 helps you work out the implications for you.

A bird's-eye view

The table on page 23 and the following pages summarises each of the main types of investment open to you. Later chapters give fuller details.

The table deals with eight key points:

Regular saving or lump sum?
Some investments are open to people who have a fair-sized lump sum of money to invest, others to people who want to save a regular amount each month or year, say. Of course, a lump sum can also be invested on a regular basis.

Some investments are flexible. The minimum amount you can invest is fairly low, so they can be used as homes for lump sums, regular savings and spare cash.

Minimum investment recommended
The minimum sensible amount you can invest is not necessarily the same thing as the minimum amount you are *allowed* to invest. For example, you can invest as little as you like in shares but the commission you must pay can make an investment of less than £1,500 to £2,000 not worthwhile.

Does it pay a regular income?
Some investments pay income direct to you at regular intervals. With others, the income is added on a cumulative basis to your original investment.

With some investments that do not automatically pay an income to you, such as single-premium bonds and National Savings Certificates, you may still be able to secure a regular income by cashing in part of your investment at regular intervals. Indeed, with some investments (such as single-premium bonds), there are often standard schemes to allow you to do this.

Some investments pay an income that is fixed when you take out the investment, for example guaranteed income bonds. With other investments, such as most deposit accounts, the income can vary after you have invested your money.

Remember that, while a fixed-income investment brings certainty, inflation may erode its real value.

You may regret a decision to go for a fixed income if interest rates in general rise; investments with interest rates that vary may turn out to have been better bets. On the other hand, if interest rates in general fall, you will feel pleased with yourself for putting your money in a fixed-income investment.

How long is the investment meant to be for?
This tells you how long you should expect to have to leave your money invested in order to get the best return. Early withdrawal often carries hefty penalties.

Can you get your money back quickly?
In some cases, you cannot get your money back quickly. So do not put your money in one of these investments unless you are certain you will be able to leave it there for the agreed period.

With other investments, you may be able to cash in early but not get back (or not be sure of getting back) what you paid in. So, if you want a certain amount of money at a certain time (e.g. to go on holiday in two years' time), you would be wise to steer clear of these investments.

Can the value of your capital go down?
Investments can be divided into two types.

- The value of the capital you invest stays the same (but, again, bear in mind the effects of inflation).
- The value may go up and down. Unit trusts, single-premium bonds and property are examples of investments in which the value of the capital invested may fluctuate. With investments like these, you stand a chance of making a capital gain but also run the risk of losing some of your money. Because the value of the capital fluctuates, the success of your investment depends very much on *when* you invest and *when* you cash in your investment.

Points about tax
This picks out particular tax points for the various investments. More details on tax are given in Chapters 10 and 11 and in the chapters dealing with each investment.

If you are a higher-rate taxpayer some investments which offer a tax-free return look more attractive, while others may offer a good rate of return before tax but may be less competitive after tax.

Where can you make the investment?
This tells you where to go to put your money in these investments.

Other comments
This gives snippets of information – for example, how some of the investments work, who might find it worthwhile to consider or avoid a particular investment, and specific tax-related advantages.

Type of investment and where to find more details	Alternative investments (e.g. stamps, antique furniture, diamonds, gold) Chapter 30	Annuities Chapter 27
regular saving or lump sum?	lump sum	lump sum
minimum investment recommended	varies	depends on age and required income
does it pay a regular income?	no – and you have to pay for insurance, maintenance and, in some cases, bank security.	yes, normally arranged at the time you buy the annuity. The older you are at that time, the higher the income
how long is investment meant to be for?	in the main, long-term investment	until you die
can you get your money back quickly?	as quickly as you can find a buyer. But you may get back less than you invested	no – once you buy an annuity, you can never cash it in
can the value of your capital go down?	yes	not applicable – you cannot get capital back
points about tax	no capital gains tax unless the value of the item at the time of disposal is more than £6,000 (post-1837 UK gold sovereigns and Britannia coins are free of CGT). If you count as a trader, you may have to pay income tax	you get interest and return of part of the capital. Interest is taxable at your highest rate of tax – normally paid after deduction of 20 per cent tax. Annuities you *have* to buy, e.g. as part of a personal pension, are *all* taxed as income
where can you make the investment?	auctions, dealers, other collectors, sometimes investment companies	life insurance company or independent financial adviser
other comments	you need expert knowledge. Watch out for dealer's mark-up	worth considering only for older people (around 70, say). Men get higher income than women of the same age because life expectancy is shorter

Type of investment and where to find more details	Commodities	Corporate bonds Chapter 26
regular saving or lump sum?	lump sum	lump sum
minimum investment recommended	several thousand pounds for direct investment; £3,000, say, for commodity fund or trust	varies – £1,500 is sensible if you buy through a stockbroker
does it pay a regular income?	no, with direct investment. Some funds and trusts pay an income – with others, you can get income by cashing units	yes – income is usually fixed at the time you buy the bond
how long is investment meant to be for?	long-term investment or short-term speculation	can be medium- to long-term, depending on the life of the bond
can you get your money back quickly?	With direct investment, you can sell at any time. With fund or trust, a few days or a month	you can sell stock at any time through a share-dealing service
can the value of your capital go down?	yes	yes – but if you hold stock until its redemption date you know what you will get back
points about tax	gain may be taxed as income or as capital gain, depending on the circumstances	interest is taxable – *accrued income* scheme may apply. Free of capital gains tax if a 'qualifying corporate bond'. Tax-free in an ISA
where can you make the investment?	commodity broker; direct from fund or trust or through financial adviser	stockbroker or other share-dealing service, independent financial advisers
other comments	investing directly in commodities is not sensible for most people. It is very risky – consider a commodity fund or unit trust instead. For legal and tax reasons, funds may be based offshore – Isle of Man or Channel Islands, say	corporate bonds can be a useful way to boost income. Many investors prefer to invest through unit trusts and other funds, rather than direct

Deposit/savings account Chapters 12 and 13	Endowment policies (unit-linked) Chapter 23
either	regular saving
varies – £1 to £10,000 or more	varies – £10 to £50 a month
interest can be withdrawn from most, but not all, types of account	normally no
any period, depending on type of account (e.g. instant access, notice, fixed-term)	at least 10 years
generally you can cash in at any time but you may need to give notice. There can be penalties cashing in a fixed-term account early	you can cash in at any time but you may get back less than you invested (and in the first year or two, you may get little or nothing)
no	yes
20 per cent tax on interest is normally deducted at source. Non-taxpayers can get interest paid gross. Starting-rate taxpayers can reclaim half the tax back. Higher-rate taxpayers have extra tax to pay. Tax-free in an ISA. Special tax rules for some National Savings accounts	insurance fund pays income tax and capital gains tax, so you pay no tax unless you are a higher-rate taxpayer. No higher-rate tax if you keep policy going for at least 10 years or three-quarters of its term, whichever is less
banks, building societies, supermarkets, post office (for National Savings accounts), Internet	life insurance company or independent financial adviser
deposit/savings accounts are referred to as 'cash' in investment speak – hence the term 'cash ISA'	limited appeal except (possibly) to higher-rate taxpayers who keep the policy going for at least 10 years or three-quarters of its term it this is less than ten years

Type of investment and where to find more details	Endowment policies (with-profits) Chapter 23	Enterprise investment schemes and venture capital trusts Chapter 11
regular saving or lump sum?	regular saving (may be monthly or annually)	lump sum
minimum investment recommended	£10 a month, say	£500 to £2,000
does it pay a regular income?	no	many of these high-risk investments in small companies are primarily for growth
how long is investment meant to be for?	10 years or more – the period is usually agreed at the outset	minimum five years for the tax breaks
can you get your money back quickly?	you can surrender the policy at any time but what you get back is often at the discretion of the company (and in the first year or two you may get little or nothing)	it may take longer to find a buyer than for shares of large, well-known companies listed on the Stock Exchange
can the value of your capital go down?	you get at least a guaranteed amount at the end of the policy (or if you die)	yes
points about tax	insurance fund pays income tax and capital gains tax, so you pay no tax unless you are a higher-rate taxpayer. No higher-rate tax if you keep policy going for at least 10 years or three-quarters of its term, whichever is less.	20 per cent tax relief on investments up to a certain level, deferment of capital gains bill on gains reinvested in these schemes, no capital gains tax when you sell, no income tax on dividends of venture capital trusts
where can you make the investment?	life insurance company or independent financial adviser	stockbrokers, independent financial advisers
other comments	often used as a way of repaying a mortgage, can be expensive, inflexible and with no tax advantage	great tax breaks, but high risk – invest money only if you can afford to lose it if the worst happens

Ethical Chapter 29	**Friendly society plans** Chapter 24
either	either
varies	£10 (maximum £25 a month, £270 a year)
some ethical investments are for income, others mainly for growth	no
ethical deposit accounts can be for any period, ethical stock-market investments are mainly medium- to long-term	10 years minimum
depends on the type of ethical investment	you can cash in within ten years but may get little or nothing back
yes, if a stock market investment	you get at least a guaranteed amount at the end of the policy (or if you die)
depends on the type of ethical investment – tax-free in an ISA	you pay no tax on proceeds, the friendly society invests the money in a tax-free fund
Chapter 29 gives sources of advice and information	friendly societies, independent financial advisers
check investment criteria carefully to make sure they fit your own aims (e.g. to avoid arms trade)	these inflexible plans have a tax-free status, but high charges on relatively small premiums can outweigh any small tax benefit

Type of investment and where to find more details	Gilts (British Government stocks) Chapter 24	Guaranteed equity bonds Chapter 26
regular saving or lump sum?	lump sum	lump sum
minimum investment recommended	none if bought through the Bank of England Brokerage Service, otherwise £1,000 is a sensible minimum	varies
does it pay a regular income?	yes – income is fixed at the time you buy the stock (or linked to the Retail Prices Index, if you buy index-linked stocks)	not usually
how long is investment meant to be for?	until stock is due to be redeemed (paid back) by the government – or until you sell, if you want to sell before the redemption date	typically five years
can you get your money back quickly?	you can sell stock at any time. It can take a day or two to get money if sold through a stockbroker, a week or so through the Bank of England Brokerage Service	usually poor value if you cash in early (not always possible)
can the value of your capital go down?	yes – but if you hold stock until redemption, you know for certain what you get back (or, with index-linked stocks, you know the current redemption value, which increases in line with the Retail Prices Index)	you get a guaranteed minimum pay-out at end of term. With some bonds, the guaranteed minimum may be less than you paid in
points about tax	interest is taxable – can be paid without deduction of tax. *Accrued income* scheme may apply. Free of capital gains tax. Tax-free in an ISA	your tax position depends on the form of guaranteed investment – often set up as single-premium investment bonds
where can you make the investment?	stockbroker, post office, high-street bank, independent financial adviser or other intermediary	direct from providers (e.g. banks, building societies, insurance companies), or through independent financial advisers
other comments	the best stock for you depends to a large extent on the rate of tax you pay. Get advice on which stock to choose, e.g. from a stockbroker or bank. Buying and selling costs less for small investments if made through the Bank of England Brokerage Service	you get a guaranteed return based on part of the rise in a stock-market index or your money back if the stock-market falls. These are complicated investments – a suitable unit trust is more flexible and might give better returns

Guaranteed income and growth bonds Chapter 25	Home income schemes Chapter 28
lump sum	lump sum (raised from mortgaging your home)
£1,000 to £10,000 but more for income bonds	normally £15,000
income bonds – yes growth bonds – no	yes – income (from an annuity) is arranged at the time you take out the scheme (the amount depends on your age and sex)
a fixed period, varying from 1 to 10 years	until you die
with some companies, at the end of the agreed period only. With others, you can cash in early – the amount is at the company's discretion	not applicable – you cannot get your money back
no (unless you cash in early)	not applicable – you cannot get your money back
tax treatment depends on how the bonds work – they can work in one of several ways. Check with the company before investing	part of the income is a return of your own capital and is tax-free
life insurance company or independent financial adviser	life insurance company, independent financial adviser, building society
your tax bill could rise, reducing your return, if you or your spouse are over 65 when you cash the bond in	mortgage-based schemes may be suitable only for people well into their 80s, following withdrawal of tax relief on new plans in March 1999

Type of investment and where to find more details	Investment trusts Chapter 22	ISAs – individual savings accounts Chapter 11
regular saving or lump sum?	either	either
minimum investment recommended	£1,000 to £1,500, say, as a lump sum, £25 to £50 with a saving scheme	varies
does it pay a regular income?	yes – most companies pay dividends. These can vary	some ISAs are for income, others mainly for growth
how long is investment meant to be for?	long-term investment or short-term speculation	cash (deposit account) ISAs – any period; life assurance and stock market ISAs – mainly medium- to long-term
can you get your money back quickly?	you can sell and get money back in a week but you may get less than you invested	depends on type of ISA
can the value of your capital go down?	yes	yes if a stock market ISA
points about tax	higher-rate taxpayers have to pay extra tax on dividend income. Non-taxpayers cannot reclaim any tax. Your are liable for capital gains tax on gain. Tax-free in an ISA	returns are free of income tax and capital gains tax – there are limits on how much you can invest each tax year
where can you make the investment?	stockbroker, bank, independent financial adviser or other intermediary; savings schemes from an investment trust management company	most financial service companies – e.g. banks, building societies, fund managers, independent financial advisers
other comments	you buy shares in an investment trust company – a company whose business is investing in other companies' shares	ISAs are a type of tax-shelter rather than an investment

Pension schemes – employers' schemes Chapter 17	Pension schemes – personal pension plans Chapter 18
regular saving	either
some schemes are non-contributory (i.e. the employee pays nothing); with others you pay a fixed percentage of your earnings	say £25 a month or £500 to £1,000 for lump-sum plans
yes – from the time you retire. Often a lump sum on retirement is paid instead of part of your pension	yes – normally from any age between 50 and 75. You can choose to have a lump sum on retirement instead of part of your pension
from the time you join the scheme until you retire or leave the scheme (income, once started, carries on for life)	from the time you begin your payments until your income starts (income carries on for life) or until you transfer to another scheme
contributions must normally stay invested until the scheme's pension age (unless you leave your job within 2 years of joining scheme)	you cannot convert a pension fund into an income (or lump sum and income) until you are 50 or over
depends on the scheme	depends on the scheme
you get tax relief on payments. Investment builds up free of capital gains tax and income tax. The lump sum taken instead of part of your pension is tax-free. The actual pension is taxable	you get tax relief on payments. Investment builds up free of capital gains tax and income tax. The lump sum taken instead of part of the pension is tax-free. The actual pension is taxable
employer	bank, building society, life insurance company, unit trust company, supermarket, independent financial adviser
you can choose to make additional voluntary contributions	start saving as young as possible to give investments longer to grow

Type of investment and where to find more details	Pension schemes – stakeholder pension Chapter 18	Pension schemes – state schemes Chapter 16
regular saving or lump sum?	either	regular saving (through National Insurance contributions)
minimum investment recommended	£20 a month	compulsory contributions depend on what you earn and whether you are employed or self-employed
does it pay a regular income?	yes – normally from any age between 50 and 75. You can choose to have a lump sum on retirement instead of part of your pension	yes, from state pension age (later if you choose)
how long is investment meant to be for?	from the time you begin the payments until the income starts (income carries on for life) or until you transfer to another scheme	you normally make payments until state pension age (income carries on for life)
can you get your money back quickly?	you cannot convert a pension fund into an income (or lump sum and income) until you are 50 or over	you cannot cash in your investment
can the value of your capital go down?	you cannot convert a pension fund into an income (or lump sum and income) until you are 50 or over	not applicable – you cannot get capital back
points about tax	you get tax relief on payments. Investment builds up free of capital gains tax and income tax. The lump sum taken instead of part of pension is tax-free. The actual pension is taxable	There is no tax relief on payments unless it is contracted-out through a pension plan. The pension is taxed as earnings, currently paid without deduction of tax
where can you make the investment?	bank, building society, employer, life insurance company, unit trust company, supermarket, independent financial adviser	payments made through employer or through Inland Revenue National Insurance Contributions Office if self-employed
other comments	start saving as young as possible to give investments longer to grow	if you earn, you cannot opt out of the state scheme altogether but employees may be able to contract out of SERPS

Permanent Interest-Bearing Shares (PIBS) Chapter 12	Premium bonds Chapter 13
lump sum	lump sum
varies from £1,000 to £50,000	£100 (maximum £20,000)
yes – interest is fixed at the time you buy	no – but you might win prizes
no set period	any period – but you cannot win a prize until that bond has been held for one month
in theory, yes, but you may get back less than you invested	allow at least eight working days
yes	no
interest is taxable – *accrued income* scheme may apply. Free of capital gains tax. Tax-free in an ISA	prizes are tax-free
via a stockbroker, not from a building society	post office, high-street bank
issued by some building societies and former building societies that have become banks	prizes are worked out to give an average return at 3.5 per cent (as at 1 September 2001). Prizes are paid monthly and range from £50 to £1,000,000

Type of investment and where to find more details	Property Chapter 28	Shares Chapter 20
regular saving or lump sum?	lump sum	lump sum
minimum investment recommended	depends on the area where you are buying	£1,500 to £2,000, say, in each company
does it pay a regular income?	rental income if you buy a property to let it out	yes – most companies pay dividends. Amounts can vary
how long is investment meant to be for?	high buying and selling costs (e.g. various professionals' fees, stamp duty) usually make property a medium- to long-term investment	in the main, long-term investment. But can also be short-term speculation
can you get your money back quickly?	it depends on the state of the housing market	you can sell shares and get money in one week – but you may get less than you invested
can the value of your capital go down?	yes	yes
points about tax	as well as income tax on the profit you make on the rent, there may (unlike your main home) be capital gains tax when you sell	higher-rate taxpayers have to pay extra tax on dividend income. Non-taxpayers cannot reclaim any tax. You are liable for capital gains tax. Tax-free in an ISA
where can you make the investment?	estate agents (solicitors in Scotland)	stockbroker, bank or other agent, e.g. accountant
other comments	few people have enough cash to buy outright to invest in property; 'buy-to-let' mortgages are widely available	buying shares of just one or two companies is very risky. Special tax rules apply if you invest in higher-risk shares through an Enterprise Investment Scheme or Venture Capital Trust – see Chapter 11

Single-premium investment bonds Chapter 22	Unit trusts and OEICs (open-ended investment companies) Chapter 21
lump sum	either
varies – but often £1,000	for lump sum, often £250 to £1,500; for regular saving, £10 to £100 a month
not usually – but most companies have schemes which let you cash in part of your investment (you can cash up to 5 per cent a year without paying tax at the time)	some are designed to pay income – the amount can vary
in the main, long-term investment	in the main, long-term investment. But can also be short-term speculation
varies – can be straight away, sometimes up to a week or a month. You may get back less than you invested	varies – you can normally sell each day (but it may take a week or so to get paid)
yes	yes
when you cash in the bond, you may have to pay higher-rate tax on the gain you've made (including any amounts you got earlier on, not taxed at the time)	your tax position depends on the investments in the fund. Tax-free in an ISA
life insurance company, independent financial adviser or other intermediary	direct from the company managing the investments or from independent financial adviser, stockbroker, bank
common varieties are with-profits bonds and distribution bonds. Limited appeal except (possibly) to higher-rate tax payers	arguably the best vehicle for people of limited means to invest in the stock market – especially when held in an ISA

3 Choosing the right home for your money

To help narrow down the choice of investments to those which would be most suitable for you, use the route maps later in this chapter. One is for lump sums, the other for savings (either on a regular basis or piecemeal).

Follow the route maps for each separate sum of money you want to invest: for example, once each for your emergency fund, for money you are willing to see fluctuate in value and for money you can invest for ten years. You will end up with a different shortlist for each sum.

For any investments you think might suit you, read the relevant chapter in the book. You should also check in the newspapers for the up-to-date rates of return being offered by the investments you have in mind.

Making your initial choice is just the start of the process. You need to monitor your investments to make sure you are still getting the best return and, as your circumstances change, you have to review your investment objectives to ensure that the investments you hold still suit you. Chapter 5 shows you how to do this.

Example 1: Saving for different needs

Roger and Rose have one child, Alex. Roger earns around £24,000 a year as a teacher; Rose does not go out to work. They want to save for a holiday next year, a new car, furniture and other household and personal items. They do not want to lock their money away for too long. They already have some money saved up in a building society instant-access account and wonder whether that is the best place for it.

First of all, Roger and Rose look at the 'Investment priorities checklist' in Chapter 1.

Both Roger and Rose have life-insurance cover. Their policies will pay out lump sums and a regular income if either partner dies. At present they have £5,000 put aside in a building society instant-access account but they feel that £2,000 is as much as they need in an emergency fund.

Roger and Rose are buying their own home and do not intend to move in the next few years; their £40,000 mortgage is low compared to the value of their house. Roger is in the teachers' pension scheme, which offers good benefits.

Roger and Rose would like to save something each month, so they have got to decide how to invest:

- their £2,000 emergency fund
- their additional £3,000, now in the building society account
- the money they manage to save in future.

They use the 'Investment strategy checklist' in Chapter 1 to help sort out their investment plan:

Age Roger is 30 and Rose 28. Rose is hoping to go back to work when Alex, their three-year-old, goes to school. Sensibly they are not going to rely on this.

Health Both are in good health.

Family Apart from Alex, there are no immediate dependants. But they feel that, if their parents were widowed or became ill, they would like to help out. At the moment, this prospect seems unlikely but it means they do not feel like committing themselves to very long-term savings, which they might not be able to keep up. They do not intend giving Alex a private education. If they did, they would consider saving in a school-fees scheme.

Expectations If Rose cannot go back to her old job, she might need retraining. This could involve some expense. There are no large inheritances coming their way, though eventually they will share in the proceeds from the sale of their parents' houses.

Tax Roger is a basic-rate taxpayer and any investment income will not put him into the higher-rate tax bracket. However, Rose does not pay tax and any investment income is unlikely to put her into the starting- or basic-rate tax brackets. It would make sense to put all their investments in her name only, so that she can make use of her personal allowance.

What they want from their investments Their main aims are to pay for a holiday next year and later for a new car; to pay for any retraining that Rose may need in a couple of years; and to be able to help out their parents, if necessary. They are not looking for income from their investments.

How much they can invest Apart from the £5,000 in the building society, they can save about £100 a month but most of this is earmarked for their holiday next year.

How long they can invest for Roger and Rose have decided to keep £2,000 as an emergency fund and they need £70 a month of their regular savings available for their planned holiday. The other lump sum of £3,000 and £30-a-month regular savings can be invested for somewhat longer. But long-term investment clearly does not suit their needs.

The range of investments they are prepared to consider Although their main aim is to find a suitable type of investment, they are interested in ethical investments, particularly those that benefit the environment.

Once Roger and Rose have chosen their investments, they keep an eye on what is happening and may move their money around from time to time. However, first they follow the route maps on the following pages to see what choices they have.

Route map for lump sums

Start here for each chunk
of your money

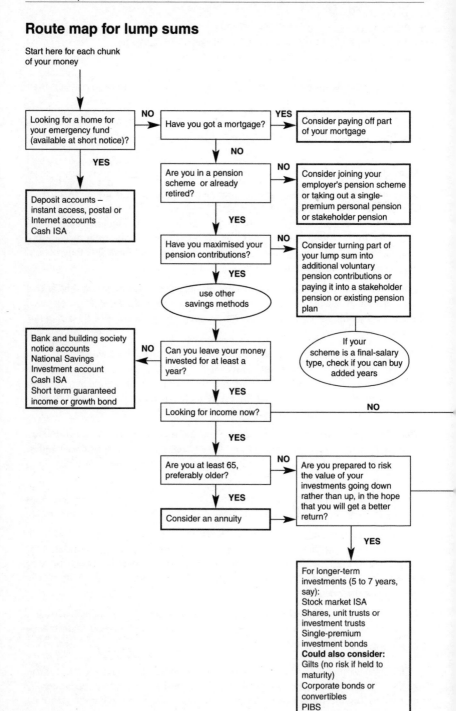

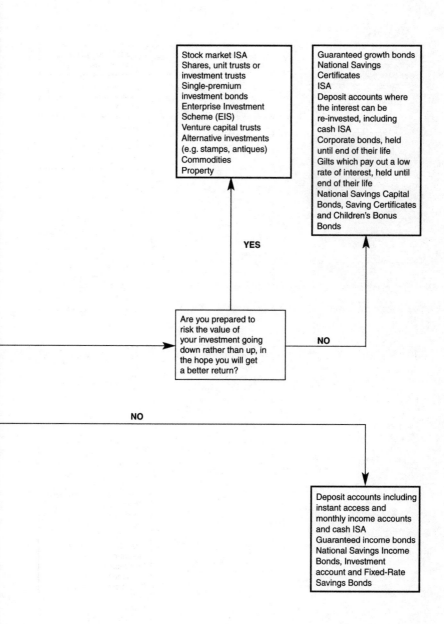

Stock market ISA
Shares, unit trusts or
investment trusts
Single-premium
investment bonds
Enterprise Investment
Scheme (EIS)
Venture capital trusts
Alternative investments
(e.g. stamps, antiques)
Commodities
Property

Guaranteed growth bonds
National Savings
Certificates
ISA
Deposit accounts where
the interest can be
re-invested, including
cash ISA
Corporate bonds, held
until end of their life
Gilts which pay out a low
rate of interest, held until
end of their life
National Savings Capital
Bonds, Saving Certificates
and Children's Bonus
Bonds

YES

Are you prepared to
risk the value of
your investment going
down rather than up, in
the hope you will get
a better return?

NO

NO

Deposit accounts including
instant access and
monthly income accounts
and cash ISA
Guaranteed income bonds
National Savings Income
Bonds, Investment
account and Fixed-Rate
Savings Bonds

Route map for savings

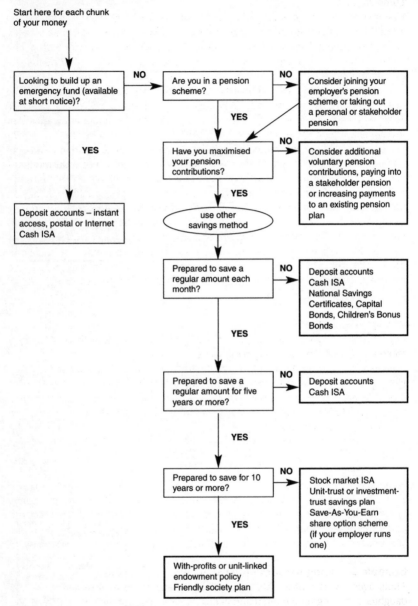

How Roger and Rose choose their investments
Lump sum
First they try to sort out what to do with their fund of £5,000. They intend keeping £2,000 for emergencies and, following the route map, find that a deposit account is the best option. They want to be able to get at their money quickly either with instant access at a branch or through the post with a postal account or by transfer to a current account with an Internet-operated account. They could use a tax-free ISA, as their £2,000 is well within the £3,000 ISA cash limit. They check on the rates of return currently offered. They choose the best-paying instant-access ISA. They will keep a close watch on rates of return in the future, in case other investments offer a better return.

Now they follow the route map again to see what they could do with the £3,000. They skip through the first few steps – they have a moderate mortgage compared to the value of their home, are in a pension scheme, are not close to retirement and can leave their money invested for at least a year. Although they do not need income now, they are not prepared to risk the value of their investment going down. They decide to put £1,000 of their long-term money into their cash ISA, and £2,000 into a top-paying deposit account. The best account they can find for a £2,000 balance is an easy-access account operated by post. It is opened in Rose's name only as she is a non-taxpayer and will be able to apply to have the interest paid gross. When the new tax year beings, on April 6, they can switch up to £3,000 to a cash ISA.

Regular saving
Roger and Rose follow the second route map to see what to do with the £100 they reckon they can save each month.

When considering the £70 a month being saved for their next year's holiday, they come to the question *Prepared to save a regular amount for five years or more?* As the answer is *No*, they decide to put the money in their newly-opened easy-access postal account.

For the remaining £30 a month, they expect to save for between five and ten years, so they choose an ethical unit trust. They can use their £3,000 stock market (mini-) ISA allowance for this – see pages 116–8.

Summary
They invest their £2,000 emergency fund plus £1,000 of their longer-term money in a cash ISA. They put the remaining £2,000 of their longer-term money in a postal deposit account. £70 of their regular monthly savings goes into the postal account and £30 into an ethical unit trust ISA.

Example 2: Saving for something special
Anne, aged 55, is a basic-rate taxpayer. She wants to go to Australia to see her daughter and her grandchildren and needs about £1,000 for the return air fare. She can afford to save around £25 a month, so will need an investment lasting four or five years to save up the fare (which may rise through inflation).

She follows the route map for savings until she gets to the question, *Prepared to save a regular amount each month?* Answering *Yes*, she moves on to consider just how long she can commit herself – not longer than five years.

She opts for a high-interest-paying cash ISA which also lets her pay in additional lump sums. She can save into this account on a regular basis to help her to be disciplined about her savings. She also decides to approach her bank manager to see whether, once she has saved for some time, she could get a 'top-up' loan.

Example 3: Investing with an eye on tax

Paul is in his late 40s, and finds himself with £50,000 from a life-insurance pay-out following the death of his wife Sheila. He lives in his own home with a £75,000 repayment mortgage, has an adequate emergency fund, a cash ISA and enough life insurance to take care of his children's needs should he also die. Paul belongs to an excellent company pension scheme (though as he joined the scheme only in his 30s, he will not quite qualify for a full pension when he reaches 65).

Despite Paul's high salary, private school fees make a big dent in his income and will continue to do so for some time. Therefore, he wants to invest some of his lump sum to increase his income while these fees continue but is worried about extra income tax he might have to pay (he already pays tax at the higher rate of 40 per cent). He also wants to invest a little with as low a risk as possible when the children are older (he is hoping to buy a boat in five years' time).

Following the route map for lump sums, he sees that it suggests he should consider paying off part of the mortgage. This could make sense for Paul – his mortgage is his second biggest outgoing after the school fees. Generally speaking, the interest rate you pay on your mortgage is higher than the interest you earn on your savings – especially after tax has been deducted from the interest (and further tax paid by higher-rate taxpayers). So he could make a net gain by paying off some of the mortgage. The only way he might outstrip the mortgage rate would be to invest in the stock market – but this involves a risk he does not want to take. Or he could switch to a lower-rate mortgage – but he would need to be careful not to incur any fees. Paul decides to repay £30,000 of his mortgage, which will give his income an immediate boost. He does not want to pay off more, because having money in investments he can cash in gives him flexibility.

Next he follows the route map for a longer-term investment until he comes to the question about whether he is looking for income now. Yes, he is. He answers *No* to the next question about age and is then asked if he is prepared to see the value of his money go down rather than up in the hope of a better return. Here the answer is *Yes*. He sees he can choose between a stock market ISA, shares, unit trusts, investment trusts, gilts, corporate bonds or convertibles and single-premium investment bonds. Deciding to give the riskier options a miss, he invests the maximum £7,000 in a maxi-ISA to benefit from the tax advantages. By investing in corporate bonds through an ISA he can increase his income without increasing his tax bill; furthermore, he is not taking as much risk with his bonds as he would with shares, as long as he is prepared to hold them until redemption. The remaining £13,000 is invested in unit trusts – ones that aim for capital growth rather than income. He plans to cash in some of his units each year to help with the school fees if he needs to, but will make sure that he doesn't make net capital gains of more than the £7,500 limit each tax year free of capital gains tax. As he approaches retirement and the school fees come to an end, he will consider making additional voluntary contributions to his pension scheme to make up for the missing years.

Example 4: Saving for a rainy day

Mike and Sue are in their late 20s, with one baby and another due soon. Mike is a basic-rate taxpayer; Sue pays no tax at all. They have little cash left over at the end of each month. They are worried because they have no savings or life insurance.

For people in their position, life insurance should come before any attempt to save money. If Mike died, Sue would have to rely on social security to make ends meet and, if Sue were to die, Mike would have a hard time looking after the babies *and* going to work. He might need to pay for child care. They realise that investment-type life insurance is not really for them. With this firmly sorted out, they decide to go to an insurance adviser to arrange protection-type life insurance to cover them should one or other partner die.

Next they think about their emergency fund, follow the route map for savings and see that they are advised to consider a deposit account and can use their cash ISA allowance for this. They go for a building society ISA. One advantage is that they get a cash card giving them access to their money round the clock from the machines outside hundreds of building society branches – useful in a real emergency.

Once they build up a large enough emergency fund, they go through the route map again and look for a somewhat longer-term investment for their additional savings. They will probably start putting money into a deposit account that pays a higher rate for higher minimum levels of investment, even if they have to give notice before withdrawing money. This account will be opened in Sue's name only, as she pays no tax.

Example 5: Investing a windfall

Marianne, 21, has just inherited £9,000 from her grandmother. She is single, lives with her parents, has a large enough emergency fund and is a basic-rate taxpayer. She reckons that some time in the future she will want to buy a home and decides to put £7,500 towards this. She decides to try to turn the remaining £1,500 into something bigger; she is prepared to take risks with it.

Marianne follows the route map for lump sums and sees that investing the £7,500 earmarked for a future home might not be easy, given that house prices are rising faster than prices in general. Accepting that she is going to have to take some risk, Marianne plumps for investing, via an ISA, in a couple of unit trusts – both growth funds with any income reinvested.

She goes back to the route map to see how she should invest the £1,500 with which she is going to gamble. She looks up the short-listed investments in the table in Chapter 2 and in the chapters later in the book. She toys with putting her money into shares but the charges mean that she could really only afford to invest in one company – a very risky idea. She decides instead to allocate the £1,500 towards improving the eighteenth-century glass collection she started a couple of years ago; even if the bottom drops out of antique glass, she will get pleasure out of the collecting.

Example 6: Investing for extra income

Amy is 80 and lives alone. She lives on her state pension and a small pension from her ex-employer. She wonders what to do with the £7,000 she has to invest, which

43

is at present in a bank deposit account. She would like to increase her income to allow herself a few more treats.

She realises that she needs to keep some of her money to act as an emergency fund but reckons she will not need more than £1,000 for this, so she switches £1,000 to a cash ISA which pays the highest rate of interest.

Amy already owns her home, so does not need to worry about getting a mortgage. As Amy is over 70, she could consider an annuity or cashing in on her home through a home income plan. She is not really tempted by a home income plan, as she may want to move home later, so she first decides to buy an annuity. But buying an annuity means losing control of her capital. Amy uses only £3,000 to invest in an annuity. The remaining £3,000 will be invested in a corporate bond unit trust that is held in an ISA. Amy also decides to give more thought to moving to a smaller house and investing any profit from the sale to give her more income. She realises also that there are heavy expenses involved in buying and selling property and that she has to allow for these before going ahead.

Example 7: Saving for retirement

Bob, self-employed, earning around £25,000 a year, and his wife, Cathy, are in their late 40s. Their three children have all left home and Cathy thinks it is time they started saving for their retirement. They do not want to rely on their business for their retirement funds.

The couple already has an emergency fund, permanent health insurance in case either of them is too ill to work and they are buying their home with a mortgage. They follow the route map for savings to the question *Are you in a pension scheme?* Bob is self-employed, and already contributes £50 a month (£600 a year) towards a personal pension plan. He asks the insurance company that runs the pension plan what he might get in the way of a pension at 65 if he maintains this level of saving. They say about £750 a month but, after inflation, this could be inadequate by the time Bob retires. So Bob and Cathy decide to step up the amount they save.

Bob can get tax relief on up to 25 per cent of his £25,000 a year, i.e. £6,250 a year or around £520 a month. He reckons that he can afford another £70 a month without too much trouble. The new stakeholder pension introduced in April 2001 seems ideal. Starting a second pension plan with a different company has the advantage that he will be spreading the investment risk.

Like many self-employed people, Bob has earnings that fluctuate from month to month and, even with these higher pension contributions, he and his wife would have something extra to save in good months. They decide to add occasional savings to their emergency fund in a building society instant-access ISA. Their emergency fund is over £2,500, so they switch it to a tiered-interest-rate account, where they get a higher rate of interest on higher balances. If the account drops below £500, they do not lose out: the interest rate falls back to the lower rate. Once their emergency fund is up to £4,000, Bob and Cathy plan to look again at their pension provision. They need to put away much more than £120 (the existing £50 plus the additional £70 a month) a month if they are not to suffer a hefty drop in income on retirement and the tax relief on increased contributions eases the burden.

Risk and how to live with it

Technically speaking, every savings and investment product carries some risk – some more than others. In practice, of course, some products are so safe that you almost have a cast-iron guarantee that you get what you were promised. For example, Government Bonds (gilts) and National Savings are backed by the British government (and your taxes), so the risk of default is remote. Similarly, institutions such as the high-street banks and building societies are require to have huge reserves of money and their activities are closely monitored by the new Financial Services Authority (FSA)* and the government, so the chances of one of these giants being allowed to go under is extremely slim. Of course, you can never completely rule out a banking catastrophe but opening a savings account with one of the high-street banks or building societies is likely to be almost completely safe for the foreseeable future.

One thing to remember is that, when it comes to savings and investments, there are two main types of risk. Many people, when they hear the word 'risk', think automatically of the risk of being defrauded or not getting all their money back. But the security of your money is just one form of risk. The other main risk is uncertainty and unpredictability. Whenever you make a deposit or investment, it is difficult to say with any degree of certainty how much you will get back when you finally cash in your investments. Share prices fluctuate, interest rates vary. Inflation is a risk, too. We cannot predict what the rate of inflation will be over the long term, so we cannot say how much our incomes will buy for us in the future.

One of the golden rules of saving and investing is that the higher the return you need, the more risk you generally have to take (see the table on page 46). But do not let that put you off. There is no need to take any more risk than is necessary and there are simple steps you can take to manage some of the risk out of your investment plan. Understanding risk means identifying your own attitude to risk and recognising the different types of risk. Then you can pick up tips for minimising the chances of things going awry.

Another golden rule is that the longer you can wait before you need to cash in your investments, the more risk you can afford to take. If your investment horizon is short term, then it is wise not to put your money at much risk – this applies to drawing an income from your investment now or needing to withdraw money quickly (your emergency fund). You do not want your available capital to shrink suddenly. This is especially important when you are coming up to retirement: the

Table 1: Markets rated for return and risk

Market	Return rating	Risk rating
Cash	2	1
Gilts	3	1–2
UK shares	4	3
US shares	5	4
Europe shares	4	3–4
Pacific shares	3	5
Japan shares	1	5

Return: 5 = good, 1 = low
Risk: 5 = high, 1 = low

Note: Performance figure ratings are based on annualised returns 10 years to 30 April 2001. Risk ratings are based on three years to 30 April 2001.

Source: Hindsight Reuters.

last thing you want is for the stock market to crash just before you retire. This chapter will help you assess the level of risk to take at different stages of your life.

If you are investing for long-term growth, you can afford to take more risk. Investing in share-based assets has proved to be the best way of providing real long-term growth that outstrips inflation and preserves the buying power of your money. There is a risk attached (see below) but, when you do invest over the long term, there is more time to recover your losses after a fall in the stock market.

Your own attitude to risk is critical. Some people are happy to live with some degree of risk if it means getting a better return in the end. Others are 'risk averse' and would simply rather not take any risk at all. Only you can judge what level of risk you feel comfortable with. A good independent financial adviser will help you to assess your attitude towards risk, particularly if you are not confident or experienced (see Chapter 7, *Getting advice*).

Savings

Security
The most obvious risk to the security of your savings is the chance that a bank or building society will go bust. This usually happens for two reasons: either there has been widespread fraud in the organisation or else the financial controls have been too weak to stop staff taking too many risks with depositors' money. The most famous recent examples are the BCCI and Barings Bank.

Banks and building societies have to be licensed by the regulators to accept deposits in the UK. This used to be done by the Bank of England and the Building Societies Commission. Responsibility for approving financial institutions and monitoring their financial wellbeing (this is known as prudential supervision) has passed to the FSA.

If a bank or building society does go bust, a deposit protection scheme guarantees that you will get back 90 per cent of the first £20,000 of your savings, i.e. £18,000. So if you have £10,000 on deposit, £9,000 of this will be guaranteed. However, if the worst did happen, you would lose anything above £20,000. This protection scheme applies to all banks and building societies regardless of size.

If you deposit money with a foreign bank with a branch in the UK, you will have to rely on the deposit protection scheme of the country where the bank is authorised (foreign banks do have the option of choosing to be covered by the UK scheme but this does not happen automatically). The scheme in the bank's home country may not be as good as the UK's.

Tips: The first thing to do if you are considering depositing money with a bank or building society, or any other financial institution, is to make sure it is authorised. You can obviously rely on the well-known high-street institutions being authorised but if you are unsure about a small institution check with the FSA.

Find out whether the bank is based in the UK or abroad. If it is authorised overseas, check which protection scheme it belongs to. If the bank has chosen not to opt into the UK scheme, you may have to rely on a weaker compensation scheme.

If you are worried about risk, do not put all your eggs in one basket. For example, if you have £40,000 to deposit, it could be a good idea to split the money between two banks or building societies. At least this way all your money will be covered by the compensation scheme. Of course, you usually find that the more you deposit the higher the interest rate you get on your savings, so splitting the money means you could lose out by getting a lower rate. You have to decide whether you would rather forgo interest in exchange for peace of mind.

Similarly, you may be reassured by size. The larger institutions generally tend to pay lower rates than average. But you may feel more comfortable with this. Smaller institutions do run a higher risk of getting into trouble and, if the worst came to the worst, you could lose 10 per cent of your savings – more if you have invested over £20,000. Again, you have to decide whether you would be willing to settle for a lower rate for peace of mind.

Unpredictability

Income from savings can be unpredictable for two main reasons. First, and most obvious, is that the interest rate paid on your savings by banks and building societies changes regularly. The main impact on savings rates is due to movements in the Bank of England's base rate. The second reason is that the real value of your savings is affected by inflation. No-one can tell how inflation will behave in future, so it follows that you cannot predict real spending power in years to come from the amounts you save.

Tips: If you want a regular, consistent income, you could choose a fixed-rate savings account (see page 126). These pay a fixed rate of interest, so at least you will know what to expect over the period. But again these products have their own risks attached. If base rates fall over the period, you will be in a good position; but if rates rise, you could find yourself stuck with an account paying a lower than average rate.

If inflation is your main concern, you could try index-linked savings products. These products guarantee to pay a rate of interest which moves in line with inflation.

Investments

Security

The most obvious risk to the security of your investments is that the financial intermediary or financial company which has your money goes bust. You can protect yourself by making sure firms and individuals are legitimate and authorised. This is covered in detail in Chapter 6, *Forewarned is forearmed*.

A recent example of the risk to investment security has been the Equitable Life saga. Following a House of Lords decision, the Equitable found that it did not have sufficient assets in its with-profits funds (see Chapter 23) to cover the liabilities owed to holders of guaranteed annuities and maintain annual bonuses at historic rates. Hundreds of thousands of with-profits policyholders with the Equitable face the prospect of having their returns on their pension funds or investment plans being severely reduced unless the Equitable can agree a deal with guaranteed annuity policyholders. It is a reminder that with-profits funds can turn into with-losses.

There is also a risk if you invest directly in shares of individual companies. Companies can go under because of fraud or simply because they were not successful enough at selling their products. Ordinary shareholders are far down the list of priority claimants on what is left of a company that has gone into liquidation. It goes without saying that small new companies are more risky than big established ones that have been listed on the Stock Exchange for many years. On the other hand, you could be lucky and invest in a new company and double your money very quickly. There is always a trade-off between risk and return.

Tips: The simplest rule is: do not put all your eggs in one basket. This is why 'collective' investments such as unit or investment trusts are so attractive for most investors. These products hold shares in a large number of companies, so if one does go bust the impact is limited.

Unpredictability

Remember, the value of investments and the income from them can go down as well as up and you might not get back what you paid in. This is the standard warning that appears on marketing literature for investments. Generally speaking, there are four different types of risk that make investing unpredictable – specific risk, market risk, currency risk and manager risk. Controlling these types of risk is a crucial part of your investment strategy. You might lose the chance of spectacular returns but on balance it is better to aim for consistently good returns combined with lower risk than to gamble with your capital.

Specific risk

This is the risk that the specific company you have invested in performs badly. For example, if you invest £10,000 in a single company and its share price falls by 50 per cent, you have a 'paper' loss of £5,000. Of course, there is the chance that the share price could instead rise by 50 per cent and in that case you would be sitting on a very nice gain.

Individual shares have different specific risk. Some fluctuate in value more than others – i.e. they're more volatile. First-time investors should be especially concerned to minimise specific risk. One way to do this is to build up a range of less risky investments first. This way, if you do fancy putting money on a share you like, any volatility will have less impact on your overall portfolio.

Tips: You can reduce your specific risk by spreading your investments across a range of shares. This way, if a company goes bust or its share price falls, the overall effect on your portfolio is minimised. For example, if you spread your £10,000 across five companies (say, £2,000 in each) and one company's share price falls by 50 per cent, the value of your portfolio drops by only £1,000. The flip side of the coin is that if the same company's share price rises by 50 per cent, your investment will rise by only £1,000 rather than by the £5,000 it would have if you had invested the entire £10,000 in the company.

This strategy is called *diversification* and simply means not putting all your eggs in one basket. The best and cheapest way to spread your risk is to invest in unit trusts or investment trusts as described in Chapters 21 and 22 respectively. But you yourself can diversify by buying a range of shares across different sectors of the market.

Market risk

This is the risk of a fall in the particular country's stock market where your shares or unit trusts are invested. When a market does fall you find usually that most shares are dragged down with it. Some companies' shares fall more than the index or average; other companies can weather the storm and their shares fall less than the index or average – this is all related to the specific risk of the individual company shares or unit trust (see above). But it is difficult for most shares to buck the overall trend or direction of a market.

This is why timing is so important. As the graph on page 50 shows, investing at the wrong time can have a huge impact on your investments. Investors on the eve of a big crash such as the famous one on 'Black Monday' in 1987 faced immediate losses of around 30 per cent in two days.

The recent turmoil in the world's stock markets provides another example of the risks involved. The fall in share prices may not have been as dramatic as in 1987, but at one stage the FTSE 100 index started a downward slide and ended up 25 per cent down from its 2000 peak.

Tips: A good way of limiting the effects of getting the timing wrong is to invest your money gradually. You can do this through a monthly savings scheme. Most unit and investment trusts offer this option and you can typically invest £50 a month. Or you could simply put your money into the stock market in chunks rather than investing it all in one go.

Investing gradually or regularly smooths out price fluctuations. Say you have £5,000 to invest. If you invest the full £5,000 on the day before a market crash, you could lose heavily. But if you invest the first £1,000 on the day before a crash, there is a good chance your next £1,000 is buying shares at the bottom just before the market rises again.

As with specific risk, you can limit the effects of market risk by diversifying. Diversification works because different types of investments and stock markets do not always rise and fall together or by the same amount. You can spread market risk by investing in a range of assets combining shares, cash and gilts and fixed-interest stocks. So, if stock markets fall, your losses should be limited by the safe

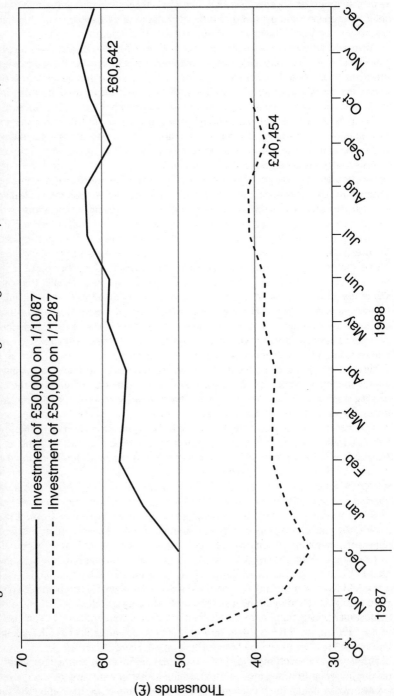

The big market crash in October 1987: how the right timing can affect your investments over a year

— Investment of £50,000 on 1/10/87
--- Investment of £50,000 on 1/12/87

£60,642

£40,454

Thousands (£)

investments in your portfolio. Again, when markets rise, the safer investments will reduce the growth you get but that is the nature of the trade-off between risk and reward.

Alternatively, you can diversify by investing in different stock markets around the world. Whenever one of the major markets crashes, this can have a domino effect on other national markets. But they do not all fall by the same amount at the same time. So, if one crashes, you may be able to limit your losses because your investments in other markets may not have fallen as much.

Diversification is a valuable tool for managing risk. If you look closely at the strategy of the big institutions that manage employers' pension funds, or insurance funds, you will see that they tend to have a carefully balanced mixture of UK shares, overseas shares, government bonds and cash.

For the ordinary investor, the best and safest way to invest overseas is through unit or investment trusts. You can choose a trust which invests solely in a country such as Germany or the USA. Or you could choose one that invests in a region such as Europe or the Far East. However, if you are an inexperienced investor, it is best to use a general international trust that spreads its investment across the globe. Once you have built up your investments in the UK, and then branched out to an international fund, you can now start thinking about single-country trusts.

Currency risk

If you do invest in stock markets outside the UK, you will be exposed to a third type of risk – currency risk. Wherever your money is invested, it will have to be converted back into sterling when you want it back. This means that movements in the exchange rate will affect the value of your investment.

Tips: Currency risk can have a big impact if you choose to invest in a single-country unit or investment trust. Even if the overseas stock market you have chosen rises in value, if the local currency falls against sterling, you could end up losing money. Of course the reverse can be true: if the stock market fell, but the local currency strengthened against sterling, you could end up making money.

You can limit currency risk by diversification. To do this, invest in an international fund which spreads its investments around the globe.

Manager risk

One form of risk that investors do not normally think about is manager risk. You need to choose the investment management company which will deliver a consistently good performance. This is more difficult than it seems. There can be a huge variation in the investment performance of individual unit and investment trust managers. You can see how great the difference can be by looking at the variation in the performance of unit trusts in the main UK sector over the past ten years. An investment of £1,000 in the best company would now be worth £8,400, while £1,000 invested in the worst would be worth only £1,600.

Most managers cannot consistently beat the index averages. For example, over the past five years, three-quarters of the unit trusts in the main UK sector have under-performed the main benchmark, the FTSE All Share Index.

Tip: If you are investing in the UK stock market, investing through an index-tracking fund can remove the risk of choosing a bad fund manager. Index funds simply track or match the movements of their chosen index, for example the FTSE

Best and worst UK All Companies unit trusts

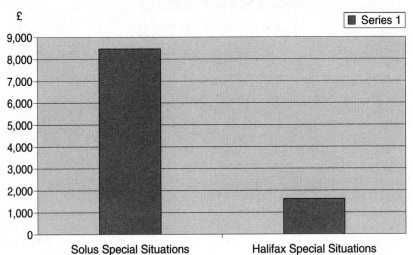

All Share Index. This may seem an unambitious goal, but because most of the 'active' managers have consistently under-performed the index, then by default this means that the index trackers should beat the average active trust over the longer term.

Some active managers will beat the index over certain discrete time periods but few seem to be able to maintain this outperformance. The evidence of history shows that around only one in ten active managers have consistently beaten the index over the long term.

It would be great if we could spot the winners at the starting gate, but FSA research indicates that past outperformance is no indication of future good performance (interestingly there is some evidence that bad performance is maintained). So rather than try to pick the winners when the odds are stacked against you, choosing an index tracker fund would seem to give you the best chance to beat the averages over the long term.

The index tracker funds also have lower charges than the active managed funds (there are no expensive fund managers' salaries to pay for a start). Charges can have a big effect on your returns when you cash in your investments.

One thing to remember about index tracker funds is that they work best with developed indices where the index reflects closely the performance of the stock-market such as the FTSE All Share Index in the UK or the S&P Composite in the USA. In other countries, where the index coverage is less comprehensive and doesn't fully reflect the performance of the local stockmarket the active managers can exploit these discrepancies and beat the index.

5

Monitoring your savings and investments

How often should I check my portfolio?

If you want your investment strategy to be effective, you must monitor your savings and investments regularly. You need to make sure your plans are still on course to meet your objectives. Remember, your needs change as your circumstances and lifestyle change, and your financial objectives at different stages of your life similarly change.

Do not assume that the best investments for you today will still be the best in a few months' or years' time. New, possibly more suitable, investments may come on the market; tax laws change, which can have a huge effect on your circumstances; inflation may be low now but, if it does rise again, you may have to save and invest more to keep your spending power. Recent forecasts for future investment growth have been revised downwards, so you may have to increase the amount you invest to ensure you have enough cash to meet your needs. This has been brought home to the millions of people who have found that their mortgage endowment policy is no longer on track to repay the mortgage. Your personal circumstances may also change dramatically. Births, deaths, marriages, changes of employment – all these major episodes in your life can affect your strategy.

Keep an eye on some of your savings and investments portfolio regularly, say on a monthly or even weekly basis. With others, you should monitor them regularly but only make adjustments over a much longer time scale. For example, if you want to maximise the return on your instant-access savings, it makes sense to switch often and chase the best rates. However, with notice accounts, your hands are tied somewhat – you cannot automatically switch or you lose interest. And, with investment products such as unit trusts, you could pay a new set of initial charges each time you switch. These charges can often be around 5 per cent, so the more often you switch the more you reduce your real returns. Each time the investments would have to make up a 5 per cent deficit.

Changing your portfolio also depends on how active an investor you want to be and how much time you have to spend on keeping up-to-date. Some people like to take an active interest, others a more long-term strategic approach. But you should check your portfolio at least once a year and carry out a major review of your strategy every three to five years.

Always remember not to get your emergency fund and other basics such as mortgage, life insurance and pension mixed up with your investment portfolio. It's easier to manage your finances over the long term if you keep these building-blocks in separate compartments. Changes in your personal circumstances will affect your priorities. Whenever you decide to monitor your portfolio, always refer back to your 'Investment priorities checklist' (see Chapter 1) to make sure these basics are covered, before you move on to your wider investment strategy. The basics are the foundation of your long-term plans.

For your emergency fund, check regularly that you have enough invested in instant-access savings accounts. Instant-access accounts generally pay lower rates than notice accounts but if you actively monitor your savings and chase after the best rates you can get the most from your money.

What to look for

Before you start to monitor your savings and investments, you need to know exactly what you should be monitoring and you will find certain tools helpful in doing it properly. This chapter tells you what to look out for, shows you how to work out what proportions of your total funds you have in different types of savings and investment and how to balance your portfolio.

Keep an eye on interest rates

One thing to watch out for is new accounts being launched with high rates. Once enough money has been attracted, often rates are allowed to slip, relative to the rest of the market.

In trying to compare the return you can get with different types of investment, one difficulty is that the rates of interest quoted with different investments are rarely comparable. This is because they make no allowance for how frequently interest is paid out. To make comparisons easier, banks, building societies and finance companies should follow a Code of Practice which lays down rules about how rates of interest should be advertised. But the Code also allows them to quote *several* different rates in an advertisement and sorting out which rate to use for comparison can be difficult. To help you compare like with like, see the box on 'The different rates – what they mean', on page 56 and Chapter 8 on *How to read financial advertisements*.

Interest rates are not always what they seem

When interest is paid out to you, you can spend or reinvest it: if you reinvest, you earn interest on the interest. The more frequently interest is paid to you, the sooner you can reinvest and the higher will be the overall return.

Suppose, for example, you invest £1,000 for a year at 5 per cent interest. If the interest is paid out once a year, £50 is all you get. But if the interest is paid out at half-yearly intervals and you reinvest it, you end up with more. This is because after six months, £25 (2.5 per cent of £1,000) is added to the £1,000, giving £1,025; in the second six months, another 2.5 per cent interest is earned on this £1,025, i.e. £25.63. The £25 plus £25.63 gives interest of £50.63 for the year – the same as you get if you put your money in an investment paying 5.06 per cent only once a year.

If the interest is paid quarterly, the return is even higher – your money grows to

Table 1: How £1,000 grows if interest at 5% is added

	yearly	half-yearly	quarterly	monthly
after 1 year	£1,050	£1,051	£1,051	£1,051
after 2 years	£1,103	£1,104	£1,105	£1,105
after 5 years	£1,276	£1,280	£1,282	£1,284
after 10 years	£1,629	£1,639	£1,645	£1,648
true annual return	5%	5.06%	5.1%	5.12%

Figures are rounded up or down.

£1,050.95. Monthly interest brings the return to £1,051.16. And these differences build up over the years, as Table 1 shows. So the true rate of return, as opposed to the 'nominal' rate (which in this case is 5%), depends not just on the amount of interest paid out but also the frequency with which it is paid out. Table 2 shows how true rates of return can differ from quoted rates.

Find the true rate of return

The rates quoted on investments where interest is added once a year are true rates of return – this applies to the National Savings Investment account, for example. The returns quoted on National Savings Certificates are also true returns which can be directly compared one with another.

However, many other investments add interest more often than once a year: with most building society accounts (other than regular savings accounts), bank deposit and savings accounts and finance company deposits, interest is added twice a year (sometimes quarterly). National Savings Income Bonds pay out income monthly, and you can ask for monthly interest with some other savings accounts. In all these cases, you need to know the true rate of return to compare them with investments paying out interest less frequently.

Table 2 sets out the true rates of return for a variety of quoted rates, when the

Table 2: True rates of return

Quoted rate	True rate if interest is paid out or added		
	half-yearly	quarterly	monthly
3%	3.02%	3.03%	3.04%
4%	4.04%	4.06%	4.07%
5%	5.06%	5.10%	5.12%
6%	6.09%	6.14%	6.17%
7%	7.12%	7.19%	7.23%
8%	8.16%	8.24%	8.30%
9%	9.20%	9.31%	9.38%
10%	10.25%	10.38%	10.47%
11%	11.30%	11.46%	11.57%
12%	12.36%	12.55%	12.68%

interest is paid out half-yearly, quarterly or monthly. The banking Code of Practice requires banks, building societies and finance companies to quote true rates in their advertising – they call them the *annual equivalent rate* (AER).

Note that with the National Savings Ordinary account, interest is paid once a year but only for complete calendar months. So, if you pay in or withdraw money during a month, the true return may be *lower* than the quoted rate.

The different rates and what they mean

Various different rates of return may be quoted in savings advertisements by banks, building societies and finance companies that follow the voluntary Code of Practice:

- **tax-free** – if interest from the account is not liable to income tax
- **net** – if you draw out the income and do not reinvest it, the rate you get with no more basic-rate tax to pay
- **gross** – the rate you have to get before deduction of tax to end up with the net rate after basic-rate tax has been deducted
- **net annual equivalent rate (AER)** – if you reinvest the income, the rate you get with no more basic-rate tax to pay
- **gross annual equivalent rate (AER)** – the rate you have to get before deduction of basic-rate tax to end up with the net compounded annual rate after basic-rate tax has been deducted at the basic rate.

If you are choosing between different investments, some paying interest after deduction of tax and some before tax, make sure you compare like with like to see which gives the better return. Suppose, for example, you want to compare the National Savings Investment account (interest paid before tax) with a building society account (interest paid after tax). The National Savings Investment account pays out interest once a year, so the quoted interest rate is the true rate of return. Compare this with the true rate of return for the building society account.

Gross rates of return

Interest on most types of savings account is now usually paid after deduction of tax at 20 per cent. There is no more basic-rate tax to be paid on the interest. If you expect to be a non-taxpayer, even after taking into account interest from your savings, you can have the interest paid out *gross* – that is, before tax – by filling in form R85 (from your bank or building society).

Advertisements for savings accounts often quote a gross rate of return to compare with the return from investments which pay interest without deduction of tax (mainly National Savings schemes). Be careful to avoid comparing gross interest rates with tax-free interest rates unless you are a non-taxpayer. (For how to work out the gross rate from the after-tax rate, see page 99.) As a general rule, you should compare gross rates of return on the same compounding basis wherever possible.

Suppose, for example, that you get 5 per cent net interest from a building society account. With a tax rate of 20 per cent, you have to earn before-tax interest of 6.25 per cent to have 5 per cent left after tax (6.25% less 20% of 6.25% = 5%). So the gross rate would be 6.25 per cent.

The ideal portfolio

Your ideal portfolio depends partly on the amount you have to invest and on your attitude to risk (see Chapter 4). The other main factor is your *age*: how long before you retire determines how much capital growth you are going to need to provide an income.

Capital growth
When you are young, the chances are you are getting an income from a job. This means you probably have no need for investments which produce a current regular income. Your main concern is to invest for the long term so that by the time you retire you have built up enough capital to provide yourself with the income you need. Share-based investments (equities) are the best method of preserving the value of your capital and making it grow.

Investing for income
As you approach retirement, your priorities change. By this time, if your growth strategy has worked to plan, you should have a suitable capital sum to provide a decent income. You need to start gradually switching your assets from share-based investments to safer investments which pay out a high income. Once you need to rely on a regular income from your investments, it is important that your capital is not overexposed to the risk associated with most shares.

But even in retirement, you find that inflation erodes the capital on which your income is built. So you need to keep some capital in lower-risk, share-based investments to preserve your money. Keeping all your money in a building society does not safeguard it from inflation.

Types of investment
The graph overleaf can help you to work out what percentage of your money should be in different investment categories. But, before you use it, you need to know which investments fall into each category.

Equities
These include shares, companies unit and investment trusts. Equities are medium- to long-term investments. The minimum period to hold equities is five years; the longer you hold them, the more chance they have to grow. Equities are risky, so you must allow them time to recover if they fall in value. They can range from medium-risk (shares in an established UK company) to high-risk (shares in a small company in the emerging Far East markets, say).

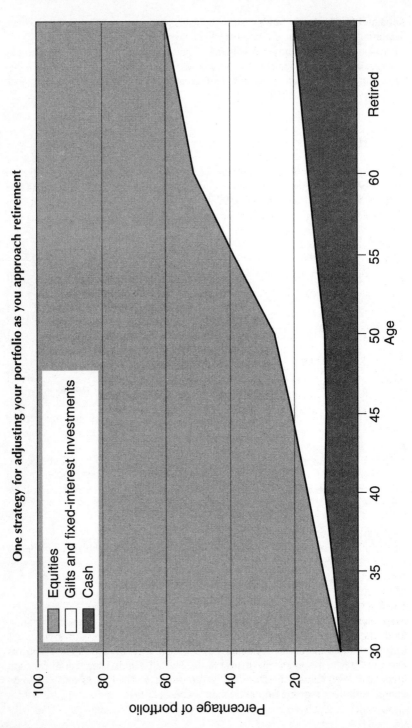

One strategy for adjusting your portfolio as you approach retirement

Equities
Gilts and fixed-interest investments
Cash

Percentage of portfolio

Age

Retired

Gilts and fixed-interest funds

These include gilts (Government-backed bonds), corporate bonds, gilt and fixed-interest unit trust and convertible funds. Fixed-interest investments are generally low- to medium-risk: they tend to be fairly safe (gilts in particular) and less volatile than shares. They are short- to medium-term investments. But do not keep your emergency fund here as their value can fluctuate.

Cash

Bank and building society savings accounts, existing TESSAs, the cash element of ISAs, money market accounts and National Savings accounts are all forms of 'cash'. Cash is the lowest-risk investment. But it is not entirely without risk: you cannot be certain what interest rate you will get and there is a risk that a bank can go bust. Cash is a short-term investment: you can usually get access to it at very short notice. TESSAs and some National Savings products are an exception, as you need to keep your money in for five years to benefit fully.

Overall balance

You can use the graph opposite to get an idea of how much you should be holding in different types of assets. Remember, this excludes your emergency fund and is after you have covered the basics, including pension, life insurance and mortgage.

This graph is only a rough guide based on a typical investor. We have assumed a retirement age of 65. If you aim to retire early or need to rely on the income from your investments before you retire, the same principle applies: the fewer years until you need the income from your investments, the less risk you should take. Similarly, your attitude to risk is critical: if you are risk-averse then you should have more in cash and fixed-interest stocks and less in equities.

Monitoring your portfolio

You should check your portfolio at least once a year: you might need minor adjustments to keep you on course. The *portfolio calculator* overleaf helps you work out what proportion of your assets you currently hold in each of the three types of investment. Set yourself a date, once a year, when you can use the calculator to check your current portfolio mix. Most investors find that the end of the tax year is the best time.

Using the portfolio calculator

The first step is to work out the value of your unit trusts, investment trusts, shares, fixed-interest investments and cash (excluding your emergency fund and pension fund). Refer to the sections under 'Types of investment' above to group your investments into the correct categories. If you have, say, £5,000 of UK unit trusts and £2,000 invested in Halifax shares, these should be added together and placed in the calculator under 'Equities: UK'. Likewise, if you hold gilts and corporate bonds, add these together and enter them under 'UK fixed-interest'. If you do not know which category your unit or investment trust falls into, contact the Unit Trust

Portfolio calculator

Type of Investment	Value	Proportion of total
(a) UK FIXED-INTEREST	£.	. . . . %
EQUITIES		
(b) UK	£.	
(c) USA	£.	
(d) Japan	£.	
(e) Far East	£.	
(f) Europe	£.	
(g) Other overseas	£.	
(h) TOTAL OVERSEAS (c+d+e+f+g)	£.	
(i) TOTAL EQUITIES (b+h)	£.	. . . . %
(j) CASH	£.	. . . . %
(k) TOTAL PORTFOLIO (a+i+j)	£.	100 %

Information Service (UTIS)* or the Association of Investment Trust Companies (AITC)*.

Once you have placed all your investments in the right categories, add them together as shown on the calculator. Then work out the proportion you hold in each – the three percentages should add up to 100 in total.

Now refer back to the graph on page 58. Compare how much you have in equities, fixed interest and cash with what the graph suggests is the ideal portfolio mix for your age group. 'Rebalance' your portfolio only if you have strayed outside the range.

This is also a good time to weed out any badly performing funds from your portfolio. One year's performance is not enough to judge a fund's merits but preformance over three to five years shows whether a pattern is emerging.

How to rebalance

If, having used the calculator, you find you have to adjust your portfolio, it is not difficult to work out how much to buy or sell.

Say you have a total portfolio of £50,000 and the graph on page 58 shows that you should have up to 80 per cent (£40,000) in equities. Having used the calculator, you find you have 90 per cent (£45,000). You should lower this proportion to around 75 per cent (£37,500) to allow a margin for error. This means that you have to sell £7,500 of equities. You could reinvest this evenly between cash and fixed-interest products or you may want to spend some money and invest the remainder.

When reinvesting, check to see whether fund managers offer discounts for switching between their unit trusts. But never let a discount tempt you if the fund's performance is not up to scratch.

Check the performance

If you want to check the performance of your investments in, say, unit trusts, you need a benchmark for comparison. Most unit and investment trusts are categorised into sectors. You can compare your fund against both the sector average and the relevant stock-market index.

However, do not rely on the figures the fund manager or a financial adviser uses when measuring performance. They may well choose time periods which flatter the performance (see Chapter 8). Always ask to see how the trust has performed over at least three or four different five-year periods. *Which?* looks at performance at regular periods – see Chapter 8. If the risk has been higher than average coupled with poor performance, it is definitely time to consider switching.

Ask to see a summary of how all the unit or investment trusts the fund manager runs have performed over the past five years. A group whose funds have generally performed above average should be able to manage money well in different market conditions.

Research from the FSA indicates that, while good past performance is no indicator of future performance, there is evidence that bad past performance is often sustained.

Forewarned is forearmed

The value of many investments and the income from them can go down as well as up, and you may not get back the amount you invest. You take a risk when you invest in shares, bonds and investment funds that the investment, you choose may do badly. There is no law to protect you against such risks, but there are laws to protect you against rogues and negligent professionals in the financial services industry. In this chapter we look at what legal protection there is to stop things going wrong and where to look for possible compensation if they do. We also outline some actions you can take to protect yourself from the rogues.

The legal framework

The Financial Services and Markets Act 2000
The Financial Services and Markets Act 2000 replaced the 1986 Financial Services Act. The Act sets out a new system of financial regulation and investor protection under the Financial Services Authority (FSA).* The FSA has brought under one authority the powers of many previously separate regulators, including:

- the Supervision and Surveillance Division of the Bank of England
- the Building Societies Commission
- the Friendly Societies Commission
- the Registry of Friendly Societies
- the Insurance Directorate of the Department of Trade and Industry
- SIB and the three Self-Regulating Organisations (SROs)
  - Personal Investment Authority (PIA)
  - Investment Management Regulatory Organisation (IMRO)
  - Securities and Futures Authority (SFA)

and the powers of regulating the investment business of:

- the Association of Chartered Certified Accountants*
- the Institute of Actuaries*
- the Institutes of Chartered Accountants in England and Wales,* in Ireland* and in Scotland*

- the Insurance Brokers' Registration Council*
- the Law Societies of England and Wales,* of Scotland* and of Northern Ireland.*

The role of the FSA
The FSA has been given several statutory objectives, two of which are particularly relevant to retail consumers. The first is to protect consumers, the second to promote the public understanding of financial services.

What are the regulations?

The FSA must ensure that people and companies are fit to do business. The following are the main components in the FSA's strategy:

Authorisation
All businesses dealing in or giving advice on investments, with certain limited exceptions, must be *authorised* to carry out their business. To become authorised, businesses have to meet certain standards. For example, they need to show they are properly run, have sound financial backing and keep adequate records. Furthermore, all staff who advise on and sell investments must pass examinations showing they have reached a minimum level of competence.

Keeping the rules
Once authorised, investment firms that fail to abide by the rules can be disciplined, fined or, at worst, have their authorisation removed and be banned from the industry. The main points of the rules are:

- Investment businesses have to take into account *your* best interests when giving you advice. This means that they are to recommend only products which are suitable for you.
- In most cases an adviser has to *know the customer*, i.e. be fully aware of your personal and financial situation. This is often done by filling in a systematic questionnaire called a 'fact-find'.
- Independent advisers must take into account the range of products on the market and your particular needs. Company representatives (or *tied agents*) have the same responsibilities as far as the range of products and services the company they are tied to provides. In either case, if nothing they can offer suits your needs, they must tell you so.
- The strict difference between independent advisers and tied agents was relaxed with the introduction of stakeholder pensions in April 2001. A tied agent (such as most banks or building societies) can now sell the stakeholder pensions of a range of providers. However, the range is likely to be restricted to a number of specified providers on the tied agent's list. Advice on stakeholder pensions from a tied agent should not be confused with independent advice, where the adviser has access to all the stakeholder pensions on the market.
- At the start of the selling process, both independent advisers and company representatives must inform you of their status.

- When you pick a pension or investment-type life-insurance policy, you must be given a *key features document* before you make your investment. Key features must also be given for investment products such as unit trusts, investment trusts and some ISAs, although these are not entirely consistent with those given out with life and pensions products. See page 265 for more details on key features documents.
- In most cases (but not when buying only life insurance or unit trusts), written *customer agreements* – also known as *terms of business* letters – are required, which give details of the services being provided and their cost, set out your investment objectives and the responsibilities of your adviser and warn you of the risks of certain investments.
- If an adviser 'cold calls' you, he or she must make it clear that he or she is hoping to sell you a financial product and make sure you are happy to discuss it. Advisers must not pretend to be doing market research.
- After you have invested in life insurance, pensions or unit trusts, you normally have a 14-day *cooling-off period* during which you can change your mind by cancelling the investment and getting your money back. But this does not apply to unit trusts or single-premium life-insurance bonds if you received no advice or if you bought either through an advertisement or in line with your customer agreement.
- *Best execution* rules apply for most transactions. This means that the firm must carry out the deal on the best terms available.
- Advertisements and illustrations of benefits have to comply with rules about comparisons, references to past performance and give necessary risk warnings. Illustrations must be based on standard assumptions about investment growth and must reflect the company's own charges for life insurance, pensions products, unit and investment trusts, ISAs and personal equity plans (PEPs).
- Proper arrangements must be made for keeping your money (e.g. money awaiting investment) separate from an adviser's money. A really determined fraudster could still run off with your money, but at least the FSA should make it easier for you to get compensation – see below.
- Some of this protection is not available to you if you are classed as a professional or business investor or if you are classed as an *experienced* investor in your customer agreement (i.e. one with plenty of recent experience in a particular field of investment). Watch out if this applies to you – read your customer agreement carefully and query it if you think your investor status should be different.

Independence

Advisers selling life insurance and unit trusts must either give completely independent advice, selecting products for you from all those on the market, or act as representatives selling and advising on a single company's or group's products. (Although you can ask a company representative to sell you another company's product, he or she cannot actually give you advice on it.) This has become known as *polarisation*. But the rules have been relaxed for stakeholder pensions – see Chapter 18. Unless you are already sure that you want to invest with a specific company (or a limited range of companies in respect to stakeholder pensions), or you are yourself collecting quotations from a handful of preferred companies, your best course is to seek independent advice. *Which?* has found that independent financial advisers give the best-quality advice, particularly those who charge a fee rather than take commission.

The status of banks and building societies can be particularly confusing. With most you can buy only the investments of a single insurance company through the branch networks: many banks and societies operate their own insurance company, others have an agreement with a separate insurance company to sell their products (i.e. they act as the company's tied agent. However, some banks and societies also run a separate independent advice service – but usually you are only put in touch with this if you ask specifically and have a considerable sum to invest.

Compensation

A compensation scheme is available if you lose money because your adviser goes bust or turns out to be a fraud (but see Chapter 12 for the protection you get with deposit accounts at banks and building societies). The scheme is financed by a levy on all investment businesses. You should be covered if your investments were made after 28 August 1988, when the scheme started. If you invested before then, you might still be covered in some circumstances.

If you find yourself in the unfortunate position of having lost money in a bankrupt investment company, you should be contacted automatically by the Investors' Compensation Scheme.* If you are not, contact the scheme yourself with any proof you have of the amounts involved. The scheme can pay up to £48,000 – full protection for the first £30,000 invested, then 90 per cent protection for the next £20,000. So, bear in mind that, in most cases, you are certain to get back all your money only if you have invested £30,000 or less.

Suing a company

You also have the right to sue a company for damages if you believe that the company has broken the rules of the regulator and as a result of this you have lost money.

How to complain

All authorised businesses must have a complaints procedure set up to deal with problems. You should approach the company in writing, providing evidence of your complaint. If you are not happy with the response you get from your first complaint or from the branch with which you were dealing, take your complaint higher – to the managing director or head office.

If your complaint is not resolved satisfactorily and you reach deadlock with the company, you can contact the FSA Enquires Unit* to find out how to formally pursue a complaint. The system of complaints and ombudsmen is currently being reorganised and may well change in the months following the publication of this book, so a call to the FSA is a good starting point.

Self-protection

Even though the regulations give you a safety net, always take precautions before deciding where and with whom to put your money. You should weigh up both the potential risks and benefits of your planned investments. Chapter 7 outlines a number of points to consider when choosing someone to advise you on what to do with your money. Here are some other things to watch out for:

- Particularly good deals – do not allow greed to overcome your common sense. Investing money is a business like any other and a competitive one at that. If you come across an adviser who promises you returns way beyond the norm, the chances are that either he or she is not planning to return your money or there is a significant risk – either way you could end up with nothing. If a deal sounds too good to be true, it probably is.
- 'Guaranteed' returns – if the sales pitch refers to a 'guaranteed return', find out exactly who or what is giving this guarantee. Words alone are not enough (especially if the company is based abroad).
- Writing cheques – wherever possible, make cheques payable to the company you are going to invest in rather than to the adviser you are dealing with.
- High-pressure selling – no deal is so urgent that you have to decide immediately whether to invest. It is your money, so do not allow yourself to be rushed into deciding what to do. Give yourself time to find out more.
- Commission – rates vary, making some investments more attractive for advisers to sell. Despite the *conduct of business rules* of the FSA, it is always a good idea to look at how much commission your adviser is getting on each proposed investment.
- Unauthorised advisers – never deal with anyone who does not have authorisation; report him or her to the FSA (you can check with the FSA who is authorised). If you find out that an authorised business is breaking the rules, report it to the FSA too.
- Being classed as an *experienced* investor – if you are, some of the protection outlined earlier in this chapter will not apply, for example the obligation on an adviser to find out your needs before giving advice.

One final warning: remember that the FSA is there to protect you against rogues and the negligence of others, not the unavoidable perils of investment. Investment is never totally risk-free.

7 Getting advice

Lots of people offer investment advice, but how good is the advice? In this chapter we look at the various sources of professional advice, what they might offer and what they might cost.

Who is offering advice?
Various groups of people give investment advice of one sort or another. For example:

- banks
- building societies
- independent financial advisers
- tied agents
- insurance company representatives
- stockbrokers.

Accountants and solicitors may also offer investment advice. Details of their services are at the end of this chapter.

In order to offer investment advice, a person must be authorised to do so. However, that does not guarantee that advisers from each of the categories outlined above will be suitable to advise you on all aspects of your financial affairs. You need to be sure you are dealing with an adviser who specialises in your area of needs. If in doubt, check with more than one adviser before acting on any advice.

What types of advice can you get?
Investment advice falls broadly into two categories:

- general advice – such as how your money should be split between different types of investment
- specialist advice – such as which shares to invest in or which kind of life insurance to buy.

It is unlikely that any adviser will offer general advice without then going on to make specific investment recommendations. You may find, however, that your adviser cannot offer more general advice but can simply offer advice on a specific type of investment such as insurance or pensions. If you are sure that you only need specific pensions advice, say, you will probably find a pensions expert will be more useful than a general investment adviser.

You may also simply want a dealing service, known as an *execution-only* service, without any advice, for example for buying or selling shares under your specific instructions. This is the only occasion on which you can deal with someone who is not authorised to offer investment advice – this may save money, as you are not paying for advice. Remember, however, if you do choose the execution-only route and do not use an adviser, you lose some of the protection you get otherwise. You lose the cooling-off rights and you cannot claim you have been given bad advice. After all, the choice was yours.

If your adviser manages all, or a large portion of, your investments for you (called *portfolio management*), you can often ask for the management to be *advisory*, where the adviser needs your prior approval to act, or *discretionary*, where he or she does not. Most advisers prefer discretionary management for larger sums of money (say, £50,000 or more), so that they can act quickly when necessary. If you decide on discretionary management, it is normal to agree certain criteria and record them in writing. Your adviser should, for example, agree a general investment strategy which suits your needs and takes account of your attitude to risk and your investment time frame. More detailed considerations – such as broad limits to your adviser's discretion (for example, investing not more than 5 per cent of your money in the shares of any one company) and whether or not your money should be invested in traded options or foreign investments – should also be decided.

Polarisation

Generally speaking advisers can either be independent and choose products from the whole market, or sell the products of just one provider either as a tied agent or a company representative. This system is known as polarisation and is designed to ensure that consumers can tell which type of adviser they are dealing with.

The Government and FSA have been consulting on relaxation of the polarisation rules to allow tied agents and company representatives to sell products of more than one provider. So far the FSA has decided to relax the rules only for stakeholder pensions, but will consider other life and pensions products at a later stage.

Choosing an adviser

It is not hard to find an investment adviser – finding the right one for you is the problem. Some general advisers, such as solicitors and accountants, normally give such advice as a sideline to their main business. Other advisers will not be interested in your business unless you have a lot of money to invest – say £100,000 or even more.

So it is best to do some homework before you go out to look for an adviser. Below is a checklist of points that you should consider to help you decide what your investment needs and aims are. In going through this checklist, you will have to put some thought into exactly what you want from your investments: whether you are willing to risk losing money in hope of a capital gain, whether you want your money available at short notice. See Chapters 1, 2 and 3 for help in sorting out your priorities. You won't always need advice. If you use a savings account to save for a holiday, say, it is up to you to shop around for the best rates yourself. But if you think your finances are in a mess and you need help to sort them out, consider getting advice. Also, some products – e.g. pensions and endowment policies – are so complex that, unless you are a confident and experienced investor, you are better off getting advice.

You should also expect to be asked about all these points by an adviser (unless your needs are very specific, for exampe you are just asking him or her to sell some shares). It is likely that your adviser will use a fact-finding questionnaire to establish your circumstances and needs. Be wary of advisers who do not ask the right questions. Not only will they be contravening the rules of the FSA*, they will not be in a position to give you suitable advice.

Checklist of points for you to consider

- age
- health
- marital status
- number and ages of children and other dependants
- size and make-up of family income
- tax position
- possible changes in financial circumstances
- regular financial commitments
- existing investments
- home and mortgage
- pension
- existing insurance policies
- how long you want to invest for
- reasons for investing: e.g. how important it is to you to get a high income or long-term capital growth
- whether you want to be able to get your money back quickly
- what degree of risk you are prepared to take with your money
- whether there are any sorts of investment you are not prepared to consider: e.g. investing in arms manufacturers.

Once you decide on your investment aims, it should be a little easier to choose a suitable type of adviser – see our guide to advisers, below, for what each type offers. When you have found the adviser you want, check that he or she is authorised. You can do this either by asking the adviser or checking directly with the FSA or the appropriate regulating body – see Chapter 6. Make sure you see more than one authorised adviser, so that you can compare what each is offering.

It is not only the adviser who should ask questions – *you* should too. It is important that you are clear about exactly what kind of adviser you are dealing with. You should find out:

- whether the adviser is independent or tied to selling the products of only one company

- whether he or she has professional indemnity insurance, which will pay out if he or she loses your money through fraud or negligence.

Another important question you should ask is how the adviser is paid. Some advisers charge a flat fee; others get commission from the companies in which you invest money. Of this latter group, it is important to bear in mind that, while the advice may seem to be free, there *is* a cost involved: the commission will be deducted from your funds. If you do pay a fee, the adviser may undertake to pass on to you any commission he or she receives. See the following pages for how each type of adviser is paid.

Make your final decision when you are satisfied on all these points. Steer clear of advisers who make fantastic claims about what they can do for your money. Investment that supposedly brings unreasonably high returns is usually fraught with risk or, worse, is fraudulent.

Once you have decided on your adviser, make sure you specify exactly what you want him or her to do, and get this in writing. Your adviser will, in most cases, have to draw up a *customer agreement* which sets out your investment objectives, the services to be provided, the responsibilities undertaken and the charges being made. Avoid making cheques out in your adviser's name if at all possible – make out your cheque to the company providing the investment. If a firm has *got* to handle your money, check that it is held in a separate client account. And if an adviser is going to be looking after your money over a long period, make sure that he or she sticks to your customer agreement. Ask how he or she will keep in touch, who will be dealing with you and how often. Expect your investment to be reviewed at least every three months and to receive a report at least once a year.

Guide to advisers

Advice is available from various sources, but it is important to remember that there are three types of adviser:

- Independent Financial Advisers (IFAs), as the name suggests, are able to search the whole market to find the best product for you. They are paid either by a fee or by commission
- direct sales staff are employed by a particular financial services company to sell that company's products
- tied agents are 'tied' to selling the products of one company, although they are not employed by that company.

In its surveys of advisers, *Which?* has consistently found that the best advice came from IFAs particularly those who charge a fee. Their independent status meant that they were able to trawl the whole market for products which suited the mystery shoppers involved.

Banks
All the high-street banks offer investment advice but they generally advise about their own investment products only.

- **What they offer** – varies from bank to bank and within banks themselves, but includes advice on the bank's own products (e.g. insurance and unit trusts), buying and selling stocks and shares, tax, pensions and portfolio management.
- **What they charge** – usually nothing if you buy life insurance or unit trusts, as the bank gets commission; normal stockbrokers' commission for buying and selling shares (maybe with an *administration fee* on top); for managing a portfolio, either a flat fee or 0.5 to 1.5 per cent a year of the portfolio's value. There could be an extra fee for tax help.
- **What to watch out for** – most banks' branches sell only their own products.
- **Who to complain to** – if you cannot get the head office of your bank to deal satisfactorily with your complaint, try the the Banking Ombudsman.* Alternatively, contact the FSA – see Chapter 6 for details.

Verdict
Useful if you want advice on, or management of, smaller sums of money – under £10,000, say. For management of larger amounts, you may have to approach a bank's investment company. Alternatively, you could go to a merchant bank, which can offer a more personalised service and usually advises only customers with large sums of money to invest.

Building societies
Building societies provide a wide range of financial services and products, for example share-dealing services in conjunction with stockbrokers. For a while some building societies offered independent advice. But most have now forged deals with investment and insurance companies to sell the products of a single company.

- **What they offer** – not all societies offer the full range of financial services the law allows them to provide, but you may be able to get share-dealing or unit-trust services (through links with other financial bodies). Some also offer independent advice through a connected company.
- **What they charge** – normally nothing, because the society gets commission from the company whose product you buy. If you are referred to another adviser, e.g. a stockbroker, you will pay that adviser's charges.
- **What to watch out for** – at branch level many building societies offer advice only on the products of a single company.
- **Who to complain to** – if you cannot get the society's head office to deal satisfactorily with your complaint, try the Building Societies Ombudsman.* Alternatively, ask the FSA for the relevant regulator.

Verdict
An obvious choice for advice on ways of investing to pay off a mortgage. Building societies are worth contacting if you want advice on their own products, instant-access accounts, or if you want to find out about any of the other services or products they offer.

Independent financial advisers (IFAs)
This term covers a range of advisers, from those who mainly sell life and pensions products through to those who deal in a wide variety of schemes. Strictly speaking,

though, they should all look at all types of investment when advising you. IFA Promotion* will send a list of six of its members in your area, with a description of their businesses. You can also contact the Society of Financial Advisers (SOFA)* or the Association of Independent Financial Advisers (AIFA).* SOFA has a useful Internet database on which you can search for specialist advisers on, for example, pensions.

- **What they offer** – includes: general investment advice, advisory or discretionary portfolio management, advice on tax and pensions, life-insurance products, shares and unit trusts and alternative types of investment.
- **What they charge** – usually nothing if they are just selling a life-insurance policy or unit trust, as they get commission. For managing a lump sum, charges range from 0.5 to 1 per cent a year of the value of your portfolio. Charges may be less for very large amounts. Instead, advisers may charge a flat fee, such as £100 a year, or a slice of your profits, or even both. Services such as tax help may cost extra. If you prefer to pay a fee for advice, the Money Management National Register of Independent Fee-Based Advisers* can provide you with a list of IFAs in your area who charge fees.
- **What to watch out for** – charges for advice can vary widely. If your adviser charges a fee, ask if it will be reduced if commission is paid on any of the investments purchased. Good fee-based IFAs will send you the fact-finding forms which you can fill in before you meet. This will mean that the adviser can focus on your needs, not waste time with basic form-filling, and save you money.
- **Who to complain to** – if you have problems, get in touch with FSA. Advisers should have professional indemnity insurance which will pay out if you can prove your money was lost through their negligence or fraud.

Verdict
Worth trying if you want general advice or someone to manage a lump sum for you (say, £10,000 plus). They should be able to advise you on all aspects of your investments. IFAs have been found to give the best advice, particularly fee-based advisers.

Tied agents
These advisers sell a wide range of products. But the products they sell belong to only one provider.

- **What they offer** – advice on life insurance and pensions, plus general insurance advice (for home, car, etc.) and sometimes tax advice and advice about unit trusts.
- **What they charge** – they earn commission on what they sell.
- **What to watch out for** – although these advisers may have their own business, remember they sell a single company's products. These advisers are not independent, so make sure you do your own homework on the company whose product they sell.
- **Who to complain to** – these advisers must be authorised by the FSA. You can approach the FSA if you have a complaint.

Verdict
Might be worth trying for basic advice but remember that they sell the products of only one company. If that company's products are poor, then you will be making a bad choice.

Insurance company representatives
Life-insurance companies often employ representatives to deal with you in person. Some companies sell their products through those representatives, press advertisements and direct mailing, others sell them only through independent advisers, others again use both methods. Some companies have a policy of passing direct enquiries on to independent financial advisers.

- **What they offer** – general financial advice. But remember they are selling the products of only one company.
- **What they charge** – representatives get commission from their company on the products they sell.
- **What to watch out for** – in the past, it was not unknown for company representatives to pass themselves off as independent – this practice is now illegal. Do not be pressurised into buying their products if you are not convinced they are right for you. Also, get quotations from more than one company. You're unlikely to save any money dealing directly with a company (rather than through an adviser); commission costs are built into the price of an investment.
- **Who to complain to** – if an insurance company's head office does not deal satisfactorily with a complaint, go to the FSA.

Verdict
Obviously, you will get advice on only one company's products, and, since many insurance companies' life and pensions products are such poor value, the chances are high that you will be sold a poor product. *Which?* has found in the past that the advice from insurance company representatives and tied agents is not of the same quality as that from independent financial advisers. But if you know you want to invest with that particular company, and you are sure you cannot get a better deal elsewhere, it may be worth trying.

Stockbrokers
These specialise in shares and gilts but many have widened their services in recent years.

- **What they offer** – mainly advice on buying and selling shares and gilts, usually unit trusts too also advisory and discretionary portfolio management (for sums starting at around £15,000, but often much more), unit trust portfolio management, their own unit trusts and Individual Savings Accounts (ISAs), investment research, general investment advice (sometimes through a subsidiary company). A *Private Investors' Directory* is available from the Association of Private Client Investment Managers and Stockbrokers.*
- **What they charge** – commission for buying and selling shares on your behalf ranges from 1 to 2 per cent of the price of the shares, plus VAT. Most stockbrokers have minimum commissions of around £20 or £25. For portfolio

management, there is an annual fee of, say, 1 per cent of the value of the portfolio. You may also be charged a small fee (around £5 per transaction) to cover the cost of complying with Financial Services Act rules. Others may have increased commission rates to reflect this.

- **What to watch out for** – charges both for buying and selling shares and for general management of a portfolio vary a lot, so it is worth shopping around. But do not expect a stockbroker to be able to choose shares that consistently do better than average; investing in shares is a risky business – see Chapter 20. Not all stockbrokers are prepared to deal with individuals.
- **Who to complain to** – the FSA.

Verdict

If you want advice on shares, gilts or unit trusts, a stockbroker may be your best bet. They are worth considering for management of a lump sum, say £10,000 plus, though some stockbrokers manage only very large sums, say £100,000 or more.

Accountants

Generally, these are not investment specialists, but they may offer independent advice or refer you to a specialist.

- **What they offer** – varies considerably but includes general investment advice, tax planning, advice on wills and trusts, sometimes advisory or discretionary portfolio management, contact with specialist advisers, e.g. stockbrokers.
- **What they charge** – their normal fees, which depend on the time spent, can vary greatly. *Which?* suggests you will typically pay £60–£100 for each hour the adviser works on your case, so shop around. They may get commission if you buy life insurance, unit trusts or shares through them. *Chartered accountants* are supposed to tell you in writing about any commission they expect to receive as a result of your investment. *Certified accountants* are supposed to tell you about any commission and deduct it from their fee.
- **What to watch out for** – although some accountants may be well qualified to advise you about investments, others may not.
- **Who to complain to** – the Recognised Professional Body (RPB) to which the accountant belongs, e.g. the Institute of Chartered Accountants in England and Wales. Check to see if your accountant has professional indemnity insurance; almost all should have this. If a large part of the practice's business comes from advising on or managing investments, it may be authorised by the FSA.

Verdict

Worth trying if you want advice on an overall investment strategy or have complex tax affairs and can afford the fees.

Solicitors

Solicitors are not generally investment specialists, but nearly all will give existing clients advice; most will give it to anyone who comes to see them. All solicitors have to give independent advice and be authorised to do so.

- **What they offer** – varies considerably but includes general advice, contacts with specialist advisers (such as stockbrokers), sometimes advisory or discretionary portfolio management, tax planning, advice on wills and trusts.
- **What they charge** – a fee based on the time spent (rates can vary, so shop around). If commission is received, it can be kept only with your permission. In practice, fees are often reduced by the amount of the commission.
- **What to watch out for** – some may be well qualified to tell you where to put your money, others may not.
- **Who to complain to** – The RPB, e.g. the Law Society.* They all have professional indemnity insurance. They may also come under the FSA if a large part of their business comes from advising on or managing investments.

Verdict

The *Which?* report on financial advice in March 1999 tested the investment advice given by 48 advisers. Independent financial advisers tended to give the best advice but *Which?* was less impressed by solicitors – only two of the six tested gave good advice.

How to read financial advertisements

Choosing the right financial product for your savings and investments is critical. Pick the right one and you could be rapidly better off; choose the wrong one and you could lose hundreds, even thousands, of pounds. Often the first, and only, step people take when choosing a financial product is to read advertisements. So it is important to know what to look out for in financial advertising, and what the pitfalls are.

Who polices advertisements?

There are three different organisations that set the rules on how financial products are advertised. You can complain directly to them if you think an advertisement is misleading.

The Advertising Standards Authority (ASA)
The ASA governs printed advertisements for savings accounts. It does not actively monitor them, but waits for members of the public to make a complaint before it takes action.

The ASA's code says that advertisements have to be legal, decent, honest and truthful. If you make a complaint, and the ASA decides that the advertisement appears to have breached its code, it will ask the company to justify its claims. If the ASA then upholds the complaint, it will tell the offending company not to repeat the claim. If the company refuses to abide by the ruling, the ASA can then ask newspapers and magazines not to accept the advertisement. (The ASA has agreed in future to use the Code of Practice adopted by the banks and building societies as a benchmark.)

As well as this, the ASA publishes a monthly round-up of its judgements; it believes the threat of bad publicity helps to keep advertisers in line. As a final and rarely applied sanction, it can refer an advertisement to the Office of Fair Trading.

In practice, the ASA has limited powers to punish companies that run misleading advertisements. Companies are free to use them while the ASA carries out its investigations. By the time the Authority makes its ruling, the offending item may have already run its course. Even if the ASA rules against advertisements, there is not much it can do to punish companies. It cannot force companies to tell customers they have been misled, nor can it fine persistent offenders.

The FSA

The Financial Services Authority (FSA)* is taking over from the Investment Management Regulatory Organisation (IMRO) and the Personal Investment Authority (PIA) the responsibility for policing advertisements for investment-based products.

Such advertisements must:

• include a warning about the risk of your losing your money
• contain a comparison of the performance of the advertised investment with some benchmark product over the past five years. If the product has not been going that long, the advertisement must include a comparison since launch.

Apart from this, companies are fairly free to choose how to display the fund's performance and which benchmark to choose for comparison (see below for things to watch out for).

The FSA does not have to reveal the outcome of complaints, unless they lead to disciplinary action against the company involved. So you do not hear why the regulator has dismissed your complaint. If companies are instructed not to repeat an advertisement, or to reword it or tone it down, this guidance is not made public.

What to look out for

It is impossible to cover all the methods financial companies use to make their products look good – marketing people can be very creative. These methods tend to be the most common.

Confusing savings with investments

The most basic, and important, rule is: know what you are getting yourself into. Take care if you are tempted by 'savings plans' which appear to offer you high rates of growth on your savings. The product advertised may well turn out to be a share-based investment plan rather than a traditional bank or building society savings account. At first glance, it is easy to be confused, especially if you are an inexperienced investor (see Chapters 1, 2 and 3 to work out your strategy).

Share-based products, such as unit trusts (see Chapter 21), are much more risky than traditional bank or building society savings accounts (see Chapter 12). Your capital is at risk through share price fluctuation and you may not get back all your original investment.

Past performance

One of the most contentious issues in the investment community is past performance. Investment firms use past performance heavily to sell their products and want to paint their funds in the best light possible (see below).

But is there any connection between good past performance and future performance? The answer would seem not. This may seem surprising given the way that investment companies market past performance and huge pension funds scrutinise past performance of investment managers. But recent research from the FSA has found that good past performance is no indication of future good performance.

However, it did find that there was a connection between poor past performance and poor future performance.

The FSA's approach on past performance seems contradictory. The FSA will be producing comparative league tables on financial products based mainly on charges. But because it has found no correlation between past and future perform- ance it will not be including past performance figures in the tables in case investors take these figures as some sort of regulatory seal of approval. However, it does not plan to outlaw investment companies using past performance to market their products, although it is looking at ways of reining in some of the more outlandish practices.

If the FSA research is right, and you feel comfortable with it, then you can discount past performance and concentrate on factors such as charges (assuming that you have chosen the right sector and the type of fund that suits your risk profile). But if you feel it is worth looking at past performance, then carry out your own research and dig deeper into the claims for past performance. There are two scenarios in which investors will need to find out their own information: first, when no information is widely available, and second (more relevant in this case), when independent information is needed to challenge claims being made by investment firms and by advisers. As the FSA will not provide the past performance information, it will be up to you to do the research to challenge the claims on past performance. The following outlines the types of claim to watch out for and tells you what questions you should ask.

Massaging the figures
Selective past performance
One problem the financial services industry faces – especially investment firms – is trying to come up with a message that will sell their products. In marketing terms, their brand awareness is quite low. Many of the big-name banks, building societies and insurance companies have names which many consumers recognise fairly easily, but this is not so true of most investment companies – apart from some of the newer entrants to the market, such as Marks & Spencer and Virgin. Even the best established and most famous of the traditional investment houses have little real brand awareness outside the active investment community.

As a result, when investment firms try to sell their products, whether direct to the consumer or through an intermediary, the biggest 'hook' they have is the past performance of their unit trusts or personal pensions. With so much riding on past performance, the temptation is to choose figures which show the firm in the best light. The financial regulators lay down two minimal rules that companies must follow when advertising their products (see page 77) but, otherwise, companies are free to choose time periods which make their investment performance look good.

One popular method of doing this is to choose a long time-frame – say 10, 15, or 20 years – over which the chosen fund has performed above average. But this does not tell the whole story. The longer time-frame can disguise the fact that an above-average return is all down to an excellent burst of performance at the start of the period. On closer inspection, you may find that the recent performance – say over the last 5 years – has been dismal.

The two charts on pages 80–1 highlight how the performance of the same unit trust can look very different, depending on how it is displayed. In the first chart, Fund A has grown by 188 per cent over the past 10 years, while the average UK growth unit trust has grown by 178 per cent. However, if you split the performance into two five-year periods (second chart), you can see the latest five-year performance does not look so good. Over the first five-year period, Fund A grew by 60 per cent while the sector average grew by only 42 per cent. However, over the second five-year period the tables were turned: Fund A grew by 69 per cent, lagging behind the sector average performance of 84 per cent. So the advertised performance, which looks so attractive over 10 years, actually relies on the first five-year performance. If you were thinking about investing in this fund, you would need to know that recent performance had slipped.

Solution
Do not rely on figures provided by companies in advertisements. For that matter, do not rely on the claims made by financial intermediaries for the funds recommended to you. They are not necessarily trying to mislead you but you have every right to ask for more figures to reassure yourself before you part with your money. Always double check and do not be afraid to ask.

You could follow the method used by *Which?* when it analyses past performance. It looks at the investment performance of a fund over four different five-year periods to allow investors to challenge the selective claims on investment managers. For example, when comparing consistency of performance up to the end of April 2001, *Which?* would use the following four periods: 30 April 1996 to 30 April 2001; 30 October 1995 to 30 October 2000; 30 April 1995 to 30 April 2000; and 30 April 1994 to 30 April 1999. Most funds are classified according to sectors, so you can compare how the fund has done against the sector average, as well as against a benchmark index.

Remember, past performance is no guide to the future but it does make sense to choose a fund that has performed consistently well. You may feel more comfortable selecting a fund which has beaten the average in all four periods. This shows that the investment manager can perform consistently above average during different stock market conditions.

Comparing share-based investments with savings accounts
Another method investment companies use when trying to promote poor-performing funds is to compare the returns with safer assets, such as bank or building society savings accounts. Over the long term, share-based investments tend to outperform cash-based savings anyway, so it is easy enough to make even the worst-performing investment fund look good against a savings account. But what you want to know is whether its investors would have done even better if they had gone to a different fund manager. Comparing performance against a savings account only excludes comparisons with the sector average and the benchmark index.

Always remember that share-based investments are much riskier than savings accounts. For example, you may come across an advertisement stating '*£1,000 of your savings would have grown to over £1,500 over five years in Fund X but to under £1,200 in the average savings account*'. This of course would be perfectly

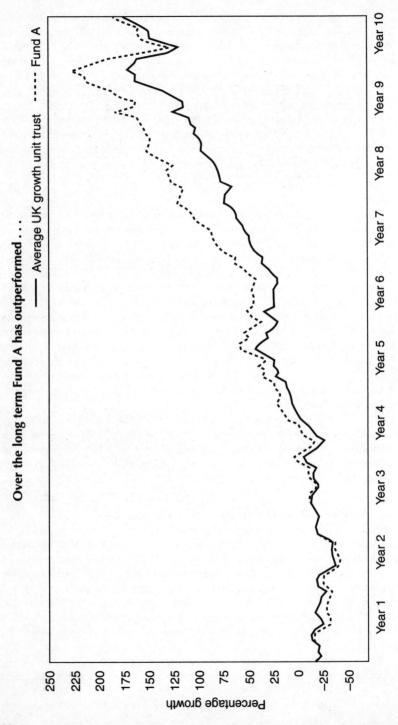

Over the long term Fund A has outperformed . . .

------ Average UK growth unit trust   —— Fund A

Percentage growth

250 225 200 175 150 125 100 75 50 25 0 -25 -50

Year 1 Year 2 Year 3 Year 4 Year 5 Year 6 Year 7 Year 8 Year 9 Year 10

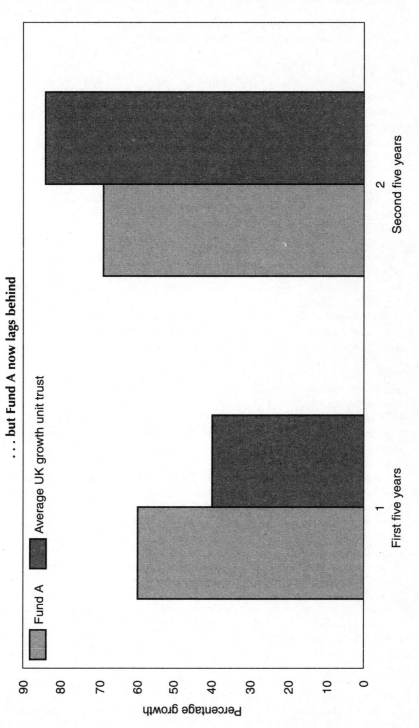

. . . but Fund A now lags behind

true – what it does not show you, though, is the fluctuations in the value of your capital in the share-based fund over the period (see the charts on pages 83–5).

Solution
If you are thinking about investing in a particular fund, never rely on simple comparisons of how the fund has done against a savings account; ask to see a comparison with a sector average or a benchmark index. And, if you are a cautious investor, ask to see how risky the fund has been. Compare the volatility of the fund with the sector average or ask for a simple fluctuation chart for the fund over the recent past.

Guarantees
Guaranteed investment products are becoming more popular. Look out for the advertisements which promise that you will benefit from rises in the stock market while guaranteeing that, if the market falls, you will still get all your money back. Some even promise you, say, 'market growth plus 40 per cent'. You might think this means that if the market were to rise 10 per cent you would get back 10 per cent plus 40 per cent – a total of 50 per cent. Not so! It would mean you would get back 10 per cent, plus 40 per cent of that 10 per cent – a total of 14 per cent. That is a big difference!

Remember, too, that 'market growth' is simply the capital growth of a particular index. This excludes dividends paid from shares – which over the long term make up a significant proportion of the return you might get from share-based investments (see the chart on page 85).

Savings accounts
The small print
Whenever you see an advertisement for a savings account which seems to pay a high rate of interest, always read the small print. The headline rate may not look so attractive once you take into account hidden penalties buried in the terms and conditions.

Some headline rates can look very attractive but this may only apply to balances above a certain amount. Similarly, on instant-access accounts the headline rate often includes a bonus. But you may find that you lose the bonus if you make more than a certain number of withdrawals in a year or if your account drops below a certain balance. These 'bonuses' can be seen as another way of using penalties to keep your money locked into the account. If you lose the bonus by making too many withdrawals, the real rate of interest paid will be lower than the interest you get on a true instant-access account.

Similarly, watch out for advertisements that show comparisons with other savings accounts. An advertised account may look as if it tops the league table. On closer inspection, you may find the quoted rate includes bonuses that you get only if you meet special conditions.

Solution
The simple advice is 'read the small print'. Watch out particularly for rates that include bonuses, or are paid only above certain balances. Check how often you can make withdrawals from accounts that claim to be instant-access. Check if the

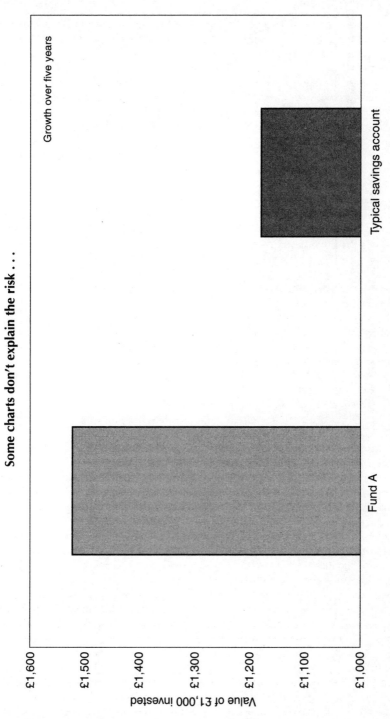

Some charts don't explain the risk . . .

Growth over five years

Value of £1,000 invested

£1,600
£1,500
£1,400
£1,300
£1,200
£1,100
£1,000

Fund A

Typical savings account

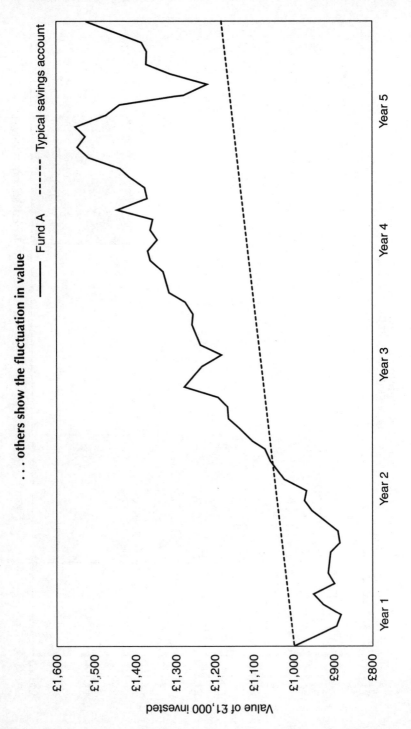

... others show the fluctuation in value

——— Fund A   ----- Typical savings account

Value of £1,000 invested

£1,600
£1,500
£1,400
£1,300
£1,200
£1,100
£1,000
£900
£800

Year 1   Year 2   Year 3   Year 4   Year 5

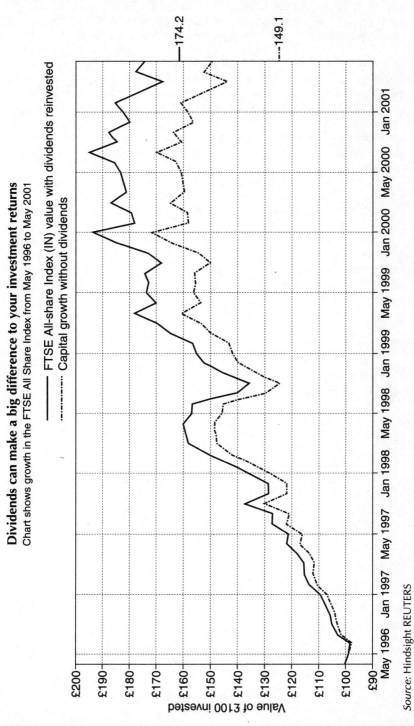

Dividends can make a big difference to your investment returns
Chart shows growth in the FTSE All Share Index from May 1996 to May 2001

—— FTSE All-share Index (IN) value with dividends reinvested
·········· Capital growth without dividends

174.2

149.1

Value of £1000 invested

£200
£190
£180
£170
£160
£150
£140
£130
£120
£110
£100
£90

May 1996 Jan 1997 May 1997 Jan 1998 May 1998 Jan 1999 May 1999 Jan 2000 May 2000 Jan 2001

Source: Hindsight REUTERS

balance has to be maintained above a certain level. Check that rates are not introductory offers on new accounts, paid for the first few months only.

Selective comparisons

You may, from time to time, see advertisements in which a bank or building society claims that its account pays a better rate than a chosen average. It may claim that the rate on its account is better than the average of, say, the top ten rival institutions. Always check what the comparison actually means. For example, the top ten mentioned may be the biggest institutions. They generally tend to pay the lowest rates anyway, so beating the average of the biggest institutions is nothing to crow about.

A variation on this is a guarantee to beat or match the average of the 'top ten'. At first glance this seems attractive but, if the advertiser guarantees to beat just the biggest institutions, it may not be worth much. You could get better rates elsewhere.

Solution

Take comparisons with a pinch of salt. Read the small print to see *exactly* what claims the advertisement is making and check them using the guidance in this chapter.

Using the Internet to save and invest

One of the biggest developments in the financial services industry in recent years has been the impact of the Internet on saving and investing. There are three points to note about using the Internet to save and invest:

First it is a rich source of information. This ranges from general guidance on saving and investing to tax information; news; comparisons of different companies' savings products, mortgages, investment funds and annuities; up-to-the-minute shares prices; and broker research. Only a few years ago, some of this information was restricted to professionals and, to gather other details, you would have had to ring round each source or tramp your local high street. Now you can review the whole – or at least a big chunk – of the market from your armchair.

Second and increasingly, you can take out products and services online and manage your accounts and investments over the web. At present, setting up is rarely an instant or complete process. In May 2000, legislation was passed to allow 'electronic signatures' (digital authority that can be sent from your computer) in place of written signatures on contracts. But this is not yet in force in many areas, including, for example, contracts for loans. Moreover, when you open an account or first make an investment, providers must comply with rules aimed at combating money laundering. In general, while you can download product details and complete application forms online, you often need to send the printed and signed form by post with the required identification documents and/or your cheque.

Finally, Internet companies themselves have been the target for substantial speculative investment. Like all stock market bubbles, this one burst. Dot.com companies' share prices tumbled and many investors pulled out nursing painful losses. While the Internet will become increasingly important in all areas of life, there is less certainty about how individual companies can turn it into a source of profit. Problems they face include:

- how to market their web sites – recently, one bank cited advertising costs running as high as £250 for each new customer
- attracting advertising revenue evidence suggests that users ignore web site advertising
- persuading customers to pay for services – so much good web information is free
- eliminating customers' fears about security – in particular, the high degree of concern about using credit cards online even though Internet purchases are at least as safe as card purchases by phone or in a restaurant.

What you can do to protect yourself

In theory, using the Internet should be the same as saving and investing through the post or by telephone. The same principles and rules apply about protection and your rights (see Chapter 6). But, in practice, there are differences simply because the Internet opens a whole new world for investors and consumers. As with any new technological evolution, there are new risks and benefits.

If you are thinking about investing over the Internet, always take these basic steps to protect yourself. Check whether an investment firm is authorised. While the Internet vastly increases the ordinary investor's opportunities, it also increases exposure to potential fraud, scams and dubious practices. The last thing you want is your money to disappear into a black hole in cyberspace.

Authorised firms have to meet certain standards set by the Financial Services Authority (FSA)* – whose new regulatory regime is expected to come into force from late 2001. (In the meantime, the rules of existing regulators apply.) Remember that you will be protected by the complaints and compensation schemes only if you deal with a firm that is authorised. The easiest way to check is to ring the Consumer Helpline of the FSA on 0845 606 1234. Once the FSA's new regime goes live, you will also be able to make an online check through the FSA's consumer web site (*www.fsa.gov.uk*). As the FSA says, even if a firm claims to be authorised, do not take the firm's word for it. Always check.

Non-UK companies

The nature of the Internet means that you are more likely to come across overseas firms advertising their investment services. The geographical barrier that normally protects potential customers does not exist for Internet investment firms, both legitimate and illegal.

Just because a web site has '.co.uk' or '.uk' in the address does not automatically mean that the firm is based in the UK. You lose all chance of recovering your investment if you send money to an illegal operation outside the jurisdiction of the UK courts.

To be legal, any overseas firm whose web site makes investment products available to UK consumers must be authorised by the FSA. In the case of firms based in the European Economic Area (see below) they will be automatically authorised in the UK if they are regulated in their home country. But remember you are protected by the systems in that home country rather than by the FSA, and these protection schemes do not necessarily match those of the FSA. So you might want to check with the overseas regulator before making any investment through the firm.

All overseas firms legally allowed to make investments available to UK customers through their web sites are listed on the FSA Register of authorised firms, so check the Register before you do business.

Beware of bogus sites

If you plan to invest using the Internet services of what seems a reputable household name, it is worth checking that the web site address is genuine. Some fraudsters copy web sites owned by legitimate firms and use similar web addresses. Look up the number in the phone book: the chances are that if you have stumbled across a bogus site the phone number given will be misleading too. The FSA has asked investors to let it know about these scams.

Countries (other than UK) in the European Economic Area (EEA)		
Austria	Greece	Netherlands
Belgium	Iceland*	Norway*
Denmark	Ireland	Portugal
Finland	Italy	Spain
France	Liechtenstein*	Sweden
Germany	Luxembourg	

* Not members of the European Union

Savings

Most of the main high-street banks and building societies now have a presence on the Internet, offering a wide range of banking services. In relation to savings, financial institutions are adopting one of two strategies.

Some, such as Barclays, NatWest, HSBC and Nationwide, have chosen to provide 'integrated' services to their customers, where if you have a traditional branch account you can use the Internet in addition to, or instead of, over-the-counter services.

Others have set up new stand-alone Internet banks, where transactions are made entirely via the Internet. Many of these new banks use quirky names with no apparent connection with banking and financial services. 'Egg', for example, was launched by the insurance giant Prudential. This deliberate policy is designed to develop a separate identity for the Internet bank from its parent company. The idea is to shake off any association with the stuffy image of the financial services industry. Other new Internet banks include Cahoot from Abbey National, IF from the Halifax and Smile from the Co-operative Bank.

Banks find Internet services attractive for two key reasons. First, many people using the Internet are young and affluent – just the customers they want to attract.

Second, online banking is much cheaper for the banks than traditional branch-based accounts. Banks can provide online services at one-tenth the cost of traditional banking, enabling the new banks to pass on the cost savings to customers through better savings rates.

Best interest rates paid on deposits

	Amount on deposit	
Type of account	£500	£5,000
Internet no-notice savings account	6.3%	6.6%
Other no-notice savings account*	5.65%	6.0%

* Branch, phone or postal.

Source: *Moneyfacts*, April 2001

However, as Internet banking matures, it seems that many customers are reluctant to commit themselves to a wholly virtual bank. The integrated-services approach appears to have the edge. As a result, some Internet banks are looking at adding a bricks-and-mortar side to their operations – for example, Egg is considering a limited branch network possibly through the 300 or so shopping centres owned by the investment side of its parent, Prudential. Other institutions, such as Allied Irish Bank, have scrapped plans for Internet-only banks.

The current intense competition is good news for customers. As the table on the previous page shows, in April 2001 Internet banks were offering the best available rates for savings and current accounts. But, as with all savings, you should regularly review your accounts and be prepared to switch if rates fall behind.

Research

Many general information and news sites on the web include guides to the best savings rates available. They include *www.ftyourmoney.com*, *www.moneyextra.com* and *www.iii.co.uk*. A definitive source is *www.moneyfacts.co.uk*, a financial information specialist.

Potential pitfalls

If a bank you've never heard of offers a particularly attractive rate on the Internet, you might feel suspicious. Lack of familiarity does not necessarily mean there is a problem, but it is wise to check with the FSA that the bank is authorised to accept deposits in the UK and which country it is based in. You will then know if the protection schemes outlined below apply in your case.

Protection schemes

Banks and building societies authorised to accept deposits in the UK belong to deposit protection schemes which guarantee that you will get back at least 90 per cent of the first £20,000 of your savings if the institution goes bust. From late 2001, these schemes are due to be replaced by the new Financial Services Compensation Scheme. This has four sub-schemes, one of which covers deposits, such as bank and building society accounts. Protection is being increased to 100 per cent of the first £2,000 you have on deposit and 90 per cent of the next £33,000 (in other words, a maximum of £31,700).

Some authorised institutions are offshoots or subsidiaries of overseas banks. In these cases, you may have to rely on the deposit protection scheme of the bank's home country, so always check. While the single European market for financial services has not yet taken off, the Internet crosses international barriers, making it much easier for the big European institutions to push pan-European products.

Ombudsmen and Codes of Practice

Banks and building societies in the UK abide by a voluntary Code of Practice and belong to the Banking Ombudsman* scheme or Building Societies Ombudsman scheme, respectively. From late 2001, these are due to be absorbed into the new Financial Ombudsman Service (FOS). However, not all overseas banks offering services in the UK have signed up. And, at the moment, the rules of the Banking

Ombudsman scheme in the UK actually rule out overseas banks from joining. All this may make it difficult to resolve complaints. Bear this in mind when you weigh up whether or not you should deposit money with an overseas bank.

Customer service

One advantage of using traditional branch-based accounts is face-to-face discussion with a member of staff to resolve problems. This is not possible with Internet banks, where you have to use the phone or email. *Which?* magazine has reported consumer difficulties in using emails this way. One particular criticism is that the Internet banks ignore emails or send customers standard emails which do not actually deal with the specific query. Customers are also charged for telephoning banks' helplines. For the time being, some Internet banks are letting customers down by providing poor service even if they offer good-value products.

Tax

If you want to deposit money with an overseas bank, check the tax position first. Interest from many offshore centres popular with UK residents (for example, the Isle of Man, Jersey and Guernsey) is paid 'gross' – in other words, without tax deducted. This can make advertised rates look particularly attractive. But bear in mind that, if you are a UK taxpayer, you must declare the foreign interest you receive and pay UK income tax on it. Even so, there can be a long delay between receiving the interest and paying tax. In the meantime, you earn extra interest on the unpaid tax, giving you a modest tax advantage.

If your interest has already had some foreign tax deducted before you receive it, you may be able to claim a credit that will reduce the UK tax due.

Investments

There are three main types of investment readily available online: investment funds (unit trusts and open-ended investment companies), shares and pensions. So far, these have nearly always been offered on a no-advice basis – so you are on your own. However, a few Internet sites are beginning to explore offering advice alongside products. For example, Egg operates a fund 'supermarket' (see page 94) and is considering links with an independent financial adviser to provide advice on its site.

A few independent financial advisers have their own sites offering online advice. One or two even have automated advice software. This works by asking you to fill in a fairly detailed online form. The programme then recommends suitable investment products by following set rules that take account of attitudes to risk, tax position and other factors.

The remainder of this chapter looks at using the Internet to invest in shares and investment funds.

Share dealing

The Internet certainly offers many new opportunities and advantages for ordinary investors who want to buy and sell shares. It is also easy to do initial research, keep track of your share portfolio and get the latest news. It is also cheap, convenient, fast and, of course, exciting.

Cost is a big factor. If you use a phone-based or postal, dealing-only stockbroking service, the commission on a £5,000 deal might range from £15.95 up to £105 – the most expensive usually include the cost of advice whether or not you seek it. By contrast, Internet charges for a £5,000 deal typically range from £9.95 to £90 with the majority in the £10 to £30 bracket. By shopping around, you can find cheap flat-rate deals at £10 to £15 and many online services have special offers, such as cut-price – or even free – dealing for a limited period.

Dealing commissions might not be the only costs. Check whether there are other charges. For example, you may have to pay a joining fee of, say, £25 to £50 a year, giving you access to research tools such as company information and analysts' research, but bear in mind there are lots of other information sites you can tap (see below). Shares are normally held in a nominee account run by your broker; otherwise there may be a £2.50 to £22.50 charge for each sale or purchase involving a share certificate.

Taking all costs into account, if you buy and sell shares only infrequently, you may do better to use a traditional postal service.

Another important reason for dealing online is *speed*. With some brokerage services, you can carry out your deal in seconds and receive confirmation through an online confirmation note. Postal services may be cheaper in some cases with the risk that by the time your dealing instructions reach your broker individual share prices may have changed significantly.

But check what sort of online service you are dealing with. Some are little different from a traditional phone-based broker – your order is simply emailed to the dealing desk. The broker then executes your order either immediately or later in the day when your order is pooled with others, reducing transaction costs. Other services connect you direct to the broker's dealing computers and your order is executed the second you hit the button – this is known as 'real-time dealing'. The benefit is that you can be certain of the price you pay or receive.

Using the Internet for research

Providing access to research on shares and stock markets is one of the biggest advantages the Internet has brought to ordinary investors.

This can come when you sign up to an Internet broker to buy and sell shares for you. But there are plenty of independent Internet sites which provide share prices, stock market news and company performance data. A number of sites have additional features allowing you to plot charts of company share prices and markets and provide links to forums and other useful sites. Many sites also provide portfolio calculators to analyse the performance of your shares.

Some sites let you register a fantasy share portfolio. You go through the motions of buying and selling shares and track how well your portfolio performs without committing real money. This way, you get a feel for buying and selling before trying the real thing.

These sites generally don't charge you for using them but most require you to register before you can use all the features provided.

The Internet investment world changes almost on a daily basis. The following sites are highly recommended by *Which?* but you should keep trying out new sites and services:

- *www.fool.co.uk* – this site comes from the highly regarded Motley Fool. It is simple to find your way around and includes a portfolio tracker service. Share prices are 20 minutes behind real time.
- *www.uk-invest.com* – well written, with up-to-the-minute share prices, the site also includes a portfolio tracker and tips on shares and unit trusts.
- *www.iii.co.uk* – the Interactive Investors International site is one of the best. It provides detailed prices (15 minutes behind real time) and an excellent investment glossary.

Which? suggests that more experienced investors should try sites such as *www.market-eye.co.uk*, *www.hemscott.co.uk* and *www.barra.com*. These sites provide more detailed information on companies, for example profit-and-loss accounts, balance sheets, stockbrokers' forecasts for company earnings and details of major shareholders. Other useful sites include *www.wisi.com* which provides detailed analysis of company sales, earnings and financial strength and so on. The site *www.hoovers.co.uk* also provides detailed information, with an additional feature that allows data to be converted into other currencies.

The more advanced sites tend to be UK versions of existing US Internet services.

Buying and selling

There are number of ways to pay for shares and receive the proceeds when you deal on the Internet. Some brokers allow you to pay by cheque when buying shares and will send you a cheque for the proceeds when you sell. By far the most common method is either to pay by debit card or to set up a cash account which the broker debits when you buy shares and credits when you sell them. These broker accounts usually pay you interest on your balance.

When you set up a cash account to trade, you need to provide proof of identity, such as a passport or driving licence, and proof of your address, for example a recent household bill or bank statement. All this has to be done by post before you can go hi-tech. Brokers generally ask you to lodge a certain amount with them to cover opening transactions and various charges. The size of this up-front deposit varies from broker to broker.

When you are choosing a broker, there are other things to consider besides cost. Check the broker's *coverage* – the range of shares that the broker handles. Most investors stick to the shares listed on the main London Stock Exchange, so there is generally no problem with coverage or availability. But if you are adventurous and determined to trade in small, risky company shares or overseas shares, you may have to do more homework to find a broker who deals in these.

When choosing an Internet broker, the most important factor – more important than cost and coverage – is *quality of service and efficiency*. Cheap dealing costs count for little if the broker is inefficient or difficult to contact when you want to deal. One way of getting an idea of broker efficiency is to ask around. Also check Internet bulletin boards.

Unit trusts

As well as shares, the Internet offers investors cheap ways of buying and selling investments in unit trusts and open-ended investment companies (either within an ISA wrapper or not). Many providers have corporate web sites through which you can invest and gather information. Some use the Internet specifically to offer low-price funds, including CAT-standard ISAs (see page 118).

Discount brokers

A way to keep down costs is to use a discount broker who will rebate some of the commission built into the initial charge you usually pay when you invest in a unit trust. A typical initial charge on a UK unit trust is around 5 per cent, including the commission paid to the broker by the fund manager who runs the unit trust. The amount of discount you get varies depending on the broker and on the unit trust.

Never let the discount on offer dictate your choice of unit trust. Saving 1 or 2 per cent on the initial charge is not worth it if you end up buying into the wrong unit trust. Do your homework and research first and decide which unit trust is suitable for you (see Chapter 21). At this point, it makes sense to look around for the best deal available.

Remember too that when you buy through a discount broker you are dealing on an execution-only basis without advice and the protection that comes with it. Chasing after discounts is a false economy if you end up with the wrong investment for your needs.

Internet investment supermarkets

Another option growing in popularity is the fund supermarket. As with most Internet developments, this originated in the USA. These supermarkets are, in principle, just the same as discount brokers but offering additional services such as decision-making software, and portfolio-monitoring services. Egg, the Prudential's Internet bank, was the first major UK company to set up an investment supermarket. Woolwich and the Interactive Investor followed suit.

Fund supermarkets are likely to become more prevalent due to a change in FSA rules in April 2001. In general, any firm selling or advising on investments like unit trusts must either stick to the products of just one company or be totally independent – a concept called 'polarisation'. However, the FSA has relaxed the polarisation rule in the case of such investments sold on a 'direct offer' basis – in other words, without advice. It is assumed that investors who buy in this way are reasonably sophisticated and unlikely to mistake a firm selling a range of companies' products for a fully independent adviser selecting products from the whole marketplace. The change opens the way for product providers more easily to offer a range of products from other companies alongside their own.

There is concern that these supermarkets are blurring the boundary between advice and execution-only services. Their basic investment profile is designed to screen funds according to your circumstances and attitude to risk. You are then offered a list of funds based on your profile from the limited range of funds on the supermarket 'shelves'.

Typically, these supermarkets rebate up to 4.5 per cent of the commission, reducing it to as little as 0.5 per cent, so it is a cheap way of buying the particular unit trusts they have in their stable. But remember that these Internet profiles are no substitute for a proper, comprehensive fact-find completed by an independent financial adviser. Morever, the funds they trade in may not be the most suitable for you. Once again, discounts may be a false economy.

The dangerous side of the Net

The basic rules of investing via the Internet are the same for investing generally. You should turn to investments only when you have satisfied your basic financial priorities, such as an emergency fund, life insurance and income protection. Next consider retirement saving, then turn to other goals. You should gradually work your way along the risk spectrum, starting off with collective investments such as unit trusts. Only then should you consider trading single shares on your own account. You should begin with major established UK shares and, once you have the experience, move on to smaller, risky companies.

If you decide to try Internet dealing, do not get too caught up in the excitement of the online-trading environment. Online investors, on average, buy and sell shares more frequently than their counterparts who use telephone or postal services – twice as often according to recent research from the USA. If you do trade frequently, remember you quickly rack up dealing costs which has a negative effect on your investment portfolio returns.

In general, if you bypass basic rules taken from the 'real' world you can get your fingers badly burned financially.

Day trading

'Day trading' is a US phenomenon which has yet to catch on to anywhere near the same level in the UK. However, a few day trading centres have now opened in London and are planned for other major UK cities. These centres have trading stations – computers equipped with the necessary software – that private investors can hire by the day. People in the US have been known to give up their day jobs to take up day trading as a full-time way of earning a living.

Investors set up Internet dealing accounts often with money borrowed from their broker which they use to buy and sell volatile shares on the same day, hoping to make quick profits. The idea, or hope, is that the shares they buy will rise during the day so that the investor can repay the loan to the broker and keep the rest as profit. If the market goes against the day trader the losses can be substantial.

Day traders favour shares in new, small companies often involved in fashionable hi-tech industries. The market in these shares is not very 'deep' and any piece of news or rumour can cause the share price to swing wildly. If it swings the right way, investors stand to make large, immediate gains.

The risks of buying volatile shares, particularly using borrowed money, should not need to be spelled out. The spread (the difference between the buying and selling prices) is usually high on small company shares and can be around 10 per cent. This means that shares have to rise by at least 10 per cent for the investor simply to break even, never mind make a profit. If the share price falls by 10 per cent, say, the total loss would be 20 per cent. Contrast this with the shares in a big established company in the FTSE 100 Index, where the spread is around 1 per cent.

Day trading is not suitable for the vast majority of investors. It is estimated that seven out of ten day traders in the USA lost money last year. Day trading should only be carried out by investors who genuinely have money to burn.

Financial regulators on both sides of the Atlantic have issued warnings on day trading. Do not confuse it with the sensible use of the Internet to do research, buy and sell shares cheaply and monitor your investment portfolio. Day trading is effectively a form of gambling, and is extremely risky. If you are determined to day trade, here are some point to remember:

- Few people actually make money. Invest only what you can truly afford to lose
- Don't rush in. Do as much of your own research and preparation as you can. Don't believe everything you read. The FSA has issued warnings about the reliability of information on Internet bulletin boards and in chat rooms (see below)
- Day trading is expensive. Traders need access to 'real-time' prices. They need to know that the prices they see on their screens are the ones they can actually deal at. The real-time dealing and quotation services are more expensive than basic Internet dealing services. Ideally, day traders also want what is known as 'level II' information. This gives not just the best available buying and selling prices, but the prices and volumes being traded by every participant in the market. Level II trading screens let day traders place their deals directly in the market without using a broker, but are currently available only for US markets not the London Stock Exchange.

Bulletin boards and chat rooms

Internet bulletin boards and chat rooms are a popular way for online investors to swap information and pick up tips. But you do need to take care. Some will be bogus or the lead into a scam. The most common scams are 'pumping and dumping', 'touting', and 'trashing and cashing'.

Pumping and dumping is simple: hucksters 'talk up' the companies they hold shares in, trying to boost the share price. Once it rises, they sell and make a quick profit. When the hype stops, the share price often falls back quickly, leaving the victims with big losses.

Some companies pay professional **touts** to recommend and push their shares on the Internet. But the shares may be more hype than substance. For example, unscrupulous directors could use a tout to boost shares to increase their own personal wealth – they might have share-option schemes. Once the share price has been boosted, they gradually off-load their shares to unsuspecting buyers.

Trashing and cashing is the opposite of pumping and dumping. Rather than shares being 'talked up', misleading or false messages may be posted on the Internet, claiming that a company is running into problems. These rumours can cause the share price to fall. Once this happens, the trasher buys the shares at a knock-down price, knowing that the price will bounce back when the rumours are proved to be untrue.

So when looking at bulletin boards:

- be suspicious – ask yourself why a complete stranger would want to share a fantastic tip with thousands of other investors
- do not trust the information you receive – do your own research, using the Internet

- be particularly suspicious of communications from people who want to share 'privileged' information with you and urge you to act quickly. Remember one of the golden rules of investment – if it sounds too good to be true then it probably is.

'Boiler room' scams

A 'boiler room' company is one where sales staff 'cold call' potential investors and pressure them into buying shares in hitherto 'undiscovered' companies.

The first approach may be through the post or via email. For example, you could be offered a free research report in a company you hold shares in – your name will appear on the easily available share register. You may receive a mail shot containing a great offer. If you sign on the dotted line, make sure you check the small print – you may be giving your consent to being contacted by the boiler room company. The next thing you know, you are bombarded by calls from the sales staff offering you great deals. They use high-pressure tactics to get you to buy the shares they are pushing. Here's some guidance if you are cold-called:

- Check the company is authorised. If it is not and something goes wrong, you have no rights to redress.
- If it is not authorised, it could mean that the company is based overseas. Leave well alone.
- Read the small print carefully. Once you sign on the dotted line, the company is within its rights to call you.
- If you are tempted by the shares on offer, do your own research to cross-check the sales team's claims.

If it sounds too good to be true, it usually is . . .

10 Tax

Whatever investment you choose, it is the after-tax return that counts. Non-taxpayers and higher-rate taxpayers should be especially careful to keep a weather eye on the impact of different tax rules. And all taxpayers should consider using special schemes, such as ISAs (Individual Savings Accounts), which are designed to encourage investment by offering tax incentives – for details, see Chapter 11.

Tax can also affect the cost of an investment. For example, tax relief can save up to 40 per cent of the cost of a payment to a personal pension – see Chapter 18.

Which taxes?
The most common tax you have to pay is income tax on investment income. A second tax to watch out for is capital gains tax. Inheritance tax does not directly affect the return you get on your investments but we give the basic rules at the end of this chapter.

Which tax hurts you most depends very much on your investment choice. If your investments produce capital gains rather than income and your returns do not exceed the annual slice of tax-free capital gains, you pay no tax at all. If you exceed your tax-free slice, the excess is added to your income and you pay tax at 10, 20 or 40 per cent, depending on the size of your total taxable income. So you should look for investments offering you the highest rate of return *after* tax, either as income or as capital gain.

Income tax

There are three ways in which investment income can be treated. It can be:

- tax-free
- taxable but not taxed before you get it
- paid with some tax already deducted.

Income tax is charged on your income for a tax year which runs from 6 April in one year to 5 April the following year. Your tax bill for 2001–2 is based on your income from 6 April 2001 to 5 April 2002.

> ### EXAMPLE 1: How tax affects investment choices
>
> Dave pays income tax at the higher rate of 40 per cent. He has a choice between two investments:
>
> - investment A will pay him an income of 7 per cent a year
> - investment B will not pay any income, but it will, he hopes, show a capital gain of 5 per cent a year.
>
> Both these figures are before tax. At first sight, investment A looks more attractive. But let us assume that investment A pays an income of £7,000. The effect of income tax at 40 per cent is to reduce this sum to £4,200. Investment B on the other hand, producing a gain of £5,000, is liable for capital gains tax. The relevant tax is also 40 per cent but the first slice of total yearly gains – £7,500 in the 2001–2 tax year – is tax-free. So Dave would pay no tax on Investment B, leaving £800 more in his pocket than Investment A.

How much income tax?

All your income is added together to arrive at your *gross income*	say £25,000
From this you deduct your *outgoings* (certain payments you make: for example, payments to your employer's pension scheme)	say £1,200
This leaves	£23,800
From this you deduct your *personal allowance* (and blind person's allowance, if appropriate)	£4,535
This leaves your *taxable income*	£19,265
Tax is charged on your taxable income	
Tax bill (£1,880 at 10% and £17,385 at 22%)	£4,012.70
From this deduct married couple's allowance (if either partner born was before 6 April 1935) or children's tax credit if applicable	£—
This leaves a *final tax bill*	£4,012.70

Rates of income tax for the 2001–2 tax year

The first £1,880 of your taxable income is taxed at the starting rate of 10 per cent. Income between £1,881 and £29,400 is taxed at the basic rate of 22 per cent. Anything more is taxed at the higher rate of 40 per cent.

Married couples

If you are married and own investments jointly with your spouse, income is assumed to be paid in equal shares, with each paying tax on half.

If you own the investment in unequal shares, the income can be taxed accordingly. You *both* have to make a joint declaration on Inland Revenue Form 17 to one of your tax offices. This sets out how the capital and income are shared between you. The different tax treatment applies from the date the declaration is made.

Husband and wife each have their own personal allowance and starting- and basic-rate tax bands. It may be worth transferring ownership of some investments from one spouse to the other, so that total income is more evenly distributed. To be effective for tax purposes, such gifts have to be outright, i.e. without strings attached. There is no capital gains tax on any gifts or sales of assets between husband and wife.

Tax-free investment income
No tax is paid on the income, interest, dividends or proceeds from:

- Save-As-You-Earn linked to an employer's share-save scheme
- Savings Certificates from National Savings (and, in most cases, Ulster Savings Certificates if you live in Northern Ireland)
- National Savings Children's Bonus Bonds
- some friendly-society savings plans
- qualifying life-insurance policies
- premium bond and lottery prizes
- tax rebates
- first £70 each year from a National Savings Ordinary account
- ISAs, maturing TESSAs and PEPs
- delayed settlement of damages for personal injury or death
- part of some annuities
- venture capital trusts.

Taxable investment income not taxed before you get it
Tax is not deducted at source from:

- National Savings Investment accounts and National Savings Income, Pensioners' and Capital Bonds
- gilts, unless you choose to be paid with tax deducted
- interest on loans you make to private individuals
- deposits at non-UK branches of building societies and UK or overseas banks
- deposits made by people not ordinarily resident in the UK
- co-operative society deposits
- credit union dividends.

How it is taxed
The interest is paid gross and you have to account to the Inland Revenue separately for any tax you owe.

Where the tax you owe is no more than £1,000 and you pay tax on other income – either earnings or a pension – through Pay-As-You-Earn (PAYE), tax on your investment income can also be collected through PAYE. In other cases, tax is collected through the self-assessment system: you make two equal payments on account on 31 January during the tax year and 31 July following the tax year. These payments are based on your tax bill for the previous year.

A balancing payment or refund may be due on 31 January following the tax year, once your actual income for the tax year is known. For example, suppose your tax bill for 2000–2001 was £5,000 and in 2001–2 tax due on your income –

including investment income – turns out to be £5,500. For 2001–2, you make two payments on account each of £2,500 (i.e. half your tax bill for the previous year) on 31 January 2002 and 31 July 2002. This means that you have paid £5,000 in total which is less than the eventual bill of £5,500, so on 31 January 2003 you must pay the final £500 (along with your first payment on account for 2002–3).

Investment income paid with tax deducted

Examples of income with some tax already deducted are:

- most interest from banks and building societies
- interest from foreign-currency deposits made at UK banks
- interest on most local authority loans issued after 18 November 1984
- interest on certain loans, e.g. loans to foreign governments
- interest on gilts, if you have not asked to have interest paid gross
- interest on company fixed-income investments (loan stocks or debentures)
- part or all of the income from annuities
- income from certain income and growth bonds
- income from certain trusts and settlements
- income from a will, paid out to you during the administration period (i.e. while the details of who gets what under the will are being worked out)
- dividends from shares, distributions from unit trusts and open-ended investment companies.

How it is taxed

With some types of saving and investments that pay interest, tax of 20 per cent may be deducted at source before you receive the income. This includes bank and building society deposits, gilts, corporate bonds and unit trusts and open-ended investment companies that invest mainly in gilts and corporate bonds.

- Non-taxpayers can reclaim tax already deducted. To avoid having to reclaim tax, non-taxpayers can sometimes arrange to have interest paid gross, without tax deducted at source. To do this, complete form R85 available from banks, building societies, post offices and tax offices.
- Starting-rate (10 per cent) taxpayers can now also reclaim half the 20 per cent tax deducted at source – ask for form R40 (SP) (M) at your tax office or Inland Revenue enquiry centre.
- Basic-rate (22 per cent) taxpayers have no more tax to pay.
- Higher-rate taxpayers have more tax to pay – at a rate of 40 per cent of the gross interest, i.e. they have another 20 per cent tax to pay.

So, for example, if you receive £80 interest after tax, £20 tax is deducted at source; the gross interest is £100. Higher-rate taxpayers must pay tax of 40 per cent of £100, i.e. £40. But they have already had £20 tax deducted at source, so will owe the balance: £20.

Shares and share-based unit trusts and open-ended investment companies come with a tax credit of 10 per cent.

- Non-taxpayers cannot reclaim this tax.
- Starting-rate (10 per cent) and basic-rate (22 per cent) taxpayers have no more tax to pay.
- Higher-rate (40 per cent) taxpayers do have more tax to pay – at a rate of 32.5 per cent of the gross dividend.

So, for example, if you receive a net dividend of £80, you get a tax credit of £8.89, making the gross dividend £88.89. (The £8.89 tax credit is 10 per cent of the gross dividend, not 10 per cent of the net dividend.) Higher-rate taxpayers must pay tax of £28.89, which is 32.5 per cent of £88.89. But they already have a tax credit of £8.89, so owe the balance: £20. For a quick way to work out how much tax is owed, higher-rate taxpayers can divide the net dividend by 4. In the example, a net dividend of £80 divided by 4 comes to £20 – the tax still owed by higher-rate taxpayers.

Points to watch
Annuities
If you have bought an annuity voluntarily with your own money (not, for example, as part of a personal pension), part of the income each year is treated as a return of capital, part as interest on the capital. Only the interest part is taxable; the insurance company will say how much this is. Non-taxpayers may be able to have the income paid out before tax. Ask the insurance company for form R89.

Discretionary trusts
Discretionary trusts pay tax at 34 per cent on most of their income. This applies whether the income is kept by the trust or paid out to you. If it is paid out to you, you get a credit of 34 per cent of the gross (before-tax) amount. If your income, including the income from the trust, is too low for you to pay tax, or you pay tax at a lower rate, you can claim back some or all of the tax deducted. Higher-rate taxpayers have more tax to pay on income paid out.

The way a discretionary trust pays tax on shares and similar investments changed on 6 April 1999. Beneficiaries and trustees should get professional advice on the tax rules.

Gilts and some other stocks
All gilts bought on or after 6 April 1998 have interest paid without tax deducted. However, you can ask to have interest paid net of tax at the savings rate of 20 per cent. Some stocks bought before this date had tax deducted at source. You can ask for interest to be paid gross.

If you sell British Government stocks before a date when you are due to receive an interest payment (normally twice yearly), part of the price you get is deemed to be the interest you would otherwise have received. It is calculated on a daily basis and taxed as income. This is known as the *accrued-income scheme* which also applies to sales of permanent interest-bearing shares (PIBS) and local authority and corporate bonds.

When you buy the stock, any accrued interest included in the price can be offset against the dividend paid, so you do have to pay tax twice on the same income. But if your holdings of all stocks covered by the scheme remain below

£5,000 *nominal* or face value in total, the above rule does not apply. In this case, any accrued income included in the price of stock you sell is considered to be part of the capital value and is not taxed as income.

Income and growth bonds
There are several different types of bond, which work (and are taxed) in different ways – see Chapters 25 and 26.

National Savings Capital Bonds
Although interest is credited to your Capital Bond each year, you do not receive it until you have held the bond for a full five years (or you cash in early). However, you still have to declare the interest and pay tax on it each year. You receive a notice of interest credited each year from National Savings.

National Savings Ordinary accounts
You and your spouse are each allowed £70 interest free of tax from a National Savings Ordinary account. But you are taxed on anything more.

Any one person is allowed only £70 free of tax, however many accounts he or she has.

Unit trust and open-ended investment companies
With the first distribution you get from a unit trust, you are likely to get an *equalisation payment.* This is a return of part of the money you first invested, so it does not count as income and is not taxable. But see page 112 for how it affects capital gains.

With an accumulation unit trust (where income is automatically reinvested for you), the amount reinvested, apart from any equalisation payment, counts as income, and higher-rate taxpayers have extra tax to pay – see page 112.

Life insurance
There are two main types of life-insurance policy for tax purposes. These are:

- qualifying policies – including most regular-premium policies, such as most endowment policies and low-cost endowment policies linked to mortgages
- non-qualifying policies – including single-premium policies.

The insurance companies' investment funds are taxed, so you do not pay basic-rate tax on policy proceeds.

You have to pay tax only if you are a higher-rate taxpayer (or would be once the gain from the policy is added to your income) and the policy is a non-qualifying policy. A qualifying policy cashed in or made paid up in its first ten years (or the first three-quarters of its term, if less) becomes a non-qualifying policy.

Your *taxable gain* is the amount you get when a policy comes to an end, *plus* any amounts you have withdrawn from the policy in the past which haven't already been taxed, *less* the total premiums paid including any subsidy you received on the premiums.

If you cash in only part of a policy before it matures, you get an allowance for each 12-month period since you first took out the policy. If you have received

---

EXAMPLE 2: Top-slicing relief

Arnold bought a £25,000 single-premium bond in December 1995 and cashed it in for £37,000 in July 2001, making a gain of £12,000. He already has taxable income for 2001–2 (after deducting allowances and outgoings) of £24,700. If his taxable income exceeded £29,400 in the 2001–2 tax year he would become liable to higher-rate tax.

Arnold can claim top-slicing relief. With this, the average yearly gain of £2,400 (the £12,000 total gain divided by the five complete years the bond ran for) is added to his other income for the year of £24,700. The total is £27,100, well within the basic-rate tax band. Arnold has no tax to pay on the proceeds of his bond.

Now suppose he made a gain of £24,000. That is an average yearly gain of £4,800 over five years. Add £4,800 to Arnold's income and you get £29,500. That is £100 over the basic-rate limit. Arnold would have to pay tax at a rate of 18 per cent – i.e. 40 per cent higher-rate tax, less the 22 per cent basic-rate tax already paid by the insurance company. Eighteen per cent of £100 is £18. Arnold's final tax bill would be £18 multiplied by 5 (for the five complete years he held the bond), i.e. £90.

Top-slicing relief would reduce Arnold's tax bill in this case. Without it, the entire £24,000 gain on the bond plus his existing income of £24,700 would come to £48,700. And 18 per cent tax on £19,300 – the excess over the basic-rate band of £29,400 – would have been £3,474.

---

more from the policy than the amount of your allowances, the excess counts as your gain. For the first 20 years of the policy, the allowance is 5 per cent of the total premiums paid so far. For each year after that, the allowance is 5 per cent of the total premiums paid in that year and in the previous 19 years.

This means that you can take a yearly income from non-qualifying policies up to the yearly allowance without paying any tax until you finally cash in the policy. Any income above the yearly allowance is free of basic-rate tax, but if you are a higher-rate taxpayer you have to pay tax at the higher rate for the year in which you take the income. If you do not use the full 5 per cent allowed in any tax year, you can use it in future years.

Any gain is added to your income for the tax year in which the policy matures or is cashed in. There is no basic-rate tax to pay on the gain, only any higher-rate tax. So if you are liable to tax at the higher rate of 40 per cent, you pay tax at 40–22 = 18 per cent.

If adding the gain to your income means that you are pushed from the basic to the higher tax bracket, you should claim *top-slicing relief*. This spreads the gain over the years that the policy has run. Your tax bill is based on the average gain for each complete year that the policy has run, multiplied by the number of years. If the average gain added to your other taxable income does not take you into the higher tax bracket, there is no further tax to pay. (See Example 2.)

Tax relief

Premiums on qualifying policies taken out before 14 March 1984 receive a subsidy of 12.5 per cent from the Revenue, irrespective of whether you pay tax. You lose the subsidy if you alter the policy in a way which increases the benefits payable. That could include taking up an option attached to the policy, for example to increase your premiums and therefore your amount of cover, to extend the term, or to convert the policy into another kind of policy. You do not lose the subsidy if the increased benefits are due to an increase that is built in, for example if premiums and cover automatically increase by a fixed percentage. But there is a limit on premiums of £1,500 or one-sixth of your total income, whichever is greater, and if you pay premiums of more than this you do not get the subsidy on the excess.

Capital gains tax

You make a capital gain (or loss) when you *dispose* of an asset. Anything you own (whether in the UK or not) counts as an asset, for example houses, jewellery and shares.

You *dispose* of an asset if you sell, give away, exchange or lose it. You also dispose of an asset if it is destroyed or becomes worthless, if you sell rights to it (for example grant a lease), or if you get compensation for damage to it (for example insurance money) and don't spend it all on restoring the damage. But a transfer of an asset between a husband and wife does not count as a disposal (unless they are separated), nor does the transfer of an asset you leave when you die. Some types of gain are tax-free altogether (see page 110), and the first slice of total chargeable gains made in a tax year is also tax-free – £7,500 in 2001–2.

Working out the gain (or loss)
To work out the basic gain (or loss) you make when you dispose of an asset, you have to:

- take the *final value* of the asset when you dispose of it – its sale price (or market value at the time, if you gave it away or sold it for less than its full worth)
- deduct its *initial value* when you got it – the price paid (or the market value at the time if you were given or inherited it). For assets acquired before 31 March 1982, you have a choice of initial value – see page 111
- deduct any *allowable expenses* you incurred in acquiring, improving or disposing of the asset, such as the costs of advertising, commission, legal fees and stamp duty.

If the answer is zero or a negative figure, there is no gain and no tax to pay. You can, however, set losses against gains on other assets. If the answer is a positive figure, you have made a gain but there are various adjustments you can make before deciding whether or not the gain is taxable.

Indexation allowance

Where you first acquired the asset before 1 April 1998, you may be able to claim *indexation allowance*. This strips out any gain in value due simply to rising prices by increasing the amount of the initial value and each allowable expense (for buying, improving or selling) in line with changes in the Retail Prices Index (RPI). You can claim this allowance for periods of ownership between March 1982 and April 1998 (but see page 111 for assets owned on or before 31 March 1982).

To work out your indexation allowance you use:

- A – the RPI for April 1998 (or the month of disposal, if earlier)
- B – the RPI for the month in which you acquired the asset or incurred the allowable expense (or March 1982, if later).

You then subtract B from A, divide by B and round to the nearest third decimal place to get an *indexation factor*. Thus:

$$\frac{A - B}{B} = \text{indexation factor}$$

You will find a list of RPI figures on page 107. However, there is no need to do the sums; a list of indexation factors for April 1998 is given on page 108. Your tax office can supply indexation factors for disposals made before April 1998.

The indexation factor, multiplied by the initial value of the asset or your allowable expense, gives you your indexation allowance. For example, say you bought shares in September 1989 for £2,000 and sold them in September 2001 for £6,000. The indexation factor for September 1989 is 0.395 (see page 108). You multiply £2,000 by 0.395, to get £790. So £790 is your indexation allowance. Your gain for capital gains tax is thus:

£6,000 (disposal proceeds) *less* £2,000 (initial value) *less* £790 (indexation allowance) = £3,210

From the £3,210 you deduct buying and selling costs. You can claim an indexation allowance for your buying costs – for example, share-dealing commission – in the same way as for the initial £2,000 value of the shares.

Where you have made a loss on an asset, you set the loss against gains made on other assets in the same tax year. You do this after deducting indexation allowance but before calculating taper relief (see below). Bear in mind that the first slice of your gains each year is tax-free (£7,500 in 2001–2). But losses must be set against all gains made in the same tax year, including any covered by the tax-free slice. Any losses you cannot offset in the tax year can be carried forward to set against chargeable gains made in a future year. Losses brought forward from an earlier year are also subtracted after indexation allowance but before calculating taper relief.

You need use only enough of any losses brought forward from previous years to reduce the later year's gains to the amount of the tax-free slice. Eventually, you should use losses to reduce your gains to the tax-free slice before claiming taper relief. You should set losses against those gains which would incur the highest tax bill: i.e. gains for which you can claim the least amount of taper relief.

Retail Prices Index

Use these figures for working out your capital gains tax bill. The RPI was rebased (i.e. went back to 100) in January 1987. We have reworked the figures for previous months so that they are comparable with the rebased figures.

	Jan	Feb	Mar	Apr	May	Jun	Jul	Aug	Sept	Oct	Nov	Dec
1982	[1]	[1]	79.44	81.04	81.62	81.85	81.88	81.90	81.85	82.26	82.66	82.51
1983	82.61	82.97	83.12	84.28	86.64	84.84	85.30	85.68	86.06	86.36	86.67	86.89
1984	86.84	87.20	87.48	88.64	88.97	89.20	89.10	89.94	90.11	90.67	90.95	90.87
1985	91.20	91.94	92.80	94.78	95.21	95.41	95.23	94.49	95.44	95.59	95.92	96.05
1986	96.25	96.60	96.73	97.67	97.85	97.79	97.52	92.82	98.30	98.45	99.29	99.62
1987	100.0	100.4	100.6	101.8	101.9	101.9	101.8	102.1	102.4	102.9	103.4	103.3
1988	103.3	103.7	104.1	105.8	106.2	106.6	106.7	107.9	108.4	109.5	110.0	110.3
1989	111.0	111.8	112.3	114.3	115.0	115.4	115.5	115.8	116.6	117.5	118.5	118.8
1990	119.5	120.2	121.4	125.1	126.2	126.7	126.8	128.1	129.3	130.3	130.0	129.9
1991	130.2	130.9	131.4	133.1	133.5	134.1	133.8	134.1	134.6	135.1	135.6	135.7
1992	135.6	136.3	136.7	138.8	139.3	139.3	138.8	138.9	139.4	139.9	139.7	139.2
1993	137.9	138.8	139.3	140.6	141.1	141.0	140.7	141.3	141.9	141.8	141.6	141.9
1994	141.3	142.1	142.5	144.2	144.7	144.7	144.0	144.7	145.0	145.2	145.3	146.0
1995	146.0	146.9	147.5	149.0	149.6	149.8	149.1	149.9	150.6	149.8	149.8	150.7
1996	150.2	150.9	151.5	152.6	152.9	153.0	152.4	153.1	153.8	153.8	153.9	154.4
1997	154.4	155.0	155.4	156.3	156.9	157.5	157.5	158.5	159.3	159.5	159.6	160.0
1998	159.5	160.3	160.8	162.6	[1]	[1]	[1]	[1]	[1]	[1]	[1]	[1]

[1] Indexation allowance only runs from March 1982 to April 1998

Indexation factors for disposals after 31 March 1998

	Jan	Feb	Mar	Apr	May	Jun	Jul	Aug	Sept	Oct	Nov	Dec
1982	n/a	n/a	1.047	1.006	0.992	0.987	0.986	0.985	0.987	0.977	0.967	0.971
1983	0.968	0.960	0.956	0.929	0.921	0.917	0.906	0.898	0.889	0.883	0.876	0.871
1984	0.872	0.865	0.859	0.834	0.828	0.823	0.825	0.808	0.804	0.793	0.788	0.789
1985	0.783	0.769	0.752	0.716	0.708	0.704	0.707	0.703	0.704	0.701	0.695	0.693
1986	0.689	0.683	0.681	0.665	0.662	0.663	0.667	0.662	0.654	0.652	0.638	0.632
1987	0.626	0.620	0.616	0.597	0.596	0.596	0.597	0.593	0.588	0.580	0.573	0.574
1988	0.574	0.568	0.562	0.537	0.531	0.525	0.524	0.507	0.500	0.485	0.478	0.474
1989	0.465	0.454	0.448	0.423	0.414	0.409	0.408	0.404	0.395	0.384	0.372	0.369
1990	0.361	0.353	0.339	0.300	0.288	0.283	0.282	0.269	0.258	0.248	0.251	0.252
1991	0.249	0.242	0.237	0.222	0.218	0.213	0.215	0.213	0.208	0.204	0.199	0.198
1992	0.199	0.193	0.189	0.171	0.167	0.167	0.171	0.171	0.166	0.162	0.164	0.168
1993	0.179	0.171	0.167	0.156	0.152	0.153	0.156	0.151	0.146	0.147	0.148	0.146
1994	0.151	0.144	0.141	0.128	0.124	0.124	0.129	0.124	0.121	0.120	0.119	0.114
1995	0.114	0.107	0.102	0.091	0.087	0.085	0.091	0.085	0.080	0.085	0.085	0.079
1996	0.083	0.078	0.073	0.066	0.063	0.063	0.067	0.062	0.057	0.057	0.057	0.053
1997	0.053	0.049	0.046	0.040	0.036	0.032	0.032	0.026	0.021	0.019	0.019	0.016
1998	0.019	0.014	0.011	n/a	n/a	n/a	n/a	n/a	n/a	n/a	n/a	n/a

Taper relief

Taper relief replaced indexation allowance in April 1998. It means that the longer you hold an asset, the greater the tax relief and the lower your tax bill. The taper relief rules make a distinction between business and non-business assets – and they are less generous for non-business assets.

You can claim taper relief for complete tax years for which you have held an asset after April 1998. However, for assets held immediately before 17 March 1998 (the date on which this relief was announced), you can add an extra year to the number of complete tax years you have held an asset.

Taper relief reduces the amount of chargeable gain. For non-business assets, the reduction kicks in after you have held an asset for three *complete* tax years. Say you buy shares in October 2001, during the 2001–2 tax year. You would then have to hold them through another three tax years – 2002–3, 2003–4 and 2004–5 – before being entitled to taper relief. For disposals after three complete tax years, taper relief reduces your gain by 5 per cent. Thereafter relief increases by 5 per cent a year until, when you have held an asset for ten or more complete tax years, you get the maximum relief of 40 per cent of your gain.

You apply taper relief *after* you have deducted any capital losses you have made in the current or earlier tax years. However, you should work out any taper relief you may be entitled to *before* you deduct losses – then you can ensure that you set losses against the gains that attract the least taper relief.

Table 1: Capital gains tax taper relief for non-business assets

Number of complete tax years after 5 April 1998 for which asset held	Taper relief	Percentage of gain which is chargeable	Example: amount of £1,000 gain which remains chargeable after taper relief
0	0%	100%	£1,000
1	0%	100%	£1,000
2	0%	100%	£1,000
3	5%	95%	£950
4	10%	90%	£900
5	15%	85%	£850
6	20%	80%	£800
7	25%	75%	£750
8	30%	70%	£700
9	35%	65%	£650
10 or more	40%	60%	£600

How much tax?

Capital gains tax is charged in the same way as tax on investment income. So if you pay only starting-rate tax you pay capital gains tax at 10 per cent. If you pay basic-rate tax you pay capital gains tax at 20 per cent. If you pay higher-rate tax you pay tax at 40 per cent (2000–1 tax rates). If your capital gains take you into

---

EXAMPLE 3: Capital gains tax to pay?

Maxine inherited units in a unit trust when her aunt died in June 1990. At that time the units were valued at £1,500. In July 2002, she sells the units for £6,300. To see if she has any tax to pay, she does the following sum:

Final value	£6,300
less Initial value	£1,500
less Allowable expenses	£ 0
Basic gain	£4,800
less Indexation allowance for period June 1990 to April 1998 (£1,500 × 0.283 – see page 108)	£ 425
Indexed gain	£4,375
Loss on another asset	£ 450
Gain before taper relief	£3,925
Number of complete tax years after 5 April 1998 for which units held	4
plus one year because units held on 17 March 1998	5
Taper relief of 15% of £3,925	£ 589
Chargeable gain	£3,336

The chargeable gain falls well within Maxine's tax-free slice for the year, so she has no tax to pay.

---

the next tax band when added to your other income, you pay tax on the excess at the rate applicable in the highest band you fall into.

Declare any taxable gains on your tax return. If you do not receive a tax return, you must tell the Inland Revenue about any gains on which you owe tax within six months of the end of the tax year (by 5 October 2002 for gains made in the 2001–2 tax year). Any tax due has to be paid on 31 January after the end of the tax year in which the gains were made (31 January 2003 for 2001–2).

Tax-free gains
The gains you make on some assets are tax-free, but any losses you make on them cannot be used to offset chargeable gains. The main tax-free gains are those on:

- your own home
- private cars
- British money (including post-1837 gold sovereigns and Britannia gold coins)
- foreign currency for personal and family expenditure (e.g. for a holiday abroad)
- personal belongings (chattels) with a predictable life of less than 50 years when you bought them (e.g. electronic equipment, machinery but also some investments such as racehorses)
- personal belongings expected to last more than 50 years (e.g. antiques, jewellery and other moveable items), unless their value when you dispose of them is more than £6,000
- gifts to charities
- gifts to some *national heritage bodies* (e.g. some museums and the National Trust)
- proceeds from life-insurance policies, unless you bought the policy from a previous holder
- *qualifying* corporate bonds including permanent interest-bearing shares (PIBS)
- gilts
- National Savings investments (though some are subject to income tax)
- shares issued after 18 March 1986 under the Business Expansion Scheme and sold more than five years after you bought them (on their first disposal only)
- shares in qualifying venture capital trusts
- shares issued under the Enterprise Investment Scheme
- futures and options in gilts and qualifying corporate bonds
- shares, unit trusts, open-ended investment companies and investment trusts held in a PEP or ISA
- damages for any wrong or injury suffered by you in your private or professional life (e.g. damages for assault or defamation)
- betting and lottery winnings
- compensation if you were mis-sold a pension between 29 April 1988 and 30 June 1994.

Points to watch
Assets owned on 31 March 1982
Only gains made after 31 March 1982 are taxable. This means that if you dispose of an asset you already owned on 31 March 1982, you can use the market value in March 1982 as the initial value, ignoring the asset's original value. But you cannot deduct expenses incurred before 31 March 1982. Alternatively, you can use the market value of the asset when you got it as the initial value and you can deduct expenses incurred before 31 March 1982.

You can elect for all your assets acquired before 31 March 1982 to be treated as though you acquired them on or after 31 March 1982, even if you acquired some or all of them before then. This election cannot be revoked.

If you do not make the election, whichever rules produce the smaller gain or loss will be used. And if you make a gain under one set of rules, but a loss under the other, it will be treated as though you made neither a gain nor a loss.

Gifts

If you give an asset away, or part with it for less than its true worth, your gain is worked out as though you had sold it for its full market value. However, there is a special form of relief available when you make certain types of gifts on which the tax is due, called *hold-over relief*. The effect of this relief is to avoid a tax bill at the time of the gift. Tax is put off until the recipient parts with the gift, although it could mean a higher tax bill then.

Gifts on which you can claim hold-over relief are:

- gifts of business assets including certain unquoted shares
- agricultural land
- lifetime gifts on which you have to pay inheritance tax.

As the recipient, you will be counted as acquiring the asset at its market value when the giver first acquired it. You can count as your own the giver's allowable expenses and benefit from the indexation rules up to the time of the gift, as well as any indexation allowance due from the time you receive the gift.

Both you and the giver must apply jointly for hold-over relief by contacting the Revenue. There's no point in claiming this relief if the giver's gains for the year (including the gain on the gift) do not exceed the tax-free slice. The giver does not save tax and the recipient might pay more.

Shares, unit trusts and open-ended investment companies

If you acquired one lot of the same type of shares in one company (or units in a unit trust) at the same time, they are treated in the same way for tax purposes as any other asset. However, if you bought shares or units of the same type in one company at different times, the Inland Revenue has special rules for deciding which ones you have sold when you come to sell them. These rules are complicated and you may need professional advice to sort matters out.

You may receive an *equalisation payment* from a unit trust. The payment is not taxable but it must be subtracted from the purchase price of the units when working out your capital gain or loss.

With an *accumulation* unit trust, the income for your units is automatically reinvested for you. This affects the purchase price of your units for capital gains tax purposes. This is complicated and you should check with the unit trust company.

Keeping the capital gains tax bill down

There are ways to minimise your capital gains tax:

- be sure to deduct from a gain, or add to a loss, all your allowable expenses
- if you have things which have increased in value, you can avoid tax by keeping the gains you make each year below the tax-free slice. Do this each year if you can – it cannot be carried forward to the next year
- if your losses for the year add up to more than your gains, carry forward the balance of the losses to set against gains in later years. So keep a careful record
- husband and wife each have their own tax-free slice. Save tax by giving assets to your spouse to dispose of – but it must be a real gift, with no strings attached.

Deferral relief

You can postpone a capital gains tax bill if you reinvest the gain in venture capital trusts within one year before or after the disposal from which the gain arose. Similarly, you can postpone tax if you reinvest in shares that qualify for the Enterprise Investment Scheme; in this case, the time limit for reinvestment is one year before and three years after making the relevant gain.

You have to pay the postponed tax when you eventually dispose of the investments in which you have reinvested. You can claim taper relief (if relevant) for the time you held the original asset.

If you dispose of Enterprise Investment Scheme shares issued after 5 April 1998 and reinvest the money in other Enterprise Investment Scheme shares, you can claim taper relief from the date you acquired the first set of shares.

Inheritance tax

Roughly speaking, inheritance tax is a tax on the value of what you leave when you die, and on some gifts you make during your lifetime. So this tax does not affect investment decisions very much. Here we give a brief outline of the rules, then look at life-insurance policies, where a little care can keep inheritance tax at bay.

When does inheritance tax have to be paid?

There may be inheritance tax to pay:

- if you die within seven years of making certain gifts (known as *potentially exempt transfers*). These include gifts to people other than your spouse (e.g. gifts from parents to children) and some gifts to trusts
- if you make a *chargeable* transfer while you are still alive, including gifts to companies and gifts to discretionary trusts
- if you die, and the value of all your possessions, plus any gifts and chargeable transfers, is more than a set amount – £242,000 in the 2001–2 tax year.

However, some gifts are tax-free (see below) and ignored by the Inland Revenue. For example, gifts between a husband and wife are normally tax-free, no matter when they are made. So if you leave all your estate of £300,000 to your spouse, the value of your estate, for inheritance tax purposes, is nil. Of course, when your spouse dies, there may be tax to pay on his or her estate.

Many other gifts you make during your lifetime will be taxable only if you die within seven years of making them.

Any gifts which are not tax-free start to clock up a running total. When your running total of these chargeable transfers (for example gifts to companies and discretionary trusts) goes above a certain level – £242,000 in the 2001–2 tax year – tax is payable at half the rate of tax due on death. At present the tax rate on death is 40 per cent, so half of that would be 20 per cent.

Any gifts made more than seven years ago are knocked off your running total, so it can fall as well as rise.

Tax-free gifts
Some gifts are tax-free only if made during your lifetime. Others are tax-free whenever they are made. Gifts that are tax-free during your lifetime include:

- gifts which are part of your normal expenditure out of income – they must be regular, and not reduce your standard of living
- gifts to people getting married, with a maximum of £5,000 from each parent of the couple, £2,500 from a grandparent and £1,000 from anybody else
- maintenance payments to ex-husbands or wives and transfers of property under the terms of a divorce settlement
- gifts of reasonable amounts needed to support a dependent relative
- gifts for the education, maintenance or training of your children if they are still in full-time education or training or not more than 18 years of age
- small gifts of up to £250 to each recipient each year
- your annual exemption of up to £3,000 a year. This is in addition to all the tax-free gifts above, except that you cannot give £3,000 plus £250 (the 'small gifts' exemption) to the same person. Note that, if you do not use the full £3,000 in one year, you can carry the balance forward for up to one year (i.e. up to £6,000 in the second year) but you must use up the current year's exemption first.

Gifts which are tax-free whenever they are made include:

- gifts between husband and wife (provided the recipient is domiciled in the UK)
- gifts to UK-established charities
- gifts to British political parties
- gifts to most museums and art galleries, universities, the National Trust, local authorities and similar bodies
- gifts of property and possessions of outstanding national interest (and where the public have reasonable access to the property or possessions), provided Treasury approval is obtained
- gifts of land in the UK made to registered housing associations after 13 March 1989
- broadly speaking, gifts of shares to a trust which will hold more than half of a company's ordinary shares and which was set up for the employees' benefit, provided the trustees have voting control.

Inheritance tax and life insurance
Regular-premium life-insurance policies are an excellent way of giving chunks of tax-free capital to your dependants, or indeed to anyone.

The premiums count as a gift but there should not be any inheritance tax to pay on them, since they are normally in one of the tax-free categories above.

What to avoid
Try to make sure that the proceeds of your policies do not count as part of your estate. If they do, they are added to the rest of your estate and your inheritance tax bill could rise.

You can avoid this by getting the policy written in trust so that the proceeds go to someone else. If a policy on your life is for the benefit of your wife (or husband) or children, the Married Women's Property Act provides a simple way of doing this. Otherwise, you need to get a declaration of trust written on the policy. Ask the insurance company what to do.

Types of policy

- Endowment policy
  what it is: a policy that pays out a lump sum on a fixed date or when you die, if this is earlier.
  useful for: people who want to give tax-free capital away in their lifetime.

- Whole-life insurance
  what it is: a policy that pays out on your death.
  useful for: paying the inheritance tax bill when you die. A husband and wife who are going to leave everything to each other could take out a last-survivor policy, which pays out on the second death (i.e. when the inheritance tax bill arrives). The premiums are lower than for a policy on a single life. A joint-life-first-death policy is useful for paying any tax bill on the first death.

- Term insurance
  what it is: a policy that pays out only if you die before the policy ends (within three or ten years, say). If you survive, it pays nothing.
  useful for: someone who will be faced with a large inheritance tax bill only if death occurs within a certain time. For example, someone who has received a gift may be caught by a tax bill if the giver dies within seven years.

This subject is covered in great detail in *The Which? Guide to Giving and Inheriting* published by Which? Books, 2001.

11 Tax-efficient saving and investing

Governments, both Labour and Conservative, have designed schemes with tax breaks aimed at encouraging particular types of saving and investing. There are currently five major schemes:

- ISA – Individual Savings Account
- TESSA – Tax-Exempt Special Savings Account (no longer available to new investors)
- PEP – Personal Equity Plan (no longer available to new investors)
- EIS – Enterprise Investment Scheme
- VCT – Venture Capital Trust.

Pension schemes and plans also have tax breaks – see Chapters 17, 18 and 19 for details.

Individual Savings Account (ISA)

Individual Savings Accounts – ISAs – became available on 6 April 1999. They replaced TESSAs and PEPs. You can no longer open a TESSA account or start a PEP. However, TESSAs opened by 5 April 1999 can continue until the end of their five-year life; PEPs opened by that date can continue indefinitely and in much the same way as before, although no new money can be invested in them.

ISAs essentially combine TESSAs and PEPs but are not nearly so attractive:

- the overall investment limits have been significantly reduced compared with TESSAs and PEPs
- the tax advantage on shares and share-based investments has been halved with a reduction in tax credit on these investments from 20 per cent to 10 per cent of the gross dividends. After 5 April 2004, the tax credit may be abolished altogether

An ISA is not an investment, but an account for holding investments in a tax-free way. You pay no income tax or capital gains tax on returns on investments held within an ISA account and do not have to put details on your tax return.

There are three ways in which ISAs can be invested.

- **Stocks and shares ISA** invests in higher-risk stock-market-type investments that can go up and down in value – such as shares, corporate bonds, unit trusts, open-ended investment companies.
- **Insurance ISA** is an investment-type life insurance (where the investments covered by a policy are in a tax-free fund).
- **Cash ISA** your money goes into deposit-type accounts with banks, building societies or National Savings.

There are three types of ISA account:

- **Maxi-ISAs** have an investment limit of £7,000 a year until 5 April 2006. A plan manager running a maxi-ISA must offer a stocks-and-shares option and can also offer the cash and life insurance options. You can invest the full £7,000 in stocks and shares; or you can put up to £1,000 in life insurance, up to £3,000 in cash and the rest in stocks and shares. Check carefully what is available with a maxi-ISA. Some plan managers only offer the stocks-and-shares part.
- **Mini-ISAs** each include just one option which can be stocks and shares or life insurance or cash. The investment limit is £3,000 a year for a stocks-and-shares mini-ISA, £1,000 a year for a life-insurance mini-ISA, £3,000 a year for a cash mini-ISA. These limits apply until 5 April 2006. The combined limits for three mini-ISAs are the same as the limit for one maxi-ISA. Be aware that, in any one tax year, you can have *either* one maxi-ISA *or* up to three mini-ISAs (one of each sort) – you cannot have both. So if you want to invest more than £3,000 in stocks and shares, do not take out a cash mini-ISA.
- **TESSA-only cash-ISA** This option is restricted to people who have a TESSA maturing after 5 April 1999. You can put up to £9,000 capital from a maturing TESSA into a deposit-account-based, TESSA-only ISA. You cannot reinvest the interest from your TESSA in the ISA.

In general, you must be a UK resident aged 18 or over to qualify for an ISA. However, from 6 April 2001 onwards, young people aged 16 and over can take out a mini-cash ISA.

Bear in mind that ISAs are mainly useful for taxpayers – for example, not many 16-year olds who stay on at school will have enough income to make them taxpayers. However, the rates offered on cash ISAs are sometimes the best available even for non-taxpayers (who get the gross rate on non-ISA accounts). And even non-taxpayers cannot normally reclaim the tax credit on shares dividends and unit trust distributions, but they can if they invest through a stocks and shares ISA.

When considering an ISA, weigh up the tax advantages against any extra charges. Usually, there are no extra charges for cash ISAs nor for stocks and shares ISAs that invest in unit trusts and similar investment funds. But with stocks and shares ISAs invested directly in shares typically there will be administration and dealing charges.

Points about ISAs
- Each tax year you can take out one maxi-ISA or up to three mini-ISAs (using different account managers for each mini-ISA if you want). In addition, you can

take out a TESSA-only ISA if you have a TESSA account maturing by 5 April 2004.
- You normally have to put cash in an ISA. You cannot transfer shares except by selling them and buying them back through an ISA – which could involve costs and in rare circumstances a capital gains tax bill. But you can transfer shares acquired under certain schemes run by your employer.
- You can make withdrawals from an ISA at any time without incurring a tax charge.
- An ISA can have a CAT mark, indicating it meets certain standards. CAT stands for charges, access and terms.

Tax-Exempt Special Savings Account (TESSA)

TESSAs ceased to be available to new savers on 6 April 1999. TESSAs opened before that date can run their full five-year course. At the end of five years you can reinvest the capital (but not the interest) in a TESSA-only ISA (see above).

Here are the main features of TESSAs.

- A TESSA lasts for five years.
- You could save up to £3,000 in the first year and up to £1,800 in each of the following four years, subject to a limit of £9,000 over the five years in total.
- The interest earned is tax-free *provided* you withdraw no more than the interest credited to your account at the time you want to make the withdrawal *less* the tax you would otherwise have paid. If you want to withdraw more interest than this, or some of your capital, the account is terminated. All the interest credited to the account then becomes taxable in the tax year that the account is terminated.
- Provided you do not overstep the mark, you are not taxed on any interest that you withdraw: the interest you cannot withdraw stays in your account (earning interest itself) until the TESSA matures.

Apart from these tax rules, the other details of TESSAs are up to each building society or bank. Some schemes are for regular and equal monthly savings (maximum £150 a month); others allow you to save as and when you like (sometimes subject to a minimum investment each time). Some do not allow any withdrawals; others do; and some automatically pay you a monthly income of as much as the Inland Revenue (and the scheme's interest rate) allows.

Banks and building societies must allow you to transfer out of one TESSA into another to chase the best interest rates (though, before you do so, check the terms and conditions for penalties). They are not obliged to let you transfer *in* though more than a half do.

You can close a TESSA whenever you like – you do not have to wait until the five years are up. But you have to pay tax on your interest and the bank or building society might charge you a penalty.

Personal Equity Plan (PEP)

PEPs ceased to be available to new investors from 6 April 1999. PEPs started before that date can be kept open indefinitely.

The attraction of PEPs is that the income from your investments in shares, unit trusts, open-ended investment companies, investment trusts or corporate bonds is free of income tax; any capital gain when you sell is also tax-free and someone else takes care of the day-to-day detail of share-ownership – buying and selling and dealing with paperwork. Some PEPs, though not all, have high charges; you need to review periodically whether the charges outweigh the tax benefits. This is particularly true for small shareholders who are unlikely to incur a capital gains tax bill even if they hold shares outside a PEP.

From 6 April 2001, the rules about which investments you can hold in your PEP have been aligned with the rules for stocks and shares ISAs. This gives you a very wide choice of shares, unit trusts and bonds from across the world. The rules on transferring PEPs have also changed so that you may now transfer just part instead of the whole PEP.

Types of PEP
You can no longer put new money into PEPs but you can still transfer your plans from one manager to another. PEPs come in many forms and the type you choose can have a significant impact on your expected return and the charges you face.

- **Advisory PEP** You choose how your PEP is invested but have the benefit of advice from the plan manager. Only a handful of managers – mainly stockbrokers – offer this type of PEP. Charges may be high.
- **Corporate bond PEP** A PEP investing only in corporate bonds and possibly preference shares too. If the PEP is invested in just one bond, you will get a fixed return. If, as is often the case, the PEP is invested in a selection of bonds (e.g. via a corporate bond unit trust), your return will be variable.
- **Corporate PEP** A PEP investing in the shares of one company, usually managed by that company or on its behalf by, say, a building society or bank. Inland Revenue rules used to distinguish between two types of PEP: general PEPs and single-company PEPs (see below). Corporate PEPs can be either general or single-company PEPs.
- **Managed or discretionary PEP** Your investment is pooled with other investors' money and the plan manager decides which companies to invest in.
- **Self-select or non-discretionary PEP** The plan manager acts on your instructions, investing in the shares, trusts or bonds that you choose. Charges for this type of PEP may be high.
- **Unit trust, open-ended investment company or investment trust PEP** A type of managed PEP. You can choose from a wide range of different funds – e.g. investing in UK shares, investing for income, specialising in the Far East – but the manager chooses the underlying shares or bonds and decides when to switch. Often no extra charges for the PEP are made over and above the normal charges of the unit or investment trust or open-ended investment company.
- **Single-company PEP** You invest in the shares of one company only. You can

sell the shares and reinvest the proceeds in the shares of another company – if the plan manager allows. From 6 April 2001 onwards, you can choose to amalgamate any single company PEPs with other PEPs you hold.

Enterprise Investment Scheme (EIS)

The Enterprise Investment Scheme aims to encourage investment in new ventures. Tax advantages when you invest in the newly issued shares of a qualifying unquoted company comprise income tax relief at 20 per cent on investments of up to £150,000 a year and freedom from capital gains tax when you eventually sell the shares. Losses can be set against gains on other assets or taxable income.

To get these tax breaks, you must invest for at least three years (five years for investments made before 6 April 2000). If you sell before then or if the company ceases within three years to qualify for the EIS, some or all of the income tax relief may be lost and any gain could be taxed. However, following a change in the 2001 Budget, relief is not lost if the company's shares become listed on a stock exchange before the qualifying period is up, provided this had not been arranged at the time you invested.

Up to half the amount you invest (to a maximum of £25,000) in the first half of a tax year (i.e. up to 5 October) can be carried back to the previous tax year, provided enough of the previous year's investment limit of £150,000 remains.

If you have made a taxable capital gain on the sale or disposal of any asset, you can defer paying tax on the gain if you reinvest it in shares which qualify under the EIS rules. You can claim this 'deferral relief' (see page 113) even if you do not qualify for EIS income-tax relief because you have exceeded the investment limits.

EIS rules allow you to invest in newly issued shares in unquoted companies trading in the UK and in companies quoted on the Alternative Investment Market (AIM). Companies which *cannot* qualify include:

- companies quoted on the main market of the UK Stock Exchange
- companies which deal in shares, provide financial or legal services or hold collectable goods (e.g. antiques, wines) for investment
- a company owned by you or one in which you (or your family or business partners) own more than 30 per cent of the business
- a company of which you are already a paid director or employee – you may, however, become a paid director provided you were unconnected with the company before you made the EIS investment
- for shares issued on or after 2 July 1997, a company engaged in property-backed activities, such as farming, market gardening, forestry, property development, hotel or retirement homes management
- for shares issued on or after 2 July 1997, a company where there is a scheme or guarantee ensuring that investors can get some or all of their money back.

Eligible shares are marketed as 'EIS shares'. They must have a sponsor who is, inter alia, responsible for ensuring that the shares are indeed eligible. You can invest either directly in companies or through a fund. If you opt for the direct route, the minimum investment is £500 per company. You should take advice before investing directly – from a stockbroker or accountant for example.

A novice investor would probably do better to invest through a fund. Your money is pooled with that of other investors and spread around several EIS companies, which helps reduce risk. The minimum investment through a fund is usually £2,000 and there is likely to be an initial fee of, say, 7 per cent of your investment.

Because EIS companies tend to be new and small, they are likely to be risky. Do not invest in an EIS unless you are happy with the level of risk and prepared to lose all your investment.

Venture Capital Trust (VCT)

VCTs are companies – basically investment trusts – which invest in a range of unlisted trading companies. They encourage investment in new ventures by addressing some of the problems investors face by:

- spreading risk across a range of qualifying companies
- increasing the chance of selling the shares by allowing the VCT itself to be quoted on the Stock Exchange.

The companies VCTs invest in are the same as those companies which qualify for the EIS (see above). But the tax breaks differ from those available to EIS investors.

You get tax relief at 20 per cent on up to £100,000 a year invested in the newly issued shares of a VCT, i.e. for every £1,000 you invest your tax bill will be reduced by £200. To qualify, you must hold the VCT shares for at least three years (five years in the case of shares issued before 6 April 2000). Dividends are generally paid tax-free. If you sell the VCT shares within five years, the tax reliefs are withdrawn.

You can get tax relief on dividends paid out by the VCT by deducting the tax credit accompanying the dividend from your tax bill for the year.

Any capital gain when the VCT shares are sold is also tax-free. But if you make a loss, it cannot be set against gains on other assets.

If you invest the proceeds of disposing of some other asset in VCT shares, you can claim deferral relief on any taxable gain. To qualify, you must reinvest the proceeds within one year before or one year after making the gain on the other asset.

By spreading your investment over a range of companies, VCTs may be less risky than some EIS investments. Remember, however, that even though the VCT itself is quoted on the Stock Exchange there may be little or no demand for its shares, so there is no guarantee that you will be able to sell when you want to.

12 Deposit accounts from banks and building societies

Banks and building societies are popular homes for people's savings. Before the conversion into banks of some of the biggest building societies, most people in the UK had a savings account with a building society. But that position has been reversed and the majority of savings are now held with banks.

It looks as if it may be bad news for consumers in the long run. Banks tend to pay out between 40 and 60 per cent of their after-tax profits as dividends to keep their shareholders happy. These dividends have to be paid for somehow and that translates into higher mortgage rates and lower savings rates for consumers. The remaining building societies are fighting back and regaining market share by offering better rates. But it is the banks that are now dominant on the high street.

On average, building societies offer better rates than banks. So if you do not have the time or inclination to shop around, a building society should be a better option than a bank. But there will be times, when you check the best-buy guides, that a bank is offering the best rate. If you do choose a savings account from a best-buy table, make sure you monitor the account closely. These accounts are often 'best buys' for a short time only and slip down the league tables once the financial institution stops promoting them (see Chapter 5, *Monitoring your savings and investments*).

If you have access to the Internet you will probably find excellent rates on offer from the Internet banks (see Chapter 9, *Using the Internet to save and invest*). Supermarkets also offer savings accounts – they can often offer competitive rates on some products. And always make full use of tax-efficient products such as Individual Savings Accounts (ISAs) – see Chapter 11, *Tax-efficient saving and investing*.

A safe home for your savings?

Building societies have traditionally been safe places to invest; they rarely run into difficulties and those that do have been quietly bailed out by others. Saving with banks, especially smaller ones, has been more risky in the past.

If a bank or building society gets into difficulties, you are guaranteed to get back 90 per cent of up to the first £20,000 of your savings; with a joint account each account-holder is separately protected up to £20,000. If you deposit money with a foreign bank in the UK, you have to rely on the compensation scheme of the country where the bank is authorised.

Offshore accounts

Money placed in most offshore accounts or held in offshore branches of UK banks or offshore subsidiaries of UK building societies is not covered by the UK protection scheme. But building societies are required by law to make good any losses that a subsidiary fails to cover. The Isle of Man runs a compensation scheme for building societies and banks similar to the UK bank scheme.

Offshore accounts present probate problems when you die. It could cost several hundred pounds and take a month or two for your savings to be released to your executors.

Basic features

Although accounts differ, they are all based on variations of three main factors:

* how you intend to *pay money in*, when and in what form
* how easily and quickly you want to be able to make *withdrawals*
* how the institution pays *interest*.

Paying money in

Some accounts have no restrictions on how you pay your money in – you can open them with as little as £1 and pay in what you like, when you like. But many do have restrictions:

* the minimum investment to open an account can vary from £1 to £50,000 or more
* some accounts once opened cannot be added to
* additions to others must be in certain multiples, e.g. in lumps of £100
* you may have to make regular, usually monthly, additions
* a maximum investment level (though rarely less than around £20,000) may apply.

Most organisations accept money over the counter at their branches or through the post. A few are linked to a network of cash machines allowing deposits outside normal opening hours. Some building societies have agents such as solicitors, insurance brokers and estate agents through whom you can deposit money. Some building societies and banks market special 'postal-only' accounts, often offering higher interest rates.

There is no legal limit on how much you can invest in any one account. Some institutions set their own limits which may vary from account to account. Occasionally this may be as low as £20,000, but it is usually not less than £100,000.

Withdrawals

Some accounts let you access your savings on demand; others require notice or lock your money for a period of time (a *term*).

To make these *notice accounts* and *term shares* more attractive, they may carry a number of concessions:

- easy access to the balance over a certain amount in your account. The 'balance-over' figure is often £10,000 and access is usually instant: that is, if you have £12,000 invested you can withdraw up to £2,000 on demand, whatever the normal conditions for withdrawals
- instant access, if you pay a penalty charge (e.g. three months' interest)
- instant access without penalty, restricted, for example, to £3,000 or one-tenth of your balance once or twice a year
- up to, say, three withdrawals a year without penalty (provided the balance does not fall below any minimum savings balance)
- a bonus of, say, 0.75 per cent if you make no withdrawals within the year.

There may be other restrictions on withdrawals:

- withdrawing only part of your savings may not be allowed
- you may have to withdraw in fixed multiples of, say, £100, or even £1,000.

Interest
How often is interest paid?
Accounts are available which pay interest yearly (occasionally even less frequently), half-yearly, quarterly or monthly. To understand how the frequency of interest affects the true rate of interest, see Chapter 5.

In most cases you can choose to have the interest:

- paid out to you, or directly into another account with the same or a different organisation
- kept in the same account to roll up (so that you get compound interest). This option is rarely available where the interest is paid monthly.

Some accounts offer a choice of interest-payment frequencies, for example half-yearly or monthly. If they do, and you choose to have your interest paid more frequently, there may be penalties, such as lower interest rates or higher minimum investments.

How are interest rates quoted?
Banks and building societies usually think in terms of gross (before-tax) rates – despite the fact that for most customers they must deduct tax before adding interest to the account.

Advertisements and rates cards often quote up to four rates:

- **Gross** – the *flat rate* before taking into account how often interest is paid, and without deduction of any tax. This is the 'contractual' rate – the rate on which (subject to the account conditions) the bank or society is obliged to base its calculations for paying you.
- **Net** – the *flat rate* after deduction of tax at 20 per cent. You usually find a phrase in the literature along the lines of 'net rates are illustrative only, based on the deduction of tax at 20 per cent'. This means that if the rates of income tax change, the bank or society is not obliged to pay you on the basis of the net rate shown.

- **Gross annual equivalent rate (AER)** – a true rate of return taking into account how often interest is compounded within the account. If interest is paid only once a year, the gross annual equivalent rate will be the same as the gross flat rate. But if, say, interest is paid twice a year, you get half the gross rate paid every six months. In the second half of the year you earn interest on the interest credited after the first six months. Over a year, the gross annual equivalent rate is higher than the gross flat rate. The gross AER is the rate at which a non-taxpayer will earn interest over a full year, provided the interest remains in the account.
- **Net AER** – the net rate compounded and what a basic-rate taxpayer earns over a full year. Higher-rate taxpayers have to pay extra tax, so reducing their effective interest rate – see below. Starting-rate taxpayers are able to claim back half the tax deducted at source.

If an AER figure is not quoted, it usually implies that interest is paid once a year and the compounded rates are the same as the flat rates.

Variable or fixed interest?

Most accounts are *variable*, which means that a building society or bank can change interest rates (up or down) on an account, whenever it likes, without giving notice or making special concessions to existing account-holders.

An overall rise or fall in rates paid by banks is usually triggered by a change in the bank base rate as set by the Bank of England. Banks tend to respond to such a change quickly, while building societies move more slowly.

Some accounts offer a *guaranteed premium* (or differential), guaranteeing to pay at least a set amount above the rate of one of the other accounts offered by the bank or building society, what happens to rates generally. Other accounts have a *fixed* rate for a period, regardless of whatever happens to interest rates generally during that time.

How is interest taxed?

Building societies and banks will normally deduct tax at 20 per cent from your interest before adding it to your account.

If you are a *higher-rate* taxpayer, you have to pay additional tax of 20 per cent (at 2001–2 rates). This tax is collected through the annual self-assessment system.

If you are a *non-taxpayer*, you do not have to pay tax on your building society and bank interest. Get form R85 from a building society, bank, post office or tax office: if you can declare that your total income from all sources (including interest) is likely to be less than your total tax allowances for the coming year, sign the form and take it to your building society or bank, which then pays you interest gross.

Any over-payment of tax can be reclaimed from the Inland Revenue. Contact your local tax office.

For more on tax and savings, see Chapter 10.

How much interest?

As a rule of thumb, the longer your money is tied up and the larger the amount you deposit, the higher the interest rate. Remember, this is a *general* rule. If you take a 'snapshot' of the rates available on all the different accounts, you may find that there are times when some of the best instant-access accounts will pay better rates than notice accounts. So shop around, if you can. Postal and Internet accounts (see Chapter 9) do not always follow this rule.

In *tiered-interest* accounts, the larger your investment, the higher the interest. Usually, if your balance grows enough to tip you into a higher tier you get the higher interest automatically. The rate is cut automatically if it falls. You usually get the highest rate your investment level entitles you to on the *whole* of your balance. Some accounts pay you the higher rates only on the amount of your money in each tier (which results in a lower average rate overall).

Some accounts pay a bonus if you satisfy particular conditions, such as not making any withdrawals for a year.

Interest is usually calculated on the balance in your account each day. In a few cases, it may be worked out on a less advantageous basis, for example your lowest balance over a month.

Types of account

Cheque accounts

Some savings accounts are now full current accounts that pay interest, provide a chequebook, cheque guarantee card, access to cash machines, overdrafts, standing orders and direct debits. Note that you probably get higher interest from an account that does not offer all these extras.

At the other end of the scale are instant-access accounts that are subject to a minimum investment and simply include a chequebook for easy withdrawals. You may have to pay fees for writing above a certain number of cheques each month or quarter. In return, you should get a better rate of interest than from an interest-bearing current account. You might get a higher rate still from an account without any chequebook.

Fixed-rate accounts

Accounts that offer a fixed rate of interest for a fixed term are a gamble because you are 'locked in' for an agreed period of time. If rates fall, you may do well; if they rise you might have been better off with a variable-rate account.

Beware of interest rates that are fixed for only part of the term of the account: such rates can fall dramatically when the fixed-rate period ends, leaving you locked into a poor-paying account.

Instant-access accounts

Many instant-access accounts have *tiered interest rates*, with minimum investment levels and tiers ranging anywhere from £1 to £50,000 or more. Even though instant withdrawals are allowed, there may still be restrictions with building society accounts: for example, you may be allowed to draw no more than £250 in cash, perhaps as little as £5,000 as a cheque; larger cash sums or cheques could take up to three days to arrange.

Beware of accounts that give you instant access only if you pay a penalty charge. Beware, too, of accounts give you instant access only to the balance over a certain amount (though if this amount is low, these accounts can still be useful if you have a large amount to invest).

Beware: a penalty charge trap

Watch out for accounts that *always* operate a penalty charge. Some of these are term shares, so you do not suffer the penalty if you leave your money invested for the full term. But some are not: if you have no way of escaping a penalty charge, it means you do not get as high an interest rate as that quoted.

Money market accounts
With many bank accounts (and occasionally a building society account), the interest is linked to the rates paid on the money markets. The rate can fluctuate frequently, in some cases every day; often it is reviewed every week.

These accounts include minimum investment stipulations and notice periods, although perhaps the most common are instant-access, high minimum investment types of account. Many offer the use of a chequebook.

Monthly income accounts
These accounts pay interest monthly to help boost incomes. They include minimum investment levels and notice periods. Though your capital is safe, your monthly income fluctuates as rates vary – unless you go for a *fixed-rate* monthly income account.

Monthly income accounts are often variations of other accounts, with generally a higher minimum investment level and a lower interest rate.

Notice accounts
Accounts allowing you access to your money at three months' notice are common. Others have shorter notice periods (down to one week) or longer ones (up to two years). Notice accounts ought to pay a higher rate of interest. But at times, to attract new savers, institutions pay much higher interest on their instant-access accounts.

Most notice accounts allow instant access if you pay a *penalty charge* of, usually, the same number of months' interest as the notice period. These accounts are useful in an emergency but can drastically reduce the effective interest rate you get.

You may have access to the balance over a certain amount in a notice account without notice or penalty. And some accounts are *tiered-interest* accounts with minimum investment levels and tiers ranging anywhere from £1 (though £500 is more common) to £50,000 or more.

Regular savings accounts
Regular savings accounts are offered by many major banks and building societies. This means that rates have become more competitive against other types of accounts. They could be useful if you need to discipline yourself to save regularly.

Regular savings offer perhaps the most complicated conditions of any account type, so check carefully that what you are being offered suits your needs. Ask:

- What are the minimum and maximum amounts I can save each month?
- Can I vary the amount I save as I like each month, or only by agreement with the society?
- Can I miss payments? How many can I miss and how often?
- Can I withdraw part of my savings? How much can I withdraw and how often?
- Are there restrictions (such as a notice period) for closing the account?
- Is there a maximum term for this account?

In general, the more restrictive the conditions you accept, the higher the interest rate.

Term accounts

These are accounts that lock your money up for a period of time, which can be anything from a few days to perhaps five years. The term is usually fixed at the time you open the account, either as a fixed amount of time (for example six months or two years), or as a fixed date (for example a term ending on 1 December 2001) and the rate of interest is usually fixed for the term.

Normally, you cannot withdraw until the account *matures* at the end of its term; if you are allowed withdrawals, you have to pay a *penalty charge* and perhaps give some months' notice as well or you are restricted to withdrawing only the balance over a certain amount. You may not be allowed to add to the account, though normally you can start another one.

Check what happens to your investment at the end of the term. It may be:

- automatically cashed in – you are sent a cheque
- automatically transferred to another account, which pays a different rate of interest
- left where it is, paying the same rate of interest, and converted into a notice account (in which case check whether you can give the required notice *before* the end of the term – otherwise the term will be longer than you originally thought, e.g. if you have to give three months' notice at the end of a one-year term share you have in effect got a 15-month term share)
- automatically reinvested for a further term (though not necessarily at the same rate); this is more likely to happen with the shorter-period bank term accounts.

TESSAs

You earn interest free of tax if you keep a Tax-Exempt Special Savings Account open for five years. TESSAs have now been replaced by Individual Savings Accounts (ISAs), but if you opened a TESSA by 5 April 1999 you can pay into it for the full five years (see Chapter 11, *Tax-efficient saving and investing*).

ISAs

Individual Savings Accounts (ISAs) are free of tax but you can invest only £3,000 in the cash element of an ISA each tax year. You can also deposit the capital (i.e. the money you invested but not any interest) from a matured Tessa. This money is in addition to the £3,000 a year. You can withdraw money at any time without losing tax benefits (see Chapter 11).

Children's accounts

Many banks and building societies have an account aimed at children. Interest rates vary from among the lowest of any account to some of the higher rates; usually the higher payers offer the fewest extras (which range from free gifts, membership of zoos and clubs to donations to charities and magazines). See Chapter 15 for more on investing for children.

Flexible mortgage accounts

This account is a type of mortgage which incorporates a current account and savings account.

It works in the following way: you pay your salary or other income direct into your mortgage account, where it pays the interest and reduces the outstanding balance on your mortgage. You can then draw whatever you need (which will increase your outstanding mortgage balance) using the normal current-account facilities, i.e. cash card, debit card and chequebook.

The benefit of this arrangement is that any excess savings you have from month to month are automatically used to reduce your outstanding mortgage (and the interest payable on it). Because your 'current account balance' is reducing your mortgage, the savings you make in interest payments are equivalent to your receiving tax-free interest on the money at your mortgage interest rate. (There is no tax to pay because you are reducing your mortgage interest payments, rather than earning interest.)

Flexible mortgage accounts are relatively new. Some people like the idea of their separate mortgage, savings and current accounts being replaced with a single account. But others are uncomfortable with this and prefer to keep their borrowings and savings well apart.

Friendly society bonds

Some (very few) building society accounts are linked with friendly societies that offer a restricted tax-free regular savings scheme. You pay a *maximum* of £25 a month (or £270 a year) for ten years and the friendly society invests the money with the building society. Because the scheme is tax-free, you make a little more interest than you would by investing directly in the building society, but not as much as you might think (only 1 to 2 per cent extra) because of the friendly society's management charge. The scheme is free of higher-rate tax, too, so is more appealing to higher-rate taxpayers. To a basic-rate taxpayer it could be little better than the best normal building society account, which would offer better access and fewer restrictions.

Permanent Interest-bearing Shares (PIBS)

PIBS, issued by building societies and by ex-building societies before they became banks, are traded on the stock market. They bear no relation to building society 'share' accounts (as the simplest instant-access accounts are often called). They work in a similar way to corporate bonds and gilts. The price you pay depends on current stock market values. You buy a regular income at a fixed rate of interest.

Unlike most corporate bonds and gilts, PIBS have no redemption date at which the issuer promises to pay back the original capital.

PIBS are traded like ordinary stocks and shares – purchased through a stockbroker. The minimum amount that can be purchased varies from £1,000 to £50,000.

The yield varies as the price of the PIBS fluctuates. But, of course, the interest rate you get is fixed at the time of purchase, according to the purchase price.

If the building society goes bust, the last people in line for the remaining assets are the PIBS-holders. And they are not covered by the compensation arrangements that protect deposits.

Making your choice

Too little income to pay tax?
You can get your interest without deduction of tax from any bank or building society account, provided you sign a declaration stating that you are likely to be a non-taxpayer in that tax year.

Looking at a large tax bill?
Consider offshore accounts. You still have to pay tax – but you may be able to arrange things so that the tax bill falls due in a year that suits you.

Investing for the long term?
Building society and bank investments are safe but, over the long term, may not make as much as more risky forms of investment. If you have a very large sum to invest for a long period, think about putting some of it into other investments – see Chapters 1 to 3.

Don't need your money for a year or so?
Term accounts look tempting but you may get as good or better rates of interest (especially on large sums) from a *notice* or even *instant-access* account, as well as easier access to your money. There is always the possibility with variable-rate term shares that the rate may go down significantly once you are locked in.

Think interest rates will fall?
Check *fixed-rate* accounts – but compare them with the best variable rates on offer before you decide whether the gamble is likely to be worthwhile. Compare with the returns on short-dated gilts held to redemption or as an alternative guaranteed income bonds.

Prepared to wait a while for your money?
A *notice* account may give higher interest than one offering instant access – often, the longer the notice period, the higher the interest will be. But do not tie up money you think you may need to get out quickly.

Can't wait, won't wait?
Try an *instant-access* account. If you have a large investment and need instant access to only part of your money, look at a notice account that gives you instant

access to money above a certain amount. Or can you make do with a short-notice account (say up to a month)?

Want a regular income?
You can draw a monthly income from any account, but it is easiest to do so from an account offering *monthly interest* – many different types offer this. If you want a fixed income, think also about other investments like gilts or guaranteed income bonds.

Want to save regularly?
A *regular savings* account is a possibility, if you need to be disciplined. The rates are good compared to other instant-access or notice accounts. Use the route maps in Chapter 3 to guide you to the other types of savings and investment available.

Expect your savings to fluctuate?
Think about an account with *tiered interest rates*. But keep an eye on your balance and what it is earning.

Choosing a home for your savings
With over 3,000 accounts and variations on accounts on offer, from scores of banks and building societies, picking the best buy is not easy. Consider first *convenience*: if you want to withdraw *and* deposit money quickly and frequently (and especially if you want current-account facilities) then you need a branch or a cash machine close to your home or place of work. For less frequent transactions, you can deal by post.

This gives you a wider range of organisations from which to choose. When comparing rates:

* note that slight differences in interest rate are important only with large investments. For example, on an investment of £1,000, 1 per cent extra on a rate will be worth just £10 a year (before tax)
* make sure you are comparing the right rate. The AER or 'true' rate is the best rate to look at if you intend depositing money for a year or more.

For more information check regular surveys and the 'Savings Monitor' in *Which?* * magazine, personal finance magazines, the personal finance pages of daily and Sunday newspapers, and summaries in the magazine *Moneyfacts.* *

13 National Savings investments

One way in which the government raises money is to borrow it from the public in competition with listed companies, banks and building societies and other financial institutions. One such investment is the wide range of government stock 'gilts', dealt with in Chapter 24. Here, we look at National Savings investments. The best known are National Savings Certificates, which are outlined below.

National Savings Certificates

There are two types of National Savings Certificates: fixed-interest and index-linked. Both produce a guaranteed tax-free return which means that they can be particularly attractive for higher-rate taxpayers. Savings Certificates increase in value by having interest added – at a pre-determined rate – at each anniversary of the date of purchase. Interest is not paid out, so you do not get it until the certificate matures or you cash it in (if this is earlier).

Fixed-interest Savings Certificates

The first of these – called War Savings Certificates – were issued in 1916. Since then, governments have brought out a new issue whenever the rate of interest on the old issue seemed too high, or too low, in the prevailing circumstances. Normally, you can buy only one issue – the current one – at any one time. In all, various governments have brought out 58 issues of five-year National Savings Certificates (by June 2001). Some certificates can be held indefinitely and, since certificates can be inherited, you do not have to have been alive and investing in 1916 in order to own some of the first issue. Some people hold a wide range of certificates. Like all National Savings products they are treated as normal assets for inheritance tax purposes.

With the early issues (up to and including the sixth), interest is added *ad infinitum* to the value of your certificates at a fixed rate of five-twelfths a month (or, with some of these issues, 112p or 114p every three months). Because the amount of interest is fixed while your original investment is rising, it follows that the rate of interest – expressed as a yearly percentage return – is going down, year by year. These now offer a miserly rate of return of under 1.75 per cent a year.

For issues after the sixth, the interest paid used to vary depending on the issue

132

and the year; the exact rates were fixed for a certain number of years at a time, for example five or seven years. Then, in 1982, the government announced that, when a particular certificate reached the end of the period for which interest rates had been set, a common rate of interest called the *general extension rate* would be paid. At June 2001 this rate was 2.4 per cent which applies to all maturing certificates which are not cashed in or reinvested and which were bought before October 1999. Certificates bought after that date are automatically reinvested in the issue which is current at the time they mature unless the holder chooses to cash them in or reinvest in a different issue.

In October 1999 National Savings also launched the first issue of its two-year Savings Certificate. As with five-year certificates, only one issue may be bought at any one time and new issues are launched whenever the rate of interest on the old issue is thought to be out of line with the prevailing circumstances. If you do not cash in at maturity, the certificates are automatically reinvested in the current two-year issue. In June 2001 two-year certificates were on their seventh issue.

Investing in Fixed-interest Savings Certificates

Anyone aged seven or over can invest directly; certificates can be held on behalf of anyone younger. You can invest anything between £100 and £10,000, so certificates are suitable for both lump sums and savings. A husband and wife can invest up to £10,000 each; if the certificates are in their joint names, however, they can invest only £10,000 between them.

If you have earlier issues of National Savings Certificates, which you held to maturity, you can reinvest an unlimited amount in the current two- and five-year issues on top of the ordinary £10,000 limit. These are called *Reinvestment Certificates* and the terms are the same as for other current two- and five-year certificates, except that if you cash Reinvestment Certificates within one year of having invested you will currently (June 2001) get interest equivalent to 3.4 per cent a year for each three months of investment. If these are cashed in early they are still paid free of tax.

How to invest

Fill in an application form NSA762 available from most post offices and banks and the National Savings* web site *www.nationalsavings.co.uk* or watch out for advertisements in the press. Your certificate showing how much you have bought will be sent to you later.

How much interest?

Interest is added to the value of your certificate over the period of its life (which is two or five years at the outset). The amount of interest added increases each year, giving you an added incentive to hold on to your certificates. Table 1 overleaf gives the details, and shows the rate of interest for each year for the 58th issue five-year certificate. If you hold the certificate for the full five years, the overall yearly rate of return works out at 3.7 per cent. This does not compare well with the rate of return on other tax-free savings products such as a cash Individual Savings Account where, in June 2001, you could earn interest of up to 6.25 per cent a year. Nor does it compare particularly favourably with the after-tax return of 4.4 per cent that a basic-rate taxpayer would receive from an account paying

Table 1: How a £100 unit of the 58th five-year issue grows

year	Rate of interest for year	£100 certificate increases by	Value at end of each completed 12-month period
1	3.40%	£3.40	£103.40
2	3.50%	£3.62	£107.02
3	3.60%	£3.85	£110.87
4	3.80%	£4.21	£115.08
5	4.21%	£4.85	£119.93

gross (i.e. before-tax) interest of 5.5 per cent. However, the compound rate of 3.7 per cent for the 58th five-year issue looks quite reasonable for a higher-rate taxpayer who would receive an after-tax return of 3.3 per cent on a normal savings account paying a gross rate of 5.5 per cent. To compare the tax-free return of future issues of saving certificates with the before-tax return from other savings products, divide the compound rate by: 0.8 if you are a basic-rate taxpayer; 0.6 if you pay tax at the higher rate of 40 per cent.

A two-year certificate (seventh issue) currently pays 3.4 per cent in the first year and 3.91 in the second. An invested £100 would give you £107.43 if invested for the full term, giving an overall yearly rate of 3.65 per cent.

What happens at maturity?
If you hold certificates which you bought after October 1999, National Savings write to you at the end of the five- or two-year period to ask you whether you want to cash them in or reinvest them in new certificates. If you do not respond, your maturing certificates are automatically reinvested in the issue of savings certificates (of the same fixed period) then current.

To cash in either all or part of your certificates before maturity or to cash in five-year certificates bought before October 1999, get form DNS502 from a post office. You should not have to wait more than a couple of weeks for your money.

What happens to your certificates if you die?
Your heirs can either cash in the certificates or transfer them into their own names. Form NSA904 from most post offices gets things under way.

What to do with earlier issues?
If you hold certificates which have already matured, it would be worthwhile cashing them in or reinvesting them because they are earning interest at the general extension rate of 2.4 per cent (in June 2001) which, although tax-free, is lower than the rate of return you could get by investing your cash elsewhere. If you still hold certificates from the first to the sixth issues (which were on sale from 1916 until November 1939), you are earning an even lower rate of interest.

However, you should be wary of cashing in earlier issues of savings certificates which have yet to mature. This is because, if interest rates generally continue to fall, the fixed interest they earn (which is unaffected by general changes in interest

Table 2: Fixed-interest Savings Certificates which have yet to mature

Issue number	Year of purchase	Rate of interest being paid in [1]:				
		2001 %	2002 %	2003 %	2004 %	compound rate %
44	1997	7.75	[2]	[2]	[2]	5.35
	1998	6.15	7.75	[2]	[2]	5.35
45	1998	5.70	7.14	[2]	[2]	5.00
46	1998	5.20	7.04	[2]	[2]	4.80
47	1998	4.20	4.46	[2]	[2]	4.00
48	1998	3.60	4.01	[2]	[2]	3.50
	1999	3.40	3.60	4.01	[2]	3.50
49	1999	3.20	3.30	3.66	[2]	3.25
50	1999	3.40	3.60	4.01	[2]	3.50
51	1999	3.50	3.75	4.31	[2]	3.65
52	1999	3.70	3.95	4.51	[2]	3.85
53	1999	4.20	4.40	5.01	[3]	4.30
54	2000	4.20	4.40	4.60	5.21	4.50
55	2000	3.85	4.05	4.30	4.86	4.15
56	2000	3.60	3.70	3.90	4.31	3.80
57	2001	n/a	3.25	3.35	3.45	3.55

[1] Starting from the anniversary of the date on which you bought the certificates.

[2] General extension rate of 2.4 per cent (at June 2001) applies if you do not cash in or reinvest at maturity.

[3] See 'What happens at maturity?' on page 134.

rates) starts to compare much more favourably with the return on other savings products. For example, 44th-issue savings certificates bought in 1998 are now earning 6.15 per cent, rising to 7.75 per cent in 2002, giving a compound return if held to maturity of 5.35 per cent. To compare rates of interest from issues which have yet to mature, see Table 2.

Index-linked Savings Certificates

These certificates are worth considering if you are worried about inflation. They guarantee that the buying power of the money you invest more than keeps pace with rising prices by linking the interest rate to the Retail Prices Index (RPI). For how they compare with index-linked gilts, see Chapter 24.

You can invest anything between £100 and £10,000, so these certificates are suitable for both lump sums and regular/occasional savings. A husband and wife can each invest up to £10,000 (i.e. up to £20,000 in all). If the certificates are in their joint names, however, they can invest only £10,000 between them. As with fixed-interest certificates, you can buy certificates which last for five years (the 20th issue in June 2001) or for two years (the 7th issue in April 2001).

If you have National Savings Certificates which you have held for at least five years, you can reinvest an unlimited amount in either a five-year or a two-year Reinvestment Certificate on top of your normal £10,000 limit. The terms are the

Table 3: How a £100 unit of the 20th index-linked issue grows

During year	Interest paid in each year on top of inflation	Annual effective rate [1]	Value at anniversary of date invested [2]
1	1.25%	3.75%	£103.75
2	1.50%	4.00%	£107.90
3	1.80%	4.30%	£112.54
4	2.20%	4.70%	£117.83
5	2.76%	5.26%	£124.03

[1] Assuming inflation runs at 2.5 per cent, this is the total amount of interest paid each year.

[2] This is the sum of money you would get if you cashed in your unit having held it for exactly this number of years, assuming inflation runs at 2.5 per cent a year.

same as for other index-linked certificates, except that if you cash in your investment within one year your investment is increased in line with the RPI and you earn interest of 1.25 per cent a year for each complete month of investment in a five-year certificate; 1.65 per cent in a two-year certificate.

How to invest
Go to a post office and fill in application form NSA763. Your certificate, showing how much you have invested, follows by post a few days later. You can also buy certificates direct from National Savings* – there are frequent advertisements in the national press. The application form is available also on the National Savings* web site (*www.nationalsavings.co.uk*).

How index-linked certificates work
If you hold a current 20th-issue five-year certificate for the full term, your overall return is 1.9 per cent a year on top of inflation. After five years, the return is equal to the RPI.

The rates on the current seventh issues before index-linking are 1.65 per cent in year one and 2.66 in year two. Assuming inflation runs at 2.5 per cent a year, a £100 unit invested for the full two years would grow to £109.52. This gives an annual effective rate of 4.65 per cent.

If you cash one in within a year of buying it, you get back only the money you invested in the first place. After a year its value is increased in line with the change in the RPI, plus extra interest since you bought it. If the certificate is cashed in early, any index-linking and extra interest is paid tax-free. These rules apply both to two- and five-year certificates.

Which month's index applies?
The level of the RPI for the previous month is announced on the second or third Friday of each month and reported in the newspapers the following day. When you buy a certificate or cash one in, the RPI figure that applies is the one announced in the previous month, which, in turn, refers to the cost of living in the month before that. See page 107 for a list of RPI figures since March 1982.

Working out how much you'd get if you cashed in now
The easiest way to find out the present value of your holding in current index-linked certificates is to look at the chart on display at post offices. But to decide whether or not your certificates are worthwhile compared with other risk-free investments, you should also consider the rate of return you are getting. The effective rate you get varies, depending on the rate of inflation and on how long you hold the certificate.

Is there any tax to pay on the gain?
No. The gain is free of both income tax and capital gains tax. This makes these certificates particularly attractive to people paying higher-rate income tax or who may have chargeable capital gains from other investments.

What happens to your certificate if you die?
The certificate can be transferred into your heir's name, even if he or she already has the maximum holding of certificates.

How to cash in certificates
Get form DNS502 from a post office. Fill it in and send it off together with the certificates in the pre-paid envelope provided. You should not have to wait longer than a couple of weeks for your money.

Can you cash in only part of your money?
Yes, you can cash in any amount you wish.

Any old National Savings Stamps?

Remember them – 10p each (or 6d and 1/– in pre-decimal days)? They were withdrawn on 31 December 1976 but you can still cash in any you have about the house. Send them to Remittance Section, National Savings* and ask for their value to be refunded.

What happens if the RPI actually falls?
The value of your certificate goes down in line with the fall in the RPI, though interest is still added. But it is guaranteed that the certificate is never worth less than its value at the previous anniversary of purchase.

What happens if the rate of inflation goes down?
A fall in the *rate* of inflation usually means that the RPI is still going up but not as fast as before; if so, the value of your certificate continues to increase but at a slower rate. The value of your certificate does not fall. What is important from the point of view of your investment is how the rate of inflation, plus the interest, compares with the rate of return you could get on other comparatively safe investments, for example bank and building society accounts.

Should you cash in old index-linked certificates?

You can but you do not have to. You can keep your money where it is and your investment will continue to be index-linked. Generally you get a much better return if you reinvest in new certificates though. It is also worth remembering that any amount you reinvest is on top of the normal limit for each issue.

National Savings accounts and bonds

In addition to National Savings Certificates, there is a wide range of other investment opportunities with National Savings,* tailored for individual circumstances and easily accessible through post offices and the National Savings* web site. An outline of the different rules that apply to different products is given below.

National Savings Ordinary account
Who can invest?

Anyone can open an account. For young children, the account can be opened by a relative or friend.

You must invest a minimum of £10 to open an account, while the maximum is £10,000, no matter how many Ordinary accounts you have. Each time you invest you must deposit at least £10.

You can open an account at most post offices using form NSA760 (also available on the National Savings* web site) – you are sent a bank book, in which a record is kept of all your transactions.

How much interest?

The rate of interest can vary, though it tends not to change often. You qualify for a higher rate of interest for each calendar month in which the balance is £500 or more. Otherwise you get the standard rate of interest. The rates current in June 2001 are 1.1 per cent for the higher rate and 1 per cent for the standard rate. Interest is worked out on each complete £1 in the account for a full calendar month. Money in your account starts earning interest at the start of the month following the one in which it is deposited. And it stops getting interest from the start of the month in which it is withdrawn. So you get most interest if you put your money in on the last day of a month and take it out on the first day of a month.

Interest is added to your account on 31 December. The first £70 interest is tax-free, and a husband and wife can each have this much interest tax-free (see Chapter 10 for more on tax).

Getting your money out

You can withdraw up to £100 at once by taking your bank book to most post offices. If you want more than £100, complete the application form available from most post offices; getting your money could take about a week. However, if you are a regular customer, you can withdraw £250 instantly at a nominated post office – check there for details.

Table 4: National Savings Investment account interest in April 2001

Investment (£)	Interest rate (%)
0–499	3.75
500–2,499	3.85
2,500–4,999	3.95
5,000–9,999	4.05
10,000–24,999	4.25
25,000–49,999	4.55
50,000 and over	4.95

Rates are gross per annum, variable and paid on the whole amount at each tier.

What happens if you die?
The money in your account can be cashed in or transferred to your heir's account. Form NSA904 gives all the details.

National Savings Investment account
Who can invest?
Anyone who can invest in the Ordinary account.

You must invest a minimum of £20 to open an account. The maximum is £100,000, no matter how many Investment accounts you have. Each time you invest, you must deposit at least £20.

Use form NSA760 (available at most post offices and from the National Savings* web site) to open an account. You are sent a bank book.

How much interest?
The rate of interest varies (the rates as in June 2001 are as shown in Table 4). You receive the highest rate of interest on the whole amount invested.

Interest is added to your account on 31 December. All interest is taxable but is paid gross – which makes the account particularly suitable for non-taxpayers.

Getting your money out
You have to give one month's notice to withdraw your money. Use the application form available from most post offices. If you withdraw money without notice, a penalty of 30 days' interest is charged on the amount withdrawn.

What happens if you die?
The investment can be cashed in or transferred to your heirs. Form NSA904 gives all the details.

National Savings Income Bonds
Who can invest?
Anyone. Bonds can also be held jointly or in trust for a larger group of individuals. Income Bonds may be attractive to non-taxpayers who want a regular income from their savings.

The minimum first and subsequent purchases is £500. The maximum holding is £1,000,000. Use the application form in the back of the Income Bonds booklet NSA767 available from post offices or the National Savings* web site.

How much interest?
The rate of interest varies (in June 2001, it was 4.85 per cent for holdings of less than £25,000 and 5.1 per cent for holdings of £25,000 and over). Interest is paid monthly. All interest is taxable and paid gross.

Getting your money out
You give three calendar months' notice if you want to cash part or all of your bond. If you need money immediately, the penalty is 90 days' interest on the amount withdrawn. For partial repayments the minimum is £500. The minimum residual holding is £500. The withdrawal form DNS201 is available from post offices.

On your death, your heirs can cash the bonds without notice and with no loss of interest. Form NSA904 gives details.

National Savings Deposit Bonds
Deposit Bonds were withdrawn from sale in November 1988. For investors who continue to hold them, the interest rate varies. In June 2001 was 4.8 per cent, added to the value of bonds each year on the anniversary of investment. The interest is taxable and paid gross.

Getting your money out
You can withdraw any amount above £50, as long as at least £100 of your original investment remains. You have to give three months' notice. Form DNS103 is available at post offices.

Your heirs can withdraw the investment without notice and with no loss of interest. Form NSA904 gives details.

National Savings Capital Bonds
Who can invest?
Anyone aged seven and over can invest. Bonds can also be held jointly by two savers. Capital Bonds can be especially attractive to non-taxpayers who do not want income from their savings. But you must be prepared to tie up your money for five years.

You have to invest at least £100 up to a maximum of £250,000, which is the total investment allowed for all Capital Bonds (excluding Series A and the Reinvestment Series). A husband and wife can each have £250,000 invested. Capital Bonds are particularly suitable for lump-sum investments or occasional savings.

Bonds can be bought at a post office or by postal application to National Savings. Capital Bond booklet (NSA768) is available at most post offices.

How much interest?
Interest is added at fixed and increasing rates to the value of your bond over its five-year life. Over the full five years the return (on the current Series Z bond – see

Table 5: How a £100 Capital Bond (Series Z) grows

During year	Interest rate	After-tax return: basic-rate taxpayer	Higher-rate taxpayer
	%	%	%
1	4.4	3.52	2.64
2	4.65	3.72	2.79
3	4.9	3.92	2.94
4	5.2	4.16	3.12
5	5.61	4.49	3.37
Compound	4.95	3.96	2.97

Table 5 works out as 4.95 per cent a year before tax, 3.96 per cent after tax at 20 per cent.

At the end of the five years you can have your bond repaid together with the full amount of interest earned. No tax will be deducted, which is good for non-taxpayers. If you are a taxpayer you have to pay tax each year on the interest even though you will not receive the interest until your bond is repaid. You will receive a notice of interest credited to your bond each year which gives you the details you need for your tax return. If you cash in your bond early you get no interest if you cash in during the first year. For subsequent years you get interest earned for complete years of holding the bond plus interest at the previous year's rate for the year in which you cash in early.

National Savings Fixed-Rate Savings Bonds
These were launched in October 1999 to replace FIRST Option Bonds. You can opt for six-month, one-year or two-year bonds.

Who can invest?
Anyone aged 16 or over. Bonds can be held jointly and in trust for personal beneficiaries of any age.

You have to invest at least £500 up to a maximum of £1,000,000. A husband and wife can each invest £1,000,000. Total holdings for each individual must not exceed £1,000,000.

To apply, get Fixed-Rate Savings Bond booklet (NSA777) from the post office or an application form from the National Savings* web site.

How much interest?
At the end of the fixed-rate period you can either cash in your investment or leave the money invested at a fixed rate for another 6, 12 or 24 months. Table 6 shows the rates that apply for six-month, one-year and two-year bonds for the three interest-rate tiers.

Table 6: Interest paid on Fixed-Rate Savings Bond

Duration of bond	£500 %	£20,000 %	£50,000 %
6 months	4.5	4.7	4.9
1 year	4.5	4.7	4.9
2 years	4.6	4.8	5

Interest is paid net of basic-rate tax and can be paid out or added to the bond. The option to have interest paid monthly is also available. Reinvestment attracts the then current rate of interest.

Getting your money out
You can cash in all or part of your investment at the expiry date without penalty. To access your investment early, the penalty is equivalent to 90 days' interest on the amount withdrawn. If a partial withdrawal is made, at least £500 must remain.

On your death, your heirs can cash in your bond or transfer it to their names.

National Savings Children's Bonus Bonds
Who can invest?
These can be bought for any child under 16 by anybody aged 16 or over. The bonds can be held until the holder is 21.

Bonds are sold in units of £25. You can invest a minimum of £25 and, in addition to holdings of Issues A to V, a child can have up to £1,000 of Issue W bonds in his or her name.

Get a Children's Bonus Bond booklet (NSA769) at your post office, or an application form from the National Savings* web site. The investment certificate will be sent to the child's parent or guardian, who will have control of the investment until the child is 16.

How much interest?
The rate of interest is fixed for five years. In June 2001 it was 3 per cent a year. A bonus added on the fifth anniversary of purchase takes the full return to 4.6 per cent.

After the first five years National Savings makes a further offer of five years' fixed interest and a bonus. The extended bond ends when the child is 21, when the final bonus is added.

The interest for these bonds is free of income tax.

Getting your money out
Bonds can be cashed in any time after the first year without notice or loss of interest. If they are cashed in before five years (unless the holder reaches 21), the bonus is forfeited. Until the holder is 16, the parent or guardian applies for repayment. Once the holder is 16, control is passed to him or her.

Pensioners Bonds
Who can invest?
Anyone aged 60 or over. Bonds can be held jointly by two people over 60. The minimum investment is £500 and the maximum £1,000,000 in each series (the maximum applies for a single or a joint holding). You can opt for one-, two- or five-year bonds.

How much interest?
The interest rate is fixed for the term of the bond and is paid as a monthly income (without tax deduction) into your bank, building society or National Savings Investment account. In June 2001, the one-year bond paid 4.75 per cent, the two-year bond paid 4.8 per cent interest and the five-year bond paid 4.9 per cent.

Get the Pensioners Bonds booklet (NSA773) from the post office or an application form from the National Savings* web site.

Getting your money out
If you apply for repayment within two weeks of the fifth anniversary of your purchase, or any other fifth anniversary, there is no penalty or notice. Otherwise you need to give 60 days' notice, and you lose interest in the notice period. A penalty of 90 days' interest is charged fron an early withdrawal. The minimum amount cashed in is £500 and £500 or more must remain. On your death, your bond is repaid to your heirs immediately with no interest penalty or transferred into another pensioners' bond.

National Savings cash mini-ISA
Who can invest?
Anyone aged 16 or over. ISAs cannot be taken out on behalf of children under 16. The interest is tax-free. You cannot transfer money from a maturing TESSA into this ISA. For more details on both ISAs and TESSAs, see Chapter 11.

How much interest?
The interest rate is variable and was 5.45 per cent in June 2001. To meet CAT standards, it is guaranteed never to be more than 2 per cent below the base rate.

You can invest up to £3,000 in the tax year 2001–2 and up to £3,000 in each subsequent tax year. The minimum you can invest is £10.

To invest by post, use the the ISA booklet NSA778 from most post offices and the National Savings* web site. You can also phone the National Savings ISA Investment Line* using a debit card and National Insurance number for identification.

You can withdraw your savings at any time by post or by phone. There is no penalty for withdrawals

TESSA-only cash ISA
The National Savings TESSA-only cash ISA was launched in July 1999 for holders of mature TESSAs. See Chapter 11 for further details.

Premium Bonds

Launched in 1956 these bonds are not conventional investment products. Instead of interest, you get the chance to win prizes.

Who can invest?

Anyone aged 16 or over can buy Premium Bonds. They are often bought in the name of someone under 16 by relations or guardians.

Premium Bonds cost £1 each, with a minimum of 100. You can hold up to £20,000 of bonds.

Application form NSA765 is available from most post offices and banks and the National Savings* web site.

How many prizes are there?

The total monthly value of the prize money is equal to interest on all bonds held for at least one month (nearly 10 billion of them) calculated at a rate of 4 per cent a year as at June 2001 but set to fall to 3.5 per cent from September 2001.

Prizes range from £50 to £1 million. All prizes are free of both income tax and capital gains tax.

There is only ever one £1 million prize each month. The number of prizes of other amounts depends on the number of bonds eligible to take part each month. (See box).

How do you know if you have won?

You are contacted by post at the last address National Savings has for you. So let them know if you move. There is over £18 million in unclaimed prizes because winners cannot be traced. If you are on the Internet, check whether any of your bonds are winning ones by entering your bondholder's number on the National Savings web site.

You are contacted in person if you have won the jackpot of £1 million.

		Estimated number (June 2001)
Higher-value prizes		
10% of each month's prize fund	£1,000,000	1
	£100,000	8
	£50,000	17
	£25,000	32
	£10,000	83
	£5,000	164
Medium-value prizes		
10% of each month's prize fund	£1,000	2,040
	£500	6,120
Lower-value prizes		
80% of each month's prize fund	£100	59,518
	£50	697,174

How do you cash your bonds?
Get form DNS303 from a post office. For each £1 invested you get £1 back, however long you have held the bond.

On your death, your bonds remain eligible for prizes for 12 months. They must then be cashed in by your heirs.

14 A comfortable retirement

For many people, ensuring an adequate income in retirement is a major motive behind saving and investing. This chapter helps you formulate a strategy to achieve this, whether you are still working, close to retirement or have already retired.

Inflation makes budgeting for retirement difficult if you are looking a good many years ahead. Currently the state retirement pension is increased each year in line with rising prices and the amount you can expect from an employer's pension should go up too. Many experts believe that the UK is entering a new low-inflation environment and are confident that there will not be a return to the high inflation of the 1970s and 1980s. But even low inflation reduces the buying power of your income over the years. With inflation at 2.5 per cent, in 25 years' time £10,000 now will be worth £5,400 in terms of today's spending power – see Table 1. The best you can probably do is to work out what you will get (and what you will need) in terms of today's pensions and prices; then make regular checks – once a year, say – that you are still on course.

Remember, too, that a number of specific developments mean that people now have to put more aside to provide for a decent retirement income. The state pension is being reduced as a proportion of average wages. In 1996, the state pension was worth 15 per cent of average salaries; in 2025, it is estimated that the state pension will be worth only 7 per cent of the average. The cost of buying a pension has also risen as annuity rates have fallen in line with long-term interest rates generally. The impact of this is that if you have a stakeholder, personal or money-purchase employer's pension, you have to invest more to provide the same level of income. If you belong to a final-salary pension scheme, external factors such as lower investment returns and annuity rates are less of a worry. This is because your employer is responsible for ensuring that you are paid the percentage

Table 1: The effect of inflation

Inflation rate	Buying power of £10,000 in today's money after:				
	5 years	10 years	15 years	20 years	25 years
2.5%	£8,840	£7,810	£6,910	£6,100	£5,390
5.0%	£7,840	£6,140	£4,810	£3,770	£2,950
7.5%	£6,970	£4,850	£3,380	£2,350	£1,640

of your salary that has been promised as pension. However, if your employer believes that current contribution rates are insufficient to meet future pension needs, you may be required to increase your pension contributions.

If your retirement income is not going to meet your needs, even after taking into account any likely shifts in spending when you stop work, you need to consider the options for boosting your retirement income. There are two main routes: building up your pension and building up other savings which you can use to provide an income when you retire. Chapters 16 to 19 look in detail at the various types of pension scheme – use these to work out how much you can expect.

Building up your pension

Everyone who has worked for long enough (and paid enough National Insurance contributions of the right type – see Chapter 16) is entitled to a basic pension – £72.50 a week for a single person, £115.90 for a married couple from April 2001. And you may get an additional state pension related to your earnings while you were working. However, state pensions on their own are unlikely to provide an adequate income in retirement, so paying into a private pension – either by joining your employer's pension scheme, if you can, or by taking out a stakeholder or personal pension – is essential if you hope to maintain a reasonable standard of living once you have stopped earning.

The major benefits of saving via an employer's scheme or personal pension plan are that your contributions get tax relief at your highest rate of tax, they grow tax-free and on retirement you can usually draw a lump sum free of tax. However, the downside is that you cannot get your money back until you retire. Rather than invest all your spare income this way, you may have to sacrifice some of the tax advantages a pension offers: you may, for example, want to help a child through higher education.

Unless you belong to an employer's scheme in which the pension is fully index-linked (such as with some public-sector schemes), you should allow for inflation in working out how well off you will be after you retire. Even if a pension from an employer's scheme or personal pension plan seems handsome when you first retire, it is likely to be less appealing ten years later. Many employers' schemes currently have some increases built in, typically 3 or 5 per cent. In future, once they start to be paid, pensions linked to your 'final pay' will have to be increased by 5 per cent (or the actual inflation rate if lower).

Personal pension plans have no built-in way of coping with inflation before or after you retire: your pension fund on retirement depends entirely on how much you have paid in, how quickly your invested contributions grow and the annuity rates when you retire. For example, to achieve a pension of £10,000 (in today's money) at age 65, a man aged 40 would need to contribute £300 a month (including tax relief) and increase his contributions by 5 per cent every year – see Table 2 overleaf.

Another pension choice you are likely to be faced with at some stage before you finally retire is what to do if you change jobs. Changing jobs may mean you end up with less pension than if you had stayed with one employer. You have three options:

Table 2: Monthly payments needed to achieve a £10,000 pension at today's prices

Age now	Man retiring at age:			Woman retiring at age:		
	50	55	65	50	55	65
25	400	280	110	440	310	130
30	560	380	140	620	420	170
35	840	540	190	930	600	220
40	1,430	800	260	1,570	900	300

Figures assume that contributions are increased by 5 per cent a year, the fund grows at 6 per cent after charges and inflation is 3 per cent.

- a *preserved pension* from the job you leave (based on the number of years you were in the scheme)
- a *transfer payment* from your old pension scheme into the new one you are joining, to increase the benefits you get from it
- a *transfer payment* into a personal pension or stakeholder scheme.

See Chapter 17 for guidance on which option to choose.

If your pension will not be enough

If you are a member of an employer's scheme, you can make Additional Voluntary Contributions (AVCs) either to your existing scheme or to a Free-Standing AVC scheme with a different pension provider. If you earn less than £30,000, you can also take out a stakeholder to top up your pension savings. See Chapters 17 and 18 for the pros and cons of each type. However, there are limits to what proportion of your income you can put into your pension.

If you have a stakeholder or personal pension plan, you can either increase your contributions to your existing scheme or make a lump-sum payment to a different plan. As with employers' schemes, there are limits on contributions to personal pension plans. However, you can increase the amount you can invest by making use of the 'carry-back' rules explained in Chapter 18.

Other ways of investing for retirement

If you have some spare money that you have decided not to tie up in a pension scheme, you can either commit yourself to regular saving, or put something away when you can spare it, say in a savings account, and then transfer it into a lump-sum investment. The first three chapters of this book will help you in making your choices. However, depending on how long there is until you retire, some investments do offer tax advantages (though none is as generous as a pension scheme).

If you can tie savings up for five years

From 6 April 1999 you can invest up to £7,000 a year (in the 2001–2 tax year) into an Individual Savings Account (ISA) which will be completely free of tax (see Chapter 11).

If you are saving for less than five years, using the cash element of an ISA is probably the most suitable. In the 2001–2 tax year you can invest £3,000 a year in this way. If you are a higher-rate taxpayer looking for a guaranteed tax-free return on your savings, it could be worth considering National Savings Certificates for higher sums – see Chapter 13.

If you can tie savings up for five to ten years

An investment that gives the possibility of capital growth (such as one based on shares) probably offers the best chance of beating inflation, and five to ten years at least gives time for your investment to recover from periods when values fall. For tax-free investment of a lump sum or regular savings, make use of your annual entitlement to an ISA. PEPs continue to attract the same tax advantages as ISAs, although you cannot make any more contributions. See Chapter 11, *Tax-efficient saving and investing*, for details about ISAs and PEPs.

Gilts (see Chapter 24) are also worth considering: capital gains made on these investments are free of capital gains tax. Taxpayers not needing income now can choose schemes that pay out only a small income.

If you can tie savings up for at least ten years

Look at investments where your capital can grow (although remember it may also shrink). Steer clear of life-insurance saving plans unless you are sure you can maintain payments to the policy; there are steep penalties on early withdrawal. These plans offer tax advantages for higher-rate taxpayers who have used up their capital gains tax allowance. But see 'Losing age-related allowance', on page 153 for possible snags. While Friendly Society tax-exempt savings plans are tax-free, the maximum contribution is small.

Widows, widowers and dependants

While planning your retirement finances, it is vital to check that your family would not be left short should you die. All but a few employers' pension schemes provide a pension for widows and dependants (and sometimes for widowers). If your family could not manage on this (together with any income from their own jobs, savings and state benefits), you need life insurance. See Chapter 23 for the different types of policy. For how to work out how much life insurance you need, see *The Which? Guide to Insurance*.

When you take out a stakeholder or personal pension plan (except where the plan has been used to 'contract out' of the State Earnings-Related Pension Scheme) there is no automatic package of benefits. However, you can choose to pay extra for life cover from a special type of life-insurance policy (you get tax relief at your highest rate of tax on premiums).

When you come to retire and you use the fund you have built up to buy a pension, you can choose to take a smaller income in return for providing a pension for your partner or children to be paid after your death.

Investing after retirement

For income later

When you first retire, your pension income may be sufficent for your day-to-day needs. In this case, your strategy should be to make your savings grow as much as you can against the day when you need the capital, either to turn it into an income to pay, for example, for nursing care or or to replace expensive durables such as a car. However, you need to balance the risk of losing your capital against the parallel risk of having it reduced by inflation. Assuming that you can afford to spread your capital over several types of investment, consider putting some in each of the following categories:

- index-linked investments, such as index-linked Savings Certificates or index-linked gilts
- secure savings schemes, such as building society and bank accounts or National Savings schemes
- investments where you have the chance of making a capital gain (but the risk of making a capital loss), such as shares, investment trusts or unit trusts. All these are covered in Chapters 20, 21 and 22.

Remember that gilts are a versatile investment. And do not assume that lump-sum investments are the only ones to consider. If a particularly attractive savings scheme is on offer, you can set up your own 'feeder' account in a bank or building society account and transfer the money across by standing order. Alternatively, buying, say, National Savings Certificates regularly will produce a stream of income as they start to mature in two or five years' time.

For income now

There are a few investments whose main purpose is to produce income:

- bank and building society monthly-income accounts (in return for lower rates of interest, many societies also give the option to have interest paid out monthly on other accounts). See Chapter 12
- National Savings Income Bonds (see Chapter 13)
- National Savings Pensioners Bonds
- guaranteed income bonds sold by insurance companies (not to be confused with the National Savings Bonds above, which work in a completely different way) – see Chapter 26
- annuities, also sold by insurance companies. Note that annuities you buy yourself (rather than ones bought on your behalf with the proceeds of a personal pension plan) are favourably taxed. Only part of the regular income is taxable; the rest is regarded as a return of your original capital – see Chapter 27
- split-capital investment trusts – broadly, these are investment companies that

When you retire, consider 'investing' some of your money in a way that cuts down expenses in the future. Consider changing your car, washing machine or other equipment for a model that costs less to run. Check your home's insulation: for example, draught-proofing single-paned windows and external doors yourself costs around £50 for an average-sized house, with potential savings of £40 or more a year.

split their shares into two basic types, income and capital shares. However, these may involve special risks (see Chapter 22).

Note that during periods of low inflation and low interest rates, minimum investments have to be high (i.e. thousands, rather than hundreds, of pounds) to pay a worthwhile monthly income. However, do not confine yourself to specialist income-producing investments. For the advantage of regular income, you may have to accept other risks, such as tying up your capital.

One of the golden rules of investment is that the higher the return, the higher the risk. And if the income on offer looks too good to be true, it probably is. Consider these ideas:

- using unit trust and investment trust companies marketing 'income' funds: they invest in companies that tend to pay high dividends
- investing in unit trusts which offer income schemes paying out a set income – remember that, to achieve this when prices are falling, they may have to cash in some of your units. Insurance company distribution bonds do the same thing
- designing your own income-producing portfolio. First choose categories of investments that achieve a sensible balance between risk, security and growth, then, where possible, buy specific investments paying income at different times throughout the year
- buying single-premium insurance bonds (see Chapter 25), which are useful for higher-rate taxpayers needing income
- using what is for most people their single biggest investment – your home. Selling it and moving to a cheaper one may give you a lump sum to invest: you could also consider mortgaging it and using the proceeds to buy an annuity (known as a home income plan – see Chapter 28). Letting out part of your home or taking in a lodger is another option. Check the legal position first with your solicitor or the Citizens Advice Bureau.

Traps to avoid

Using up capital too fast
You cannot tell for certain how long you are going to need an income. You have to take into account how much your investments are likely to earn, how fast

inflation erodes your income's purchasing power and how long you are likely to live. For how inflation can affect your income, see page 146.

Failing to monitor your investments

Jumping on to the latest investment bandwagon is unwise for people seeking income in retirement – and, in any case, switching from one scheme to another normally incurs extra costs, such as unit trust initial charges or early redemption penalties. Be especially wary of advisers who recommend frequent changes in your existing investments – known as 'churning'. This earns commission for them, but incurs costs for you, and is in breach of investor protection rules.

Even so, you should still check regularly that your investments are working as well as they can for you, taking particular account of the way you are taxed and any changes in the financial world or your own circumstances. See Chapter 5 for advice on how to monitor your investments.

Forgetting that things may change

If either husband or wife dies, pension income may drop sharply, forcing the surviving partner to depend more upon investments (unless life insurance fills the gap). What happens to any jointly held investments and savings accounts depends on whether they are held by 'joint tenants' or 'tenants in common'. In England and Wales, in the absence of any other arrangement, it is assumed that jointly owned property is owned by joint tenants. This means that when one owner dies the whole account or investment automatically passes to the other, irrespective of any will and whether there is a will or not. In Scotland, this may not be the case – check with your solicitor or investment provider.

The surviving partner's investment priorities are almost bound to change. He or she may be particularly at the mercy of inflation and should beware of putting too much in an investment, such as a building society account, which is secure but whose real value, over time, is eroded by inflation. Instead, the surviving partner should consider index-linked investments such as index-linked gilts and index-linked National Savings Certificates or, if there is enough capital to risk, investments such as shares, which have a chance of beating inflation.

Selling at the wrong time

When a long-term investment matures – for example a pension or some types of life-insurance policy – you may lose out badly if the stock market happens to be low at the time. One way to reduce the risk is to ask the company if you can transfer your money to a safer (probably more pedestrian) fund, some time before maturity. See Chapter 5, on how to plan to switch your investments as you get closer to retirement. Things like shares or unit trusts you can, of course, sell at any time. But, if at all possible, avoid being forced to sell them when their value is very low, by making sure that you always have a safer investment to fall back on until prices improve.

Buying at the wrong time

You need a crystal ball to avoid this trap completely, particularly when you invest in schemes that provide a fixed return, such as a fixed-interest savings account or annuity. These usually have penalties if you close the account early; so, if you buy a long-term scheme at a time when interest rates are low, you could lose out badly should interest rates then rise. This is a particular problem with annuities. Annuity rates have fallen dramatically and stayed at low levels over the past four to five years. This has been bad news for people retiring recently. Compared to someone retiring on the higher rates available in the mid-1990s, they have a reduced income to live on. Once you have bought an annuity, you cannot usually get any of your money back. Annuities usually involve very large sums of money (for example, when your personal pension plan investment fund is converted into a pension on your retirement, you are technically buying an annuity).

However, the annuity market-place is also competitive, with some companies offering much better rates than others. Therefore, shop around as many companies as possible or, if you can, consider waiting or even deferring your pension until rates improve. One new option is an income drawdown plan. Consult your financial adviser.

Losing age-related allowance

If you are aged 65 or over at any point in the tax year, you can claim a higher tax-free personal allowance, which is higher still if you reach 75 or over: you can claim up to £5,990 (£6,260 if you are over 75) in the 2001–2 tax year. You may also be able to claim a higher married couple's allowance provided either you or your spouse reached the age of 65 by 5 April 2000. The figures for 2001–2 are £5,365 or £5,435 if either of you is aged 75 or over. The higher married couple's allowances are restricted to 10 per cent tax relief in 2001–2.

You start to lose your age-related allowance once your 'total income' (see Chapter 10) rises above a certain limit – £17,600 in the 2001–2 tax year. The extra allowance is reduced by half the amount by which your 'total income' exceeds the limit but is never reduced below the level of the basic personal and married couple's allowance. Note that even if a married man gets a higher married couple's allowance based on his wife's age (because she is older than him), it is *his* total income that determines the amount of allowance received.

If your 'total income' is above the limit, consider tax-free or favourably taxed investments – including those investments where the return comes mainly in the form of capital gain – that do not swell your income.

Cashing in part of some life-insurance policies

If you invested in a single-premium life-insurance policy (for example an insurance bond), and you are getting age-related allowances, be careful. Although any taxable gain you make when you cash in this type of life-insurance policy is free of basic-rate income tax, it is counted as part of your investment income for the year – and increasing your income can mean less age-related allowance and so more tax.

See Chapter 23 for more on the taxation of single-premium life-insurance policies.

 # Investing for children

Choosing an investment for someone under 18 involves much the same principles as for an adult, including how much there is to invest, how long you want to invest it for and what rate of tax will be paid on the income. But the range of investments to choose from is not the same as for adults.

- Not all investments allow children to invest in their own name. Some have age limits (7 or 16 are common), while others are not open at all to anyone under 18. However, even for a child below the age limit, you can usually invest on the child's behalf.
- Investments open only to children usually offer perks and free gifts to win the custom of the next generation of money magnates.

When investing for a child (we use this term for anyone under 18), follow the guidance in Chapters 1 to 3 on deciding your investment strategy and finding a shortlist of likely investments. Then use the table on pages 156–7 to eliminate any investments that require too high a minimum investment.

How tax affects your choices

Which investment to choose depends very much on the child's (or, in some cases, the parents') tax position.

Until a child reaches 18 or gets married at a younger age, all income that comes from investing money given to the child by a parent is taxed as the parent's income – unless it is £100 a year or less, in which case it is taxed as the child's income. The £100 rule applies to gifts from each parent: a child can have tax-free investment income of £200 a year arising from parental gifts. But once the £100 income is exceeded in respect of gifts from just one of the parents, all the income taxed as the income of that parent. Note that these limits also apply to interest earned on money given by a parent for a child over 16 to invest in a cash-only Individual Savings Account (ISA). This is to stop parents using a child's ISA allowance to increase their own tax-free savings.

Any other income the child gets is taxed as the child's, whether it comes from investments handed on by grandparents, earnings from a paper round or appearance fees from advertisements. Children have the same personal allowance (£4,535 for the 2001–2 tax year) as adults.

If a child is a non-taxpayer, it makes sense to consider investments that pay interest out before tax. Examples are most National Savings products and bank or building society accounts, where non-taxpayers can register to have interest paid gross. This saves the bother of having to reclaim tax later. If there is any likelihood of tax being payable, it might be sensible to invest gifts from parents separately from other gifts and keep a record of all monetary gifts made. Alternatively, parents should choose tax-free investments for the money they give to their children – see Chapter 11.

Capital gains tax

If you hand over assets (such as shares or your second home) to your children, or put them into a trust, you *dispose* of what you have given. As a result, there may be some capital gains tax to pay (and, possibly, inheritance tax). The asset is valued at its market value at the time you make the gift. For the rules about capital gains tax, see Chapter 10.

Bear in mind that the first £7,500 (for the 2001–2 tax year) of net capital gains you make from disposing of assets during a tax year is tax-free.

Once a gift has been made, how much capital gains tax has to be paid on any further gains depends on whether the child controls the investment, or whether the gift is held in trust – see page 158.

Gains made by a child

Capital gains made by a child are taxed as the child's gains, including gains on investments arising from parental gifts. The normal rules for working out capital gains tax apply; so, for example, the child can make £7,500 of gains in the 2010–2 tax year without paying tax.

Special investments for children
Banks and building societies

Banks and building societies know that today's young savers are tomorrow's consumers of financial products: loans, insurance, investments. They aim to catch them young. Some offer higher rates of interest to young savers; others tempt the nation's youth with perks such as books, badges, magazines, school gear. Some offer both. A few also now offer cash cards to children aged around 13 or over – though with no overdraft facilities.

Some gifts are designed to help children learn about money and draw up budgets. You might find them worthwhile even if the rate of interest is not top of the league. However, if it is interest you want, do not let the goodies distract your attention from the best rates going. Accounts usually give instant access. Some do not allow withdrawals before a given age.

Since most children are non-taxpayers, do not forget to register to get the bank or building society account interest paid before tax. Complete form R85 (available from the society or bank). If you fail to register as a non-taxpayer, you can still apply to your tax office to reclaim the tax deducted at source.

National Savings

National Savings Children's Bonus Bonds can be bought by anyone over the age of 16 for anyone under 16 and can be held until the holder reaches age 21. If children under 16 want to invest their own money in the bonds, they must enlist

Table 1: Which investment suits your child?

Type of investment	Age child can operate account in own name [1]	Minimum investment
Gilts bought through post office	7	none [2]
Gilts bought through stockbroker	18	none – but £1,000 a sensible minimum [2]
National Savings Certificates	7	£100
National Savings Ordinary account	7	£10
National Savings Investment account	7	£20
National Savings Fixed-Rate Savings Bonds	16	£500
National Savings Income Bonds	7	£500
National Savings Capital Bonds	7	£100
National Savings Children's Bonus Bonds	16 – bonds for a child aged under 16 must be bought by a person aged 16 or over	£25

Premium Bonds	16 – bonds for a child under 16 must be bought by a parent, guardian or (great) grandparent	£100
Building society or bank instant-access account	varies – often 7	normally £1 to £10
Building society notice account or term shares	varies – often 7	£500 upwards
Friendly Society 'baby bonds'	16	usually £25 a month
Individual Savings Account (ISA)	16 – earliest age a child can open his or her own ISA.	normally £10
Life-insurance policies	varies widely – often 16 to 18, can be younger	often £15 to £20 a month; lump sum usually £250 to £1,000
Shares	18	none – but £1,500 a sensible minimum [2]
Unit trusts and OEICs	varies – usually 18	usually £250 to £500, but can be less

[1] See page 158, if the child is too young to invest in his or her own name.
[2] You have to pay commission each time you buy or sell, so investing or withdrawing small amounts may not be worthwhile.

the help of an adult. For full details of how these bonds work, see Chapter 13. To get the best return, they must be held for five years. The return is tax-free, so they are particularly worth considering if the child is a taxpayer or if he or she is likely to breach the £100 limit above which income from parental gifts is taxed as the parent's (see page 154).

Friendly societies

Friendly societies offer similar products to life-insurance companies. They also offer children's savings plans, often called 'baby bonds', which are aimed at people under the age of 18.* Children can invest in a plan themselves or an adult can on their behalf. Baby bonds work in the same way as savings-type insurance policies (see Chapter 22) and usually last for ten years. The maximum investment is small – £25 a month or £270 a year.

Investing on a child's behalf

Children must reach a certain age before they can open many types of investment themselves, but you can often buy the investment on the child's behalf before that age. Check how withdrawals or other transactions can be made before the child reaches the appropriate age. For example, a building society, bank or other institution will often act on the child's own signature at the age of seven. Usually, a parent or other guardian living with the child can make the withdrawal on his or her behalf before this age.

Most unit-trusts and open-ended investment companies do not register investments in the name of anyone aged under 18, though a few do this from the age of 14. However, they usually allow units to be bought in the name of an adult, with the account 'designated' for a particular child. The adult runs the account but it is treated for tax purposes as the child's. On the child's eighteenth (or fourteenth) birthday, the trust can be transferred to the child's name.

If you have a lump sum to invest, you may still be able to invest it in the form of regular premiums. For example, friendly societies often allow you to pay with a lump sum, which is invested in a 'temporary annuity'. This produces a regular amount to pay the premiums. Alternatively, you can simply put a lump sum in a building society or bank account and make regular payments by standing order.

Trusts

If you are planning to give substantial amounts of money to a child, you may be worried that he or she might squander it. A way out of this problem is to set up a trust for the child. A trust is managed by *trustees* for the benefit of those for whom it was set up, the *beneficiaries* of the trust. The people setting up the trust (the parents, say) can act as trustees. Alternatively they can appoint friends or relatives

---

* These should not be confused with the proposed government scheme under which, once approved by Parliament, all new-born babies receive a bond worth £250 or £500.

or a professional adviser such as a solicitor or accountant as trustees. Below we give brief details of how a trust is set up and look at some shortcuts you can take.

A trust can have more than one beneficiary. You can, for example, set up a trust for the benefit of all your ten grandchildren (plus any more that come along). In this chapter we assume a trust has only one beneficiary but what we say holds equally well for more than one.

The trustees may be given the power to invest in specified investments, or to invest *as they think fit*. If they are not given these powers, there are special rules about how they can invest the money.

However, putting money into a trust could mean an inheritance tax bill – see pages 160–1.

Setting up a trust

The rules concerning trusts are extremely complicated, so ask a solicitor with experience of setting up trusts to draw up a *trust deed* for you. This specifies who the trustees are, who is entitled to benefit from the trust, when income and capital are to be paid out, ways in which the trustees can invest the money.

Even a fairly straightforward trust might cost several hundred pounds to set up and there could be a charge each year from any professional trustees for running the trust (as much as £100 or more, say). So it is probably not worth setting up a trust unless you plan to give a lot of money to your children (at least £10,000, say) and feel the cost of setting up and running the trust is outweighed by tax savings.

There are two basic types of trust:

- **Interest-in-possession trusts** (also known as 'fixed-interest' or 'life-interest' trusts) give a particular person or people the right to the income from the trust or the equivalent of income (e.g. the right to live in a rent-free home). The trustees have no choice but to hand over the income to the beneficiaries at the times stated in the trust.
- **Discretionary trusts** leave to the discretion of the trustees which of the possible beneficiaries should be paid income. They may also be free to decide which beneficiary should get capital. If the trustees have the power to accumulate income, i.e. not to pay it out at all (until the trust ends), the trust is called an *accumulation* trust. An *accumulation-and-maintenance* trust is a type of accumulation trust from which income can be paid out only for the maintenance, education or benefit of the beneficiaries until the beneficiaries get an *interest in possession*.

Once you have set up a trust, you cannot normally change your mind and take the money back. Also, although you can indicate to the trustees your preferences about how they should manage the trust's affairs, the trustees do not have to follow them. The trustees have a duty to follow the intentions of the trust but have the final word on how this is achieved.

If you think you or your family could benefit from a trust, you should discuss it with a solicitor or other professional adviser.

Tax on income from interest-in-possession trusts

An interest-in-possession trust pays tax at the basic rate on its income. Any income paid out of the trust comes with a tax credit of the amount of tax deducted (22 per cent of the before-tax income for the 2001–2 tax year).

If the trust was set up by the parents, the income counts as theirs and they get the 22 per cent tax credit. If the trust was set up by anyone other than the parents, the income counts as the child's and the child gets the tax credit.

If the parents (or child, as the case may be) do not pay tax, or pay less than the tax deducted, they can claim tax back. If the highest rate of tax the parents (or the child) pay is 22 per cent, the tax liability on income from the trust is automatically met by the tax credit. If the parents (or child) pay tax at 40 per cent, they have to pay extra tax, calculated on the income paid out plus the tax credit.

Tax on income from discretionary trusts

These pay tax on their income at a special rate: 34 per cent for the 2001–2 tax year.

As with an interest-in-possession trust, any income paid out is taxed as either the parents' income (if the trust was set up by the parents) or the child's income (in any other case). But, with a discretionary trust, the income comes with a tax credit of 34 per cent of the before-tax amount of income (25 per cent for dividend income and income from share-based investments). Whether or not there is more tax to pay (or whether a rebate can be claimed) depends on whether the parents' (or child's) top rate of tax is more or less than 34 per cent. If the top rate is *less* than 34 per cent, it would be worth asking the trustees to pay as much income out as possible, as tax could then be claimed back from the Inland Revenue. With an accumulation trust, if the income is accumulated and not paid out until your children are 18 or over, there is no further income tax to pay; but neither you nor your children can claim tax back.

Gains made by a trust

Trusts pay capital gains tax at a flat rate of 20 per cent for an interest-in-possession trust, 34 per cent for a discretionary trust (including an accumulation-and-maintenance trust). But the first £3,750 (for the 2001–2 tax year) of net capital gains is free of capital gains tax. This lower tax-free limit for trusts means that trusts are often liable for more capital gains tax than is an individual.

If a beneficiary becomes entitled to some or all of the assets of the trust, for example on reaching the age of 18, this counts as the trust disposing of the assets. If there are gains, capital gains tax may have to be paid by the trust. However, there is no capital gains tax for the beneficiary to pay and he or she cannot reclaim any capital gains tax paid by the trust.

Inheritance tax on gifts to trusts

If you make a gift to your child (or set up a trust under which he or she benefits) it normally counts as a gift for inheritance tax purposes. But some gifts you make are free of inheritance tax. For brief details of how inheritance tax works, see Chapter 10. The taxation of trust funds and settlements can be very complicated – one reason for getting professional advice if you are setting up a tailor-made trust.

In general, the value of the money, property or whatever you put into the trust counts as a gift. With gifts to the following types of trust, there may be an inheritance tax bill only if you die within seven years of making the gift (in the same way as for any other gift):

- an accumulation-and-maintenance trust
- a trust for disabled people
- an interest-in-possession trust.

Note that gifts to trusts count as tax-free if they would be tax-free when made to an individual (for example if made out of normal spending).

Inheritance tax on trusts
Interest-in-possession trusts

Anyone with the right to income from an income-in-possession trust or the equivalent of income (such as the right to live in a rent-free home) is considered to own the trust's capital – or part of the trust's capital, if the rights to the benefits are shared. When a person's right to the trust's benefit goes to someone else, this is considered to be making a gift. For example, your son may have the right to income from a trust once he reaches 18. If this right passes to his younger sister when he reaches 21, he is considered to make a gift at that time. The gift is valued as the share of the trust's capital which he is considered to own at the time the right to the income is transferred. Inheritance tax is due if the son dies within seven years of the gift; but this tax is paid by the trust.

When the trust finally comes to an end, and the capital is handed over to beneficiaries who until that time had only the right to the income, there is no more inheritance tax to pay.

Discretionary trusts

Discretionary trusts (other than accumulation-and-maintenance trusts – see below) may be charged inheritance tax even if payments are not made out of the trust. Inheritance tax is automatically charged on everything in the trust every ten years – the *periodic charge*. The rules for calculating the periodic charge are complex.

When payments are actually made from a discretionary trust's capital (or if fixed interests are created), the trust is also charged inheritance tax. The value of what is paid out or turned into a fixed interest is charged at the rate of tax which applied at the last periodic charge. However, this rate is scaled down in proportion to the time since the last ten-yearly charge: so if it has been one year since the ten-yearly charge, the rate is one-tenth of the rate at the last ten-yearly charge. If the payment from the trust is made within three months after a ten-yearly charge, there is no tax to be paid.

Accumulation-and-maintenance trusts

Payments of capital from accumulation-and-maintenance trusts may be free of inheritance tax and these trusts may be free of the ten-yearly tax bills. To qualify, a trust must be for the benefit of one or more people under the age of 25, who must get the capital of the trust (or at least the right to the income, or use of the trust property) on or before their twenty-fifth birthday. If any income is paid out before this, it must be used only for the maintenance, education or training of the

---

EXAMPLE 1: Single-premium life-insurance band

John and Susan pay tax on the top slice of their income at 40 per cent. They have £5,000 from a with-profits endowment policy, which they want to invest for their ten-year-old daughter, Sally. They do not want her to have the money until she is 18.

They consider whether to set up an accumulation-and-maintenance trust but they decide that the amount they are investing does not justify the expense of setting up a tailor-made trust. So they put £3,000 into a single-premium life-insurance bond taken out on John's life. The proceeds are payable to Sally and the policy will be handed over to her when she is 18, so that any gain counts as hers for tax purposes. John and Susan invest the remaining £2,000 in unit trusts on behalf of Sally. The income (assuming it is below the £100 per-parent threshold – see page 154) – and any gains are taxed as Sally's.

The £5,000 counts as a gift for inheritance tax purposes. However, John and Susan have not used their tax-free quota of £3,000 each for this year (see page 114) and between them can give £6,000. So they can invest the money for Sally without fear of inheritance tax. And there is no inheritance tax to pay when the investments are handed over to Sally.

---

beneficiaries. In addition, payments from the trust are free of inheritance tax only if the children who benefit have a grandparent in common or the trust is less than 25 years old.

Shortcut trusts
There are ways of making sure that money you invest for your children is held in trust for them without going to the expense of setting up a tailor-made trust.

Life-insurance policies
You can take out a life-insurance policy on your own, or the child's other parent's life, with the proceeds made payable to your child. The insurance company should be able to advise you of the options available and has standard forms for setting up various types of trust. The policy can be a single-premium one (for example a managed bond) or a regular-premium one (for example a unit-linked savings plan or an endowment policy).

The premiums you pay count as gifts for tax purposes but probably come into one of the tax-free categories – see page 114. There is no inheritance tax to pay on money paid out by the policy and, if the policy is handed over to the child after the age of 18, any taxable gain on the policy is taxed as the child's, not the parent's. However, if the policy ends before it is handed over, the gain is taxed as the parent's.

Planning for education

Having to worry about the cost of financing your offspring's education is no longer the preserve of parents choosing fee-paying rather than state schooling. The introduction of tuition fees and the abolition of the student maintenance grant in the 1999–2000 academic year mean that parents whose children go to university may also have to fund fees and, possibly, make a contribution towards upkeep.

Planning for university costs
How much you are expected to contribute towards a student's
tuition fee and upkeep is decided by a means test of the parents' income (or the student's if over 25, married or self-supporting). In the 2001–2 academic year, the most parents are expected to contribute is the tuition fee of £1,075 and 25 per cent of living costs – see Table 2. The student loan provides the remaining 75 per cent of living costs. No parental contribution is required if parental income is £20,000 or less and the student can apply for the maximum student loan available.

Under the present system, both fees and living costs are increased each year in line with price inflation as measured by the Retail Prices Index (RPI). Table 3 gives an estimate of the most you have to contribute in future academic years using the most expensive option of a student studying in London and assuming that inflation continues to run at its current level of 2.5 per cent.

To work out the total cost of funding a university education, add up the relevant figures for the 'maximum parental contribution' for each full academic year (i.e. all years before the final year) and then add the maximum for the final year. For example, if your son or daughter would be off to college in the 2010–11 academic year, you can see that the maximum you may have to contribute is £2,810 in the first year, £2,880 in the second year and, assuming a three-year course, £2,749 in the final year which gives a total of £8,642.

How to meet the cost of a university education
If you do not think that you will be able to meet university costs out of income and you do not want to borrow the money to finance your parental contribution when the time comes, the alternative is to plan ahead.

Table 2: Maximum parental contribution for the 2001–2 academic year

| Contribution in all years except final year | | | |
Place of study	Tuition fee	Living costs	Total
London	£1,075	£1,175	£2,250
Elsewhere	£1,075	£955	£2,030
Living at home [1]	£1,075	£755	£1,830
Contribution in final year			
London	£1,075	£1,020	£2,095
Elsewhere	£1,075	£825	£1,900
Living at home [1]	£1,075	£660	£1,735

[1] The contribution for a student who lives at home is the same even if studying in London.

Table 3: University costs in the future

Academic year starting in September	All years except final year			Final year		
	Tuition fee £	Living costs £	Maximum parental contribution £	Tuition fee £	Living costs £	Maximum parental contribution £
2001	1,075	1,175	2,250	1.075	1.020	2.095
2002	1,102	1,204	2,306	1.102	1.046	2.147
2003	1,129	1,234	2,364	1.129	1.072	2.201
2004	1,158	1,265	2,423	1.158	1.098	2.256
2005	1,187	1,297	2,484	1.187	1.126	2.312
2006	1,216	1,329	2,546	1.216	1.154	2.370
2007	1,247	1,363	2,609	1.247	1.183	2.430
2008	1,278	1,397	2,675	1.278	1.212	2.490
2009	1,310	1,432	2,741	1.310	1.243	2.553
2010	1,343	1,467	2,810	1.343	1.274	2.616
2011	1,376	1,504	2,880	1.376	1.306	2.682
2012	1,410	1,542	2,952	1.410	1.338	2.749
2013	1,446	1,580	3,026	1.446	1.372	2.818
2014	1,482	1,620	3,102	1.482	1.406	2.888
2015	1,519	1,660	3,179	1.519	1.441	2.960
2016	1,557	1,702	3,259	1.557	1.477	3.034
2017	1,596	1,744	3,340	1.596	1.514	3.110
2018	1,636	1,788	3,424	1.636	1.552	3.188
2019	1,677	1,833	3,509	1.677	1.591	3.267
2020	1,719	1,878	3,597	1.719	1.631	3,349

If you already have savings and investments, the simplest approach is to earmark a lump sum of around £6,500 for each of your children destined for further education. This is the total cost of a three-year course in today's money. So provided the lump sum grows at a rate equal to or greater than inflation, it should be more than enough to meet the amount you expect to contribute. But, if you want to play safe, set aside a sum equal to the current cost of a four-year course which is £8,845.

Which type of investments you choose depends both on how long there is to go until your child goes to university and how much risk you are prepared to take. With fewer than five years, deposit-based investments such as cash Individual Savings Accounts (see Chapter 11), savings accounts from banks and building societies (see Chapter 12) and tax-free National Savings Certificates (see Chapter 13) are probably most suitable.

If there are more than five years to go, equity-based investments are an option provided you move them into less risky investments a year or so before you need to spend the money.

If you do not have a lump sum you can set aside to fund university costs, you

Table 4: School fees

Academic year starting in September	Average yearly fees:		
	Day school £	Weekly boarding £	Full-time boarding £
2001	6,216	11,982	14,208
2002	6,632	12,761	15,117
2003	7,077	13,590	16,085
2004	7,551	14,474	17,114
2005	8,057	15,414	18,210
2006	8,597	16,416	19,375
2007	9,173	17,483	20,615
Total	**53,303**	**102,121**	**120,724**

Figures assume current levels of school fee inflation (6.5%).

need to start saving on a regular basis. The easiest way to work out how much you need to save is to take the current cost of a three- or four-year course, divide by the number of years before your child is set to start at university, then divide again by 12 to get a monthly amount. Your choice of investment is the same as if you have a lump sum to invest.

Planning for school fees

In general terms, planning for school fees is the same as planning to fund the cost of putting your child through university – except that the costs are higher and the length of time you have to pay fees for is much longer. You should also be aware that school fees tend to go up at a rate which has traditionally been higher than general inflation. In the 12 months to January 2001, school fees in general rose by an average of 6.5 per cent – well ahead of price inflation of 2.5 per cent.

Table 4 shows the average yearly cost of sending your child to three types of fee-paying school and gives the total cost of seven years of secondary education assuming that fees continue to rise at their current rate.

How to pay

Although two thirds of fee-paying parents manage to fund fees from current income, this can be hard going. So if there is time in hand, look at ways of saving now for the future.

Various insurance companies and investment advisers specialise in arranging schemes to provide the money needed for school fees or further education. These schemes are often based on investment-type life-insurance policies and annuities. Broadly speaking, they fall into two groups:

- **capital** schemes, where you invest a lump sum now to provide fees in the future
- **income** schemes, where you save on a regular basis to build up the money needed to pay fees.

165

Depending on your circumstances, a mixture of the different types may suit you best.

There is nothing magical about such schemes. They are simply a way of investing money in order to make a set of payments some time in the future. The income they produce may turn out to be less than, or more than, enough to pay the fees. They use the same range of investment that you might well choose to invest in yourself if you were arranging to save up for school fees independently. However, there has to be careful timing of the investments to make sure that the money is around when the fees are due and there are tax complications to take into account. So, although you can go it alone, you may decide it is best to make your investments through a special scheme.

Where to go for education-funding schemes

A reputable independent financial adviser should be able to help you or put you in touch with an insurance company or adviser specialising in such schemes. Alternatively, you could try the Independent Schools Information Service (ISIS)* for help. But get quotes from more than one source – different schemes suit different people – and ask how any adviser is paid: they may get commission for selling particular products, or they may give you the option of paying a fee, reduced by any commission received.

Cutting the cost

Many schools offer scholarships to academically, musically or artistically gifted children, subject to entrance-exam results. These can help pay part or all of the fees. A leaflet on grants and scholarships is available from ISIS.* If you have already chosen a school, ask the bursar.

Some employers may help with fees, especially for staff posted overseas. There are schemes, for example, for parents working for the Diplomatic Service or serving in the armed forces. Financial help from an employer can count as a taxable fringe benefit in some cases – check with the Inland Revenue.

Capital schemes

The amount you need to invest will depend on how long there is until the fees start and what the fees are expected to be. If you have a newly born child, you should think about investing a lump sum of at least £60,000 to £70,000 to pay for private boarding secondary education (assuming fees go up from current levels by 6.5 per cent a year).

Tax

The amount of income tax and capital gains tax you pay depends on the investments on which the scheme is based and your own circumstances. See the relevant chapter for more details.

How much inheritance tax has to be paid and when depends on who gives the money.

- **If the parents give the money** Payments made by the parents solely for the *maintenance, education or training* of their children are free of inheritance tax. However, if the money is not held in trust or if it is held in trust and the parents keep the right to cash in the scheme, there may be inheritance tax to pay if the parent who gives the money dies. The cash-in value of the investment forms part of his or her estate and will be taxed in the normal way. If the parent gives up the right to cash in a trust scheme, and the money remains in trust for the child to be used for his or her maintenance, education or training, the money does not form part of the parent's estate.
- **If someone else (e.g. grandparents) gives the money** If the grandparents (or whoever) do not set up a trust scheme, the money they eventually pay over for school fees may count as gifts for inheritance tax. If they do set up a trust scheme – and give away the right to cash in the scheme – the money they invest in the first place may count as a gift for inheritance tax purposes. If they keep the right to cash in the scheme, what counts as a gift is the cash-in value of the scheme when fees start being paid. This will almost certainly be higher than the value of the original investment.

Composition fees

With many private schools, you can pay school fees in advance by what is known as a *composition fee*. In this case, the school then invests the money, often in an annuity which starts paying out when the child goes to school. The amount you have to pay could be either fees frozen at current levels or reduced fees. But check what happens if you decide to send your child to a different school.

Income schemes

There are a number of different ways in which these schemes can be set up. Most involve saving regularly by taking out a series of investment-type life-insurance policies, which mature year by year as the fees become due.

For example, suppose you plan to send your child to private school in ten years' time for five years. You could take out five with-profits endowment policies which end after 10, 11, 12, 13 and 14 years respectively. For the first ten years, you pay a flat amount (the premiums for all the policies). From the eleventh year onwards, the premiums start to tail off as each policy ends.

If you expect your income to go up over the years, you might prefer to pay premiums which increase rather than decrease. In this case, it may be best to take out five ten-year policies in successive years. Your premiums increase each year up to the fifth year, stay level for the next five years, then tail off as policies end.

Some companies use unit-linked policies (see Chapter 23), unit trusts, open-ended investment companies and investment trusts to provide part or all of the fees. With all these, there is the risk that the value of your investment will fluctuate. If their value is low when you want to cash in your investment, you might get less than hoped for.

What happens if you change your mind about sending your child to private school? If the policies are being held in trust (which gives a possible inheritance tax advantage – see above), the money from the policies must be used for the benefit of the child. If they are not being held in trust, you can either cash in the policies or keep them as a form of saving.

As with capital schemes, the amount you need to invest depends on how much time there is before your child goes to private school and what the fees are expected to be. For example, if you hope to provide private boarding secondary education for a child who is a baby now, you need to think about investing around £5,000 to £8,000 a year (assuming fees go up from current levels at 6.5 per cent a year).

Tax
The amount of income tax and capital gains tax you pay depends on the investments on which the scheme is based and on your own circumstances.

If the parents pay for the scheme, there is no inheritance tax to pay on the premiums or on the money paid out by the schemes. If people other than the parents pay and as long as the scheme contributions are paid out of their normal income or count as tax-free for some other reason, there is no inheritance tax to pay. If there are life-insurance policies being held in trust for the child, if the person who set up the scheme dies there is no inheritance tax to pay. If the policies are not being held in trust, the proceeds on death count as part of the person's estate.

Failed to plan?
If you have left it too late, or the fees are more than you anticipated, you may be able to borrow the money for the fees. But first compare the monthly cost of any loan with the outlay if you pay as you go. You may be able to meet the cost out of your income. The occasional overdraft may be cheaper and you are committed to paying off loans for years to come.

Banks and insurance companies offer special loan packages for school fees, which usually involve a second mortgage on your home. The money is lent to you as the fees fall due and you repay it after, say, 25 years (or when you retire) with the proceeds of an investment-type insurance policy. As you draw more of the money to pay the fees, the monthly cost (insurance premiums plus interest) rises.

If you can manage most of the cost out of day-to-day income but need to top it up with more than an overdraft, you could ask your bank or building society for a straightforward loan. If you have an investment-type life-insurance policy, you may be able to borrow from the insurance company on the strength of it.

16 Pensions from the state

Latest statistics (1998/9) show there are some 10 million pensioners in the UK receiving the basic state pension. Of them 5.5 million also have income from SERPS, 6 million from an occupational pension and 7 million from investment income including personal pensions and retirement annuity contracts. Average annual income (net of taxes) for a single pensioner is around £7,332 from all sources including earnings from employment.

Your pension is one of the most important ways of saving for the future. Understanding how state pensions work is particularly important. Unless you know roughly what you are going to receive from the state, you are ill-prepared to sort out the rest of your savings and investments.

State pensions are in the process of being changed fundamentally. The government recognises the inadequacy of the state basic pension alone but is reluctant to increase it across the board because of the cost to the taxpayer and the disincentive it gives to people making their own savings for retirement. Instead, the government has introduced the minimum income guarantee (see page 170) to give means-tested top-ups to pensioners on low incomes and, from April 2003, intends to replace this with the pension credit (see page 172), which combines means-testing and an incentive to make your own savings. In the meantime, from April 2002, a new state second pension (see page 171) replaces SERPS. As many people as possible are to be encouraged to opt out and make their own savings, especially through the stakeholder pension schemes now available.

In this chapter we explain the choices facing you concerning the state pension; for employers' schemes see Chapter 17 and for your stakeholder and personal pension plan choices see Chapter 18. If you have an old-style personal plan, called a retirement annuity contract, see Chapter 19. For how pensions tie in to planning your savings and investments for retirement, see Chapter 14.

The current state pension system

There are currently three main parts to the state system. Your state pension may be made up of:

- a flat-rate *basic* pension
- a small *graduated* pension based on earnings from 1961 to 1975

- an additional pension based on your earnings since April 1978, known as the *State Earnings Related Pension Scheme (SERPS)* pension.

The amount of these pensions is increased each April in line with changes in the Retail Prices Index (RPI) up to the previous September.

You start to get these pensions when you reach the *state pension age*. At present, this is 65 for men. For women born before 6 April 1950, state pension age is 60. It is being progressively increased for women born after that date until it reaches 65 for women born on or after 5 April 1955.

If your income from these pensions and all other sources (for example, private pensions, your savings) is below the minimum income guarantee (MIG), you may be eligible to claim income support to bring your income up to the level of MIG. In the 2001–2 tax year, the MIG is set at £92.15 a week if you are a single person and £140.55 a week if you are a couple (whether married or unmarried).

Basic pension

Anyone who has paid enough full-rate Class 1, Class 2 or Class 3 National Insurance contributions, or has been given credits, qualifies for this pension. There are complicated rules to work out whether you have paid enough in contributions but you are pretty certain to qualify for the full basic-rate pension (£72.50 a week for a single person and £115.90 for a married couple in the 2001–2 tax year) if you have paid full-rate contributions for nine-tenths of your *working life* (broadly, between 16 and 65 for a man and for a woman born after 5 April 1955 or between ages 16 and 59 for a woman born before 6 April 1950). If you have contributed for a quarter or more of the years in your working life, you may qualify for a reduced pension. If there were periods when you were not working but receiving benefits such as Jobseeker's Allowance (or the earlier Unemployment Benefit), Incapacity Benefit (or the old Sickness or Invalidity Benefit), Maternity Allowance, or Invalid Care Allowance, you would have been credited with contributions for these years.

Since April 1978, if you stayed at home to look after children, or an elderly or sick person, the number of years needed to qualify are reduced. This is called *home responsibilities protection*.

Some married women rely on their husband's National Insurance record, rather than their own, for a basic pension – see page 172.

You can check on your basic pension and your graduated and SERPS pensions too by using the Department of Social Security's (DSS) Retirement Pension Forecast and Advice Service.* You need to get form BR19 from your local Benefits Agency or the DSS web site (*www.dss.gov.uk*), fill it in and send it to the address on the form. The Service can tell you how much pension you are entitled to so far, how much you might get by the time you retire, and anything you can do now to increase your entitlement. For example, in some cases it is possible to make up gaps in your contribution record by paying voluntary Class 3 contributions.

If you are saving for retirement through an employer's pension scheme, stakeholder scheme or personal pension, you may get a *combined pension statement* from the scheme. This shows your likely state pension at retirement alongside the potential pension you are building up through the scheme.

Graduated pension

People who were employed in a job between 1961 and 1975 may have a small graduated pension payable on top of the basic pension.

Between April 1961 and April 1975, there were two kinds of National Insurance (NI) contribution: a flat-rate one paid by almost everyone in employment and a graduated one paid by people who earned more than £9 in any one week.

For each £7.50 a man contributed during those years, he gets a unit of pension, which is now worth 9.06p a week (in 2001–2). If you are a woman, it will have taken £9 of contributions to earn that 9.06p a week. The rules were set in this way because women have, up to now, had an earlier state pension age than men and they live longer on average. The graduated pension has been increased since April 1978 with rising prices. But it is never going to be large.

The DSS keeps records of how many *units* of pension each person has earned. You can check with it for your own position using the Retirement Pension Forecast and Advice Service (see above).

Many people were *contracted out* of the old graduated scheme because their employers ran their own pension schemes. But when the graduated scheme was wound up, many employers got rid of their liabilities by paying the money back into the state scheme. Again, you can ask the DSS about this.

State Earnings Related Pension Scheme (SERPS)

This is a supplement to the basic pension for employees paying the full NI contribution. It started in 1978 but the government has cut back on it for people retiring from 6 April 2000 onwards. Many people are *contracted out* of SERPS – see page 178.

What you get from SERPS, and what you pay, depends on your earnings. We tell you later in this chapter how the scheme works and how to find out what you will get. If you are contracted out of SERPS, the benefits from your contracted-out scheme replace SERPS. We explain the different methods of contracting out too.

State Second Pension

From a future date, expected to be 6 April 2002, SERPS is to be replaced by a new state scheme called the State Second Pension (S2P).

Initially S2P is an earnings-related pension, but to boost the pension built up by people on low earnings, it provides a set pension for everyone earning up to a lower earnings threshold (£9,500 at 1999–2000 values but to be increased each year in line with earnings inflation).

After a few years – possibly five (i.e. April 2007) – S2P converts to a flat-rate pension based on earnings at the lower earnings threshold (£9,500 adjusted). But the change does not apply to anyone aged 45 and older at that time – they continue to build up earnings-related S2P.

Employees are covered by S2P but not the self-employed. Special rules credit you with pension (based on the lower earnings threshold) if you are unable to work because you are caring for young children, an elderly person or an invalid or, in some cases, if you yourself are suffering from a long-term illness or disability.

The aim of S2P is to provide adequate pensions for people on low or modest earnings. Although if you are a higher earner you may belong to S2P too, you will usually be better off contracting out into an employer's scheme stakeholder scheme or personal pension.

For details about how S2P pensions will be calculated, see page 175.

Pension credit

From April 2003, the government intends to introduce a pension credit to replace the minimum income guarantee (see page 170). The credit both guarantees a minimum level of retirement income and, to some extent, rewards you if you have made your own savings for retirement.

From April 2003, the minimum guaranteed income is expected to be around £100 a week for a single person and £154 a week for a couple. If your income from the state basic pension and other sources comes to less, you qualify for a pension credit to bring your income up to that level.

In addition, where your income is more than the state basic pension (because, for example, you have some state second pension or a stakeholder pension) but no more than the guaranteed income, you get extra pension credit of 60p for each £1 of income above the state basic pension up to the guaranteed minimum income. However, the pension credit is reduced by 40p for each £1 by which your income exceeds the guaranteed minimum.

For example, suppose in 2003 you have a full basic state pension of, say, £77 a week plus a private pension of £21 a week and the income guarantee is £100 a week. Your income from all sources comes to £98. This is less than the guarantee, so you get pension credit of £2 to bring you up to £100. But you also get credit of 60p for each £1 of income above £77 – in other words 21 x 60p = £12.60. So your total pension credit is £14.60. Your retirement income including the credit is £77 + £21 + £14.60 = £112.60.

To see how the credit is reduced as your income increases, suppose you have state pension of £77 plus other income of £35. Your total income is £112, which is above the minimum income level. However, you still get pension credit of 60p for each £1 of income above the state basic pension up to the minimum income limit. This is (100–77) x 60p = £13.80, reduced by 40p for each £1 above £100 – in other words 12 x 40p = £4.80. Your net pension credit is £13.80 – £4.80 = £9.00 and your retirement income including the credit is £77 + £35 + £9 = £121.

Married women

If you pay the full-rate National Insurance contribution, you are treated in exactly the same way as a man or a single woman. If you have had to spend time at home caring for children, or elderly relatives, you can qualify for a basic pension with a shorter contribution record under *home responsibilities protection* (see page 170).

However, some married women and widows still pay the reduced-rate contribution, which used to be called the *small stamp*. No one has been able to *start* doing so since 1977. If you become divorced, you are no longer eligible to pay at the lower rate. Reduced-rate contributors qualify for a state pension only on their husband's record (in the same way as married women who have paid no contributions). They have to wait until a husband starts to receive his pension. These women cannot qualify for SERPS. The pension for a dependent wife is approximately three-fifths of the rate the husband is getting (a maximum of £43.40 in the 2001–2 tax year).

Table 1: How much SERPS pension you can inherit

Date on which husband or wife dies	Date on which husband or wife reaches (or would have reached) retirement age	Percentage of husband's or wife's SERPS pension you can inherit
Before 6 October 2002	not applicable	100%
On or after 6 October 2002	5 October 2002 or earlier	100%
	6 October 2002 to 5 October 2004	90%
	6 October 2004 to 5 October 2006	80%
	6 October 2006 to 5 October 2008	70%
	6 October 2008 to 5 October 2010	60%
	6 October 2010 or later	50%

If the man has retired, and his wife is under 60, he can draw a dependant's allowance for her too, provided she is not earning or drawing an employer's (occupational) pension of more than £53.05 a week in 2001–2. If she is over 60, the pension is the same amount, but it is paid direct to her. Earnings and occupational pension are not taken into account once she is over 60.

Widows and widowers

Up to April 2001, women under retirement age, but not men, can get help from the state if they are widowed. The help stops if you remarry. If your husband had paid enough NI contributions, you qualify for various benefits, depending on your age and whether you are looking after children. For details, get leaflet GL1 *Widowed?* from your local Benefits Agency.

From April 2001 widows benefits have been replaced by new bereavement benefits, which can be claimed by widowers as well as widows. The new benefits for widow(er)s who are not caring for children are less generous than the old widow's benefits but, if you are already claiming the old benefits when the new system is introduced, you can continue under the old system.

If you are widowed after reaching state pension age, the rules have long been the same for both men and women. You can usually use your late husband's or wife's NI record to enhance your state basic pension up to the maximum a single person can have.

Whether widowed before or after retirement, if you receive widowed parent's allowance or retirement pension, you can inherit some or all of any SERPS pension for which your deceased husband or wife qualified. The amount you can inherit depends on when death occurs and the age of your spouse – see Table 1. The sum of the inherited SERPS and any SERPS pension you have in your own right may not come to more than the maximum SERPS a single person can have.

For example, suppose a husband dies in November 2002 aged 59. If his birthday is in May, he would have reached retirement age of 65 in May 2008, so his wife may inherit 70 per cent of his SERPS pension.

Is it worth deferring your pension?

You can earn extra state pension by putting off drawing your state retirement pension. Under current rules, you can do this for up to five years after pension age. For each week you postpone drawing the pension, your total state pension is increased by one-seventh of 1 per cent – or 7.5 per cent a year. You do not get any increases in the state pension for any weeks when you are drawing other state benefits such as Jobseeker's Allowance. Any graduated pension, and any SERPS benefits (see above), must be deferred along with the basic pension. They are increased in the same way.

A wife cannot claim a pension on her husband's contributions until he starts drawing the state pension. If he puts it off, her part of the pension is postponed too and increased by the same percentage as her husband's.

Once you're five years over state pension age, you must start taking your pension and no longer have the option to earn increases.

If you have already started drawing your state pension, you can cancel your retirement *once* before you reach five years over state pension age and earn increases in your pension from then on.

Is it worth deferring your pension in this way? If you give up the full basic pension in 2001–2, you lose about £3,770 over the year. In return, your pension next year is 7.5 per cent higher – some £283 a year in terms of 2001–2 money. You need to carry on getting that extra £283 a year (increased each year in line with inflation) for 13⅓ years before you recoup the full £3,770. A single man aged 66 could, on average, expect to break even on the deal. But, as he got older, deferring the pension would look less attractive: by the age of 70, he could expect to live 11 years more – too few to recoup the pension given up. Deferring the pension looks a better deal for women, who have a longer average life expectancy than men, and for married men whose widows would continue to benefit from increased pensions even after their husbands had died.

From 2010, the terms on which you can earn extra pension are due to change. You will then be able to earn an extra 10.4 per cent pension for each year you delay and defer your pension for as many years as you like.

Working out SERPS and S2P

The additional state pensions, SERPS and S2P, are complicated. The simplest way to find out how much pension you might get is to contact the Retirement Pension Forecast Service (see page 170). However, here we give a broad-brush outline of how these pensions are worked out.

SERPS

SERPS pensions are based on your earnings for all the tax years:

- from either 6 April 1978 or, if later, the year in which you reached 16
- up to the year before you reach state pension age (see page 170).

Table 2: Maximum SERPS pension you can build up

Year in which you retire	Maximum post-April 1988 SERPS as a percentage of earnings between the lower and upper earnings limits
2000–1	24.5%
2001–2	24%
2002–3	23.5%
2003–4	23%
2004–5	22.5%
2005–6	22%
2006–7	21.5%
2007–8	21%
2008–9	20.5%
2009–2010 and after	20%

You are in SERPS only if you count as an employee. But years when, say, you are unemployed or at home caring for children or elderly dependants are zero years for SERPS purposes. They reduce the overall SERPS pension you get.

Years when you earn less than the *lower earnings limit* (£72 a week in 2001–2) also count as zero years. Similarly, the years from the introduction of S2P (expected to be 6 April 2002 onwards) count as zero years for SERPS purposes.

Your earnings for each tax year between the lower earnings limit up to the *upper earnings limit* (£575 a week in 2001–2) are recorded and revalued in line with average earnings up to the year before you reach state pension age. These are called your *surplus earnings* for each year.

If you retired before 6 April 2000, your annual SERPS pension is basically one-quarter of the sum of your surplus earnings divided by the years from 1978–9 (or reaching 16) to the year before state pension age.

If you retire after that date, your period in SERPS is divided in two:

• the years from 6 April 1978 (or reaching age 16 if later) to 5 April 1988. You still get one-quarter of the sum of the surplus earnings for this period divided by the years from 1978–9 (or reaching 16) to the year before state pension age
• the years from 6 April 1988 to the year S2P is introduced (or reaching state pension age if earlier). The sum of these surplus earnings is multiplied by a fraction that is progressively reduced from one-quarter to one-fifth – see Table 2. The answer is as usual divided by the years from 1978–9 (or reaching 16) to the year before state pension age.

Your SERPS pension is reduced for any periods during which you are contracted out (see page 178).

S2P
S2P pensions are based on your earnings for all the tax years:

• from either 6 April 1978 or, if later, the year in which you reached 16
• up to the year you reach state pension age (see page 170).

EXAMPLE 1

Fred reaches state pension age in 2002–3. He has been in SERPS since 1984. His SERPS pension is based on the period from 6 April 1978 to 5 April 2002 – in other words, 24 years.

The sum of Fred's revalued surplus earnings for the period 6 April 1984 to 5 April 1988 is £106,100. Taking a quarter of this and dividing by 24 gives SERPS pension of £1,105 a year.

The sum of Fred's revalued surplus earnings for the period 6 April 1988 to 5 April 2002 is £241,200. This is multiplied by 23.5 per cent and divided by 24, giving SERPS pension of £2,362 a year.

In total, Fred's SERPS pension is £1,105 + £2,362 = £3,467 a year or £66.67 a week.

However, earnings for the years before the introduction of S2P (probably 6 April 2002) count as zero for S2P purposes. For the years from 6 April 2002 onwards, your earnings are divided into three bands – see Table 3. If you earn less than the lower earnings threshold or have no earnings because, say, you are caring for children or elderly dependants or, in some cases, you yourself have a long-term illness or disability, you are credited with earnings at the lower earnings threshold (£9,500 at 1999–2000 values).

Each band of earnings is revalued in line with earnings inflation up to the year before you reach state pension age. Then each revalued amount is multiplied by a given percentage. The percentage also varies according to when you reach state pension age – see Table 4.

The three totals – one for each earnings band – are then added together and divided by the number of tax years from 1978–9 (or the year you reached 16, if later) to the year in which you reach state pension age.

Table 3: Earnings band for S2P pension

Earnings Band	Description	Example based on 2001–2 earnings limits but 1999–2000 earnings thresholds
Band 1	Earnings from the lower earnings limit up to the lower earnings threshold	Earnings from £3,744 a year to £9,500
Band 2	Earnings above lower earnings threshold up to second earnings threshold	Earnings from £9,501 to £21,500
Band 3	Earnings above second earnings threshold up to upper earnings limit	£21,501 to £29,900

Table 4: Percentage of each earnings band used to work out your S2P pension

Tax year in which you reach state pension age	Earnings multiplied by this percentage:		
	Earnings band 1	Earnings band 2	Earnings band 3
2003–4	46%	11.5%	23%
2004–5	45%	11.25%	22.5%
2005–6	44%	11%	22%
2006–7	43%	10.75%	21.5%
2007–8	42%	10.5%	21%
2008–9	41%	10.25%	20.5%
2009–10 onwards	40%	10%	20%

EXAMPLE 2

It is May 2020. Jan has reached state pension age of 65. The number of years since 6 April 1978 comes to 42. Jan was over 45 when the S2P scheme became flat-rate for younger people, so she continued to build up an earnings-related pension based on three bands of earnings.

Over the years since April 2002 that she has been in the S2P scheme, her earnings have averaged around £26,000 a year. Each year's earnings are divided into bands and revalued. The total for each band is multiplied as follows:

- her revalued earnings for band 1 total £103,600. These are multiplied by 40 per cent to give £41,443
- her revalued band 2 earnings are £207,000. These are multiplied by 10 per cent to give £20,700
- her revalued band 3 earnings are £90,000. These are multiplied by 20 per cent to give £18,000.

The sum of these answers comes to £41,443 + £20,700 + £18,000 = £80,143. This is divided by 42 (the years since 6 April 1978) to give an S2P pension of £1,908 a year or £36.70 a week.

Once S2P has been running for a while – say, five years – it becomes a flat-rate pension scheme for everyone under age 45 at that time. The flat-rate pension is worked out as above but based only on band 1 earnings. In other words, someone who is in the S2P scheme from age 16 through to state pension age gets a pension equal to 40 per cent of the lower earnings threshold (40% x £9,500 = £3,800 a year or £73.08 a week at 1999–2000 levels).

Your S2P pension is reduced for any periods during which you are contracted out. This will work in broadly the same way as contracting out of SERPS (see below).

Contracting out of SERPS

If you are contracted out, a lower percentage of your National Insurance goes towards the state pension scheme. The remainder, called the *rebate*, is intended to be used for the contracted-out pension. From April 1997, the amount of rebate depends on the type of scheme through which you are contracted out:

- **Employer's final-salary scheme** There is a flat rebate equal to 4.6 per cent of earnings between the lower and upper earnings limits – 3 per cent of the employer's contributions, 1.6 per cent of the employee's.
- **Employer's money-purchase scheme** In 2001–2 the rebate is 2.2 per cent flat rate plus an age-related element from 0.1 per cent at the age of 19 to 6.8 per cent from the age of 51 onwards. A constant 1.6 per cent of the rebate represents a refund of the employee's contributions.
- **Personal pension plan** In 2001–2 the rebate is a 3.8 per cent flat rate plus an age-related element from 0.1 per cent at age 17 to 5.2 per cent from 50 onwards. Again, 1.6 per cent represents a refund of the employee's contributions. The age-related element was increased from 6 April 1999 onwards to compensate for the effect of pension funds being unable to reclaim tax on dividends since 2 July 1997. The rebates for personal plans are higher than those for an employer's money-purchase scheme to compensate for the fact that the rebate is paid later into a personal plan and for the higher costs of running personal plans.

Contracting out with a pensions promise

If you contract out through an employer's final-salary scheme, you are promised a certain amount of pension in place of the SERPS pension you are giving up.

For periods of contracting-out before 6 April 1997, you get a *guaranteed minimum pension (GMP)* which is broadly equivalent to the SERPS pension. At retirement, GMPs you have built up are deducted from the full SERPS pension you would otherwise have had and the difference is the SERPS pension you actually receive. The calculation is repeated each year to take account of increases in GMPs and SERPS. The result is that you could never lose out by contracting out in this way – your GMPs plus SERPS always equalled the full SERPS pension you would have had had you not contracted out.

From 6 April 1997 onwards, the link with SERPS is broken. Contracted-out final-salary pensions you build up from then onwards must (for most scheme members) be at least equivalent to the benefits from a 'reference scheme' (a model pension scheme which the government has devised). The benefits include a retirement pension and widow's or widower's pension, together with increases to pensions up to a maximum of 5 per cent a year. Under this system, especially if inflation is higher than 5 per cent during most of your retirement years, you might end up with a lower pension than you would have had under SERPS. In practice, the reference scheme benefits are fairly generous and it is probable that you will not lose out.

Another significant change as a result of switching to the new system is that, for benefits built up from April 1997 onwards, it will no longer be possible to separate contracted-out from non-contracted-out benefits. If you transfer post-April 1997 contracted-out rights out of a final-salary scheme into a scheme which offers *protected rights* (see below), you lose the right to any non-contracted-out benefits, such as a tax-free lump sum at retirement, which the original scheme might have offered.

Contracting out with a Contracted-Out Money-Purchase (COMP) scheme

Since April 1988, employers have been allowed to contract out their workers in an alternative way, with what is called a *Contracted-Out Money-Purchase (COMP)* scheme. Here they guarantee only the amount of money going *in* as contributions: there is no guaranteed minimum pension or requirement to match the benefits from a reference scheme (see above).

The money is used to create *protected rights* – a retirement pension from state pension age plus a widow's or widower's pension, with pensions (once paid) increasing in line with inflation up to a maximum of 5 per cent a year. These money-purchase pensions (see page 183) turn out to be worth whatever the pension fund can buy given *annuity rates* at the time. If only the minimum contribution is going in, no other benefits are possible. Special restrictions on how the money is invested cover your protected rights, and each person must have an individual account that can be identified. Remember that you give up your SERPS rights for those years you are contracted out and the COMP pension could be greater or less than what you would have had from SERPS.

Contracting out with a rebate-only personal pension

Introduced in July 1988, this pension allows you to contract out of SERPS, outside your employer's scheme. You can take out a rebate-only plan if:

- your employer does not have a contracted-out pension scheme *or*
- your employer has a contracted-out scheme, but you do not belong to it *or*
- your employer has a contracted-in scheme, whether or not you are a member of it *or*
- your employer has arranged a *group personal pension scheme (GPPS)*. In this case, each employee individually decides whether or not to contract out.

If you take out a rebate-only plan, your National Insurance rebate (plus tax relief on the part which represents a refund of your own contributions) buys you *protected rights*, on a money-purchase basis (as with COMP schemes – see above). These entitle you to a pension at state pension age (no earlier) and a pension for your spouse on your death. If you want extra pension or a different pattern of benefits, you must pay extra. You *give up* your SERPS rights for the years you are in a rebate-only plan. The resulting pension may or may not exceed the pension you would have got under SERPS. It all depends on the performance of your chosen plan.

If you have a rebate-only plan, you pay full-rate National Insurance contributions. At the end of each tax year the DSS calculates what your rebate is and pays it over to the pension provider to credit your pension fund.

Is contracting out a good idea?

If you were contracted out through an employer's final-salary scheme before April 1997, you could not lose out. Moreover, most such schemes aimed to provide pensions better than just the GMPs required by law. Although the link with SERPS and the absolute guarantee are now lost, you are still unlikely to lose.

The position is less clear-cut with money-purchase employer schemes and personal pension plans. The rebate has to be invested and whether or not it produces better benefits than SERPS depends on a variety of factors discussed below. However, do not leave or fail to join a contracted-out employer's money-purchase scheme simply to join SERPS – in most cases, the scheme offers you a whole package of benefits and you are likely to lose by belonging to SERPS. Where you have the choice of contracting in or out of SERPS independently of your membership of an employer's scheme, or where you have a personal pension plan, consider these factors:

- **Size of the rebate and the benefits to be provided** Obviously, the larger the rebate, the more likely it is to produce a large enough fund to match or exceed SERPS benefits. Note that from April 1997 the state has ceased to pay for inflation-proofing for these pensions once they start to be paid, so the rebates have to 'buy' more benefits.
- **Your view about investment returns** Whether or not the rebate helps you buy a better pension than SERPS depends largely on how well your fund grows. The more optimistic you are about investment returns, the more attractive contracting out will seem. And the more willing you are to accept a degree of risk, the greater your scope to choose investments with a higher potential return.
- **Plan charges** With some money-purchase employer schemes, the employer pays the costs of running the scheme separately, so charges do not eat into your own fund. Where the employer's scheme is run by an insurance company or in the case of personal pension plans, charges are met out of the contributions and/or investment returns. The rebates on their own are relatively small compared with the contributions which you would ideally pay into a personal pension plan, so any flat-rate charges have a proportionately very large impact on your pension savings.
- **Your age** From April 1997, rebates are age-related but, in order to keep down costs, the government has capped them at 9 per cent for people in their late 40s and older. As you reach these ages, contracting out of SERPS looks progressively less attractive. The rebate is insufficient to produce a large enough fund to replace SERPS. However, if you are already contracted out, it is often better to remain contracted out: penalties and/or other charges can eat heavily into your contracted-out plan.
- **Your gender** Protected rights are worked out using *unisex annuity rates* – in other words, for a given lump sum, men and women get the same amount of pension at any given age. This means that women born on or after 6 March 1955, who have a state pension age of 65, get more or less the same deal as men from contracting out. But for women born before then, contracting out is less attractive than for men of the same age. These women retire earlier and so give up more SERPS pension.

There is no easy way to judge the impact of all these factors. If you are unsure about what to do, seek advice from an independent financial adviser.

Pensions from employers

From October 2001, all employers with five or more employees must by law make a pension scheme available to you through your workplace. This may be:

- an employer's scheme set up and run by the firm you work for
- a group personal pension scheme (GPPS). These are simply personal pensions (see Chapter 18) but your employer has arranged with the pension provider to offer the plans to eligible employees. And your employer may have negotiated a special deal – for example, lower than normal charges or more flexible contribution terms. If this is the only pension scheme available through the workplace, your employer must contribute to the scheme on your behalf by paying in an amount equal to at least 3 per cent of your pay
- a stakeholder pension scheme. This too is a personal pension but it meets certain minimum conditions regarding low charges, flexible contributions and penalty-free transfers (see page 193). There is no obligation on the employer to contribute.

You do not have to join any of the pension schemes offered but usually an employer's scheme is the best way to save for retirement not least because your employer pays a part of the cost. If there is no employer's scheme, you have to weigh the options. Consider, in particular, whether your employer pays into whatever scheme or plan you choose and whether charges eat heavily into your savings.

The remainder of this chapter focuses on employer's pension schemes. For details about group personal pension schemes and stakeholder pension schemes, see Chapter 18.

Stakeholder pension schemes

'Stakeholder pension scheme' is commonly used to refer to personal pension plans that meet the conditions set out on page 193. However, employer's money-purchase pension schemes (see page 183) that meet the conditions may also register as stakeholder schemes.

An employer's pension scheme may be *contributory*, which means you pay a proportion of your pay into the scheme each week or month. Common contribution rates are 4 or 5 per cent (normally your employer will be paying at least the same or often more). Alternatively, the scheme may be *non-contributory*, with all the contributions coming from the employer on your behalf. Provided the scheme meets certain conditions laid down by the Inland Revenue, it gets favourable tax treatment. You get tax relief on any contributions you make, you pay no tax on any contributions made by your employer and the pension fund itself pays no tax on capital gains. Some of the scheme's income is also tax-free. The eventual pension is taxable as your income but you can take part of the benefits as a tax-free lump sum.

To work out how much you get from your pension scheme, you need to know what kind it is. The types covering most people are *final-salary* schemes and *money-purchase* schemes, explained below. Other kinds are summarised later in the chapter.

Final-salary scheme

With a final-salary scheme, the number of years you have been a member of the scheme and your yearly earnings at the time you retire (or averaged over the few years before then), decide the size of your pension. Many schemes pay one-sixtieth of your final salary for each year of membership. Others pay one-eightieth.

Under the Inland Revenue's rules, the maximum pension you can get is two-thirds of your final salary. If the pension scheme was set up before 14 March 1989 and you joined it before 1 June 1989, there is no limit on the final salary that can be taken into account. Otherwise, there is a limit (the 'earnings cap') of £95,400 in the 2001–2 tax year, normally increased each year in line with price inflation. Some employers set up 'top-up' schemes to cover earnings over the limit but such schemes receive less favourable tax treatment.

Employers' pension schemes commonly set 65 as a normal retirement age, but this can vary widely between the ages of 60 and 75.

In what is known as a *fast-accrual* scheme, if you were in the scheme before 17 March 1987, you can get the maximum pension after only ten years' service. But if you changed employer after that date, this maximum can be reached only after 20 years.

For most people, the benefits are assumed to build up over 40 years. So, if you reach normal retirement age after 40 years' membership of a scheme that pays one-sixtieth of your final salary for each year, you can retire on two-thirds final salary. Even if you retire after 45 years in the scheme, you can still only have a two-thirds pension.

The higher your final yearly earnings, the higher your pension from the scheme. But pension scheme rules define 'salary' differently. Some include bonus, commission and overtime, others exclude these. The Inland Revenue no longer allows income from *share option* schemes to be counted. 'Final' is also defined differently, for example:

- average earnings in the best three consecutive years out of the last thirteen, *or*
- basic salary in the last year before you retire (or the last but one year), plus the

average of your 'fluctuating emoluments' such as bonus or commission over the last few years, *or*

• average yearly earnings over the last few years (most often three or five).

Check in your scheme booklet exactly how your employer's scheme works. You have a legal right to know this information.

People who left a final-salary scheme before retirement used to get a raw deal because their pensions could be frozen at the level they were at on leaving. The position is much better now, because their pensions must be increased to protect them at least partially against inflation during the period between leaving and retiring. Even so, the treatment of early leavers is a weak spot in final-salary schemes compared with money-purchase schemes – see below.

Taking account of the state basic pension

Some final-salary schemes make a deduction, either from the final salary used to work out your pension or from the pension itself, to allow for the fact that you get some basic pension from the state. Often the way this is done is to take away an amount equivalent to the lower earnings limit from your pay before contributions and therefore pension entitlement are calculated. But schemes vary, so check what yours does. If the normal retirement age in your job is earlier than state pension age, any deduction for the state pension ought not to be applied until you reach the official retirement age for the state pension. If you are forced to retire early because of ill-health, it is particularly important that it should not apply.

Money-purchase schemes

From 6 April 2001 onwards, an employer's money-purchase scheme can be opted into the contribution and benefits rules that apply to personal pensions – called the 'Defined Contribution' or DC regime (see Chapter 18). At the time of writing, it is not clear how many schemes are likely to take this course. This chapter concentrates only on those that stay within the normal rules for employers' schemes. If your scheme does opt into the DC regime, you should read Chapter 18.

The money-purchase scheme is popular with smaller companies and becoming more widespread for new employees of large employers too.

Your employer – and you, if it is a contributory scheme – pay contributions which are fixed as a percentage of your salary. (If the scheme is covered by the 'earnings cap' rules – see opposite – only earnings up to £95,400 can count in the 2001–2 tax year.) The contributions are invested and on your retirement the proceeds are used to buy a pension. How much pension you get depends on how the investments have performed and what level annuity rates are at when you retire. (In theory, the scheme rules can allow you to delay the purchase of an annuity and draw an income direct from the fund under the *income drawdown* rules – see page 200. However, in order to do this, you usually need to transfer to a personal pension or stakeholder scheme.)

For pensions built up from 6 April 1997 onwards, the pensions (once they are being paid) must increase in line with inflation up to a maximum of 5 per cent a year. This is called *limited price indexation*.

The Inland Revenue's restrictions on maximum pension, lump sum and other benefits apply to *all* types of employers' schemes, including money-purchase schemes. But there are special rules for *simplified* money-purchase schemes. For example, if a scheme limits the total contribution to 17.5 per cent of earnings (on top of any National Insurance rebate), there need be no limit on the amount of benefit. So, in theory, if a simplified scheme did exceptionally well, you might end up with a pension bigger than your earnings (not normally allowed). There are also various restrictions on other benefits, on the way a scheme like this is run, and on when the benefits may be taken.

With a money-purchase scheme, you do not lose out on leaving your job; though no more will be paid in, the fund simply continues to receive interest and dividends on the amount already in there. If you felt that it was going to produce a better return on your investment than the current managers, you could transfer it to a new employer's scheme or a personal pension plan. But you would need to look carefully to see how much you lose by leaving the existing scheme, especially if you have been in it for only a few years.

Though they are nothing new, *hybrid* schemes are now being introduced by more employers, either final-salary schemes with a guarantee that you will not do worse than on a money-purchase basis with a given level of contributions, or money-purchase with a guarantee of at least a certain pension level worked out on the final-salary basis. If the guarantees are at a reasonable level, these hybrid schemes can give you the best of both worlds. They protect the pensions of early leavers and provide protection against inflation, in line with increases in earnings, for those who stay to claim their pensions.

Other sorts of employer scheme
Average-pay schemes
With these, your pension is based on your pay in each year you belong to the scheme; there is usually a graded scale of earnings. For each year that your pay is in a particular earnings band, you get a fixed amount of pension. As you move up the earnings scale, the amount earned in pension rises. The yearly pension you eventually receive is the total of all the little bits of yearly pension you have earned in each band, so there is no protection against inflation in these schemes.

Revalued-average schemes
By contrast with average-pay schemes, these work in a similar way to SERPS and do give some protection against inflation. Your earnings are revalued to take account of the rise in earnings (or sometimes only prices) between the date you earned them and the date you retire. Your pension is then based on your average revalued salary over all your years in the scheme.

Flat-rate schemes
Flat-rate schemes provide a fixed amount of pension for each year's membership of the scheme.

Inflation-proofing
Retirement can last a long time, particularly for women. On average, men retiring at 65 can expect 14 years of retirement; women retiring at 60 have an average 22 years and, at 65, 18 years. You want an adequate pension not just at the time you retire but later in your retirement too. A pension of, for example, only half your

final pay but with full inflation-proofing can soon overtake an apparently better pension of two-thirds of your final pay with no protection against rising prices.

In public-sector jobs, such as in the Civil Service, most pensions are guaranteed to increase in line with the rise in the RPI. In the private sector, not many schemes offer this. Many have in the past promised to increase pensions by a certain percentage each year. Often this was 3 or 4 per cent or, if less, the increase in the RPI. While inflation is low, this percentage is adequate but provides poor protection at even modest rates of inflation. For pensions built up from 6 April 1997 onwards, schemes *have* to increase them by rises in the RPI up to 5 per cent a year. Most larger schemes are applying the increase to the whole of a pension rather than splitting it into pre-1997 and post-1997 segments.

Some schemes, particularly those run by large companies, have in any case tended to give increases that do not fall far short of inflation. In periods when pension schemes have been flush with money, many have done a 'catching-up exercise' for older pensioners, increasing their pensions to the real level they were at when they retired. But there is no guarantee that this policy will continue indefinitely.

Tax-free lump sums

When you retire, you can normally exchange part of your pension for a tax-free lump sum. With some schemes, especially in the public sector, you automatically get a smaller pension and a lump sum. You can have up to one-and-a-half times your earnings as a lump sum, subject (where it applies) to the £95,400 earnings limit for 2001–2. You may also be subject to a cash limit on the lump sum of £150,000 if you joined your scheme between 17 March 1987 and 1 June 1989.

If you have a choice, should you go for a tax-free lump sum or more pension? If the pension is usually increased generously, but this is not guaranteed, be wary of exchanging any of it for a lump sum. But, if this is not the case, it may pay you to exchange as much as possible of your pension for a lump sum, and then buy an annuity – see Chapter 27 – or invest it in other ways to provide you with an income. An annuity is an investment where you swap a lump sum for a regular income – in this case payable for life. Annuity rates at the time you make the swap determine the amount of income you get. For example, with a level annuity, the income is fixed for life according to the interest rate at the time you buy the annuity. Your after-tax income from the annuity may be worth more than the pension you are giving up. This is because the whole of the pension you give up is taxable. By contrast, part of each payment from the annuity you buy counts as return of capital and that part is tax free.

Other benefits from your employer's scheme

An employer's pension scheme may provide other benefits besides a retirement pension, such as:

- a pension if you are forced to retire early because of ill-health; this is usually more generous than the pension paid if you retire early of your own accord. Or a permanent health-insurance scheme may provide long-term benefit for anyone who is off sick for a long spell
- a pension for your husband or wife if you are the one who dies first

- pensions for children or other dependants you leave on death
- life insurance if you die before retirement age, which can be as much as four times your earnings (subject to the earnings cap if it applies).

In some cases, whether they are members of the pension scheme or not, permanent health insurance and life insurance are provided for all employees.

Additional voluntary contributions (AVCs)

Additional voluntary contributions (AVCs) are a way of topping up your pension savings. From 6 April 2001, saving through a stakeholder pension scheme could be the better option – see opposite.

All employers' pension schemes must allow members to make AVCs. These build up extra pension and other scheme benefits (except that AVCs started on or after 8 April 1987 cannot be taken as a lump sum). Employers offer a range of AVC schemes and some – but not many – match the members' extra contributions with their own. The most you can put into an employer's pension scheme and AVC scheme altogether is 15 per cent of your earnings in any one tax year (or 15 per cent of £95,400 in 2001–2 if you earn more than the earnings cap). However much you put in, you cannot have more than the final two-thirds pension allowed by the Inland Revenue. If you over-contribute, any excess AVCs are returned to you at retirement after a special tax deduction: 33 per cent in 2001–2. Non-taxpayers, starting-rate or basic-rate taxpayers cannot reclaim any of this tax, and higher-rate taxpayers have extra to pay at a higher-than-usual rate.

You are entitled to make contributions to other schemes run by commercial pension providers, such as an insurance company, outside your employer's scheme. These scheme are called '*free-standing AVCs*', or *FSAVCs* for short. The limits on what you can pay and the pension you can have are the same as for AVC. Excess FSAVCs are returned at retirement after a tax deduction. If your employer's scheme is contracted in, you can also use an FSAVC for contracting out of the state scheme. This alternative to a rebate-only personal plan is less tax-efficient because you do not receive tax relief on the National Insurance rebate this way.

For AVCs or FSAVCs made from 8 April 1987, *if your scheme allows it,* you can start and stop contributions as you like, reduce the amount or pay in windfall amounts.

As already noted, AVCs cannot normally be used to increase the tax-free lump sum from the pension scheme. However, some final-salary employers' schemes (particularly in the public sector) offer 'added years' schemes. With these, your AVCs buy extra years of membership. This means that an increased number of years is used in the formula that works out how much pension and other benefits you qualify for. Added-years AVCs boost the tax-free lump sum along with the other benefits.

Other ways to top up your pension

In the past, you could not simultaneously pay into both an employer's pension scheme and a personal pension plan. From 6 April 2001 this changed. Provided you do not earn more than £30,000 a year and you are not a controlling director of your firm, you can belong to your employer's pension scheme and also pay up to £3,600 a year into stakeholder pension schemes and/or personal pension plans.

Stakeholder schemes and personal pensions are described in detail in Chapter 18, but it is worth noting here that, unlike all FSAVC schemes and most AVC schemes, stakeholder schemes and personal plans can provide a tax-free lump sum at retirement as well as pension and other benefits. In addition, stakeholder schemes have low charges (see page 193) which makes them better value than FSAVC schemes and many AVC schemes. The only circumstances in which AVCs are likely to have the edge are where your employer matches your AVCs by paying extra towards your pension as you do and where the scheme on offer is an 'added years' scheme (see opposite).

The main drawbacks with all pension schemes, whether AVCs, FSAVCs, stakeholder schemes or personal plans, are that your money is tied up until at least age 50 and the bulk of it can be withdrawn only in the form of taxable pension. A more flexible alternative is an individual savings account (ISA). Like pensions, ISAs benefit from tax advantages. Although they take a different form, the ISA tax breaks are worth much the same as pension tax advantages, except where the pension scheme lets you take a tax-free lump sum.

Table 1 on page 188 summarises the main features of the various ways you can top up the pension from your employer's pension scheme. Note that, while the two-thirds limit on pension applies to AVC schemes topping up your employer's pension, it does not not apply to additional income from personal, stakeholder and ISA-based pensions.

Changing jobs

If you leave an employer's scheme (whether or not you also leave the job) within two years of joining, you have no rights to a pension from the scheme. Instead you can be offered a refund of your own (but not your employer's) contributions. If you had been contracted out of SERPS at any time before 6 April 1997, there is generally a deduction from your refund to cover the cost of buying you back into SERPS. Tax at a special rate of 20 per cent is deducted from whatever remains.

If you have been in an employer's scheme for more than two years, you must be given a *preserved pension*. You can choose what to do with this pension:

- You can leave the preserved pension in your old employer's scheme. In general, pension rights built up since 1 January 1985 must be increased between the time you leave and the time you retire in line with changes in the RPI up to a maximum of 5 per cent a year. The exception is any guaranteed minimum pensions (GMPs): different rules mean that your employer and the state between them fully protect your GMPs against inflation. While no obligation exists on schemes to increase pre-1985 benefits, your scheme may increase the whole of your benefits, or provide protection in excess of 5 per cent inflation.
- Alternatively, you can take a *transfer value* to a new employer's scheme, a stakeholder scheme, a personal pension plan or a *Section 32* policy. A transfer value is the lump sum needed now to provide your preserved benefits. A Section 32 policy, a special type of personal pension plan, accepts only a single lump sum and is used to provide a guaranteed minimum level of pension. Other names for it are *buy-out plan* or *transfer plan*. If you have a preserved pension

Table 1: Ways to top up your pension

	'Added years' AVC scheme	Other AVC scheme	FSAVC scheme	Stakeholder scheme	Personal pension	ISA
Tax relief on what you pay in	yes	yes	yes	yes	yes	no
Tax relief on dividends and similar income earned by your investment	not applicable	no	no	no	no	yes, until 2004
Tax relief on other income and capital gains earned by your investment	not applicable	yes	yes	yes	yes	yes
Take proceeds whenever you like	no	no	no	no	no	yes
Take proceeds as tax-free lump sum, if you choose	part	no (except pre-1987 schemes)	no	part	part	yes
Whole of proceeds tax-free	no	no	no	no	no	yes
Low charges	yes	sometimes	not usually	yes	not usually	yes if you choose a 'CAT standard' ISA – see page 118

in a scheme you left after January 1986, your previous employer must agree to a request for transfer. If the scheme is wound up, you lose the right to transfer and the administrators must buy you an annuity.

Special rules govern a transfer between two public-sector jobs, which mean you are unlikely to lose out. With a transfer to a private-sector employer, your new employer will:

- if he or she runs a money-purchase scheme, invest the transfer value in the same way as new contributions *or*
- if he or she runs a final-salary scheme, possibly agree to pay you extra pension in your retirement – normally fixed in pounds and not increased in line with future pay increases *or*
- give you a credit of so many years' membership of the scheme. This is unlikely to be the full number of years that you had been in the old employer's scheme, because the benefit you get from it may be different and it is based on your expected salary at retirement (rather than salary at the time of leaving the old scheme). If you are offered credited years, try to negotiate a deal so that the pension you get (in pounds) is guaranteed to be no less than the amount you would have had from the old employer's scheme. This should prevent you from losing if you change jobs again.

If you are transferring a pension that has been contracted out of SERPS, there are special rules. If you are transferring a guaranteed minimum pension (see page 178) into a Section 32 policy, it must guarantee to pay at least as much. On the other hand, if you are transferring it into a personal pension plan, its money value is turned into *protected rights* within the personal pension plan. This means that it can be used only in certain ways. In return, you are giving up the guaranteed benefits that the guaranteed minimum pension gave you. If you transfer post-April 1997 pension rights from a contracted-out employer's final-salary scheme to a scheme or plan offering protected rights, you lose any benefits not included within protected rights (for example tax-free lump sum from the previous scheme).

How safe is your pension?

In late 1991, it was learned that the late Robert Maxwell had, in effect, stolen over £400 million from company pension schemes in his business empire. This raised serious doubts about the organisation and regulation of company pension schemes and, after a government inquiry, Parliament passed the Pensions Act 1995. This introduced a new system of pension regulation based on three pillars:

- **Occupational Pensions Regulatory Authority (OPRA)*** Although this body does not proactively monitor schemes, it has wide-ranging powers to investigate schemes and take action where something is thought to be going wrong.
- **Trustees** Pension schemes (other than unapproved schemes and the public-sector statutory schemes set up by Act of Parliament) continue to be run as trusts to which trust law applies. However, trustees have been given much more explicit duties and responsibilities and if they fail in their duties run the risk of hefty penalties. Schemes are also required to let members choose one-third of

the trustees. But the employer can opt out of this rule, though he or she must follow an elaborate procedure to give members the chance to object to the opt-out.

- **Scheme advisers (e.g. scheme actuary and lawyer)** Their duties have been tightened up and, in particular, if they suspect that anything about the scheme is amiss, they are required to 'blow the whistle' to OPRA.

The Pensions Act also introduces a compensation scheme for members of pension schemes with insufficient assets to pay pensions through dishonesty or fraud on the part of those running the scheme. The scheme does not pay out for losses due to negligence or incompetence.

Pension-scheme frauds are in fact relatively rare. The risk of retiring having saved too little for an adequate pension is much greater, and an employer's scheme is usually the best option. However, you can take steps to help ensure the safety of your pension: take an interest in your scheme, get to know who your scheme trustees are, consider becoming a trustee yourself, read all the information sent to you, ask questions and make sure that you are given satisfactory answers. If your scheme fails to give you the answers you need, you can get help from the Office of the Pensions Advisory Service (OPAS).*

Which scheme should you join?
Employers' final-salary schemes (contracted out)
If you are in a good employer's scheme based on final salary and *contracted out* of SERPS, you should think seriously before deciding to leave and go it alone with a stakeholder scheme or personal pension plan. Your pension would no longer be based on final salary and would depend instead on two uncertainties: how well your money has been invested up to your retirement date, and interest rates at that time. A sudden change in the fortunes of the stock market, like the crash in share values in October 1987, or a drop in the interest rates which dictate *annuity rates* (i.e. the pension you can actually buy with your fund) could mean a big change in your pension. (Of course, this applies also to employers' money-purchase schemes.)

It is likely that, if you go outside the scheme, your employer will say that you must also provide your own death-in-service benefits and disability benefits. Find out about this before taking any decision and shop around to compare the costs; if you are over a certain age, you may find that replacing benefits costs more than your contribution to the employer's scheme as a whole.

Before taking any decision, find out whether the employer allows you to rejoin the pension scheme if you change your mind. In many cases, one change of mind is allowed, but no more. Some employers put an upper limit on the ages at which people are allowed to join or rejoin, perhaps 45.

Employers' final-salary schemes (contracted in)
If your employer's scheme is contracted in, then you may want to contract out of SERPS. You can do this, without leaving the employer's scheme, through a stakeholder pension scheme or rebate-only personal pension plan (or an FSAVC scheme, though because of a difference in the tax rules this is not recommended). The arguments in favour of employers' final-salary schemes are much the same whether they are contracted in or out.

Employers' money-purchase schemes

If your employer runs a money-purchase scheme, you may feel that you could do better with your own money-purchase stakeholder scheme or personal pension plan. But find out how much your employer is putting into the scheme and what administrative charges (if any) are being deducted. Doing your own thing is likely to mean paying your own charges as well. And, with an employer's COMP scheme, part of the money goes straight in each month when the payroll calculations are done. With a personal pension, the whole National Insurance rebate is held back by the DSS until after the end of the tax year. On the other hand, while there is this delay in earning dividends or interest, rebates to personal plans are now considerably higher than those for COMP schemes.

Stakeholder pension schemes

Employers who run their own pension scheme are unlikely to contribute to a stakeholder scheme, unless you are in a sufficiently senior position to bargain for special treatment. As many employers contribute twice as much as the employee to the employer's pension scheme, only the very young or very lucky are likely to build up more pension through a stakeholder scheme than an employer's scheme (unless the benefits from the latter are poor).

But at least stakeholder scheme charges are low and if you change jobs there is no penalty. Some stakeholder schemes may be limited to employees of a particular firm, in a particular industry or belonging to a particular union. But even if you have to switch to another stakeholder scheme, there are no penalties for making the transfer. So far most stakeholder schemes are not dependent on a particular job or membership of a particular group, so you can keep the same scheme when you change jobs.

If you earn no more than £30,000 and are not a controlling director, consider topping up your retirement savings by paying up to £3,600 a year into a stakeholder scheme in addition to your contributions to your employer's scheme.

Personal pensions

Similarly, unless you are a senior employee, employers who run their own pension scheme are unlikely to contribute to your personal pension. However, if no employer or stakeholder scheme exists, the employer must make a contribution of at least 3 per cent of your pay to any group personal pension being offered through the workplace.

Unlike stakeholder schemes, personal pensions often have relatively high costs. Some of these cover the charges of setting up the plan and are deducted in its early years. This makes the plan a particularly poor deal if you keep it only for a short time.

If you belong to a group personal pension scheme and leave your present employer, you can probably carry on the plan but any special terms – for example, low charges or flexible contributions – may cease. If your employer has been contributing to the plan and you change jobs, his or her contributions will stop and, if there is a minimum contribution limit, you have to increase your payments to keep the plan going.

If you earn no more than £30,000 and are not a controlling director, you can contribute up to £3,600 a year into a personal pension plan in addition to belonging to an employer's scheme. The main reason for choosing a personal pension is if you want a wider range of investment choices – for example choosing for yourself which stocks and shares to hold – than stakeholder schemes generally offer.

Verdict

Overall, unless you are under 30 or so, intend to move jobs rapidly and have no dependants, a reasonable employer's scheme is likely to be the best for you. If you take out a stakeholder scheme or personal pension plan in the early years of your working life, you ought to aim to move back into an employer's scheme in your 30s or when you get married.

If you run your own business as a company, you can set up your own employer's scheme (for example, an executive pension plan) – contact an insurance company or independent financial adviser for advice. If you are self-employed, you have to use a stakeholder scheme or personal pension plan – see Chapter 18.

If you are not able to join an employer's scheme, a stakeholder schemes may be the best option for you. But if you are already committed to making regular contributions to a personal pension plan, be wary of switching to a stakeholder scheme – there may be hefty charges for stopping your personal plan.

Unapproved pension schemes

Your employer may offer you membership of an *unapproved pension scheme*. This does not attract the favourable tax treatment of an approved scheme but can be more flexible, because there are no restrictions on the amount and type of benefits – you can even take the whole lot as a lump sum, if you choose. They are especially useful as 'top-up' schemes if your earnings exceed the earnings cap (in which case, you are also ineligible to have a stakeholder scheme alongside your employer's scheme). Unapproved schemes work in one of two ways:

- *Unfunded schemes* Your employer simply pays you benefits at the time you retire. These will be taxed as income.
- *Funded schemes* Your employer pays contributions which count as a taxable fringe benefit on which you have to pay tax. They are invested, usually in a trust, in which case any income and gains are taxable (though generally only at the basic rate of tax – whatever your own tax rate). When the benefits are paid, they are tax-free.

18 Stakeholder and personal pensions

An employer's pension scheme is usually the best way to secure adequate retirement income. But if your employer does not offer one, or you are self-employed, what do you do? This chapter outlines your two main options – a stakeholder scheme or personal pension.

These schemes for individuals are offered mainly by insurance companies but also by other providers, such as banks, building societies, friendly societies and unit trusts. Stakeholder schemes operate on the same general principles but are subject to specific conditions. Both stakeholder and personal pensions work on a 'money purchase' basis, so the pension you get depends on:

- how much is paid in
- how well the invested contributions grow
- how much is deducted in charges
- annuity rates at the time you want to start drawing a pension.

What are stakeholder pensions?

Personal pension plans that are designed to ensure you get value-for-money can be registered as 'stakeholder schemes'. Features of a 'stakeholder scheme' must include:

- **low charges** Charges must total no more than 1 per cent a year of the value of your pension fund. This must cover all the costs of running the scheme and managing your investments, as well as giving information and basic advice. If more detailed advice warrants an extra fee, this must be set out in its own contract and charged for separately
- **low and flexible contributions** The minimum contribution must be no higher than £20, whether it is a one-off payment or a regular contribution. You cannot be required to make contributions at regular intervals – it is up to you when or how often you pay
- **portability** You must be able, without penalty, to transfer out of a stakeholder scheme into another stakeholder scheme or pension arrangement. Stakeholder schemes must accept transfers
- **simplicity** If you do not choose an investment for yourself, the scheme must

include a default investment option to determine how your money is invested. Typically, this is a 'tracker' fund (see page 204)

- **keeping you informed** The scheme provider must send you an annual benefit statement at least once a year showing you in straightforward terms the value of your rights under the scheme. If the scheme's charges alter, you must be informed within one month of the change.

Employer's money-purchase schemes (see page 183) that meet the above conditions can also register as stakeholder schemes. The main difference between an employer stakeholder scheme and a personal stakeholder scheme is that you can belong to the former only while you are working for the particular employer, whereas personal stakeholder schemes are not usually linked to a particular job.

From October 2001, employers with five or more employees who do not already offer a pension arrangement must arrange access for you to a stakeholder scheme through your workplace (see page 181). In most cases, this is a personal stakeholder scheme. But, even when your employer has set up a stakeholder scheme, you retain the option to take out your own scheme through a provider of your choice.

Who qualifies?

If you are self-employed, you must make your own pension arrangements. Personal pension plans and stakeholder schemes are the main ways of doing this.

In the past, you could not simultaneously belong to your employer's pension scheme and have your own personal pension plan, unless:

- the personal plan was a *rebate-only plan* used to contract out of SERPS (see page 179)
- you had other earnings not from the employer running the pension scheme – for example, freelance income or earnings from a second job.

From 6 April 2001 onwards, for most people these restrictions have been swept away. Now, nearly everyone can invest up to £3,600 a year (and sometimes more) in these types of pension scheme – see page 196. That includes employees already members of their employer's scheme and earning no more than £30,000 a year who are not controlling directors of their company (see Chapter 17). Even children can invest up to £3,600 a year in a pension scheme.

Why save through stakeholder or personal pensions?

All pension schemes and plans benefit from generous tax breaks that either cut the cost of your savings or boost their growth. Personal plans and stakeholder schemes have the following advantages:

- the amount you pay in is treated as if it has had tax relief at the basic rate already deducted. The scheme provider claims the tax back and adds it to your

---

EXAMPLE 1

Mary is a non-taxpayer. In September 2001, she pays £50 into a stake-holder pension scheme. This is treated as a contribution net of tax relief at the basic rate (22 per cent in 2001–2). The *grossed-up* contribution is £50 x 100% / (100% – 22%) = £64.10. The scheme provider claims the difference (£64.10 – £50 = £14.10) from the Inland Revenue and adds it to Mary's scheme. In effect, Mary has received a bonus of £14.10 boosting the value of her £50 to £64.10.

---

scheme. This happens even if you are a non-taxpayer or pay tax at less than the basic rate (see Example 1)

- if you are a higher-rate taxpayer, you can claim extra relief on anything you pay into your scheme (see Example 2)
- some of the income earned by your savings builds up tax-free (but not dividends from shares and similar income)
- capital gains earned by your savings build up tax-free
- you can take part of the proceeds of the scheme as a tax-free lump sum (but the rest must be taken as taxable pension).

The disadvantage of saving through a pension scheme or plan is that you cannot get your money back until you have reached at least age 50 and, even then, the bulk of your savings must be taken in the form of a pension. This means pension schemes and plans are not the place for money you might need for some other purpose – for example, buying a home (but see 'Pension mortgages' on page 205) or paying school fees.

On the other hand, do not delay the start of savings for retirement. It takes a

---

EXAMPLE 2

In June 2001, Sanjay pays £5,000 into a personal pension plan. This is treated as a payment from which tax relief at the basic rate (22 per cent in 2001–2) has already been deducted. The grossed-up contribution is £5,000 x 100% / (100% – 22%) = £6,410. The plan provider claims the difference (£6,410 – £5,000 = £1,410) from the Inland Revenue and adds it to Sanjay's plan.

As Sanjay is a higher-rate taxpayer, he can claim extra relief through his tax return. Higher-rate relief on £6,410 would be £6,410 x 40% = £2,564. But Sanjay has already had basic rate relief of £1,410, so he now claims extra relief of £2,564 – £1,410 = £1,154.

In total, £6,410 has been invested in Sanjay's pension plan at a cost to Sanjay of £5,000 – £1,154 = £3,846.

---

long time to build up an adequate pension and the money you save earliest has most time to grow. For example, starting to save £1,000 at age 39 could provide a pension (in today's money) of £4,800 a year at the age of 65. But, on the same assumptions, if you delayed until age 55, your £1,000 a year would produce just £1,500 a year.

How much can you save?

The quid pro quo for the tax advantages of personal pension plans is that rules limit the amount you can save. These rules changed significantly from 6 April 2001 onwards. The new rules apply to personal pension plans taken out both before and after 6 April 2001. Called the *DC regime,* they apply also to stakeholder schemes and some employers' schemes – see below.

The DC regime

'DC' stands for 'defined contribution', which is another name for money purchase. Under DC rules, you can pay up to £3,600 a year in total into any of the following:

- personal stakeholder schemes
- personal pension plans
- employers' money-purchase schemes that have been opted into the DC regime. These may or may not be registered as stakeholder schemes. (Other employers' schemes are covered by different rules described in Chapter 17).

The £3,600 limit applies to your grossed-up contributions – in other words, including tax relief at the basic rate. So, in 2001–2, you can pay net (after tax relief) contributions of (100% – 22%) x £3,600 = £2,808.

The £3,600 limit is available to everyone, regardless of age or earnings. You can pay up to that limit even if you have no earnings at all and anyone else can pay into your scheme for you. For example, a husband might pay into his wife's scheme, a parent can pay into a scheme for a child, a disabled person might pay into a scheme for a carer.

If you have earnings, you may be able to pay more than £3,600 a year into the various pension plans outlined above. The maximum you can contribute is set as a percentage of your earnings, which varies with your age – see the table on page 198. The cap on the amount of earnings taken into account is set at £95,400 in 2001–2 and is usually increased in line with inflation each year.

Under the 'carry back' rule, you can elect to have contributions paid in one tax year treated as if they had been paid in the previous year. To do this, you must both pay and elect for carry-back by 31 January during the tax year. For example, for a carry-back from 2001–2 to 2000–1, you must pay the contribution and make the election no later than 31 January 2002.

Carry-back is especially useful if, say, you run your own business. There is often a delay before you make up your accounts and so know how much you can afford to pay in age-related contributions. Carry-back is also useful if tax rates fall. You get relief at the rates applying in the tax year to which you carry back the contribution.

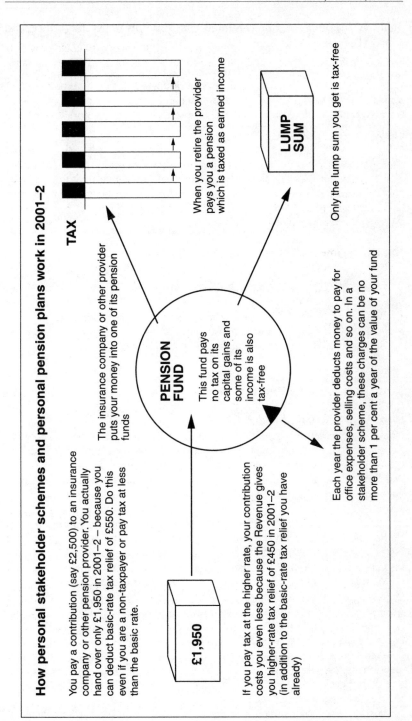

How personal stakeholder schemes and personal pension plans work in 2001–2

You pay a contribution (say £2,500) to an insurance company or other pension provider. You actually hand over only £1,950 in 2001–2 – because you can deduct basic-rate tax relief of £550. Do this even if you are a non-taxpayer or pay tax at less than the basic rate.

If you pay tax at the higher rate, your contribution costs you even less because the Revenue gives you higher-rate tax relief of £450 in 2001–2 (in addition to the basic-rate tax relief you have already)

£1,950

TAX

The insurance company or other provider puts your money into one of its pension funds

PENSION FUND

This fund pays no tax on its capital gains and some of its income is also tax-free

When you retire the provider pays you a pension which is taxed as earned income

LUMP SUM

Only the lump sum you get is tax-free

Each year the provider deducts money to pay for office expenses, selling costs and so on. In a stakeholder scheme, these charges can be no more than 1 per cent a year of the value of your fund

Table 1: Maximum earnings-related contributions under the DC regime rules [1]

Your age at the start of the tax year (6 April)	Percentage of earnings you can contribute to pension schemes in the DC regime	Earnings where maximum contribution is more than £3,600
Up to 35	17.5%	£20,571
36–45	20%	£18,000
46–50	25%	£14,400
51–55	30%	£12,000
56–60	35%	£10,286
61–74	40%	£9,000
75 and over	You can no longer contribute	

[1] Everyone can pay up to £3,600 a year regardless of earnings.

In the past, you may also have used the 'carry forward rule' that let you mop up unused contribution relief from earlier tax years. From 6 April 2001 onwards, this rule has been abolished. However, by carrying-back a contribution paid in 2001–2 to the 2000–1 tax year, you have a last chance to use up any carry forward relief under the old rules. For more about this, see page 218.

Your pension and other benefits

What your scheme provides

Unlike most employers' pension schemes, personal pension plans and personal stakeholder schemes do not automatically provide a package of benefits. They are geared towards providing you with a retirement pension and tax-free lump sum. If you want to add other benefits, such as life cover or a pension for your widow or widower, you must either pay extra or accept a cut in your pension or tax-free sum.

If you die before retirement, with most plans and schemes, a lump sum equal to the value of your fund or your contributions plus interest is paid out to your heirs. If you want a higher life cover than this, you can pay for separate life insurance. Under the new DC rules, for life cover started on or after 6 April 2001 up to 10 per cent of the contributions you make can be used to pay for life cover. Unlike conventional life insurance, your DC contribution towards life cover qualifies for tax relief in the same way as the rest of your contributions.

If you have a personal pension plan and you had already taken out life cover under the plan before 6 April 2001, a different limit applies. You can pay up to 5 per cent of your earnings towards life cover (whether or not you are also contributing towards the pension) and these payments qualify for tax relief just like any other pension contribution. Remember, however, that paying for life cover reduces the maximum you can save towards your pension.

At retirement, you can choose whether to have a pension that, say, increases with inflation or, if you die first, carries on being paid to your husband or wife. The price of these benefits is a reduction in your retirement pension. For details, see pages 213–4.

When can you start receiving the pension?

Generally speaking, at any time between the ages of 50 and 75. (The government has discussed raising this to around 80, but no decisions have been taken.) You may need to specify a 'retirement' age when you start the plan. More often, you can decide nearer the time. People in certain occupations can retire earlier, and you may also be able to do so if you become too ill to carry on working – though the pension payable is at a very much reduced rate. If you have several plans, you can start receiving the benefits from each at different times. (We use *retire* in this chapter to mean *start receiving the benefits of the plan*, whether or not you actually stop work at the time.)

From April 2001, the tax rules changed. You can now have more than one pension date with a single plan. This means you can use part of the fund to buy an annuity on one date and further tranches to buy further annuities at dates of your choosing up to age 75. This is particularly useful if you want to ease out of work gradually, taking part of your pension now, say, and adding the rest once you give up work completely. You need to check whether your plan provider offers this particular option.

Another way to achieve the same effect is if your plan is divided into many segments (technically each segment is a separate plan). You can convert different segments into annuities at different times to achieve a pension which grows as necessary. This arrangement is called 'phased retirement'. There are usually extra costs involved in setting up your pension this way, so it is generally not suitable unless you have a reasonably large pension fund.

How your pension is worked out

Pension providers calculate benefits in different ways, depending on how your pension plan is worded.

A *deferred annuity* plan talks in terms of the pension you get from a certain age. This is based on the amount you paid into the scheme. For example, if you pay in £1,000 for 26 years from age 39, the provider might quote a pension of £10,000 a year if you retire at 65.

A *cash-funded* plan (much more common) talks in terms of the amount of money that accumulates to buy your pension with. For example, if you paid in the same amounts as in the example above, the plan may say that a cash fund of £94,000 would have accumulated by the age of 65.

Remember that these examples in pension providers' proposals are nearly always illustrative and rarely guarantee.

With a cash-funded plan, when you retire, the fund is usually used to buy an *immediate annuity* that pays you an income for life. The income you get depends on the company's annuity rate for your age and gender when you retire and the type of annuity you choose. This will specify how much pension you get each year for each pound in your fund, usually in terms of annual pension per £10,000 in the fund. So, for example, your pension might be £880 per £10,000 (8.8 per cent) for a 65-year-old man. Therefore, your pension might be 8.8 per cent of your cash fund of £94,000 which is £8,272 (though you might swap part of this for tax-free cash). It all depends on the annuity rates at the time you retire.

Usually, you do not have to take up the annuity offered by the provider with whom you built up your pension fund. Most personal plans give you an *open-market option* which means you can shop around with your pension fund and buy the annuity from another company. Usually, this is worth doing because some companies specialise in annuity business and others do not.

Personal finance pages in newspapers and magazines often list the top annuity rates available. You can also check out the best rates through the specialist publisher Moneyfacts* or through an independent financial adviser (contact IFA Promotion*, the Institute of Financial Planning*, the Society of Financial Advisers (SOFA)* or the Money Management National Register of Independent Fee-Based Advisers)*. Some IFAs are annuity specialists, for example Annuity Direct* or the Annuity Bureau*. If the company with which you built up your fund offers a guaranteed annuity rate, check carefully what you are giving up before deciding to use your open-market option.

If annuity rates are low at the time you want to retire, you might face the stark choice of either locking into a low pension for life or putting off your retirement in the hope that annuity rates will rise some time in the future. Since May 1995 there has been another option called *annuity deferral and income drawdown* which some providers offer. You put off buying an annuity up to the age of 75 and in the meantime take an income direct from the pension fund. You have the normal choice about whether to take a tax-free lump sum at the time you start to draw the income. The maximum income you can take is the amount which would have been provided by an annuity for a single person according to tables published by the government. The minimum is 35 per cent of that amount – for example, if the maximum is £10,000 a year, the minimum would be £3,500. The income is reviewed every three years to check that enough remains in your pension fund to provide an income at the same level throughout retirement. It may have to be increased or reduced at this review. So choose this option only if you can cope with a fluctuating income. The pension fund remains invested until you switch to an annuity, and you have the same investment choices as you did when building up your pension fund, though often the self-investment route (see page 205) is a good option. To make this option worthwhile, you usually need to choose investments which involve some risk to your capital, so annuity deferral and income drawdown are unlikely to be suitable for you if your pension plan is your only source of retirement income. There are also ongoing charges while your pension fund remains invested, making this option viable only if you have a reasonably large fund built up – say, £100,000 or more. You should take financial advice before going down this route.

From April 2001, you can stagger the time at which you convert your pension fund into annuities instead of converting it all in one go. For example, you might choose to convert half your fund into an annuity and continue drawing an income from the remaining half until that too is converted to an annuity by age 75.

The types of plan

There are several hundred different personal pension plans. The main variations are in:

- who is providing the scheme
- how often you pay contributions
- how your money is invested
- the level of charges deducted from the plan.

Individual pension accounts (IPAs)

From 6 April 2001, if your pension provider offers this facility, you can organise your pension fund using a new arrangement called an individual pension account (IPA).

IPAs can be used with personal pension plans, stakeholder schemes, occupational money-purchase schemes and free-standing AVC schemes. You pay money in the normal way into whichever of these arrangements you choose and the normal contribution limits and other rules for that arrangement apply. But, instead of the pension manager investing the money on behalf of you and other savers, your contributions go into your own IPA.

The IPA is run by an IPA manager (which could be the same firm as the pension manager or a different one). The money in your IPA can be invested in any of the following:

- unit trusts and open-ended investment companies (OEICs) – see Chapter 21
- investment trusts (see Chapter 22) provided no more than half its investment funds are borrowed money
- gilts (see Chapter 24)
- similar investments established in other countries in the European Economic Area (EEA).

Depending on how the IPA is organised, the investments could be chosen by the IPA manager, by you from a 'menu' offered by the IPA manager or by you on your own.

IPAs are intended to be flexible, allowing you to switch investments simply and to transfer an IPA easily from one pension arrangement to another.

Only relatively few of the personal pension plans on offer are registered as stakeholder pension schemes. This is because, to qualify for stakeholder status, the scheme charges must be capped at 1 per cent a year. This is a lot lower than the level traditionally charged for most personal pension plans. Many providers have said that offering stakeholder schemes at such low cost and often for very small investments is simply not economic. The main providers of stakeholder schemes are firms that believe they will be able to sell in large enough volumes to keep costs down and those that sell no-frills products direct to the public usually on a no-advice basis.

Who is providing the scheme?
From July 1988, banks, building societies, unit trusts, insurance companies and friendly societies have all been able to offer personal pension plans. In practice, they have remained very much the province of the insurance companies and a few friendly societies. While banks and building societies do offer pension plans, these are usually either the products of their own insurance subsidiaries or of another insurance company. Only a few unit trusts offer pension plans. The government is hoping that a wider range of providers will offer stakeholder pensions.

At retirement, only insurance companies and friendly societies are allowed to offer the pension itself, but you do not have to stay with the company that has been running your plan up to retirement. With most plans, you can shop around for the best pension (annuity) rates using your open-market option. With a rebate-only plan, you must be given this option. You should always investigate using your open-market option because some companies specialise in providing competitive annuities, while others do not.

How often you pay contributions
Traditionally, you have the choice of either a single-contribution plan, to which you pay a single lump sum, or a regular-contribution plan, where you commit yourself on a fixed basis. But a growing number of companies now offer completely flexible plans which allow you to make contributions as and when you want, on either a regular or ad hoc basis. Stakeholder pension schemes *must* let you pay what you like (subject to a minimum which may not be more than £20), when you like. The pros and cons of regular versus flexible payments are:

- **discipline** A regular-contribution plan commits you to saving steadily. Often (but not with stakeholder schemes), there are penalties if you stop making the payments or reduce them, so you have a strong incentive to keep the plan going. This makes it more likely that you achieve your target retirement income
- **adapting to changing circumstances** A flexible plan, or taking out single-contribution plans as and when you can afford it, lets you tailor your retirement savings to your changing financial situation. This can be particularly useful if you are self-employed and make varying profits from year to year, if you are not in secure employment, or if you are a woman who plans career breaks or a switch to part-time working while bringing up a family
- **coping with crisis** Similarly, if you might not be able to work because of illness or redundancy, a flexible or single-contribution plan does not tie you into payments you can no longer afford.
- **charges** In the past, charges for regular-contribution plans have often been high, especially where your contributions were small or made only infrequently. However, charges have been coming down because of the introduction of stakeholder pension schemes. The maximum charge for a stakeholder scheme

is 1 per cent of the pension fund per year. So personal pensions which carry on making high charges have to justify this in some way – for example, by offering a wider choice of investment funds. Unless you are satisfied that you are getting additional benefits or options which you want, you should not pay extra.

How your money is invested
Below, we give the details of four main types of plan. For which type to choose, see 'Planning your pension' on page 206–7.

With-profits
Your contributions go into the provider's fund to be invested in, for example, shares, gilts and property. The plan guarantees from the outset your minimum pension (if the policy is a deferred-annuity one) or your minimum fund with which to buy an annuity (if it is cash-funded). These minimum amounts are low but, as the provider makes profits on its investments, it announces increases in the minimum you are guaranteed. Once these *reversionary bonuses* are announced – usually every year – they cannot be taken away. An additional one-off *terminal bonus* is included at the time you retire. While estimates of the size of this bonus may be given in your annual benefits statement, the actual amount is not decided until your retirement date.

With-profits investments provide a half-way house between safe, but generally low-returning, deposits and higher-risk, but potentially more rewarding, shares. The scheme provider smoothes the returns from the underlying investments and tries to keep bonuses fairly stable from year to year. But the bonuses you get depend not just on investment returns but also a host of other factors that affect the profitability of the provider's business – for example, claims against it, costs of attracting new business, dividends paid to shareholders. This makes the calculation of bonuses – particularly terminal bonuses – complex and obscure. Since the closure of Equitable Life to new business (following the discovery that guarantees given to planholders could cost the business £1.5 billion that Equitable had failed to set aside), there has been mounting concern about the lack of transparency surrounding with-profits investments.

Unit-linked and unit trust
Nearly all unit-linked plans are cash-funded. Your contributions buy units in one or more of a number of funds offered by the insurance or unit-trust company. The most common types of fund are:

- equity funds – invested in shares, directly or through unit trusts
- fixed-interest funds – invested in gilts, company loan stocks and other fixed-income investments
- property funds – invested in office blocks, factories, shops
- cash funds – invested in bank deposit accounts and other investments whose return varies along with interest rates in general
- managed funds – invested in a range of the options listed above, in proportions decided by the investment managers.

Each fund is divided into a number of units, the value of each of which is the total fund divided by the number of issued units. So the unit price goes up and down as the value of the investments in the fund itself fluctuates.

With most providers, there is a choice of funds to invest in and you can switch between them.

Unitised with-profits
This cross between a unit-linked and a with-profits scheme is being increasingly offered by providers either as a completely separate plan or as one of the range of funds available with a unit-linked plan (in which case it is usually called a 'with-profits fund'). Contributions are allocated to units in a fund, with bonus units added to reflect investment performance. Once added the bonus units cannot be taken away. However, when your plan matures or you decide to transfer it, the company does reserve the right in exceptional circumstances to revise the value of your units downwards (called a 'market-value adjustment' or MVA). This means that unitised with-profits plans are not as secure as the original with-profits version.

Deposit administration
This type of scheme is provided particularly by building societies and works rather like a deposit account. Your contributions are put into an account with the provider, with interest added from time to time. The interest rate varies with the general level of interest rates. There may be a guaranteed minimum amount, sometimes linked to the mortgage rate. Since the value of your fund, in pounds, cannot go down, it is often sensible to switch your pension savings into this type of fund (or to the cash fund in a unit-linked plan) as you near retirement.

All deposit-administration schemes are cash-funded, with a few guaranteeing a minimum cash fund at retirement. The amount of pension depends on annuity rates at the time you retire, though many policies do guarantee a minimum annuity rate at retirement.

Tracker funds
These invest in a range of shares which mimic the performance of a particular stock-market index, such as the FTSE 100 Index. Relatively little buying and selling of shares once the fund has been set up means that costs are lower than for an actively managed fund. For this reason, tracker funds are likely to be a popular default fund for stakeholder pension schemes (see page 194).

Generally tracker funds are considered suitable for people who do not like too much risk. But you do need to look carefully at the index being tracked. Provided the index covers a broad spread of companies and industries, risk should not be high. But, if the index becomes dominated by a few large companies or one or two particular sectors, you could end up with too many eggs in one basket. Some pundits think that the FTSE 100 Index is now risky to track because of the dominance of information technology and communication companies. Choosing a fund which tracks a broader index, such as the FTSE Eurotop 300, could be a better option.

Self-investment
Some providers offer pension schemes where you yourself select the individual shares and other investments which make up your pension fund. These pensions are often known as self-invested personal pensions or SIPPs. Charges for self-invested schemes are usually higher than for managed schemes. This is generally an option only if you have a reasonably large sum to invest (say, £100,000 or more). You must be confident about your abilities to select investments to perform well.

The level of charges
The plan provider deducts a variety of charges from your plan to cover its administrative costs and provide its profit. Charges have often been criticised for their size and the arrival of stakeholder pensions has put welcome pressure on personal plan providers. For example, surveys by *Money Management* show that, in 1998, with a 20-year, £200-per-month regular-contribution plan, charges reduced the size of your pension fund by 17.7 per cent on average. In 1999, the average reduction was down to 14.8 per cent and, by 2000, 14.4 per cent.

As a basis for comparison, it is worth noting that even the 1 per cent a year maximum charge for a stakeholder scheme is equivalent to a reduction in your eventual pension fund, assuming 7 per cent a year growth, of:

* 2.5 per cent over 5 years
* 5.1 per cent over 10 years
* 7.8 per cent over 15 years
* 10.7 per cent over 20 years
* 13.7 per cent over 25 years.

Some stakeholder schemes, and a few personal pension plans, charge less than the maximum.

A high-charging plan is not necessarily a bad plan but clearly your investment has to work harder to overcome high charges.

Other options

Pension mortgages
It is possible informally to link your pension and your mortgage. What happens is that you take out an interest-only mortgage. You also pay your pension scheme contributions, receiving tax relief on them. At retirement, you use your tax-free lump sum to pay off the capital on the mortgage.

Pension mortgages are tax-efficient but do have some disadvantages. They can tie you to one provider, who may not offer the best rates or returns, and you may have to take the pension at a fixed date, which may be inconvenient. You commit yourself many years ahead to a particular use for your tax-free lump sum. And, unless you have separate funds from elsewhere to repay the capital early, you lock yourself into a specified term for your mortgage (i.e. up to the age at which you plan to take your pension). If you end up borrowing for more years than you would using a non-pension mortgage, this inflexible scheme could cost you a great deal.

You may find that having a pension mortgage creates problems if later on you join an employer who has a good pension scheme. You might want to stop paying into the personal pension plan. You would then need to make a new arrangement for paying off the mortgage.

There may also be difficulties in keeping up payments to the pension plan if you become unemployed and so cannot afford to keep up the payments. You can buy insurance to cover the payments – but only for a limited period. With a mortgage linked to the employer's pension scheme (which is also possible but unusual), there is the added problem of rearranging the scheme if you leave that employment.

Above all, taking a pension mortgage could reduce your income in retirement. If you use part of your pension fund to repay a mortgage, there is less available to provide a pension for you.

Although the tax advantages are considerable, they do not necessarily outweigh the disadvantages. Think carefully before deciding to take out a pension mortgage.

Rebate-only personal pensions

These policies allow you, if employed, to contract out of SERPS. While you cannot have more than one rebate-only personal pension in any one tax year, you can pay additional contributions to it and add as many ordinary personal pension plans on top as you like. In practice, if your *only* pension provision was a rebate-only plan, your pension would be poor and inflexible, so it is not recommended. You also forgo the chance of a lump sum at retirement, or of retiring at any age earlier than state pension age.

The contributions to a rebate-only plan are made up of:

- the National Insurance rebate. From April 1997 this comprises a flat-rate element plus an age-related element – see Chapter 16.
- tax relief on your rebate which comes to roughly another 0.45 per cent of your earnings in the 2001–2 tax year.

These contributions are paid over by the Department of Social Security (DSS) after the end of the tax year. They are not counted by the Inland Revenue against their limits for tax relief, explained on page 196. For whether or not a rebate-only plan would be a sensible choice for you, see Chapter 16.

Planning your pension

Stakeholder or personal pension?

Over the years, personal pension plans have had a bad press because they were generally inflexible and expensive. Stakeholder pension schemes have been introduced to address these problems. Stakeholder schemes must meet conditions (see page 193) that ensure they offer you value for money.

So do not choose a *non-stakeholder personal pension* plan unless either it matches the stakeholder terms or it offers you additional options or benefits. These might include the facility to choose between a particularly wide range of investments or to make your own choice of stocks, shares and other investments.

What contributions to a rebate-only personal plan will buy you

In 2001–2, you can contribute extra payments up to £3,600 (more if your earnings are high enough – see page 198)

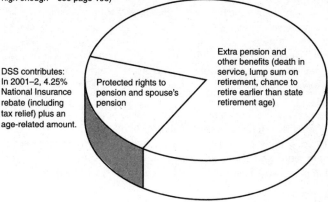

DSS contributes: In 2001–2, 4.25% National Insurance rebate (including tax relief) plus an age-related amount.

Protected rights to pension and spouse's pension

Extra pension and other benefits (death in service, lump sum on retirement, chance to retire earlier than state retirement age)

If you can take out a personal pension plan through a *group personal pension scheme* at work, this may be a better option than arranging your own stakeholder scheme. In such cases, your employer may contribute to the plan on your behalf or negotiate a special deal on charges and flexibility.

If you are already paying into a personal pension, *do not switch to a stakeholder scheme* without first getting advice either from the plan provider or an independent financial adviser. You may already have paid the bulk of the charges for the personal plan and, if you now transfer to another scheme, you could suffer a hefty penalty. But, if you decide to increase the amount you save, consider whether it would be worth putting the extra into a stakeholder scheme.

Which type of plan?

Deposit-administration plans and the *cash funds of unit-linked plans* are dependent on levels of interest rates. So they look good when interest rates are high. As you near retirement and have a unit-linked policy, you can *switch into the cash fund or a deposit-administration scheme*. This is useful if you are worried about units going down in value. The pension itself remains dependent on annuity rates when you retire.

For the longer term, the choice is between *with-profits* and *unit-linked plans*. With-profits plans are the less risky. Although the guaranteed pension or cash fund is initially low, it is reasonably certain to be increased steadily over the period to retirement. However, many insurance companies have been piling a large proportion of the 'profits' into the terminal bonus, which is not guaranteed and can be held static or cut. Even future rates of reversionary bonus can be reduced if a company falls on hard times. This tendency is even more pronounced in some schemes which *offer guaranteed annuities* (in other words, promise that the annuity rate at retirement will not be less than a certain level even if general annuity rates are then lower). A few such companies (notably Equitable Life) have had their fingers burned. When Equitable Life's attempt to cut terminal bonuses to planholders of guaranteed annuity schemes was ruled illegal, the company had to raise money in other ways to meet the cost of guarantees. It did this primarily by paying no reversionary bonus to any policy holder for a period of seven months. This high-profile case may reduce the number of guaranteed annuities on the market.

If you go for a *deferred-annuity scheme*, your pension does not suffer if annuity rates are low at the time you retire (though some companies will increase your pension if annuity rates are high). With *unit-linked policies* (apart from the small number of index-linked ones available), the return is much more dependent on when you make your payments and when you start taking the benefits. So the level of risk is higher.

Some pension plan providers offer an investment option called a *lifestyle fund*. With this, the fund is initially invested in shares, bonds and cash in proportions appropriate to your attitude towards risk and length of time until retirement. As you get closer to retirement, the fund manager automatically increases the proportion invested in bonds and, later on, in cash to reduce the investment risk.

How much to pay in
With stakeholder schemes, any minimum contribution may not be higher than £20. With regular-contribution personal pension plans, many companies set a minimum regular contribution of, say, £250 a year or £25 a month. The minimum for a single-contribution policy could be £500 or £1,000, but can be a good deal higher for a scheme specially tailored for senior people on high salaries. The maximum you can pay is the maximum amount you can get tax relief on, explained on page 196.

Organisations selling pension plans and schemes give very accurate-looking and impressive figures showing the pension you are likely to get from each pound you pay from a certain age. But these quotations are only estimates, based on assumptions about future investment returns set, in most cases, by the Financial Services Authority. Nor, except with rebate-only plans, do they take account of inflation, which can be devastating (though you get a separate, and rather confusing, statement about inflation).

For example, if you start paying £1,000 a year into a regular-contribution policy at age 35, you might imagine yourself living in comfort on the £14,800 a year the insurance company quotes you. But if inflation averaged 3 per cent over the rest of your working life, the buying power of this pension at 65 would be only £6,100 a year. Ten years after retirement, if inflation continued at 3 per cent, it would be worth only about £4,500 a year.

Yearly rate of inflation	Pounds you will need in future to match each pound today in				
	10yrs	20yrs	30yrs	40yrs	50yrs
	£	£	£	£	£
2%	1.2	1.5	1.8	2.2	2.7
4%	1.5	2.2	3.2	4.8	7.1
6%	1.8	3.2	5.7	10.3	18.4
8%	2.2	4.7	10.1	21.7	46.9

This makes it extremely difficult to know how much you should pay in to your pension. But you should consider the following:

- how much income you will have after retirement from other sources, such as state retirement pension, from selling your business or from part-time work
- the age you intend to retire at – the older this is, the more pension you get for each pound you pay in
- inflation after retirement. At age 65, you can expect, on average, to live to 80 if you are a man, 83½ if you are a woman. You still want your pension to have reasonable purchasing power in your old age, so your pension in the first year of retirement needs to be much higher in pounds than you would think. Alternatively, you can give up some pension in the early years of retirement in order to have a pension which increases each year – see 'Level or increasing pension?' on page 213.

Using the table on page 208 you can work out the value of pension you will need for various rates of inflation. For example, if you think you will need a pension of £10,000 a year (in today's money) in 30 years' time and you reckon inflation will average 4 per cent over that time, you will need to get £10,000 × 3.2 = £32,000 a year from the scheme to achieve this.

To take account of inflation both before and after retirement, use the number of years up to your 70th or 75th birthday, say, even if you intend to retire younger.

You might find that you cannot possibly afford the contributions for a pension of the amount you work out. The best you can do is to save the highest amount you can and, if you have an opportunity to do so, to set aside extra amounts in future. Bear in mind that you cannot pay in more than the Inland Revenue limits allow. If you need to save above those limits, consider topping up by saving through another tax-efficient investment, such as an Individual Savings Account (ISA). If you are an employee, can you persuade your employer to contribute to your personal pension plan?

When to start

If you are aiming to get a pension at age 65 of two-thirds of your final salary (which is the most that someone in an employer's scheme is allowed to have) you need to pay the full percentage of earnings allowed by the Inland Revenue each year from about age 44 onwards (see Table on page 198).

However, it is unwise to leave starting a scheme as late as this. There may be years when you can afford only a small amount in contributions perhaps because of ill-health or redundancy; you may need life insurance or a pension for your dependants; you may need to retire before 65; inflation may be high in the first few years of your retirement. So, unless you are confident of substantial income from elsewhere, you should certainly start paying for your pension by your early 30s.

A good strategy might be to start contributing when you first start work and carry on paying in as much as you can until family commitments catch up with you. Cut back during the years you are heavily committed to other spending. Then boost your pension savings again once those commitments ease off. This way some contributions work for you right from the early years of your working life – and they are the ones which work hardest.

With the introduction of the DC regime (see page 196) from 6 April 2001, up to £3,600 a year of contributions are no longer linked to earnings and anyone can pay into someone else's stakeholder scheme or personal pension plan on their behalf. This opens the way for, say, parents and grandparents to start pension schemes for children, giving them a head start in building up an adequate retirement pension.

If you stop paying

You may need to stop paying into a regular-contribution personal pension plan, perhaps because you find yourself short of cash. Most personal pension providers let you miss one or two payments but there may be a limit at which the policy has to be made *paid up*. This means that your money remains invested in the fund and you get a pension when you retire. But it will be smaller than if you had kept paying. If your plan has been running only a few years when you stop paying contributions, you may find it has a low value or is even worth nothing at all.

You can often reinstate a policy within a year or so of its being made paid up. With with-profits plans, you may have to pay all the contributions you have missed and perhaps a fee as well. But this could be worth doing if the guarantees on your old policies are better than they would be on a new one, or if the old policy is a retirement annuity contract with the higher level of lump sum available. Make sure you qualify for tax relief on the contributions.

If you expect your earnings to fluctuate from year to year, do not choose a regular-contribution plan. Instead go either for a series of single-contribution plans or a plan which is flexible and allows payments to be made on an ad hoc basis.

All stakeholder schemes allow flexible payments and the ability to stop and start contributions without penalty.

When you plan to retire

Under current rules, unless your job is recognised as having a lower retirement age, you must start to take the benefits from a stakeholder scheme or personal pension plan some time between your 50th and 75th birthday. There are only a few types of people who may be allowed to retire early, such as various groups of sportspeople and athletes with retirement ages of 35 or 40.

There is no need to stop working in order to draw your pension and lump sum.

If you have become too ill to work before the lowest age at which you can retire, you can start taking the benefits then, but the amount will be much reduced. This is because you will have been paying in for a shorter period and will expect to draw out for longer.

With some plans, you have to say at the outset when you intend to retire, though you can change your mind later. Other plans have a standard retirement age but you can still retire when you like within the age range allowed. Always make sure you do not lose out by changing your mind about when to retire.

Phasing your retirement

You may not want to stop work suddenly but would rather slide out gradually over a period of years. If so, you may want to supplement your earnings over a number of years by drawing a small amount of pension, increasing year by year until you draw your full pension when you stop working altogether. See pages 199–200 for details of how to use your pension in this way.

Choosing a plan

There are hundreds of different personal pension plans to choose from. Choosing is not easy and, if this is going to be your main way of saving for retirement, it might be sensible to spread your investment over more than one plan, though each extra scheme you take out means an extra administration charge.

To find out for yourself which policies offer which features, see the most recent edition of the *FT Personal Pensions* published by FT Finance* (it is costly, so ask your public library to get hold of a copy). This gives useful comparative details on most plans.

From some time in 2001, the Financial Services Authority is making comparative information tables available on its website* and by calling the FSA Consumer helpline*. These list the features of different providers' products and allow you to search out those with features you want. Personal pensions and stakeholder schemes are among the products due to be covered by the tables.

There is no reliable way of knowing how successful each company's investment performance will be. With *with-profits* policies, you could check what you would get from different companies if current bonus rates were maintained. A company with relatively high reserves may be better placed to maintain its bonus levels in the future.

With *unit-linked* and *deposit-administration* schemes, the past is, again, little guide to the future, nor are current growth rates a reliable indicator. A large body of current research suggests there is no link between good past investment performance and good future investment performance, especially over the long time periods that typically apply to pensions. There is some weak evidence that investment funds that have historically performed badly may perform badly again or even close down. It is probably sensible to avoid a fund with a consistently bad record over the immediate past.

Plan providers issue illustrations giving an example of the benefits your plan might produce, but these should be used with care. The FSA lays down the assumptions about investment performance, and all providers must base their illustrations on the same standardised growth rates. However, since January 1995 plan providers use their own charges, so comparing illustrations from different providers for the same contributions and benefits shows you how the costs compare. A high-charging provider is not necessarily a worse choice than a low-charging one, but the high charger will have to make the investments work harder to overcome the extra charges, and you need to know why that provider's investments are expected to do so much better.

Gathering information about plans and making comparisons is time-consuming. You can save yourself work by going to an independent financial adviser – make sure you choose one who specialises in pensions business (see Chapter 7, *Getting advice*). A good pensions adviser has access to computer databases that make plan comparisons straightforward once you know the type of features you want. Bear in mind that independent financial advice is not free.

The clearer your own ideas of what you want before you visit an adviser, the more effectively you and the adviser can decide on the most suitable course of action for you. You may also increase your chances of getting good advice if you go to more than one adviser. You can get a list of advisers in your area by contacting IFA Promotion*, the Institute of Financial Planning*, SOFA* or the Money Management National Register of Independent Fee-Based Advisers*.

The security of your plan

Insurance companies are currently covered by the Policyholders' Protection Act (shortly to be absorbed into the Financial Services Compensation Scheme). If the company fails, the Policyholders' Protection Board, set up by the government to administer the Act, has to try to get another company to take on the policy. Provided you carry on paying the contributions due and, in the opinion of the Board, the amount involved is not excessive, the Act guarantees that you get at least 90 per cent of the amount guaranteed at the time the company went bust.

However, you get no guarantees of future bonuses from the new company that takes over your policy. So, since you could lose quite a lot if your company goes bust, it is prudent to stick with a large, well-established company.

Very few insurance companies do go bust. Sometimes they get taken over instead, and sometimes, if they get into financial trouble, they have to cut their bonus rates. The guarantees remain, but the rate of growth on the policies is slower than expected.

Other pension providers are covered by other compensation funds that are also shortly to be amalgamated into the Financial Services Compensation Scheme. However, in some cases these cover smaller amounts than the Policyholders' Protection Act. Providers have to abide by rules laid down by the Financial Services and Markets Act 2000 or earlier legislation – see Chapter 6.

The Financial Services Compensation Scheme is a new single compensation scheme covering most financial products and services. It is to be divided into sub-schemes broadly in line with the various compensation schemes it replaces, with broadly similar levels of compensation.

Your choices at retirement

When to retire

Once you reach an age at which you can start taking the benefits under your plan – usually between 50 and 75 – you can start your policy. Before committing yourself, find out your level of benefits so that, if necessary, you can postpone your decision.

Shopping around for a higher pension

With all rebate-only personal pensions and nearly all other personal pension plans and stakeholder schemes, you do not have to take your pension from the providers with which you have been saving. When you retire, you can shop around to see if you can use your *open-market option* to get a better deal for your money.

If you want to do this, you first have to find out the value of your cash fund. If the policy is a deferred-annuity plan, the provider has to work out (using what is called its *commutation* rate) the number of pounds of fund allocated for your pension. You then compare these benefits with those you could get if you switch providers. If, over the years, you take out a number of different plans, you can transfer them all at retirement to the insurance company offering the best package of benefits.

To find the best company for you, contact one of the independent financial advisers that specialise in annuity business, such as the Annuity Bureau* or Annuity Direct.*

If annuity rates are low at the time you want to retire, you might consider a flexible annuity or annuity deferral. But these options do not suit everyone, so get advice before deciding on this route.

Lump sum

When you retire, you can normally choose to have a reduced pension and a tax-free lump sum. You may be glad to have a lump sum to spend at the start of your retirement or you can invest the money and draw on it later. You could even, if you use the money to buy an *immediate* annuity, end up with a higher after-tax income than the pension you give up. This is because only part of such an annuity is taxable.

The personal pension rules let you take a quarter of your fund (after some deductions) as a lump sum. But if you have a rebate-only personal pension as part of the plan you cannot take any of it as a lump sum – it must all be paid as pension. The same rules apply to personal pension plans that are registered as stakeholder schemes.

Level or increasing pension?

The buying power of a level pension is quickly eaten away by inflation. You can instead choose a pension that increases each year. It is, though, smaller to start off with. For example, a pension for a 65-year-old man that increases by 5 per cent compound each year starts off at around two-thirds of the amount of a level pension. Although the increasing pension catches up with the level pension in about 10 years, it takes about 18 years before you actually receive the same *total* number of pounds in pension.

Some providers offer pensions which are linked to an index – often the Retail Prices Index (RPI). But a pension that is increased in line with such an index starts off much lower than a level pension. If it starts off at half as much when you retire at 65, it has to increase by an average of 20 per cent a year for you to receive the same total buying power by the time you reach 75.

Another option is to choose an investment-linked annuity. With these, the income you get depends on the performance of underlying investments. Consequently, the income fluctuates and can fall as well as rise. A with-profits annuity is normally less risky than a unit-linked annuity. See Chapter 28 for details of how these annuities work.

An investment-linked annuity is suitable only if you can cope with an income that varies from year to year. For example, you might have income from elsewhere to fall back on or the pension might be large (which would require a pension fund at least into six figures). If you cannot cope with this, choose an ordinary annuity.

Unless you expect inflation to return to high levels, you might be better off choosing a level annuity rather than one which increases or is linked to the RPI. But, to cope with higher prices later on, make sure you save some of the pension you get in the early years of retirement.

If you have a rebate-only personal pension as part of your policy, that must be increased by a certain amount – by inflation up to a maximum of 5 per cent each year from April 1997, by up to 3 per cent before then.

A pension for a dependant after you die

There is only one way in which you can be certain of providing an income for a dependant – typically your husband or wife, but perhaps an unmarried partner, child, elderly relative, and so on – if you die after you start drawing the pension. Choose to have a pension paid as long as you or someone else is alive (called a *joint-life, last-survivor* annuity). The pension may continue at the same level, or it can be higher while you are both alive. A joint-life pension (if the man is 65 and the woman 60 and the pension stays level) might be around 25 per cent lower than a pension payable on one life only for the man, 7 per cent lower than that for the woman alone.

A poor alternative is to choose to have the pension paid for a certain period (often five or ten years) whether you live that long or not. Bear in mind that, as the guarantee period passes, the amount your survivors receive declines. Once the guarantee period expires, they get nothing. So do not look on this as adequate protection for dependants.

With a rebate-only personal pension, the policy must provide for a pension of half of what you would get, for your widow or widower (but not an unmarried partner) after your death – even if you are not married at the time when you retire.

If you opt for annuity deferral and income drawdown and you die before switching to an annuity, a surviving dependant has three choices: he or she can use the fund to buy an annuity; continue to draw an income direct from the fund until either he or she reaches the age of 75 or the date at which you would have been 75, whichever comes sooner; or take the fund as a lump sum after deduction of tax at a special rate of 35 per cent.

19 Retirement annuity contracts

Before 1 July 1988, when personal pensions in their current form were introduced, the only tax-efficient vehicle for individuals to make their own pensions provision was the *retirement annuity contract*. Many of these contracts are still in operation. This chapter describes the rules which govern them. It also describes specific rules applying to a post-July 1988 personal pension plan where you have carried back a contribution made in 2001–2 to the 2000–1 tax year in order to use up carry-forward relief (see page 218).

Retirement annuity contracts were abolished in 1988 for new savers. They have many features in common with post-1988 personal pension and stakeholder schemes. They work on a money purchase basis, so the pension you get depends on:

- how much is paid in
- how well the invested contributions grow
- how much is deducted in charges
- annuity rates at the time you want to start drawing a pension.

Why keep a retirement annuity contract?

Like other pension schemes and plans, retirement annuity contracts have a number of tax advantages:

- you get tax relief on what you pay in. Contributions are paid *gross* – i.e. without deducting any tax relief. You claim relief through your tax return or tax office. This means that, unlike personal pension plans, non-taxpayers and starting-rate taxpayers do not get any bonus added to their savings (see page 195). With retirement annuity contracts, you get tax relief only against tax you actually pay
- some of the income earned by your investment is tax-free – but not share dividends and similar income
- capital gains on your investment build up tax-free
- at retirement you can take part of your fund as a tax-free lump sum, the rest must be drawn as taxable income.

If you are one of the many people who still hold retirement annuity contracts, you have the choice of continuing to pay into your contract or instead making future payments to a personal plan or, since 6 April 2001, a stakeholder scheme. You can also choose to transfer savings built up in a retirement annuity contract to a stakeholder scheme or personal pension plan. Your decision hinges on the advantages and disadvantages of the different types of plan which are mainly:

- unless your earnings are high (see opposite), from age 45 onwards you can contribute more to a stakeholder scheme or personal pension plan than to a retirement annuity contract
- if you have high earnings (see Table 1 for figures), you can pay more into a retirement annuity contract
- you may be able to take a larger tax-free lump sum from a retirement annuity contract (see page 219)
- the earliest you can draw a pension from a retirement annuity contract is usually age 60. You can reduce the age to 50 by transferring to a stakeholder scheme or personal pension plan
- retirement annuity contracts do not offer *annuity deferral and income drawdown* (see page 200). You can take advantage of this option by transferring to a stakeholder scheme or personal pension plan
- charges for a retirement annuity contract are likely to be higher than charges for stakeholder schemes and some personal pension plans.

Before transferring from a retirement annuity contract or stopping payments to it, you should get advice from the contract provider or an independent financial adviser. Transfer penalties or ongoing charges for a paid-up contract might outweigh the benefits of making the switch.

You cannot use a retirement annuity contract to contract out of SERPS.

How much can you save?

You can pay into a retirement annuity contract only if you have 'net relevant earnings' – basically, your taxable profits if you are self-employed or, if you are an employee, your earnings including the value of most fringe benefits.

The most you can pay in each year is a given percentage of your earnings that varies with age – see Table opposite. Unlike personal pension plans, there is no cap on the earnings you can use for this purpose. This means that, if your earnings are high, you can pay much more into a retirement annuity contract than a stakeholder scheme or personal pension plan. The final column of Table 1 shows the level of earnings at which your contributions to a retirement annuity contract can be higher than contributions to a stakeholder scheme or personal pension plan.

Carry-back

You can opt to have a contribution paid in one tax year treated as if it had been paid in the previous year. You have until 31 January following the year in which the contribution was actually paid to make this decision. For example, you have until 31 January 2003 to decide whether to carry back a contribution paid in 2001–2 to the 2000–1 tax year.

Table 1: Maximum contributions to a retirement annuity contract

Age at the start of the tax year (6 April)	Percentage of earnings you can contribute	You can pay more to a retirement annuity contract than a stakeholder scheme or personal pension plan if you earn more than
Up to 35	17.5%	£95,400
36–45	17.5%	£109,029
46–50	17.5%	£136,286
51–55	20%	£143,100
56–60	22.5%	£148,400
61–74	27.5%	£138,764
75 and over	you can no longer contribute	

If you had no net relevant earnings in the previous tax year, you can carry the contribution back one more year. For example, suppose you pay the contribution in 2001–2 but had no earnings in 2000–1. You can then carry the contribution back to 1999–2000.

You get tax relief at the rates for the tax year to which you have carried back the contribution.

If you are in business and there is a delay in working out your net relevant earnings, the carry-back option is useful. It is also worthwhile if tax rates were higher in the earlier tax year.

Carry-forward

If, in any tax year, you have not made the maximum possible contribution, you have unused contribution relief. You can carry this unused relief forward for up to six years. This means you can make an extra large contribution that uses up all of the current year's contribution relief and then some or all of the relief carried forward.

In the 2001–2 tax year, you can use up relief carried forward from as long ago as 1995–6.

You can combine the carry-back and carry-forward rules. For example, you could pay a large contribution in 2001–2 and opt for it to be carried back to 2000–1. The contribution can then be set against the relief available for 2000–1 and unused relief brought forward from as long ago as 1994–5.

Your pension and other benefits

What your scheme provides

As with stakeholder schemes and personal pension plans, retirement annuity contracts do not automatically offer a package of benefits. They are geared towards providing a retirement pension and tax-free lump sum at retirement. If you want to add other benefits, you must pay extra or accept a reduction in pension.

If you die before retirement, most contracts pay out a lump sum to your heirs equal to the value of your pension fund or your contributions plus interest. If you

---

Carry-back and carry-forward for personal pensions

From 6 April 2001, carry-forward has been abolished for personal pensions (and other pension arrangements in the DC regime – see page 198). However, the rules still allow you to carry back a contribution made in one year to the previous tax year. By carrying back a contribution made after 6 April 2001 to the 2000–1 tax year, you have a last chance to scoop up unused carry-forward relief.

The carry-back rule for personal pensions is now different to the rule for retirement annuity contracts. With a personal pension plan, the contribution must be paid and the option to carry-back made by 31 January during the tax year. So to carry a contribution back to 2000–1, you must pay it on or before 31 January 2002.

The carried-back contribution is then treated as if it had been paid in 2000–1 and, once the contribution relief for that year has been used up, you can scoop up unused relief carried forward from as long ago as 1994–5.

After 31 January 2002, it is no longer possible to use the carry-forward rule and any unused relief from earlier years is lost.

---

want to add extra life cover, you can pay for separate life insurance. Up to 5 per cent of your net relevant earnings can be used to pay for life cover (whether or not you are also contributing towards the pension) and qualifies for tax relief in the same way as other contributions.

At retirement, you can add, for example, pension increases or a pension for your widow or widower by choosing the appropriate sort of annuity. Your annuity choices are the same as those for stakeholder schemes and personal pension plans – see pages 213–4.

When can you start receiving your pension?

The minimum age at which you can start to draw a pension is usually 60, though there are earlier ages for some occupations, such as professional footballers and deep-sea divers. If you are unable to work because of ill health, you may also be able to start your pension earlier.

How your pension is worked out

This is the same as for stakeholder schemes and personal pension plans – see page 199 – except that retirement annuity contracts do not have the *annuity deferral and income drawdown* option.

The types of plan and planning your pension

The range of plans on offer, how to choose between them and your investment choices are basically as described for stakeholder schemes and personal pension plans on pages 201 to 205.

Your choices at retirement

When to retire

You can start to take a pension from a retirement annuity contract at any age between 60 and 75. You do not have to stop work to be eligible.

You could gradually ease out of work by using *phased retirement*. This involves splitting your contract into many segments and converting a few segments at a time into pension, leaving the rest invested. Phased retirement usually involves extra costs so is unlikely to be suitable if you have less than, say, £100,000 in your pension fund. Get advice before going down this course.

If you want to start your pension before age 60, you have to transfer to a stakeholder scheme or personal pension plan. All other aspects of your pension are then subject to the stakeholder/personal pension rules described in Chapter 18. Get advice before making any switch.

Shopping around for a higher pension

Your contract may give you an *open market option* allowing you to shop around other providers for your annuity. Usually, this enables you to secure a higher pension because not all companies specialise in annuities.

However, if you do buy your annuity from another provider, this counts as a transfer to a personal pension plan. This might reduce the amount of tax-free lump sum you can have. If so, you need to weigh that up against any increase in pension as a result of shopping around.

Lump sum

The maximum tax-free lump sum you can have from a retirement annuity contract is whatever amount would be three times the remaining pension payable after the lump sum has been deducted from your fund. (There is also a cash limit of £150,000 for contracts taken out after 17 March 1987 though, in practice, this has been easily circumvented by splitting contracts into separate segments.) This compares with a limit of one-quarter of the fund for most stakeholder schemes and personal pensions.

Level or increasing pension?

See page 213.

A pension for a dependant after you die

See page 214.

Investing in shares

Two decades ago, only 3 million people in the UK directly held shares. Now, the figure is around 16 million. Three factors have prompted this dramatic rise in private share ownership:

- the privatisation of state-owned assets, including the sell-off of British Telecom, British Gas and water and electricity companies
- more significantly the conversion of mutual building societies to banks, starting with Abbey National in 1989 and including other giants, such as the Halifax, Woolwich and Alliance and Leicester in 1997, whose 13.2 million members were given free shares. At the end of 2000, 2.6 million Bradford and Bingley members were also given free shares
- the growing popularity of employee share-ownership schemes which give employees a stake in the company for which they work, for example most companies in the FTSE 100 now offer these.

Investing in shares through direct purchase in UK stock markets can be risky. Many individuals found this out in early 2000 when they were left holding 'dot.com' shares as their prices collapsed. But, held for the medium- to long-term, shares tend to outperform lower-risk investments, such as savings accounts, gilts and corporate bonds.

To reduce risk, you need to be prepared to invest in shares for a reasonable length of time – at least five years. You should also spread your money around a number of companies in different industries. You can also consider different financial markets around the world.

If you are not attracted to the risks of direct investment in shares, consider investing indirectly. This way you pool your money with that of other investors and spread your risk. Your money is invested in a wide range of companies through two main methods, unit trusts or investment trusts, dealt with in Chapters 21 and 22 respectively. Other ways of investing in shares are detailed at the end of this chapter.

What is direct investment?

When you invest directly, you buy a company's shares and thereby participate in its performance. Generally speaking, if the company performs well, the value of your share increases. If its performance is poor, your share value decreases.

So long as you hold the shares and the company performs well, you can expect two sorts of return:

- *income* – the company pays out an income (called dividend) to its shareholders. The hope is that, as company profits rise, this income increases over the years.
- *capital gain* – the share price of the company rises over the years. This may happen if, for example, the company's prospects improve. But you should not expect the share price to rise steadily.

Looking at what has happened in the past gives some idea of the ups and downs of investing in shares but, of course, not necessarily what will happen in the future. The chart on page 222 shows how the value of the London stock market has varied between 1990 and 2001, using the index of share values of the 100 biggest companies in the UK published daily by the *Financial Times* – the so-called 'FTSE 100' or 'Footsie'. As you can see, it has been a bumpy ride – for example at the beginning of 2001 it fell by almost 20 per cent. Within the market as a whole some shares will have produced a smoother performance, while others will have been even more volatile. The success of your investment depends crucially on when you buy the shares and when you sell, and no one has a cast-iron method of forecasting the right moment to buy and sell.

Spreading your investment

Three major factors influence the share price of any company. First, its profitability and, as important, expectations of future profitability. Second, the industry the company operates in. You may believe that BP, say, is the best-performing oil company but, if the oil sector is depressed because of a glut in oil supply, you may do better not investing in oil companies at all. Third, general economic factors – inflation, fear of recession, fear of a 'trade war' between countries or blocs of countries – may push the market lower overall. All these factors must be considered before investing in shares and reviewed regularly afterwards. If you can choose the right company in the right sector at the right time, you can do very well indeed, but timing is critical and if you get it wrong you could do very badly.

If you buy shares in more than one company, your chances of an extreme result reduce. And, if you spread your money over the shares of at least 10 companies covering different sectors of the market, the chances of them all doing much worse than average are further reduced. In this way, you reduce both company risk and sector risk. You can also go one step further by spreading your investments over different countries. The benefit is that the outcome of your investment does not depend entirely on the UK stock market. The risks then become the cost of converting into foreign currencies and the likely lack of detailed information about company prospects.

But, remember, share prices fluctuate both individually and on average. So, even if you invest in a wide spread of shares, you cannot be sure that the value of your share investment will not fall, particularly in the short or even medium term.

Because of buying and selling costs, it makes no sense to invest small amounts in shares – less than about £1,500 to £2,000 per company, say. So, to get a good spread, you need at least £15,000 to invest directly in shares.

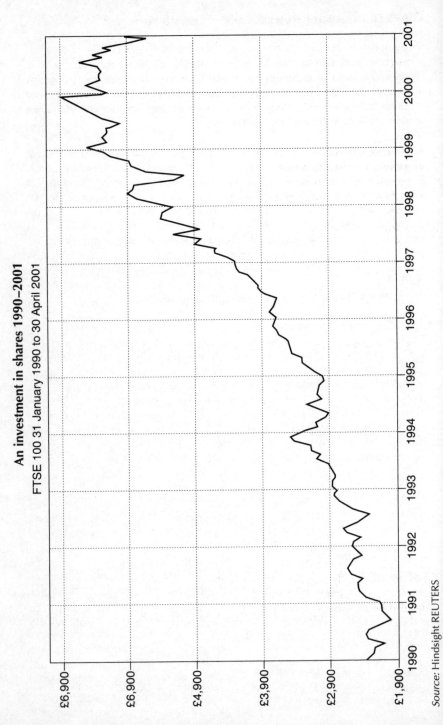

An investment in shares 1990–2001
FTSE 100 31 January 1990 to 30 April 2001

Source: Hindsight REUTERS

Ways of choosing shares

If you make the decision to buy shares, you are still faced with the problem of choosing which ones. Amateur investors often seek professional advice (see Chapter 7) from a stockbroker, for example, or from the business pages of a newspaper. But, to help you understand this advice and to assess its worth, you might want to know something about the different methods of choosing shares used by advisers. There are four main ways:

- fundamental analysis
- technical analysis (chartism)
- quantitative analysis
- general observations and personal views.

Fundamental analysis

At any given time, a company's shares have an intrinsic or 'fundamental' value. This value depends normally on the earning capacity of the company, which in turn depends on such things as the quality of management and the outlook for the industry and for the economy as a whole. If the current market price of the shares is lower than what you think the intrinsic value should be, the share is one to consider buying. The expectation is that the share price will eventually rise to reflect the intrinsic value.

Stock market research analysts use fundamental analysis to calculate a precise intrinsic value for a share, based on detailed estimates of the company's future earnings. They use any information that can be obtained, for example by visiting companies, talking to the management and analysing company reports and accounts. Obviously, this is much more difficult for individuals to do.

The accounts may reveal important facts about the company's performance including sales, costs of sales, level of overheads and investment in new products. By working out the relationships between various factors, analysts build a picture of the company's financial position. One commonly used ratio is earnings per share or EPS (see box). A second is the price/earnings ratio (see 'What the papers say' on page 231). The financial position of one company is usually compared with other companies in the same industry. In addition, by studying the broader economic background, predictions are made about how well, or badly, particular industries (such as heavy engineering, retail or financial) or even whole countries are going to fare.

But there are problems. The information available is far from comprehensive and not sufficiently standardised. Information in accounts is largely historic and potentially misleading. For example, the accounts may not give a sufficiently detailed breakdown of where a company's profits are coming from. One part of the business may be subsidising other parts. Yet this might just be the type of company you should avoid.

Technical analysis (chartism)

Technical analysis is concerned with the behaviour of the stock market, i.e. the rises and falls in share prices over time, rather than the details of a company's

---

A few examples of common terms and ratios

Earnings per share (EPS)

EPS is the amount of profit per share from the *ordinary* activities of the company, after tax and all other charges. It does not include any profit (or loss) made outside the company's normal business (called extraordinary items), say the sale of land by a manufacturing company. The EPS is worked out by dividing the ordinary post-tax profits by the total number of shares issued.

Profit margin

This is worked out by finding what the pre-tax profit of the company is as a percentage of its sales.

Return on capital employed

This is worked out by finding what the profit of the company is as a percentage of its assets, i.e. the sum of the value of its property, machinery, stock, what it is owed by its customers and other relevant assets.

---

performance. The method normally includes the study of charts, hence the term *chartism*.

As in other markets, the assumption is that investors, collectively, have all the available facts about companies and that movements of share prices accurately and quickly reflect this knowledge. But technical analysts believe that share prices do not move instantly to take account of the information, and so they can predict price movements.

The method involves studying charts or graphs showing the range of prices at which each company's shares are bought and sold. The share price record of a company can indicate periods when investors have displayed confidence (or lack of it) in the company, and have built up (or sold) large holdings of its shares. Chartists argue that these graphs can tell them when such periods are about to recur. They are looking for *trendlines* and for significant shapes like *head-and-shoulders* patterns. If the share price of a company has completed a head and shoulders (see chart opposite), a chartist would say it is time to sell that share.

Quantitative analysis

This is a highly mathematical method of share analysis that concentrates on the riskiness of a share. It looks at the past performance of individual shares relative to the market as a whole. Those shares that perform better than the market do so because they are riskier investments than those which perform in line with the market. Beta analysis, which is a commonly used part of quantitative analysis, is a means of measuring the risk.

A share which has moved exactly in line with the FTSE All Share Index is said to have a beta of one. But some shares and unit trusts go up and down more than average. These are described as *aggressive* – i.e. when the index goes up, the share or unit trust goes up relatively more; when the index goes down, it goes down relatively more. The value of beta for aggressive shares or unit trusts is more than

A typical chart

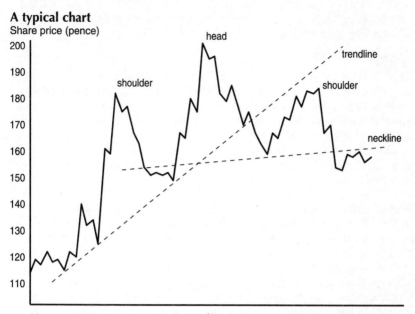

Share price (pence)

one. Other shares and unit trusts are *defensive* – i.e. they go up and down less than the average (and their beta value is less than one). This means that when the index goes up, the share or unit trust goes up less than the average and, when the index goes down, it goes down less than the average. Many shares and unit trusts fall somewhere between the two extremes. The beta of a share is a measure of how much its rate of return is likely to be affected by general stock market movements.

Some people use this analysis so that, if they think the general level of prices in the stock market is going to rise, they can invest in shares with high betas because their prices will (they hope) go up correspondingly more. And if they think share prices in general are going to fall, they switch to shares with low betas, whose prices should fall less than average. This analysis can also help establish the right mix of investments for an individual, taking into account the amount of risk he or she wants to take.

General observations and personal views

Of course, you can choose your shares by your own observations. For example, you may see people spending more money in the high street and decide to invest in the retail sector, or you may read about a company you think has a good product or the right approach. Professional investors often dismiss a gut feeling about a company or market in favour of more sophisticated methods. They may make a great deal of money by taking a contrary approach: when everyone else is buying, it is time to sell.

For most individual investors, it may not be possible to get sufficient information to follow this approach for short-term trading. Careful reading of the financial press and following share price movements may give you the ability to spot when a share is 'over-bought' or 'over-sold'.

Verdict

There is no effective, reliable, proven and generally usable method of picking out which individual shares are going to be winners. All the methods described above depend, to some extent at least, on looking at how shares have fared in the past. But past performance is not a reliable guide to the future. A share can perform well for many months, then fall in value unexpectedly overnight and vice-versa.

This does not mean, however, that you cannot make a sensible choice of shares. Your *share portfolio* should reflect *your* objectives and circumstances and preferred level of risk. In broad outline, here are some guidelines:

- You need to look at shares as part of your overall financial planning.
- Decide what your objectives are, because different shares are likely to suit different objectives. For example, you may (or may not) attach importance to drawing an income from your investment.
- Decide on your time horizon for any given investment. For private investors, it is generally recommended that you hold shares for at least five years.
- Choose shares which carry the degree of risk you are willing to accept. If you want to speculate, you could invest in a collection of very risky shares and be prepared to trade short term. On the other hand, if you are investing for the long term, divide your money among the shares of a spread of companies and industries.
- Consider reducing the influence of the stock market on your total range of investments by putting some of your money into less risky options, for example, building society accounts, gilts or corporate bonds (see Chapters 12, 24 and 26). And look at the possibilities of investing some of your money overseas to give yourself a spread of geographical areas and currencies.
- In general, the best policy is likely to be *buy and hold.* Research in the USA has found that investors who switch from traditional to Internet dealing suffer a marked fall in their returns. It is thought that one reason for this is the increased frequency with which online shareholders trade. Quite apart from the greater potential for mis-timing your deals, trading in this way often increases your total dealing charges, eating into any profit you do make.

For more detailed information on choosing shares see *The Which? Guide to Shares* by Jonquil Lowe, published by Which? Books.*

Buying and selling shares

You can buy or sell shares by going to a stockbroker. A *Private Investors' Directory* is available from the Association of Private Client Investment Managers and Stockbrokers (APCIMS).* Alternatively, you can go to a bank or building society, many of whom own or have agreements with stockbroking firms. You can also buy and sell shares over the Internet (see Chapter 9). Whichever method you choose, the procedure is more or less the same.

Novice investors should probably stick to shares that are quoted in the main marketplace, i.e. those with a full listing on the London Stock Exchange.

Other market places include Techmark, also part of the overall London Stock Exchange. This specialises in stocks involved in new technologies, including telecommunications and the Internet. The London Stock Exchange also runs the Alternative Investment Market (AIM) which in effect replaced the old Unlisted Securities Market in 1995. AIM is for small companies which may not qualify for (or do not want) a full listing on the London Stock Exchange. Companies in this market are likely to be relatively new and probably represent a higher risk for investors than those quoted in the main market.

In early 2001 the London Stock Exchange gave private client stockholders direct and cheaper access to over 100 US and European stocks. This scheme is to be extended to cover the top 300 European and top 100 US stocks.

Buying shares

Suppose that you find a broker and decide to buy 600 Newco Electronics shares. You look at the share price lists in the morning paper, where Newco shares are quoted at 300p.

This price is normally the previous day's 'closing' price – the price being quoted towards the end of Stock Exchange business. The price quoted is also normally a middle price. For example, if the price for Newco is 300p, it probably means that the *offer* price (the price at which you could have bought Newco) was, say, 303p, while the *bid price* (the price at which you could have sold) was, say, 297p. The difference between the two figures is called the *spread*.

One way to place your order is simply to ring up and say, 'Buy me 600 Newco Electronics.' The broker takes this as an order to buy this number of shares at the best (i.e. cheapest) available price *now*. Or you can give the broker a *limit*. Suppose you decide the shares would be a good buy at 295p but no more. You ring up your broker and say, 'Buy me 600 Newco, at 295p or less.'

You lose nothing by setting a limit and you protect yourself from the risk of buying at a higher price than you expected. However, it is no use setting too low a limit: you waste your time and the broker's as well. Also make sure your broker knows how long you want your limit to stand – your order may be held as 'good-till-cancelled' or have a standard time limit – perhaps as long as one month or as short as the day you have placed your order.

But remember, once you have placed your order, it is too late to change your mind: you have made an unwritten and enforceable contract. For the most actively traded shares the broker contacts the Stock Exchange Electronic Trading Service (SETS), which on 20 October 1997 became the main way of trading in the shares of the UK's major companies. This 'order book system' matches buyers and sellers electronically. When first introduced, SETS did not cover small orders (for example, fewer than 500 or 1,000 shares, depending on their price) but from June 1998 even the smallest trades can be dealt with through SETS. However, if you want longer than three days (the standard settlement period for SETS trades) to settle your deal, it must be handled outside the SETS system (called dealing 'away from the book'). In that case, your broker deals directly with a market-maker (in effect, a share wholesaler, called a 'retail service provider'). Similarly, if your order is for shares not yet traded through SETS your broker deals directly with the market-makers. Remember the price the broker quotes to you does not include commission, stamp duty or other dealing costs.

At the broker's office, a contract note is made out for the shares you have bought. You should get this on the following day or soon after; check it at once to see that the details are correct. Keep this contract note safe, as evidence of what you have paid for the shares. It looks something like the example shown opposite.

Selling shares

As with buying shares, there are two kinds of order that you can give to your broker. You ring up your broker and either say 'Sell 600 Newco Electronics'; or you set a limit – 'Sell 600 Newco Electronics if the price reaches 320p.'

The contract note for a sale looks much like the contract note for a purchase. Brokers' charges usually range between 1 and 1.9 per cent on a deal of up to, say, £7,000, with a typical minimum commission of £20 or £25 but no stamp duty. Some brokers also charge a flat fee, such as £2.50 or £10, which they call a 'compliance levy'.

When the contract note for your sale has been made out, the broker sends it to you. If you still hold certificates for the shares, you complete a transfer form and return it to the broker with the certificates. If your shareholding is registered through CREST (see page 230) there are no forms to sign.

Rolling settlement

In July 1994 the settlement system changed from 'account' to 'rolling'. When rolling settlement was first introduced, the settlement date was ten working days after the transaction date (known as T+10). While many brokers still deal T+10 for private investors, the settlement period was reduced to T+3 in February 2001, and this may be reduced still further to T+1.

These shorter settlement periods mean you have to act quickly after you sell shares to return the share certificate and signed transfer form to your broker. The shares must be delivered promptly to the new owner. To make this possible, the market-maker may have to go back to the stock market and buy more shares – and can charge you the extra costs incurred. As the settlement period becomes shorter, this process, called 'buying-in', may become more frequent.

Nominee accounts

To avoid being caught out with too little time to complete the formalities of the sale of your shares, you may want to consider a 'nominee' account. If you trade through the Internet (see page 230), normally you must use the broker's nominee account.

Stockbrokers' nominee companies hold shares on your behalf. Legally the shares are yours and you are still liable for any capital gains tax payable when they are sold. The advantage is that, when you decide to sell the shares, you still get a contract note but the settlement is completed by your stockbroker transferring your shares from the nominee company. Remember, though, that stockbrokers charge you for setting up a nominee account. Particularly if you buy and sell shares only occasionally, it may be cheaper to settle transfers yourself.

ABC STOCKBROKERS AND COMPANY

A member firm of The London Stock Exchange
Regulated by The Securities and Futures Authority**

CONTRACT NOTE

UNIQUE CODE No.	DATE & TAX POINT	EXECUTED AT
6405/97Z	25 APRIL 2001	12.00

F MURRAY ESQ

WE HAVE <u>BOUGHT</u> ON YOUR BEHALF AS AGENTS,
FOR SETTLEMENT ON 2 May 2001

600	NEWCO ELECTRONICS		
	ORD £1	295P	£1,770.00*
600			£1,770.00
	TRANSFER STAMP	9.00 †	
	COMMISSION	29.21 ‡	
	TOTAL CHARGES		£38.21
	DUE TO US		£1,808.21

COMMISSION DETAILS
£1,770 AT 1.65%

signed by:

DIRECTOR

for and on behalf of ABC Stockbrokers and Company

UK RESIDENTS SHOULD RETAIN THIS CONTRACT NOTE AS
THEY MAY REQUIRE IT FOR CAPITAL GAINS TAX

BARGAIN No.	REFERENCE No.
0928	01435

Subject to the Rules and Regulations of The London Stock Exchange
including any temporary regulations made by or under the authority of
The London Stock Exchange – or The Securities and Futures Authority**

* Consideration The name sometimes given to the amount you pay for the shares (or get for them if you are selling) before the various deductions are made. In our example, the consideration is £1,770.

† Stamp duty This is the main government duty on the deal. It is charged at £5 per £1000 up to £10,000. And for amounts above £10,000 at a rate of 0.5% rounded up to the next multiple of £5. In this example, the duty is £10. There is no stamp duty when you sell shares.

‡ Commission The rate of commission varies depending on individual broker's charges and the size of the consideration (see above*).

PTM Levy If the cost of shares is £10,000 or more, an additional charge of £2 is made – this is a levy for the Panel on Takeovers and Mergers and applies on both sales and purchases.

** The Securities and Futures Authority is being absorbed into the new single regulator, the Financial Services Authority (FSA) due to take place in 2001. For a while, either name might appear on the paperwork. But, in case of problems, the regulator you should contact is the FSA.

CREST

CREST, a computerised settlement system, was developed to replace the outdated paper-based Talisman system and brought into full operation in April 1997. Trading for about 90 per cent of all stocks is settled through CREST. Rather than holding a paper certificate, you have an electronic entry in a company's share register, in much the same way that your current account is logged at your bank. When you buy or sell shares the transfer happens electronically, enabling settlement to take place very rapidly.

If you choose to keep your shareholdings in paper certificates, you need to arrange delayed settlement with your broker in order to complete the paperwork – say T+10 or even T+25. This may incur an additional charge to cover the extra administration involved.

Buying and selling through the Internet

There are two types of share-dealing service available through the Internet, both generally have lower charges than telephone ones. The first is basically an email system which merely offers another way to send your order to your broker. As with placing your order by phone, the broker gets the best price available for you but you do not generally know in advance what that price will be. You can set a limit as described above. However, the web site may also give you access to a wealth of information, such as moving share prices during the day and company reports.

You can also be linked via the web to a trading computer. This way you see the real-time share price at which you can buy or sell. If you go ahead, the deal is processed immediately and you normally get your contract note shortly after, via email. Commission for online dealing is often lower than that for traditional telephone dealing but watch out for membership or management fees.

The number of private investors trading by Internet – which has obvious benefits of lower cost, access to a wealth of information and instant dealing – has been increasing rapidly over the last year. In April 2000, around 10 per cent of all trading done by private investors was being carried out this way. But do not get carried away! Until you have some experience, it can be difficult to absorb and interpret all the information correctly. Here are some tips for dealing successfully through the Internet:

- Check the contract carefully before you sign up with an Internet broker. In particular, make sure you understand all the charges.
- Have a few practice runs before trading for real.
- Make sure you check your order before you hit the trade button.
- Make sure you hit the trade button just once – jerky finger moves can result in your buying or selling twice over.
- If you are essentially a long-term investor, do not be tempted to trade too often – dealing charges will eat into your profits.
- If you want to speculate by buying and selling often, do not risk any money you cannot afford to lose.
- Beware of 'day trading' – buying and selling large amounts of stock within the day in order to make a large profit from small price movements. This is very risky. Research in the US shows that most day traders lose money.

- Steer clear of 'margin trading' – this means paying only part of the purchase price and borrowing the rest. This magnifies your profits but, if the deal goes against you, you have to stump up extra to cover the losses, which could be large.

For more information on Internet dealing, see Chapter 9.

What the papers say

Shares pages of daily newspapers contain useful information.

Let us suppose you want to find out about Newco Electronics. The relevant section of the newspaper would look something like this:

ELECTRONIC & ELECTRICAL EQUIPMENT

	Notes	Price	+ or -	52 week high	low	Volume '000s	Yield	P/E
ABB B SKr	♣	£8⅞	+¼₆	£9⅛	£4⅞	-	1.8	22.1
Advanced Power	‡	49½	......	72½	28	-	2.5	18.9
Alba	†	310	+2½	333	165	6	2.2	15.7
ALSTOM UKDR		£18¾	......	£21¼	£11⅛	0.730	-	20.4
Amstrad	†	55¼	+¼	57	27	874	1.1	16.0
Arcolectric	♣	59	......	80¼	40	-	2.9	13.0
Arlen	♣	28xd	......	34¼	18	33	4.6	-
AromaScan		18½	-¼	19¼	3¾	400	-	-
BICC	♣	99xd	+½	182½	36½	98	6.1	24.5
Cnv Prf		105¾ xd	+¼	124	83¼	-	10.2	-
Bowthorpe		482½ xd	......	590	306½	138	2.5	17.7
Blick	♣	187½	......	460	162	10	7.9	10.9
CML Micro		92½	......	189½	69	-	7.6	8.2
Channel		4	......	15½	3½	13	-	-
Chloride	♣	79	......	79¼	39¼	237	1.5	19.5
City Technology	♣†	228½	+1	270	155	52	3.2	31.1
Critchley Grp	♣†	382½	......	912½	310	-	3.9	9.6
DRS Data Res		24	+2½	24	9½	-	-	-
Delta	♣N	154½	+2	311½	98	97	5.2	10.5
Densitron		37	......	55½	15½	-	-	-
Dewhurst A	♣	56½	......	66½	47½	-	5.6	5.4

Each column has a specific meaning:

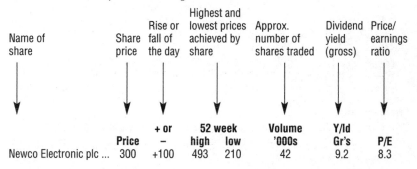

Name of share	Share price	+ or - Rise or fall of the day	52 week high low Highest and lowest prices achieved by share	Volume '000s Approx. number of shares traded	Y/ld Gr's Dividend yield (gross)	P/E Price/ earnings ratio
Newco Electronic plc ...	300	+100	493 210	42	9.2	8.3

This data is the minimum you need to decide whether or not to buy or sell shares in a listed company. What do the various indicators mean?

The share price

This is usually the previous day's closing mid-market price in pence. If these are shares traded through SETS (see pages 227–8), the closing price is a weighted average of the deals done in the last ten minutes of trading before the market closed at 4.30pm. If the shares are not traded through SETS, the closing price is that of the last deal done before the 4.30pm. close.

+ or –

The price change from the previous trading day, expressed in pence.

Volume

This shows the number of shares, to the nearest thousand, traded through the Stock Exchange Electronic Trading Service (SETS): see page 227. This shows whether any price movement has been as a result of a higher volume of activity in the market or whether, in a 'thin' market, it is largely due to market-makers changing their prices to encourage buyers and/or sellers to trade.

Dividend yield

Shareholders receive their share of the company profits as dividends. These come in the form of dividend warrants: in effect cheques, with 10 per cent deducted for tax. Dividends can also be credited direct to your bank account. Newco Electronics last year declared a post-tax dividend of 24.8p per share, the equivalent to 27.6p per share before tax. For more details of how dividends are taxed, see 'Investment income paid with tax deducted', in Chapter 10.

The dividend of 27.6p is 9.2 per cent of the share price of 300p. Therefore the *gross dividend yield* on your money is currently 9.2 per cent a year. This gives you a comparative figure for when considering other investments. Remember, though, that, in general terms, if the price rises, the yield at the new price falls.

Companies usually pay dividends twice a year (as long as they have earnings to distribute). About six to eight weeks before each dividend is paid, the company declares a dividend, i.e. announces what it is to be. A week or two later, the company's shares go *ex-dividend* (the share price is marked 'xd') and the register of shareholders is temporarily closed. The coming dividend is paid only to those people who are on the register of shareholders on the day it was closed. Anyone who buys shares in the company after they have gone ex-dividend does not get the coming dividend and if you sell your shares before they have gone ex-dividend you have to return the dividend to your broker.

Companies rarely distribute all their net profit, retaining some to finance expansion of the business.

Price/earnings ratio

When you buy shares you are acquiring the right to benefit from a corresponding share in the company's yearly stream of earnings. The price/earnings ratio (or PE ratio for short) is a way of expressing at what expense (or how cheaply) you are buying that stream of earnings.

To work out a PE ratio, first work out the earnings per share, i.e. divide the company's after-tax profits for ordinary shareholders by the number of shares. The

Newco Electronics plc

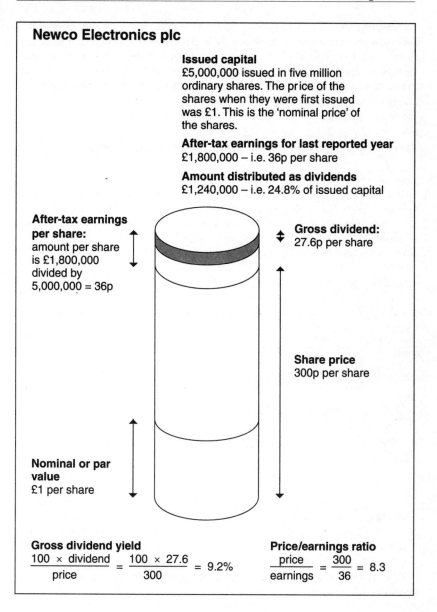

Issued capital
£5,000,000 issued in five million ordinary shares. The price of the shares when they were first issued was £1. This is the 'nominal price' of the shares.

After-tax earnings for last reported year
£1,800,000 – i.e. 36p per share

Amount distributed as dividends
£1,240,000 – i.e. 24.8% of issued capital

After-tax earnings per share: amount per share is £1,800,000 divided by 5,000,000 = 36p

Gross dividend: 27.6p per share

Share price 300p per share

Nominal or par value £1 per share

Gross dividend yield
$$\frac{100 \times \text{dividend}}{\text{price}} = \frac{100 \times 27.6}{300} = 9.2\%$$

Price/earnings ratio
$$\frac{\text{price}}{\text{earnings}} = \frac{300}{36} = 8.3$$

PE ratio is found by dividing the current market price of the share by the earnings per share.

Take our Newco Electronics example. The company's earnings in the last reported year were £1,800,000 which, since the company has five million ordinary shares, works out at 36p for each share. Each share actually costs 300p at current prices, so to buy earnings of 36p a year, you have to pay 300p. Newco Electronics has, therefore, a PE ratio of 300 divided by 36 = 8.3.

Remember that the PE ratio is not an absolute guide to the relative value of any particular share. Use it particularly to compare companies in the same industry.

Dividend cover

Some newspapers also show the *dividend cover* – i.e. how many times the company could have paid its dividend out of the profit for that year. This is usually calculated as the earnings per share divided by the net dividend per share. In the case of Newco, this comes to 36p divided by 24.8p which equals 1.45. Once again, this information is best used for the purpose of comparisons.

New issues

If a company is not quoted on a stock exchange, it may be difficult to buy or sell its shares. You have to find an individual or an organisation that is prepared to deal with you. When the company decides it wants to make a better market in its shares, it may offer shares to the public and become quoted on a stock exchange.

One method for marketing a new issue is an *offer for sale* by an *issuing house*, often a merchant bank. The issuing house puts advertisements in newspapers giving details of the company and offering a stated number of shares at a stated price (the *prospectus*). The advertisement normally includes an application form. If you want to buy some of the shares, fill in the form saying how many you want, and send it with a cheque for the value of the shares.

If the issue is over-subscribed, i.e. more shares are asked for than are on offer, the shares are allocated by the issuing house (there are a variety of ways of doing this).

A more commonly used alternative to making an offer for sale is to sell new shares through a *placing*. This means institutional investors and other market professionals are invited to take up the new shares without the shares ever being offered direct to the public.

Scrip (or bonus) issue

As a company grows, its share price may increase so much that it becomes too unwieldy to trade easily. So the company may make an extra issue of free shares to its existing shareholders. This is called a scrip or bonus issue or capitalisation. If, for example, you have 500 shares in Newco Electronics, and the share price is 300p each, your shareholding is worth £1,500. If the company makes a one-for-one scrip issue, you get another 500 shares, making 1,000 in total. But the share price instantly falls to around 150p each, so your shareholding is still worth £1,500. In practice the share price is unlikely to fall to exactly 150p.

Rights issue

Occasionally, a company may decide to raise more money from its shareholders, perhaps to finance a new investment. One option is to make a rights issue to its existing shareholders. This means the company offers the right to invest more money in exchange for new shares.

In this case, the company sends you a document, telling you what it is raising money for and enclosing an application form for new shares. Do not ignore this document – it is valuable. If you do not understand it, ask a professional adviser.

As a shareholder you have four choices:

- do nothing
- pay up
- sell your rights to the new shares on the stock market
- sell part of your rights and take up part (but remember this reduces your proportion of the company's capital).

What you do depends on whether you have the cash and, in the light of company's plans, whether you want to increase your investment.

Suppose, for example, you have 500 shares in Hightech Power and the share price is 400p each, so your holding is worth £2,000. The company makes a one-for-one rights issue at 200p each. If the company has three million shares already issued, it is raising £6 million by the rights issue (three million shares at 200p each). The market value of the company before the rights issue is £12 million; afterwards it is £18 million. The share price after the rights issue will be:

$$£18 \text{ million} \div 6 \text{ million} = £3 \text{ each}$$

If you do nothing, your 500 shares are now worth only £1,500, so on the face of it you appear to have lost £500. However, all UK companies must sell rights that have not been taken up and send you the proceeds. If you take up your rights, you agree to buy 500 new shares at 200p. So you would pay £1,000. You would then have 1,000 shares altogether. At the new market price of 300p, these would be worth £3,000. Alternatively, you can sell your rights to the new shares on the stock market – in theory, for £500. This is worked out by taking the new share price from the old one, i.e. £4 – £3 = £1 per share.

Your fourth choice is to sell part of your rights and use the proceeds to buy the rest of the new shares, maintaining the same level of investment in the company.

Mergers, demergers and takeovers

One company may decide it would like to acquire another company and it therefore offers to buy the shares from the company's shareholders. For example, suppose Hightech Power decides to take over Newco Electronics. Hightech sends you a document offering to buy your shares and giving information such as:

- what Hightech is offering in cash, its own shares or a mixture of the two
- why Hightech wants to buy Newco
- a profit forecast for Hightech
- the date on which the offer closes.

If the takeover is registered by Newco, further documents are sent to you – with the possibility of a third company intervening. You often need to consult a professional adviser but remember you have to pay fees.

Mergers come in and out of fashion. So, too, do demergers. This is where companies split their range of businesses into component parts. As a shareholder, you have no decisions to make – in place of your current shares, you are given a basket of shares in the component companies. If 'focusing' works, the new pattern of shareholding should be ultimately more profitable. But, if your are a small shareholder, you may be left with very small, and uneconomical, holdings in each of the new companies.

Other ways of investing in companies

Loan stock and debentures
Companies can raise money by issuing *company loan stock* or *debentures*. They work like gilts – a fixed rate of interest and a fixed repayment date are set for the loan. Because they are riskier than gilts, you can expect the return to be higher. For more details see Chapter 26.

A variation is *convertible loan stock*. This starts out as a loan when the company first gets the money. But the person holding the loan stock has the right to convert it or part of it into an agreed number of shares on a fixed date (or between certain dates). This means the price of the convertible loan stock rises or falls with that of the shares.

Preference shares
Some companies have *preference* shareholders, though these are becoming less common. A fixed rate of dividend is usually paid on preference shares. There are different types of these shares, which include, for example, cumulative preference or stepped preference. Each type of preference share has different terms, so check carefully before investing.

Warrants and options
High risk and specialist investments traded on the stock market include *warrants, options* and *traded options*. These are not recommended for the ordinary shareholder and are outside the scope of this book. If you are interested, seek professional advice.

Other ways of buying shares

Employee share schemes
Some employers encourage their employees to invest in the company through employee share schemes. There are currently four main types:

- **All-employee share schemes** From July 2000, employers can offer a new type of all-employee share scheme. Under the scheme, your employer can give you up to £3,000 of free shares, which may be linked to performance targets at work achieved by you personally or by a team or division to which you belong. In addition, out of your pre-tax pay you can buy up to a further £1,500 of 'partnership shares' and your employer may award up to two 'matching shares' for every partnership share you buy. Provided you keep the shares in the scheme for at least five years, you pay no income tax or National Insurance on them.

- **Approved profit-sharing schemes** These are open to all employees who have been with the company for a qualifying period (no longer than five years). A portion of the company's profits is set to buy ordinary shares, which are then allocated to employees. All employees must be eligible to participate on the same terms. The maximum one employee can get is shares with an initial value of £3,000 – or 10 per cent of earnings, if this figure is higher – with an overall cumulative limit of £8,000 per year. There is no tax to pay when the shares are allocated and, if you keep them for three years, there is no income tax to pay on the money you make from selling them. These schemes are being closed. From 5 April 2002, no new awards can be made.
- **Company Share Option Plans (CSOPs)** These give you the option to buy your company's shares at a future date(s) (usually three years) and at a set price. If the market price has risen above the option price, you make an immediate profit. Under CSOPs, provided the exercise price is not lower than the share price at the time the option is granted and the maximum value of shares is £30,000, the profit is tax-free.
- **SAYE share option schemes** Again, these are open to all employees with five years' service or more. These are the most popular schemes – most firms in the FTSE 100 offer them. They are the lowest-risk share schemes. Employees agree to pay a fixed monthly sum up to £250 (minimum £5) into a Save-As-You-Earn (SAYE) account for a set period – three, five or seven years. At the end of the period a tax-free bonus is added to your savings – which can be as high as 18 times the monthly sum after seven years – and the whole sum is available to buy shares at a pre-determined option price.

Verdict: Share option schemes are recommended – unless the company is in difficulties.

The Enterprise Investment Scheme

Under the Enterprise Investment Scheme (EIS) rules, you can claim income tax relief at 20 per cent on the amount you invest in companies up to a maximum investment of £150,000 each tax year. For more details, see page 120.

Verdict: EIS companies are likely to be risky. Only invest if you are prepared to lose the lot.

Venture Capital Trusts

An investment in a Venture Capital Trust (VCT) gives you similar tax breaks to investing through the EIS. It is less risky because a VCT has a range of investments in unquoted trading companies. The VCT itself is a quoted company, so selling your investment is likely to be much easier. For more details see page 121.

Verdict: Do not let the tax advantages alone encourage you to make a riskier investment than you would otherwise make. Look at your financial planning as a whole and seek financial advice.

Investment clubs

A growing number of people, often friends or work colleagues, club together to share their investment skills and create their own small-scale unit trust. You share profits and losses among the group. There are currently over 8,500 clubs in the UK, with numbers increasing dramatically since 1996.

Each club decides its own rules and method of dealing but the general principles are:

- Each member pays an initial lump sum into the club and thereafter an agreed monthly amount (typically £25).
- Club members meet regularly to discuss their views on the stock market.
- As the cash builds up, the club buys and sells shares selected by the members (in an agreed and democratic way).
- Each member's proportion of the fund depends on his or her payments. As members pay into the club, they are allocated units reflecting the value of the fund at the time (this system is similar to unit trusts).

Although for legal and practical reasons membership is limited to a maximum of 20 people, you may be able to join an existing club. In practice, most people who develop an interest in investment clubs start their own with friends and family.

ProShare Investment Clubs (PIC)* is a national association of investment clubs. While membership of PIC is voluntary, its manual (£29.50) gives an easy-to-read and detailed guide to how investment clubs work, with a step-by-step guide to setting up and running a club, guidance on tax and tips for avoiding potential pitfalls. PIC also publishes a quarterly newsletter for its members and runs competitions to find the best-performing clubs.

Individual Savings Accounts (ISAs) and Personal Equity Plans (PEPs)

If you buy shares through an ISA or have a PEP, remember that gains on them are tax-free and, until April 2004, you can claim the tax already deducted from dividends. See Chapter 11 for more information.

21 Unit trusts and open-ended investment companies

Since their inception in the 1960s, unit trusts have traditionally been used to invest in shares. Today some unit trusts invest in gilts and international bonds, corporate bonds, a few invest in other unit trusts. They can also be used to invest in deposits and short-term loan stock, property, futures, options and commodities or a mixture of all these investments.

For most investors, investing in a unit trust is less risky and more convenient than investing directly in shares. The paperwork is minimised and you gain the advantage of specialist advice (though that is no guarantee of success).

The return you get from a unit trust is in two parts:

- **Income** – this is made up of dividends and interest from the securities in which the unit trust invests and interest from cash on deposit. It can be either paid out to you or reinvested automatically to buy more units.
- **Capital growth** – if the price of shares in which the unit trust has invested rises, the value of your units rises too.

One benefit of using unit trusts is that the managers do not have to pay capital gains tax on any gains made within the trust – see 'Tax', on page 252.

This chapter looks at the points to consider before investing in unit trusts and the choices open to you. Then it explains how prices are calculated and what charges you can expect to pay.

The chapter also looks at alternatives to unit trusts: open-ended investment companies (OEICs), which are structured differently but offer you basically the same type of investment as unit trusts; and the even newer exchange-traded funds (ETFs), which may be a better choice in some circumstances. Another option to consider is investment trusts, which also give you a stake in a portfolio of different shares and/or other investments – see Chapter 22.

Timing your investment

Investing in unit trusts is riskier than many types of investment, for example building society accounts, because the value of your capital can fluctuate. But, although there is a chance of your losing money with a unit trust, the hope is that you get a better return. You can see from the diagrams in this chapter that investors in unit trusts have had a bumpy ride over the years. So, just like shares again, the success of an investment depends very much on when you invest and when you cash in your investment. If you invested in a typical unit trust in February 1994 and cashed in around July the same year, you would have lost about 10 per cent of your money but, if you had continued with your investment over a longer period, you would have done well. The chart on page 244 shows the average of all major UK unit trusts compared with an ordinary bank or building society savings account over the last ten years.

For the long term or short term?

There are two schools of thought about how long you should invest in a unit trust.

- You invest for a long time (at least five years) and stick pretty well to the same trust (or trusts) *or*
- You invest for a shorter time and move your money in and out of unit trusts or from trust to trust as the prospects alter.

For most small investors, the former is probably the better strategy. Generally all equity investment, either direct or via a unit trust, should be considered on a long-term basis for at least five to ten years. Switching your money in, out or between trusts, can be expensive (see 'Charges', on page 251). The longer you stay invested, the more time you have to recover the charges. Unless you are prepared to take the chance of getting the timing wrong, you should think of unit trusts as long-term investments.

Size of investment

The minimum you can invest in most unit trusts varies between £250 and £1,500 or, for regular saving, from £10 to £100 a month.

Which unit trust to choose

The diagram on page 245 shows how the outcome of an investment in unit trusts can vary depending on the trust you choose. (For example the performance of the average UK unit trust has been significantly different to the average Japanese trust.) No magic formula exists to tell you which trust will do best – several popular systems are tested later on in this chapter. And you cannot automatically expect that an investment adviser or newspaper can pick a trust which is going to perform well. But the step-by-step guide below should help you narrow down the choices.

Different investment strategies

From June 1999, the Association of Unit Trusts and Investment Funds (AUTIF)* has implemented a major reclassification of unit trusts and OEICs to make it easier for investors to compare competing funds. The main change has been to adopt two main categories: trusts designed for growth; and trusts providing income. AUTIF reviews the classifications regularly and made further minor changes from April 2000. The different categories of trust are listed below:

Growth Funds
Capital Protection
UK Money Markets
Guaranteed/Protected
Capital Growth/Total Return
UK All Companies
UK Smaller Companies
**Japan
**Japan Smaller Companies
**Far East including Japan
**Far East excluding Japan
**North America
**Latin America
**North America Smaller
  Companies
**Europe including UK
**Europe excluding UK
**Europe Smaller Companies
*Cautious managed
*Balanced managed
*Active managed
*Global Growth

*Global Emerging Markets
UK Equity & Bond
*Global Equity & Bond

Income Funds
Immediate income
UK Gilts
UK Corporate Bond
UK Other Bond
Money Market
*Global bonds
*Managed Income
UK Equity and Bond Income
Growing income
UK Equity Income
*Global Equity Income

Specialist Funds
Specialist
Property
*Pension Funds
Index 'Bear' Fund

* These funds invest in a range of stock markets across the globe.
** These funds invest in a specific region.

In addition, there are several types of fund which are all included in the relevant sector above but may also be separated out into one of the following groups:

Fund of funds
UK large capitalisation (cap)
  companies
UK mid cap companies
Ethical
Institutional

Index trackers
Index-linked bond
Technology and Telecoms
Recovery and special situations
Futures and options

These categories help to divide some thousand unit trusts into comparable groups. Before you invest, you need to check which category the fund falls into. The name of the fund helps identify some differences but you need to check the specific details before you buy. Some are explained below. (Further changes to the classifications are planned for later in 2001.)

UK All Companies
These are the most popular types of unit trusts (often called 'general' funds). At least 80 per cent of their assets must be in UK shares and the main aim of each fund is capital growth. However, they usually provide income as well which you can either receive or reinvest.

Index tracker funds

As the name implies, these are designed to track a particular stock market index. Most tracker funds follow the UK market and are measured against either the FTSE All Share Index or the FTSE 100 Index. There are others which track overseas markets. Under the AUTIF classification system, tracker funds are allocated to the relevant sector. For example, funds tracking the FTSE 100 or FTSE All Share Index can be found in the UK All Companies sector described above and a tracker following the Dow Jones Index in the North America sector.

Trackers can never exactly track their chosen index, because of management charges and dealing costs, but they do offer a share-based fund without any intervention by fund managers. As a result, the management charges tend to be lower.

Research published by *Which?* shows that around three-quarters of all 'active' UK trusts consistently underperform a benchmark such as the FTSE All Share Index over a five year period. Even fewer beat the index consistently over the longer term. So, unless this track record is reversed, you are probably better off choosing a tracker fund. Some active trusts have performed consistently better than the average, and you may want to try to spot these. If you have a lump sum of, say, £1,500 or more to invest, you should look at investing in Exchange Traded Funds (ETFs) as an alternative to a tracker unit trust or OEIC – see page 255.

Equity Income funds

These funds are often called *High Yield, Extra Income* and the like. They invest at least 80 per cent of their assets in UK shares and aim to provide a yield which is more than 10 per cent above the yield of the FTSE All Share Index.

Managed funds

These funds invest in a range of different assets and stock markets around the world. So they may include a combination of bonds, cash and investments in UK and international stock markets. Under the AUTIF classification, they are divided into three sectors. Funds in the Active Managed sector allow the manager discretion to invest the whole fund in shares but at least one-tenth of the assets must be in non-UK shares. In the Balanced Managed sector, only up to 85 per cent of the fund can be invested in shares; once again, at least 10 per cent must be in non-UK shares and at least half the assets must be denominated in sterling or euros. Funds in the Cautious Managed fund are restricted to a maximum 60 per cent in shares; again at least half must be denominated in sterling or euros; there is no requirement to hold non-UK shares.

Small companies

As the name suggests, these funds invest in smaller companies. For example, in the UK Smaller Companies sector, at least 80 per cent of the fund must be invested in companies included in the FTSE Small Cap Index or have a market capitalisation less than that required for the index. Smaller companies can be more risky, matched by better potential for long-term growth.

Equity and Bond funds

As the name suggests, these funds invest in a mixture of shares and bonds, including gilts, preference shares and loan stock. Because bonds tend to be a lower-risk investment than equities, these funds can be attractive to investors who are not prepared to invest in a pure equity product. Equity and bond funds usually produce a higher income than an equity income and growth fund; some invest for high income.

International funds

Some general funds (often called *international funds*) invest in several different stock markets around the world, so the fortune of your investment is not so tightly tied to the UK stock market. This means the overall performance of the fund should be more stable than one investing only in the UK stock market. However, international funds are subject to an additional risk: currencies can fluctuate as well as share prices.

Specialist sector funds

These funds invest in particular industries, such as financial or energy. The aim is *long-term capital growth*, but there may be wider than average day-to-day price fluctuations. Managers are warning you that you could be in for a bumpy ride.

Specialist regional funds

These unit trusts invest in certain overseas stock markets, usually Europe, Japan, the US, Hong Kong, Singapore and Australia. A typical fund might aim to achieve growth of capital through investment in the Far East in countries such as Japan, Hong Kong, Australia and Singapore.

You should not expect specialist regional funds to move in line with the UK stock market. The Japanese and other Far Eastern economies, for example, have shown both excellent and disastrous performance over the last ten years. This is why specialist regional funds often appear at the top and the bottom of tables showing unit trust performance.

Note that funds that invest overseas are also affected by the caprices of the currency market – the unit price of an overseas trust tends to rise if the exchange rate of the pound goes down, fall if the exchange rate of the pound goes up.

Funds of funds

Not a very common type of fund, but one to be careful of because of the charges. The idea behind 'funds of funds' is that one unit trust invests in other unit trusts, with the aim of providing a managed investment for more cautious investors. With over 1,000 unit trusts to choose from, there is a good argument for leaving the selection to a professional fund manager. There are rules about how such unit trusts can be invested. They cannot invest in another fund of funds and must invest in at least five unit trusts. There are no limits on management charges, but charges in both tiers of the fund must be disclosed. These funds cannot make an initial charge but you still have to pay this when it invests in other unit trusts. However, the managers of funds of funds are allowed to make a yearly charge.

These two levels of charges mean that returns may be reduced. However, since

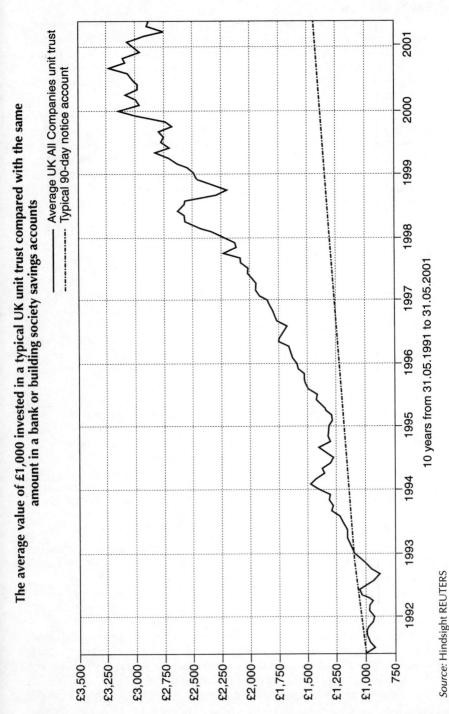

The average value of £1,000 invested in a typical UK unit trust compared with the same amount in a bank or building society savings accounts

—— Average UK All Companies unit trust
-·-·-·- Typical 90-day notice account

10 years from 31.05.1991 to 31.05.2001

Source: Hindsight REUTERS

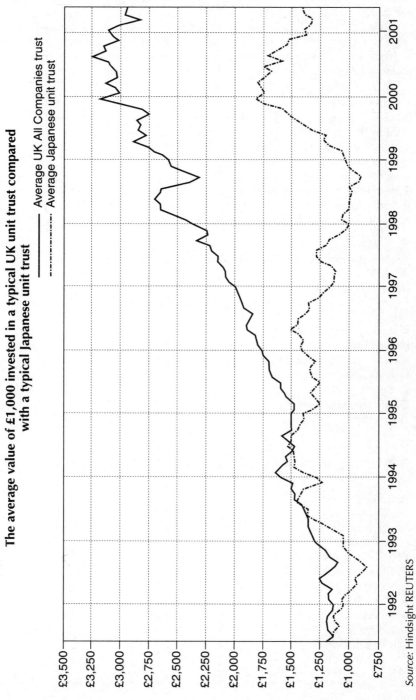

The average value of £1,000 invested in a typical UK unit trust compared with a typical Japanese unit trust

—— Average UK All Companies trust
·–·– Average Japanese unit trust

Source: Hindsight REUTERS

245

funds of funds spread your investment among a number of trusts, risk is also reduced.

Some OEICs include umbrella funds investing in a wide range of subfunds. You buy into the umbrella fund and, without first selling your shares, must be allowed to switch from one subfund to another. This can be useful if you want the freedom to alter your investment strategy from time to time.

Verdict: which type of fund?

To select the right type of fund for your needs you must consider whether you want income or capital gain, how much risk you are prepared to take and how long you want to invest for. Remember, if you are not willing or able to take any risk, keep your money in a safe, savings-based account. If you want to invest for a short time (say, one to three years) and are looking for a higher income, stick with a money-market or bond fund. If you are investing for longer (at least three years) and are prepared to take some risks, consider a bond or balanced fund. If you are investing for at least five years look at equity funds which offer you the right

Best- and worst-performing unit trusts and OEICs over five years

Name of fund	Average annual growth	value now of £1,000 invested*
Best performers		
Fidelity American	32.39%	£4,070.14
Solus UK Special Situations	29.75%	£3,680.64
INVESCO Inst North American	24.54%	£2,997.98
CF BioTech	23.38%	£2,860.16
Close Beacon Investment	23.25%	£2,846.04
TU European	22.45%	£2,754.71
Fidelity American Special Situations	22.17%	£2,723.34
Marlborough Special Situations	22.06%	£2,711.10
Threadneedle Amer Select Gth C1	21.69%	£2,669.72
Exeter Capital Growth	21.18%	£2,614.33
Worst performers		
Old Mutual Asian	−10.06%	£588.46
Baring Japan Growth	−11.00%	£558.35
Baring Eastern	−11.18%	£552.59
HSBC Asian Growth	−11.19%	£552.20
Merrill Lynch Pacific	−11.85%	£532.03
Friends Prov Asian Growth	−12.15%	£523.12
Schroder Seoul	−12.32%	£517.99
Scot Widows South East Asia	−13.21%	£492.38
Fidelity ASEAN	−13.87%	£473.68
Old Mutual Thailand	−28.33%	£188.92

Over five years to 1 April 2001.

*Calculated on a buy-to-sell basis with net income reinvested.

balance of income and capital gain for your needs. Investing in overseas unit trusts entails currency risk (see Chapter 4), so start off with UK-based unit trusts. Only consider specialist funds if you have other investments and are prepared to take a higher risk.

How to choose a unit trust

There is no magic recipe for choosing a unit trust. Past performance is no guide to the future, but it may be sensible to choose a trust which has performed consistently well over the long term and, if possible, through different economic conditions. Here is our guidance on favourite theories for picking a winner which financial advisers and newspaper tipsters may use. The verdicts are general: there are always exceptions to a rule.

'Small funds do best'
We looked at how all UK trusts had performed over four-year and nine-year periods. The results showed that you could rely on neither large funds nor small funds to be consistently good performers; but small funds tended to move more in line with UK stock markets than larger funds.

Verdict: Size is not a particularly useful criterion for picking a unit trust.

'Go for last year's winners'
We looked at the performance of all UK trusts over five 12-month periods and found no evidence that, just because they had done well in the past, the trusts would do well in the future. The table of the best- and worst-performing trusts over a five-year period illustrates at least one reason why this should be the case – the best *and* worst performance should come from the highest-risk funds, i.e. the specialist funds.

Verdict: Past performance never points you to the next year's winners. Use past performance only to find those trusts that have above-average performance in the long term.

'Go for last year's losers'
When we tested the theory, consistent investment in previous years' losers (over five years) looked to be a good way of losing money. The results were more promising when we invested in the bottom five and held them for five years. But, again, by concentrating on those trusts with extreme performance (in this case extremely bad performance) you end up with specialist trusts.

Verdict: Unless you are prepared to take the risk, avoid the trusts that produce extreme performance (good or bad).

'New is best'
We looked at new trusts launched each year over a five-year period in each unit trust sector and compared them with other trusts in the particular sector. There was an initial benefit which did not last.

Verdict: A newly launched trust may have some initial benefit compared with others in its sector. It is not guaranteed (and it may not compare well with unit trusts in other sectors).

'Pick a management company'

We looked at trusts managed by companies with at least five trusts, and measured their performance over one, five and 17 years. There was no evidence that good performance in one period means good performance in the next.

Verdict: A unit trust's performance could change because the individual manager of the fund has changed. If you do believe in going for the 'best' managers, you need to keep a very close eye on developments. Some surveys estimate that, on average, a fund manager stays with the same trust for only three years.

'Look for investments in small companies'

Some evidence from studying the UK and US stock markets supports this view. However, we looked at trusts whose names suggested that they specialised in this sort of investment. Only over the longest period at which we looked (17 years) was there the possibility that investing in smaller companies improved performance by comparison with other similar trusts. Recent evidence is that small-company trusts lag behind those investing in medium and large companies.

Verdict: The only evidence to back up this theory is over the very long term.

A step-by-step guide to choosing a unit trust

Although there is no certain way of choosing the unit trust that will perform best, you can narrow down your choice among the bewildering number available by following the steps below. But be warned – it is a long job. You could ask advisers to do it for you – see page 250.

Step 1 Make sure a unit trust really is a suitable investment for you – see Chapters 1 to 3. Bear in mind that the success of your investment depends very much on when you buy and when you sell.

Step 2 Work out how much risk you are prepared to take with your investment. You may decide to invest in more than one trust, in which case decide what level of risk you want to take for each amount.

Step 3 Decide which types of fund to go for. You may want to consider a fund that holds cash, a tracker fund or bonds, particularly as corporate bonds are allowable for Individual Savings Accounts (ISAs) – see 'Equity and Bond funds', on page 243.

Step 4 Do you want to invest a lump sum or a regular amount each month?

Step 5 Find out when you can deal. With a few unit trusts you cannot deal daily and this may be inconvenient.

Step 6 Still left with lots of unit trusts to choose from? Look at the different management and fund performance figures, and compare charges. Taking these factors together should narrow your choice.

Step 7 If you are still undecided, look at the investments the funds hold. Ask the company to send you the manager's report and the scheme particulars.

Getting information
From the company
If you want information about a unit trust, ask to see the latest *manager's report* and the *scheme particulars*. The content of each of these documents is laid down by the Financial Services Authority (FSA) – see Chapter 6. The scheme particulars have to be revised once a year, or more frequently if a major change occurs in the unit trust. The managers of the unit trust have to produce a report every six months. From these two documents you should be able to find out most of what you want to know.

The manager's report should, among other things, tell you what the objectives of the fund are, how the fund has done over the last six months, how much income will be paid out and what changes have occurred in the investments. It should also include information about the highest buying and lowest selling prices for the last ten years (or, if less, since the fund began).

The scheme particulars give the name and address of the manager, the trustee, the investment adviser for the fund (if there is one), the auditor and the registrar (if there is one). You can also read about the fund's investment policy, what, if any, the borrowing powers of the fund are, and details of its valuation, the charges and expenses of the fund.

From newspapers and magazines
Daily prices of most unit trusts are listed in several newspapers. An entry might look like this:

Westover income 494.8 523.2 0.3 3.83.

This tells you the name of the unit trust and (in the order above) yesterday's selling price, (494.8), yesterday's buying price (523.2), how much the price has changed since the previous day (0.3) and the yield (3.83) – see 'Size of income', on page 252. Once a week the initial charge is shown as a percentage of the price.

Magazines such as *Money Management,** *What Investment** and *Moneywise** give other details, for example what £1,000 invested five years ago is worth now.

You can get an information pack from the Unit Trust Information Service, run by the Association of Unit Trusts and Investment Funds (AUTIF).*

Internet sites
Many fund managers now have Internet sites from which you can get details of their unit trusts and even invest. Fund supermarket web sites give detailed information about a wide range of different trusts and facilities for online investment. If you simply want to compare performance and risk ratings, try *www.micropal.com* or one of the many personal finance web sites carrying this data. To find web sites about unit trusts, visit *www.find.co.uk* (a directory of many financial web sites) or use a search engine.

From investment advisers
In Chapter 7 we looked at sources of professional advice, many of which help you in choosing unit trusts. But remember that it is up to you to evaluate their advice.

Both independent advisers and unit-trust company representatives can sell you unit trusts, generally on commission.

If you buy from one of these groups as a result of a recommendation, you have the right to cancel the investment within 14 days of receiving a notice of your rights. This is discussed in more detail in Chapter 6. What you get back is the price you would have paid if you had bought on the day you decided to cancel, plus the initial charge.

Investing in unit trusts

Units
When you invest in a unit trust you buy units directly from the management company. When you cash your investments, you sell units back to the management company (it *has* to buy them from you). The management company puts the cash you pay for units into the fund and it is used to buy investments, such as shares.

Prices
A unit trust has two prices. These prices are based on the value of the investments in the trust fund which is usually calculated once a day. The higher price (the buying price) is what you pay to buy units. The lower price (the selling price) is what you get if you sell units. You usually buy or sell at the price worked out when the fund is next valued (called the *forward* price), which means that, as with shares, you do not know the exact price until the deal is done. But some funds deal at the *historic* price – the price calculated when the fund was last valued. Others may use a mixture of forward and historic pricing. In this case, if the valuation is done at noon, deals done in morning and afternoon use that price as forward or historic respectively.

Prices are worked out using a method set out in the FSA's rules. To arrive at the offer price, the company finds out the best available price it would have to pay to buy the investments currently in the unit trust fund. It adds dealing costs, accrued income less charges and management expenses. This sum divided by the number of units the trust has issued gives the maximum offer price the company can charge.

The lowest bid price, i.e. the price the company has to pay you for your units, is worked out in a similar way. Again, the company must use the best available price for the investments in the unit trust fund.

The difference between these two prices is called the *spread*. A typical spread for actively managed trusts is around 6 per cent, which includes initial charges; tracker funds and bond funds will have a much smaller spread.

Actual deals can depend on their size or volume – with unit trust managers charging or bidding at the top or bottom of the permitted range. So, for example, if many unit-holders are selling, the management company can shift the unit prices downwards to discourage selling and attract buyers. One consumer safeguard is that the company cannot alter the pricing basis mid-way through the dealing period.

Buying and selling

As with shares, you can buy or sell over the telephone or Internet, by letter or through a company representative or independent adviser. Note that an order over the telephone is just as binding as one made in writing. If the fund is dealing only at the prices worked out at the next valuation, you can, of course, set a limit on the price you are prepared to pay for units or accept if you sell them.

If you are selling, once the unit trust manager has received your unit trust certificate or other relevant evidence of ownership, you get the money in five days.

Charges

There are three different sorts of charges. These are:

- **initial charge** – often 5 per cent and included in the spread between the bid and offer prices. Some companies have cut their initial charge to as little as 1 per cent; others have dropped it in favour of an exit charge. Tracker funds and bond funds tend to have much lower initial charges.
- **annual management charge** – often in the range 1 per cent to 1.5 per cent a year, but can be higher, especially if the initial charge is low. This charge is usually taken from the income of the fund. The trust deeds allow some funds, after giving the required notice, to raise charges to 2 per cent or 2.5 per cent.
- **exit charges** – often 4 per cent if selling within the first year, reducing to 0 per cent if you hold the units for three or four years.

Management of the unit trust

There may be three groups of people involved. A management company handles the administration and advertising. An investment adviser – usually from the same company though sometimes from an independent stockbroker – decides how the fund should be invested. Third is the trustee (see below).

Under the Financial Services Act (see Chapter 6), there is a procedure for handling complaints about unit trusts. Contact the unit-trust company first. If you are not satisfied with the company's resolution of your complaint, the manager refers you either to the office of the Investment Ombudsman* or the Personal Investment Authority (PIA) Ombudsman Bureau*. These Ombudsman schemes are being absorbed into the new Financial Ombudsman Service*.

Trustees

For investors, the benefit of trustees is that they are independent of the management and hold the assets of the fund in trust for the unit-holders. This means that if anything happens to the management company the assets of the fund are safe-guarded. Over a dozen companies, mainly banks, act as trustees to hundreds of different unit trusts.

Trustees have several roles. First, the trustee keeps all the cash and investments of the fund in its name.

Second, the trustee makes sure that the managers stick to the terms of the trust deed and the scheme particulars – see above. The trust deed includes the following information:

- the name of the fund and its investment aim
- the currency of the fund
- when income of the fund is paid out.

Third, the trustee checks that the unit-price calculation has been done correctly and cancels and creates units.

Finally, the trustee checks that the management company is operating within FSA regulations.

Income

There are two different types of units a trust can issue, reflecting the needs of different investors:

- distribution or income units
- accumulation units.

With distribution or income units, investments held in the unit trust fund receive income in the form of share dividends, interest from gilts, and so on. The management company takes its regular charge from the income and usually pays out what is left to unit-holders in the form of *distributions*. If it is not paid out, the money is reinvested through the fund for the benefit of the unit-holders. There are usually two distributions a year with some trusts paying quarterly or monthly.

With accumulation units, the unit price is simply increased to reflect the amount of income retained.

With many unit trusts, you can buy either type of unit.

Tax

Dividend distributions from a unit trust come with a *tax credit*. The effect is that if you are a starting-rate or basic-rate taxpayer there is no income tax to pay on the distribution. If you pay tax at the higher rate, you have to pay more tax through your annual self-assessment. If you are a non-taxpayer, you cannot claim tax back.

Unit trusts investing largely in gilts, bonds or cash funds pay *interest distributions* rather than *dividend distributions*. Interest distributions are paid with tax at the savings rates already deducted. Again, you get a tax credit.

While there is no capital gains tax liability when managers sell shares *within* the funds, the normal capital gains tax rules apply to unit-trust investments – see Chapter 10 for details.

Size of income

If you are buying a unit trust as a way of getting an income, look at the *yield* of the fund. The higher the yield, the higher the income you receive.

To calculate the yield, the amount of the distribution per unit is divided by the unit price. This is then multiplied by 100 to give a percentage. For example, if the distribution per unit is 3p and the unit price 60p, the yield is $3 \div 60 \times 100 = 5$ per cent.

Of course, if you were to buy units when the price was lower, say 50p, the yield on your investment would be $3 \div 50 \times 100 = 6$ per cent.

Note that the yield usually quoted is gross of 20% tax.

Stabilising your income from unit trusts

Unit-trust prices, like shares, go up and down. To provide stability of income, some unit-trust companies have *withdrawal schemes* that allow you to receive income either as:

- a percentage, say 5 per cent, of the original amount you invest, so you can be certain you get the same income each year, *or*
- a percentage, say 5 per cent, of the current value of your investment. In this case, the income would still go up and down each year and can only be stabilised by buying or selling units. This is generally not recommended.

If you decide a withdrawal scheme could be useful, you need to check the minimum investment which can be as high as £15,000.

Some unit-trust groups organise regular income schemes, where you invest in three or more unit trusts, each with a different month for paying income. In this way, you can get a regular, if varying, monthly income.

Size of investment

For lump-sum investments, all unit trusts ask for a minimum investment when you first invest – usually not less than £250. If you want to increase your investment, you can usually do so by smaller amounts.

Some unit-trust companies will let you invest a regular amount, such as £25 a month. This is known as a *savings plan*.

One advantage of a savings plan sometimes cited is *pound-cost averaging*. What this seems to show is that you can get a bargain by investing regularly. If the unit price goes up and down, the average cost of your units will be less than the average of unit prices – when the unit price is low your fixed sum of money buys more units than when it is high. But there is nothing magic about this, it just shows the advantage of not having to worry about timing your investment correctly. And do not forget you still have to worry about when you should cash in your investment.

If you already hold shares, you could swap these for units through a *share-exchange scheme*. The unit-trust company will usually do one of two things with your shares:

- Put them in one of its funds, if the fund already holds that company's shares. In this case, in exchange for the shares, the company may give you units equal to the price it would have to pay that day through the stock market. As this is more than you would raise selling the shares yourself, this seems to be a good saving.
- Similarly, if the company does not want to put them in a fund, the company often pays the selling costs.

Most unit-trust companies have these share-exchange schemes. But do not let quite small savings push you into a poorly performing unit trust.

Cost of switching

With the growth of more and more specialist funds and specialist advisers, an increasing number of companies lets you switch your investment from one trust to another for a lower-than-normal initial charge. This can reduce the initial charge to as little as one per cent.

Open-ended Investment Companies (OEICs)

From January 1997 investment managers have been able to sell a new type of collective investment scheme called an OEIC (pronounced 'oik'). These funds are neither unit trusts nor investment trusts but are similar to both. An OEIC is a company rather than a trust (as an investment trust is) but it can issue (or cancel) new shares like a unit trust and is covered by similar investor protection rules.

Most differences between an OEIC and the other types of trusts are technical and make little difference to investors. With OEICs it is considered necessary for UK fund managers to sell their funds on the same terms as other continental or US-managed funds, thereby opening their markets to international investers.

Pricing
One area where OEICs differ is in the way they are priced. Like other continental investment funds, they are traded on a single price for both buyers and sellers. Managers' charges or dealing commissions are shown separately.

The single price is based on a valuation of the fund, as with a unit trust (but without any price leeway for the bid/offer spread). This is unlike an investment trust, where the price is dictated by supply and demand for its shares. The OEIC's single price is simpler to understand and its charges are more transparent.

Which type of fund?
Once you have decided to invest in a collective fund, your decision should still be dictated, to a major extent, by the underlying investments rather than the fund structure. Use the step-by-step guide in this chapter to help you. Only once you know what type of investment you want, should you consider which kind of fund you should buy. What is available limits your choice.

Conversion from other trusts
Many of the major unit-trust companies have already converted their range of trusts to OEICs and more plan to do so in the future. As an existing investor, you will be consulted on this change and my be able to refuse permission. If conversion does happen, there is unlikely to be any major difference in the way your unit trust performs. But check the information you receive from the fund carefully before making your decision, particularly if the conversion includes a change in the investment aims and objectives.

Where can you buy them?
Like unit trusts, you can buy OEICs directly from the fund manager. If the manager has elected to list the company on the London Stock Exchange, you can also buy them there. If you have any doubts about the new OEICs, consult an independent financial adviser.

Exchange Traded Funds (ETFs)

In April 2000, the first Exchange Traded Fund (ETF) went on sale in the UK. An ETF is a tracker fund (see page 242) which is set up as a company, with shares bought and sold on a stock exchange.

ETFs are different from Investment trusts (see Chapter 22). Like unit trusts, they are open-ended funds. This means that ETF shares are created or cancelled to meet changes in demand.

Pricing

Because the size of the ETF varies, its price is not affected by the relative weight of buyers and sellers (as is the case with an investment trust. So the ETF behaves more like a unit trust or OEIC, with the price reflecting the value of the investments in the fund.

Which type of fund?

To date ETFs have all been tracker funds and, at the time of writing, the only ETF so far launched in the UK tracks the FTSE 100 Index. However, plans exist to launch further funds tracking a wider range of indices – some experts predicted that this could be as many as 80 ETFs by the end of 2001, but by mid-2001 only 7 had been launched in the UK. Fund managers are also looking at the possibility of launching non-trackers (in other words actively managed) ETFs.

How can you buy them?

You buy ETFs like any other stocks and shares.

What do they cost?

The big advantage ETFs have over other types of investment fund is their low-charging structure. In the USA, they have become very popular, with large volumes of ETF shares traded every day. As a result, the spread between the buying and selling price of the shares has been driven to as little as 0.1 per cent. UK ETFs are expected to have low spreads too.

In addition because ETFs are tracker funds, they have low management costs. As a result, the annual management charge is as low as 0.35 per cent of the fund per year for the UK's first ETF. This makes them competitive, though some tracker unit trusts and OEICs also have charges at or below this level.

The main drawback is that, like other shares, you have to pay dealing charges to a broker – see page 251. This makes small purchases – below, say, £1,500 – uneconomic.

Who should consider ETFs?

ETFs are definitely worth thinking about as a competitively priced alternative to other types of investment fund. But if you have only a small lump sum to invest or want to save regular small sums, stick to unit trusts or OEICs – or consider investment trust savings schemes (see Chapter 22).

22 Investment trusts

Investment trusts, like unit trusts, are a way of investing in shares, gilts, bonds and property throughout the world. An investment trust can hold a number of different types of investment in a range of industries and countries.

Unlike unit trusts, are investment trusts are investment funds set up as limited companies and floated on the London Stock Exchange. When an investment trust is created, its shares are sold to investors in the usual way. The money raised is solely used to buy shares, bonds, property and other investments. The investment trust's Memorandum and Articles and prospectus – the documents that set up the company – specify the investments the trust can invest in and the return it aims to make.

You can invest in investment trusts for income, capital growth or both. Holders of investment-trust shares receive dividends from their shares and, as the value of the fund rises, the value of the shares should also rise. Some types of share pay very small dividends, some in a split-capital trust (see page 259) are designed to provide no dividends at all, so not all types of investment-trust shares trusts are suitable for investors looking for an income. Equally, some types of investment-trust shares are not suitable for investors who want growth.

Investment trusts are like unit trusts or shares in that the value of your investment can fall as well as rise.

Investment trusts versus unit trusts

When it comes to choosing between unit trusts (see Chapter 21) and investment trusts, there are a number of differences to consider. Investment trusts are *closed-end* funds. This means that, once an investment trust is created, the number of shares is fixed and cannot be altered (except in the case of a rights or scrip issue – see Chapter 20). The money raised forms the trust's capital and investors cannot add to or take money from the trust's capital. The value of the investment trust's shares depends entirely on the demand for its shares. This is very different from a unit trust, whose managers create units when you want to buy them and buy units back from you when you want to sell them.

Pricing

This difference between unit trusts and investment trusts has important consequences for the way the trusts are priced. Unit trusts are priced according to the value of the assets they hold. The price of investment-trust shares is determined by supply and demand for them on the stock market.

A low demand could pull the price of the shares down to a level that does not reflect the full value of the invesments held by the trust. In fact, most investment-trust shares tend to sell at a price below the *net asset value* of the trust. This is known as a *discount to net asset value*. Occasionally, the shares of very popular investment trusts sell for more than the *net asset value*. This price is *at a premium*.

The discount or premium moves in an unpredictable way and varies over time, from sector to sector and trust to trust. For example, in March 2001 the average discount in the UK Growth and UK Growth and Income sectors was around 10 per cent. In the UK Smaller Companies trusts, it was 14 per cent. But in the UK High Income there was a premium of 12 per cent.

Discounts can be bad news for the investor if the discount increases during the time you hold the shares. If, for example, you buy shares in an investment trust at the launch (when there is no discount), you may find, when you come to sell your shares, that they are trading at a discount, thus preventing you from realising the full capital value of the underlying assets. However, over the long term the movement in discounts generally has a smaller effect compared to the change in the price of the trust's share.

The Association of Investment Trust Companies (AITC)* publishes information about the net asset value and discounts of most investment trusts. Discounts and premiums to net asset value are also commonly published in share listings in newspapers and magazines.

Selling assets

Another important difference between unit and investment trusts may be seen when stock market values are falling rapidly. As unit-trust investors rush to cash in their investments, managers have to sell assets to pay back the investors. As the stock market is spiralling downwards, managers may have to sell the best shares first. This can accentuate the downward spiral both of the market itself and of the units held by investors.

In the same circumstances, investment-trust managers are under less pressure to sell their investments and can take a more strategic view.

Borrowing money

Because investment trusts are companies, they can borrow money on behalf of their investors. Unit trusts are not allowed to do this. When an investment trust invests borrowed money, the result is known as *gearing*.

Gearing is a double-edged sword. If the investments bought with the borrowed money produce a greater return than the interest payments, the additional return makes the assets owned by shareholders rise more quickly. But the opposite can also be the case. If share prices generally start falling, a heavily geared trust – i.e. one which has borrowed large amounts of money – can quickly fall in value.

Most investment trusts involve some degree of gearing. The amount an investment trust has borrowed can be seen in the trust's annual report. The AITC publishes information on the level of gearing for most investment trusts.

Costs

The costs of investing in a unit trust are fixed by the trust managers and usually consist of an initial charge of, say, 5 per cent plus an annual charge of between 1 and 1.5 per cent. The costs of investing in an investment trust vary according to how you buy. Unless you buy very few investment-trust shares, the cost of commission is almost certainly less than the charges made by a unit trust.

However, to make a fair comparison you also need to take into account the cost of the *spread* i.e. the difference between the lower *bid* price at which you can sell shares and the higher *offer* price which you can buy them. Just like shares in other listed companies and unit trusts, the spread represents a cost to the person investing in the shares. In addition to day-to-day movements, the spread in investment-trust share prices is generally related to the size of the trust, the liquidity of shares (that is, how easy and often shares are traded and popularity. Regularly traded) shares tend to have smaller spreads.

This means that it is hard to say whether investment trusts are cheaper or more expensive than unit trusts. While the spread for a popular investment trust would probably be less than 1 per cent, it could easily be as high as 10 per cent for shares traded infrequently. Always check first.

Reinvesting income

Unit trusts usually let you to reinvest the income from your investment directly back into the unit trust. If you are investing solely for capital growth, this is particularly useful. Investment trusts do not have this facility, unless you buy shares through a saving scheme, an existing PEP or an ISA, where some managers allow it.

Specialisation

Unit trusts can be set up at little cost and promoted much more easily than investment trusts. This explains the wide range of unit trust open to investors.

Investment trusts require a full stock-market flotation, which is expensive and subject to vigorous regulation. As a result there are fewer of them.

Different types of investment trusts

Investment trusts, like unit trusts, break down into many different types of investment specialisation, for example:

- **Global** – with less than 80 per cent of assets in any one geographical area and at least 20 per cent of assets in UK-registered companies. Global trusts break down into four varieties: growth, growth and income, smaller companies and high income.
- **UK** – with at least 80 per cent of assets in UK-registered companies. Like the global trusts, they are divided into growth, growth and income, smaller companies and high income.

Other categories cover North America, Japan, the Far East, Europe, emerging markets, Latin America, and non-geographical specialisations including biotechnology, life sciences, endowment policies and financial products.

Split-capital investment trusts

Split-capital trusts are a variation on traditional investment trusts. They enable you to tailor investment returns more closely to your particular financial goals.

In a split-capital investment trust, different classes of shares give different kinds of returns. In the simplest form, the trust is divided between *income shares* and *capital shares*. People with income shares receive all the income from the fund, people with capital shares receive all the capital growth. Investors can buy both income and capital shares.

So that investors in the capital shares can be certain of realising the full value of their investment, split-capital trusts are wound up at the end of a fixed period; otherwise the price of capital shares might be constantly at a discount, preventing investors from getting back their return.

The maximum life of these trusts is usually no more than ten years and you can buy shares on the stock market with less time to go until wind-up. So capital shares can be useful for medium-term financial goals, for example paying for your children's education, but not for long-term goals, such as building up a retirement fund.

Income shares will produce a higher income than other shares. And if the fund grows, the income produced will also grow. This may also result in the price of the shares rising, giving investors some capital growth if they sell their shares on the stock market. However, at the end of the term the trust pays back only a predetermined sum – sometimes less than the original amount invested. Some income shares pay back a proportion of capital growth, others a token penny. Consider carefully what the income shares are offering. It may look as if you are getting a very high current yield, or income, but this may be at the expense of an in-built capital loss.

The income from income shares is not guaranteed – it may be higher one year and fall back the next. Preference shares offer you more certainty. They pay a fixed income (provided the trust earns enough to pay the promised amount, which will usually be the case) which is paid before any dividends to other shareholders. Stepped preference shares pay an income which is set to increase year by year. Preference shares also receive a pre-set amount of capital when the trust is wound up – again before any capital can be distributed to other shareholders.

Capital shares behave very much like heavily geared investments. This means that, when the market is rising, they rise much more quickly than other investments. The reverse is the case when the market is falling. This makes them a risky investment over the short term. But if you are investing for capital growth over the longer term, capital shares in an investment trust are worth considering. Remember that capital shares rank lowest in priority for repayment when all other classes of shareholders have received their entitlement.

A lower-risk way to invest for capital growth is to choose zero-dividend preference shares – often just called 'zeros'. These preference shares pay no income during the life of the trust. The return is a fixed amount of capital paid out when the trust is wound up. It must be paid before any remaining capital can be distributed to other shareholders. This makes zeros lower-risk than other capital shares and a suitable choice if you are saving for definite medium-term commitments, such as paying school fees or university fees and accommodation.

Warrants
Many new investment trusts' shares are issued with warrants attached, and many existing investment trusts have issued warrants in recent years. When you buy a warrant you have the *right*, but not the *obligation*, to buy shares at a fixed price (the exercise price) at some time in the future. Because you have bought the right to buy shares, rather than the shares themselves, the cost is much less but the risks are much higher. If you do not exercise the warrants (agree to buy the shares) before the final exercise date the warrants become worthless. Most warrants tend to be sold at a premium, i.e. the cost of buying a warrant and exercising it immediately is more than the cost of buying the shares directly.

You do not have to hold warrants until their exercise date. You can sell them on the stock market before then. This could be worth doing if the market price of the warrants has risen since you bought them.

Warrants are 'geared' investments. The amount you pay for the warrant is a lot less than the price of the related shares. But, if the share price rises, the price of the warrant will tend to increase by a similar-sized amount. This may give you the opportunity to sell the warrant at a profit which is, in percentage terms, a lot higher than the profit you would have made if you had simply bought the related shares.

For example, suppose you buy 1,000 warrants in ABC Investment Trust at 100p each (total outlay £1,000), while the related shares cost 600p each. If the share price rises by 12.5p the warrant price might rise by, say, 9p. Selling the warrants gives you a profit of 9p × 1,000 = £90 (ignoring dealing costs). In percentage terms, this is a profit of 9 per cent on your £1,000 outlay. If instead you had bought the shares, you would have paid 1,000 × 600p = £6,000. Your profit would have been 12.5p × 1,000 = £125 which is only 2.1 per cent return. Buying the warrants has magnified your gain. But equally, if the related share price falls, the warrant price will tend to fall by a greater amount in percentage terms, so magnifying your losses. This makes warrants a high-risk investment – get advice before investing.

Who should invest in investment trusts?

Whether they are the right investment for you depends on how much you have to invest (see 'Buying investment trust shares' below), over what time period you are investing, what kind of return you hope to get from your investment and how much risk you are prepared to tolerate. Ultimately, your choice of investment will also depend on how you think different investments and markets are going to perform in the future.

How long are you investing the money for?
Investment trusts are medium- to long-term investments. Because investment-trust companies invest in a number of different shares, the share price is less likely to make sharp short-term moves up or down than the shares of individual companies.

What are your investment objectives?

If you are looking solely for *capital growth,* over the medium to long term an investment trust or a unit trust would be a suitable investment. If you are looking for capital growth over a period of five years or more, then investment in a capital growth fund or capital shares from a split-capital investment trust could be worth considering.

If you are looking for a *moderate income* and want some capital growth, for example to compensate for inflation, then an investment in a general investment trust might be the answer.

If you are looking to *maximise income,* the income shares of a split-capital trust could be worth looking at. But bear in mind that you may have a built-in capital loss or a high risk of losing part of your capital. A way round this could be to put part of your money into income shares and the rest into other investments designed to provide capital growth and so replace the capital you lose through the income shares. Constructing this kind of portfolio can be complicated, so get financial advice.

How much risk are you prepared to accept?

If you need to be certain of being able to draw out your capital at any moment, investment trusts are not for you. In the longer term, if you are prepared to ride out fluctuations, investment trusts could be a suitable investment. Emerging-markets and venture-capital trusts are relatively high-risk. The more general a trust, the less risk involved. A general global trust, which spreads your investments worldwide, is likely to be less risky than a trust that invests in only a few countries.

Buying investment-trust shares

There are two ways to buy investment-trust shares. As with any other share, you can buy them through a stockbroker or other intermediary. You can also buy the shares from the management company through its own investment-trust savings scheme (see below).

Stockbroker

The cost of buying and selling shares from a stockbroker means that it is impractical to buy shares worth less than, say, £1,500 to £2,000. Most stockbrokers charge commission, with a minimum charge per transaction – see Chapter 20.

Savings schemes

Many investment-trust managers run savings schemes for their investment trusts, set up to encourage private investors. While companies are not allowed to advertise their own shares (except when they are first issued), investment trusts can advertise their savings schemes. The cost of buying investment-trust shares through a savings scheme is normally much less than buying through a stockbroker. Most savings schemes charge less than 1 per cent of your investment in commission; some charge no commission at all, just stamp duty. Investment-trust savings schemes have minimum investment levels: most are either £25 a month or £250 as a lump sum.

Information about savings schemes is available from the AITC. Many of them are advertised in the national weekend newspapers.

Share exchange schemes

Some investment trusts operate share exchange schemes whereby you can swap your holdings of individual shares for shares in an investment trust. There is a charge for selling and buying the shares, but this may be less than you would pay for a sale on the stock market. Share exchange schemes might restrict the shares they are willing to accept – for example, only shares in the FTSE 100 Index.

A share exchange may be worth considering if you have built up a haphazard collection of shares through, say, privatisations and building society conversions.

Tax

The shares of investment trusts are taxed in the same way as other shares. Dividends are subject to income tax and capital growth in the value of the shares can lead to a capital gains tax bill (see Chapter 10).

23 Investment-based life insurance

Investment based on a life-insurance policy is one of the most popular forms of personal investment in the UK.

There are two ways of investing – with regular premiums or with a lump sum. Lump-sum policies are sometimes called single-premium bonds or investment bonds. For more details, see Chapter 25.

The regular premium versions of both with-profits and unit-linked policies represent poor value because of the high upfront charges and punitive surrender penalties. But there has been particular concern about with-profits policies. In February 2001 Consumers' Association published a damning report questioning the way in which these funds are managed. The Equitable Life saga highlighted the risks involved in with-profits funds. (This is explored in more detail later.)

Basing an investment on an insurance policy usually means locking your money away for a long time or, if you end a policy early, getting a poor return. So think carefully before investing this way. You need to take care with investment-based life insurance policies, particularly the regular premium policies. These policies are very inflexible and if you have to surrender the policy early you could pay a high penalty. You need to be sure that you will be able to maintain payments. Based on current projections it will take up to 10 years to break even on an endowment policy.

The most common type of investment-based policy is the regular-premium *low-cost endowment* policy with a fixed term. These policies are linked to interest-only mortgages for the purpose of buying a home. If you die during the term of the policy, the guaranteed death benefit pays out the amount you borrow: your mortgage. However, the guaranteed sum on maturity is significantly less than the mortgage so as to keep premiums affordable. Whether or not there will be enough to pay off the mortgage depends on how well the policy does. Many people who took out these policies in the 1980s and 1990s are now being asked to increase their premiums to make sure that the policies pay out enough. For more about this problem, see below.

A *non-profit endowment* policy is rare nowadays. With a non-profit policy, you agree to save for a certain period, which must be ten years or more. The policy gives a poor, but guaranteed, return. You get the amount guaranteed if you save to the end of the agreed period. Your heirs get the same amount if you die within the period. You get no bonuses on the guaranteed amount.

A regular-premium *whole-life* policy is investment-linked insurance that may be worth considering in some circumstances, for example to pay inheritance tax on your death – see Chapter 10. Some whole-life policies pay out a fixed sum with no investment return but, unlike term insurance, you may get a surrender value if you cash in before you die. A whole-life policy should be made out so that the proceeds go to your heirs, not to you. Otherwise, the proceeds could form part of your estate and become liable to inheritance tax. The policy is written 'in trust', which the insurance company arranges for you.

With whole-life policies, you agree to pay premiums for the rest of your life or up to a certain age, often 85. Premiums can rise after ten years and at set intervals after that. The policy pays out only when you die, not at the end of the premium-paying period. The insurance company agrees to pay out a fixed sum (plus bonuses if the policy is a with-profits one). You can cash in your policy at any time, but even after a very long time, the cash-in value is likely to be fairly low. People who live to a ripe old age often find that the pay-out on death is less than the premiums paid.

If what you want is life cover to protect your family from financial hardship in the event of your early death, you should consider *term insurance*. Term insurance has no investment element. With term insurance, you insure for an agreed period. If you die within that period (the term), the policy pays out. If you survive, the policy pays nothing. For a given amount of cover, term insurance is usually much cheaper than other types of life insurance. You can take out a term-insurance policy that pays a tax-free lump sum or a tax-free income (a *family income benefit* policy) if you die within the term.

Some investment-based policies provide virtually no life insurance. For example, single-premium policies normally pay out only slightly more than the value of the units if you die – such as 101 per cent of the value of the units.

Unit-linked insurance was attractive to some investors in the past because of the favourable tax rules – in particular, tax relief on the premiums you paid. Over the years, the tax rules have changed. Nowadays, investing through an Individual Savings Account (ISA) in unit trusts, open-ended investment companies or investment trusts (see Chapter 11) has clear advantages over unit-linked insurance. The return from the money you invest is free of tax, and charges can be lower. But if you want to invest more than the limits for an ISA (£7,000 in the 2001–2 tax year, £5,000 subsequently), unit-linked insurance may be worth considering if you are a higher-rate taxpayer *and* you tend to pay capital gains tax. Even then, though, its usefulness is debatable.

Buying a policy

Anyone selling you an investment-based life-insurance policy must operate within the investor-protection rules (see Chapter 6). They are normally paid by commission on the policies they sell and this amount should be shown in the *key features* document.

The key features document must include:

- the nature of the policy or plan, including its aims, what commitment is required from you (e.g. regular savings for a minimum time period) and the risks inherent in the policy
- an illustration of the return you could expect based on growth rates laid down by

the Financial Services Authority. The illustration needs to include the company's charges and your relevant details: age, sex, amount of cover you want

- statements clearly showing that the illustration is simply an example and is not guaranteed and a warning that inflation will erode the values (i.e. buying power) given in the illustration
- a description of the main terms of the policy or plan, set out in question-and-answer format
- tables showing the amount you could get back if you stopped the plan early, showing what would happen in the first five years and the last five years (to show the importance of the initial charges and any terminal bonus)
- a statement that over the lifetime of the policy the effect of charges is to reduce the rate of growth of your investment
- a warning that if you cash in your policy you may get back less than you have paid into it in premiums
- the amount of commission to be paid to an adviser if you use one.

The final payout may bear no relation to the illustration provided when you buy. This is based on standard growth rates laid down by industry regulators, but using the company's own charges. The final payout is not guaranteed, nor are the growth rates from which the final payout is calculated. Only the death benefit is guaranteed.

Life insurance or other funds*

Investing in investment-based life insurance is similar to investing in other investment funds such as a unit trust, open-ended investment company or investment trust. The advantages or disadvantages of either investment depend largely on taxation and how the charges compare.

If you invest in a unit trust or open-ended investment company, you pay income tax and capital gains tax on investment returns according to your own personal liability. Since everyone can make a certain amount of gains (£7,500 in the 2001–2 tax year) before having to pay capital gains tax, many investors do not ever pay this tax. And those who do not pay income tax can reclaim the tax deducted at source on income from some types of unit trust and open-ended investment company.

By contrast, life-insurance companies pay income tax and capital gains tax on investment returns, and this cannot be reclaimed, regardless of the investor's tax position.

Special features to look out for

Regular-premium plans and flexible-cover plans (see page 275) may offer some of these features:

- **Waiver-of-premium option** – you stop paying premiums if you become ill or disabled over a long period (more than six months, say) and cannot continue with your normal job. If you have a joint policy and either partner is ill or disabled, some companies do continue the plan for you.
- **Total disability cover** – some companies pay out the death benefit if an accident or illness leaves you unable to work again.

* Unit trusts, open-ended investment companies, investment trusts.

	Life insurance	Other funds
Income tax	Paid at the basic rate by the life-insurance company and *cannot* be claimed back by non-taxpayers: by further tax payable by higher-rate taxpayers	In ISA, 10% tax credit on share-based funds reclaimable, other income is tax-free; outside ISA, non-taxpayers can reclaim tax where deducted at 20%, starting-rate taxpayers can reclaim half the tax deducted at source, higher-rate taxpayers have further tax to pay
Capital gains tax	Paid by the insurance company and cannot be reclaimed	Not paid by the fund-management company
At the end of a plan	No tax is payable on qualifying policies (tax has already been paid within the funds)	Capital gains tax is charged according to personal liability – you get a tax-free allowance (£7,500 in the 2001–2 tax year); no tax if fund is held in ISA
Cashing in a plan early	If policy has been going less than 10 years or ¾ of the policy term, whichever is less, higher-rate taxpayers may pay the difference between the higher and basic rate of income tax on any gains	

- **Accidental death benefit** – if you die as the result of an accident, the plan pays out an extra lump sum.
- **Inflation linking** – you can increase your cover (or premium) in line with changes in the Retail Prices Index (RPI).
- **Special event cover** – a further plan can be taken out, or your cover can be increased, on marriage or the birth (or adoption) of a child, without your having to prove you are still in good health.
- **Family income benefit** – if you die, the plan pays out a regular tax-free income for a given number of years rather than a lump sum.
- **Low-start option** – for the first year of your plan, premiums are reduced to, say, half the normal amount. Then they increase by, say, 20 per cent a year for 5 years or 10 per cent a year for 10 years and are level for the rest of your plan. Note that this option usually costs more in the long run.
- **Stop-start option** – if you are made redundant or suffer financial hardship, you may be allowed to stop paying premiums for a limited period (up to two years, say) and keep your policy going. Eventually, you have to make up for these missed premiums at a later date.
- **Increasing or extending options** – you may be able to increase your cover or extend the term of the policy without having to prove that you are still in good health.
- **Term insurance** – if you die within a given period, the plan pays out an extra

lump sum. Check, though, that it is not cheaper to take a separate term-insurance policy.

Some whole-life plans give you the option of building in permanent health insurance which pays out if you are off work through illness, or cover against critical or terminal illness or major medical expenses. This may be convenient but if you need this cover you could get it more cheaply by buying a separate policy from another company. Watch out, too, for any differences in the tax treatment of such plans: they may be 'non-qualifying' in tax terms, which means that higher-rate taxpayers may have a tax bill when the policy pays out. Non-qualifying whole-life plans are often called 'universal life' plans.

If you already have a unit-linked policy
Over the years, unit-linked policies have changed a great deal. If you already have a unit-linked policy, you may find it is different from the types of policies now available and described in this chapter. It would be unwise to cash in an old-style policy in favour of a new one without considering the surrender value and the cost of setting up a new policy. What is more, your life cover is certain to be more expensive now that you are older than when you took out your policy.

The government still subsidises the premiums on policies taken out before March 1984 – see page 277.

Choosing a company
Sadly, there is no foolproof way of picking a company whose policies are going to perform better than those of other companies. In particular, just because a company's funds have done well in the past, it does not mean that they will do as well in the future. But, when choosing a company, there are a number of things to watch out for, in particular the *key features document* (see pages 264–5 for more details).

Friendly societies
You can buy savings-type life insurance from friendly societies as well as insurance companies. Friendly societies were originally self-help organisations, providing financial protection such as sickness benefits for their members. Nowadays the larger societies also offer with-profits endowment policies and unit-linked savings plans which operate in the same way as insurance-company policies.

As well as conventional savings policies, friendly societies can offer 'tax-exempt savings plans' where your premiums are invested in a tax-free fund and the maturity value is free of tax. There are strict limits on the amount you can invest, with a maximum premium of £270 a year (£25 a month). Partly because of the cost of administering small policies, friendly societies' expenses tend to be high. A society's investment performance has to be particularly good to make up for this.

If things go wrong
It is important to realise that, although the performance of your policy depends upon the performance of a fund of investments, investors do not own the investments. However, insurance companies are covered by the Policyholders' Protection Act.

The selling and marketing of these plans are covered by the investor-protection rules – see Chapter 6.

With-profits policies

The life and pensions industry manages £765 billion-worth of funds on behalf of investors in the UK. It controls over 40 per cent of all personal sector holdings of long-term savings and investments. Of the £765 billion managed by life-insurance companies, just over half, £400 billion, is held in the 'with-profits' funds run by some of the biggest household financial names: £300 billion of the with-profit funds is managed by the shareholder-owned PLCs such as the Prudential, Legal & General, Royal & Sun Alliance and Norwich Union with the rest run by the remaining mutual life insurers such as Equitable Life and Standard Life.[1] Over 10 million investors have a stake in with-profits funds through an endowment plan used for saving or paying off the mortgage, saving for retirement through a personal pension or company scheme or saving via with-profit bonds. On top of the individual contracts, substantial numbers of customers belong to employers' pension schemes also invested in with-profits funds.

A with-profits policy allows you to invest in a mixture of shares, gilts, corporate bonds, property and so on. 'With-profits' refers to the way in which investment returns are added to your policy. The policy-holders get a share of the profits the insurance company makes on its investments. These are paid in the form of bonuses added to the guaranteed minimum payout on your policy. There is usually some form of smoothing applied to avoid sharp variations in bonuses from year to year. An exceptionally good year on the stock market does not necessarily lead to an increase in the bonus rate, nor a bad year on the stock market to a decrease in the bonus rate.

The funds themselves come in two main forms:

- **conventional with-profits funds**: premiums are invested in a similar range of assets to a managed fund. As the fund grows, policyholders share in the profits through the addition of annual (or reversionary) bonuses. Once added these bonuses cannot be taken away, *provided that contributions are maintained until the end of the contract.* The unique selling point of with-profits funds is that they are meant to be lower risk than unit-linked funds because policyholders are protected from direct exposure to the volatility of the stock markets. Life companies do this by holding back some of the profits earned each year for a rainy day, thereby smoothing out returns over the term of the contract. At the end of the contract a terminal bonus is added to the guaranteed benefits built up through the addition of the annual bonuses. This bonus is at the complete discretion of the insurance company.
- **unitised with-profits funds (uwp)**: these are another form of with-profits contracts and are becoming increasingly popular. Like a unit-linked fund, premiums buy units in the fund, but most importantly the units grow in value through the addition of annual bonuses which represent only a part of the investment return. Terminal bonuses continue to be used.

In terms of new business, the conventional with-profits business is being outstripped by unitised with-profits and unit-linked funds. However, it remains the

[1] Consumers' Association estimates, source data Cazalet Financial

case that the bulk of assets under management is with profits of one form or another.

Bonuses

There are two sorts of bonuses, regular and terminal. *Regular* bonuses (usually called *annual* or *reversionary* bonuses by the insurance companies) are added to your policy's guaranteed sum. They cannot be taken away once added.

Suppose, for example, that the company announces a compound bonus of 3 per cent and your original guaranteed sum is £6,000. At the end of the first year, your bonus would be £180 and the new guaranteed sum would be £6,180. At the end of the second year, if the same bonus rate is announced, the bonus is 3 per cent of £6,180, which is £185. The new guaranteed sum becomes £6,365.

Some companies add different rates to the original guaranteed sum and to the reversionary bonuses already added to the policy. For example, a bonus of 3 per cent might be added to the original guaranteed sum and a bonus of 5 per cent to the reversionary bonuses already announced.

There is no guarantee that a bonus will be added each year. Reversionary bonus rates have generally fallen since 1990.

Life-insurance companies usually also pay a *terminal* bonus as well as reversionary bonuses. This is a one-off bonus added at the end of the policy, either the end of the savings period or on earlier death. If you cash in your policy early (see page 277), you may get no share of the terminal bonus.

These terminal bonuses can vary widely from one company to another and from year to year, depending on the current market value of the insurance company's investments. On 25-year policies, as much as 60 per cent of some top-performing companies' payouts may be made up of terminal bonuses.

In fact, terminal bonuses have been rising as reversionary bonuses have fallen. This has undermined the traditional claim made for with-profits policies: that your policy grows steadily and smoothly in value.

What sort of return do you get?

The return you get depends on your age, your sex and your health. A younger person would get a slightly better return than an older person, a woman a slightly better return than a man, and a healthy person a better return than someone in poor health. This is because life insurance is tacked on to the investment, and the life-insurance company deducts some money from the premium you invest to pay for the life insurance.

The returns you could have got in the past vary widely from company to company. For example, during 2001 the best-performing company could be paying out nearly half as much again as the worst-performing company for the same amount of savings. It is impossible to know in advance which is going to be the best-performing policy, and strong past performance can be a poor guide to choosing a policy.

Problems with with-profits funds

With-profits funds are marketed to investors as a lower risk way to invest. They are supposed to protect investors from falls in the stock market by 'smoothing' investment returns from reserves built up over the years. In theory they are supposed to be 'better' than other investment vehicles that invest directly in the market, for example unit trusts. But many experts, including Consumers' Association, believe that for most investors with-profits policies, particularly long-term contracts, are not delivering. This is for a number of reasons:

The corporate governance and regulatory framework for with-profits funds is weak. The directors have a clear duty to maximise shareholder returns but have no corresponding duty in relation to policyholders. There is little regulation of the way in which funds are managed other than through the amorphous concept of 'policyholders' reasonable expectations' – 'PRE'. This has not been defined in law, and in practice is decided by life-insurance companies and their actuaries. So the industry is allowed therefore to set the rules and how they will be applied.

The exact operation of the funds is not transparent. Although the PRE has been defined as the investment returns less any charges and other transfers, with-profits funds are not required to disclose crucial details, such as the amount of the charges and the actual allocations made to policyholders. This is in contrast with unit trusts and unit-linked funds where performance can be tracked daily.

It is made even more difficult for policyholders to assess the success of their investment because of the two-tier bonus system. The information life companies must provide – with-profits policy guides – are incomprehensible even to experts. There has been a shift in emphasis between annual bonuses, which have been falling consistently for the last ten years, to terminal bonuses, which have steadily increased. This means that terminal bonuses can now be equal to 200 per cent of the guaranteed fund and so make up to two-thirds of the total return on a 25-year contract. Terminal bonus amounts are then heavily marketed to investors.

Table 1 shows how much terminal bonuses are worth in relation to the guaranteed element.

Most investors on long-term contracts, however, never benefit from high terminal rates or smoothing – the key features of with-profits – as these are only realised at the end of the contract. It is estimated that on 25-year contracts, only 30 per cent of policyholders maintain payments until maturity.

Nearly half of these endowments are surrendered within ten years, yet policyholders face huge penalties if they surrender or transfer their fund in the early years. A policyholder with a 25-year endowment who cashed in his or her policy

Table 1: Terminal bonuses increase as a proportion of total return the longer the contract term

	10-year contract		15-year contract		20-year contract		25-year contract	
	Total return £	TB %	Total return £	TB %	Total return £	TB %	Total return £	TB %
Highest	11,276	35	26,251	79	57,629	133	124,750	178
Average	9,860	28	21,799	43	47,517	79	101,491	138
Lowest	9,023	11	19,069	16	41,592	52	84,047	85

Source: *Money Management*, April 2000

in 2000 after investing for 7 years would have earned a return of minus 2 per cent a year, while a similar unit trust grew by 10 per cent a year. Even if they had managed to hold on for 10 years, the return would have been only 3.9 per cent a year, just marginally better than an instant access savings account, and much worse than a similar unit trust which grew by 11 per cent a year (see chart on page 272).

The same story applies to personal pensions. The introduction of stakeholder pensions has forced down charges so personal pensions have actually improved. But, given that almost 40 per cent of personal pensions are transferred or have lapsed within four years, even now many investors are guaranteed to get a negative return if they choose to transfer to a similar scheme with a different company see Table 2.

Table 2: Projected transfer values of with-profits personal pensions

	1 year	2 years	3 years	4 years	5 years
Premiums paid	2,400	4,800	7,200	9,600	12,000
Average transfer value	1,991	4,171	6,696	9,461	12,413
% return	−30	−13	−4.7	−0.7	1.3

Source: *Money Management*, October 2000, £200 per month premium, 25-year plan

'Orphan assets'

Another example of the ability of companies to manipulate investment returns is the existence of so-called 'orphan assets' – reserves built up over the years that are no longer required. Most have been built up because of chronic underpayment to policyholders in the past due to an unduly prudent approach by actuaries. Orphan assets are currently valued at £45 billion – £30 billion held by shareholder-owned companies and a further £15 billion held by the remaining mutuals.

Previous government policy has been that these orphan assets generally should be divided up between policyholders and shareholders on a 90:10 basis – policyholders should get 90 per cent and shareholders 10 per cent. But the latest division of orphan assets in the Axa case approved in the High Court saw policyholders getting only 30 per cent.

These orphan assets are attractive to the other big shareholder-owned with-profits companies. If the Axa case sets a precedent for the whole industry, policyholders would lose out on around £18 billion. This comes at a time when millions of policyholders are facing shortfalls on their mortgage endowments and/ or seeing their annual bonuses being cut on their pension plans.

The Equitable Life

The problems with the way with-profits funds are regulated is highlighted by the Equitable Life saga. Following a House of Lords ruling, the Equitable found that it did not have enough assets to cover its guaranteed annuities liabilities without cutting bonuses to other policyholders. This was compounded by the fact that the management of the funds lacked transparency so policyholders could not appreciate the level of risk they ran. The Equitable is renowned for being the insurance

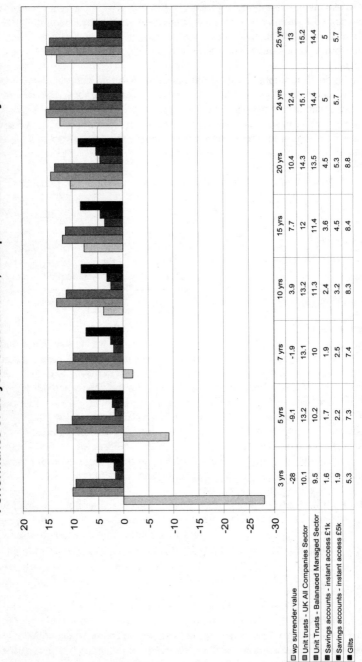

Performance of 25-year endowments, £50 per month to February 2000

	3 yrs	5 yrs	7 yrs	10 yrs	15 yrs	20 yrs	24 yrs	25 yrs
wp surrender value	-28	-9.1	-1.9	3.9	7.7	10.4	12.4	13
Unit trusts - UK All Companies Sector	10.1	13.2	13.1	13.2	12	14.3	15.1	15.2
Unit Trusts - Balananced Managed Sector	9.5	10.2	10	11.3	11.4	13.5	14.4	14.4
Savings accounts - instant access £1k	1.6	1.7	1.9	2.4	3.6	4.5	5	5
Savings accounts - instant access £5k	1.9	2.2	2.5	3.2	4.5	5.3	5.7	5.7
Gilts	5.3	7.3	7.4	8.3	8.4	8.8		

Source: *Money Management*, April 2000, Hindsight REUTERS, Consumers' Association calculations

company of choice for the professional classes such as solicitors and accountants. The company is also a popular choice for company AVC schemes. Yet even these classes of customer, who might be expected to be well informed and confident in their dealings with financial issues, were unable to discern the true extent of the gaping hole in Equitable's balance sheet. Now that the extent of the potential damage has become known, policyholders are finding it hard to act on the information. The ability of with-profits actuaries to impose market value adjusters (MVA) means that policyholders face the choice of either sticking with the Equitable with all the risk that involves, or cutting their losses and paying a 15 per cent penalty for switching providers.

The Equitable case brings home the fact that with-profits are also 'with-losses'. As we went to press the new management is trying to construct a compromise deal to restore Equitable's fortunes.

Is a with-profits policy suitable for you?

In principle, with-profits policies, with their wide mix of investments (shares, property and fixed-interest investments), provide a safer home for your money than, say, unit trusts alone. But the dominance of life-insurance companies, including their links to company pension schemes, and their practices means that many investors have no option but to invest in with-profits or unit-linked plans. Recent history shows that, where choice is available, particular care needs to be taken before signing up to a long-term with-profits policy.

Unit-linked policies

Your money buys units in a fund of investments run by an insurance company or friendly society, less a deduction for charges. As the value of the investments in the fund fluctuates, the unit price goes up and down.

Most companies run a number of funds. The main types are:

- equity funds investing in the UK, or other regions, such as North American funds, European funds or Far Eastern funds
- fixed-interest funds
- cash funds investing in short-term loans, bank deposit accounts, or other money-market investments
- unitised with-profits funds, i.e. where you buy units in a company's with-profits funds – the policy terms vary considerably from company to company, and there may be hefty penalties if you cash the units in or take early withdrawals
- property funds investing directly in properties (usually commercial)
- managed funds which invest in all types of investments.

Equity funds may be invested through a unit trust, and managed funds may be invested in a selection of unit trusts.

Unit values can go down as well as up, and the unit values of funds in different geographical or industrial sectors can rise and fall at different times. In general, the more specialised a fund is, the more you should avoid putting all or most of your money into it. Consider spreading your money across different funds or putting it into a managed fund, with its broad spread of investments.

Keeping track of your investment

You can follow the fortunes of your investment by looking up the unit price in a newspaper (the *Financial Times* lists most companies' unit prices – look under the section headed 'Insurances' in the *FT Managed Funds Service* section).

Buying and selling

Buying and selling units in a unit-linked insurance fund is the same as buying and selling units in a unit trust (see Chapter 21), and you can switch your money between the company's funds fairly easily. However, if you cash in your policy early, there may be heavy penalties.

Each unit normally has two prices. What you pay for the units (the *offer* price) is usually between 5 and 6 per cent more than what you can sell your units for (the *bid* price).

Switching

The majority of insurance companies allow you to switch your money from one fund to another, for example from the equity fund to the property fund, without paying their initial charge again. This could prove to be a useful facility for active investors who want to maximise returns as the prospects of different countries, markets or types of investment change.

Most companies make some charge when you switch, typically £15 each time you move. But most companies allow you one free switch a year. There may be a minimum amount you can switch, usually £250, £500 or £1,000.

Policy wording

The policy document is the contract between you and the insurance company, so it makes sense to see a copy before you invest. Check that most of the following points are spelled out:

- how the fund is valued – for example, it might show that stocks and shares are valued at the market prices quoted on the stock exchange
- that property in the fund is valued by an independent valuer, such as a surveyor
- the maximum period between valuations
- how unit prices are worked out
- the charges the company makes, and the other costs it can deduct from the fund
- that you will not be double-charged if your fund invests in other funds run by the company
- what happens to the fund's income.

Unit-linked regular-premium plans

With a unit-linked regular-premium plan you agree to pay premiums at regular intervals. In return, the insurance company uses some of your money to pay for life cover and expenses. The rest is invested in the funds of your choice.

You can select a plan that lasts for between ten years and the rest of your life (a few plans last for fewer than ten years, but they are not common). You can choose, within certain limits, the amount you think your dependants would need were you to die before the end of the policy.

If you die during the period of your plan, the life-insurance company guarantees that the life cover will pay out a set amount of death benefit. However, your dependants would receive the full value of your units if this is more than the death benefit.

The amount of death benefit payable under your policy depends on the length of your plan and the premiums you pay as well as your age and state of health when you take out your plan.

Unit-linked regular-premium plans fall into three main categories:

- *maximum investment* plans – for minimum life cover and high investment
- *endowment* plans – for higher life cover and longer-term investment
- *flexible-cover* plans – the percentage of your premium that provides investment, and the percentage that provides the life cover, can be varied throughout your life.

Maximum investment plans These plans may also be known as capital-accumulation plans. 'Maximum' investment means that virtually all your money is invested, with the amount used to buy life insurance (and the level of life cover) kept low. The plans usually last for ten years, but on maturity some plans give you the option to carry on the policy while drawing an income, providing you keep paying premiums of at least half the largest annual premium paid during the initial ten-year term. The minimum premium can be as little as £10 per month or as much as £100 per month, and there is usually no limit on the premium you can pay.

These plans usually provide the minimum life cover under the 'qualifying' rules. A low level of life cover means that the maximum amount of your premiums can be invested.

Endowment plans These plans, often called savings plans, can last for up to 25, or even 30 years. They may provide a higher level of life cover than other plans. Minimum premiums for these policies vary from £10 a month to £50 a month.

These plans are accepted by many lenders as a way of repaying a mortgage, but there are more attractive types of mortgage scheme than an endowment mortgage.

Flexible-cover plans Sometimes called flexible whole-life plans, these plans last throughout your life, though you may have to pay premiums only until a given age, 85, say. Depending on the size of the premium and your age and state of health at the start of the plan, you can choose the amount of cover you want.

You can alter the level of cover and premiums to suit your needs during the various stages of your life. Some plans include a variety of benefits and insurance that you can add on to the plan as and when you need them.

Monitoring your investment
With longer-term policies and whole-life policies, life-insurance companies keep an eye on your investment to make sure its value is sufficient to provide the

expected payouts. This is done by reviewing your policy, usually after ten years and then every five years.

During the last few years your policy may be reviewed once a year. Some companies suggest you invest in a cash fund during the last five years so that if share prices fall suddenly near the end of your plan, you do not lose any of the money you have made.

If the growth of your investments has fallen below the expected rate, you probably have to pay higher premiums (at the rate applying to your age at the time) or accept reduced benefits.

On the other hand, if the growth of your investment is greater than the expected rate, you may be able to reduce your premiums or build up a larger sum. In practice, you are more likely to have to worry about a shortfall. For example, many mortgage borrowers who took out policies in the 1980s and 1990s to cover their capital repayment now need to increase premiums or pay extra money into another investment, such as a unit-trust ISA.

Charges on regular-premium plans
The costs of administration and life insurance are met by deductions from your premiums in the first few years.

For example, with an endowment plan you might get a unit allocation of 55 per cent in the first year or two. In other words, just under half of your premiums are going towards administration costs and life cover during that period. Your unit allocations depend on the length of your plan, the amount of life cover and the premiums you pay.

Remember that there is also a difference between the price at which you buy and the price at which you sell units, usually 5 to 6 per cent. Also, a management fee is deducted from the fund, usually between 0.5 and 1.5 per cent a year. Companies now have to tell you how their current charges reduce the value of your policy, assuming you keep it for the whole term. You get this information built into the *key features document* (see pages 264–5) that the company must provide before you buy. It is shown as the 'Reduction in Yield' (RIY). The smaller the RIY the better, but charges can go up or down during the life of the plan and if you cash in early, are much higher.

How regular-premium policies are taxed
There is normally no tax to pay on the lump sum you get back from a regular-premium policy, provided you do not cash in the policy (or make it *paid-up* – see below) within its first ten years or within the first three-quarters of the period you insured for, if this is shorter. This is because it counts as a *qualifying policy*.

The lump sum is tax-free in your hands but the insurance company has already paid tax on the money in its funds; with some plans, a *capital gains tax deduction* is shown on the statement you get when the plan matures. You cannot claim this tax back, even if it is below your annual capital gains tax-free slice.

If you do cash in a policy before it has had time to become a qualifying policy, and you pay tax at the higher rate (or would do when the gain on your policy is added to your income), there may be some tax to pay – see page 282. The amount of the gain is normally the amount you get less the total of the premiums paid.

There is no basic-rate tax to pay on the gain, because the life insurance fund has already paid tax.

Any gain on cashing in a policy counts as part of your 'total income', which is used to work out the age-related allowances you can get. So, if you are 65 or over during the tax year, be careful about cashing in an endowment policy before the end of the agreed saving period. It may mean a reduction in your allowances and more tax to pay.

For how single premium policies are taxed, see page 282.

Before 14 March 1984, when you took out an endowment policy you also got tax relief (really a premium subsidy) on what you paid for the policy. You can carry on getting the premium subsidy on a policy that you took out before that date, as long as you have not changed the policy to give you more benefits – for example by extending its term or increasing its cover. The amount of the subsidy is currently 12.5 per cent.

Ending a regular-premium policy early

To get the best return on a policy, you have to keep it going for the period you originally agreed, often 10, 15 or 25 years. But your financial life could be drastically altered during this time – through marriage, divorce, having children, moving home, being made redundant or starting your own business, for example. So you may find yourself wanting to end the policy early.

There are a number of options:

Cashing in your policy

The *cash-in value* (also called the *surrender value*) of regular-premium policy is usually decided entirely at the discretion of the insurance company.

Cashing in a policy early can reduce considerably the return on your investment. With a few companies, you get nothing back if you cash in your policy within its first two years. Even after five years, you are lucky to get back as much as you have paid in. And on a 25-year policy you are unlikely to break even within ten years.

Making the policy paid-up

You stop paying the premiums but do not get the proceeds until the end of the original term. With a with-profits policy, the insurance company reduces the guaranteed sum for which you are insured. This new guaranteed sum, called the *paid-up value*, is paid at the end of the period you originally insured for (or when you die, if this is earlier). Most insurance companies offering this option continue to add bonuses to the paid-up value of a with-profits policy.

With a unit-linked plan, you may be allocated only the number of units that you could buy with the money you would get if you actually cashed in your plan. Alternatively, go for a plan that is broken up into a series of mini-policies. Then, if your circumstances change, you have the option of cashing just some of your units, keeping your plan going and paying a reduced premium.

Not all companies will make a policy paid-up, because of the tax implications (a qualifying policy may become non-qualifying if the premiums are not maintained, see page 000).

Getting a loan on it

Many insurance companies will consider lending you money, using your policy as
security for the loan. Generally, the maximum loan is between 75 per cent and 90
per cent of the cash-in value (see above). Some companies will not make a loan of
less than a certain amount, say £100 to £250. If you are considering a loan, check
the current rate of interest and compare it with what is available from other
sources.

Selling your policy

You may be able to sell your with-profits policy on the traded endowment policy
market. Usually, to be eligible, policies must have a surrender value of at least
£1,500 and have been running for seven or more years. When you sell, the buyer
takes over payment of the premiums and gets the benefits on maturity (or when
you die). It is not usually possible to sell a unit-linked policy.

If your policy has a second-hand value, you could typically get 10 to 20 per
cent more than the surrender value, in some cases considerably more. But even
second-hand values can give policy-holders a poor return on their money.

There are three ways to sell your policy: at auction, to a market-maker or via an
intermediary. Selling to a market-maker or through an intermediary may be the
easiest option but you might get a better price at auction. If you decide to auction
your policy, get quotes from a market-maker first to work out a realistic reserve
price.

One firm that auctions policies is H. E. Foster & Cranfield.* If the policy is sold,
the firm currently charges a fee of £50 plus a commission of one-third of the
difference between what the policy sells for and its cash-in value. If the highest bid
is below the cash-in value or whatever you set as a reserve price, you can
withdraw the policy from sale.

You can contact the Association of Policy Market Makers (APMM)* or the
Association of Policy Traders (APT)* for information.

What should you do?

If you need the cash, you have to choose between cashing in your policy, getting
a loan on it or selling it (if it is a with-profits policy). If you do not need the cash,
but can no longer afford the premiums, you can also consider making your policy
paid-up.

The best choice for you depends on your particular circumstances. The first
thing to do is to ask the insurance company to tell you:

• the policy's cash-in value
• details of any loan you can use your policy to secure (e.g. rate of interest
  charged and how much you can borrow)
• the current sum guaranteed by the policy
• the current rate of bonus if it is a with-profits policy
• the paid-up value and whether bonuses continue to be added to this value.

Then you have to work out for yourself the best course of action. One possibility
worth considering (if you do not need cash now) is to get a loan from the company
just to cover the policy premiums. You could consider getting a loan each year

until the policy matures. This preserves your life-cover insurance and gives you full value for the premiums you have already paid. A further option is to reduce the term of your policy.

Single-premium bonds

With these policies, you hand over a lump sum to the insurance company. The company takes part of the money to cover its expenses and to provide you with a little life insurance. The rest of the money buys units in whichever investment fund you choose.

The current tax rules give single-premium bonds some advantage for higher-rate taxpayers who have used up their capital gains tax allowance. But an ISA, where the return is totally free of tax, would be a better choice for most people. Single-premium bonds may be useful for higher-rate taxpayers who want to draw an income from the bond.

With most insurance-company funds, the income earned by the fund's investments is generally put back into the fund to buy more shares, property or whatever.

You can normally arrange to cash in part of your investment from time to time, on either a regular basis (under a withdrawal scheme) or an irregular basis. If you are a higher-rate taxpayer, cashing in part of your bond could possibly lead to a bill for income tax, but paying tax at the time can generally be avoided if you withdraw no more than 5 per cent (one-twentieth) of your original investment in any one year.

You often have to cash in a minimum amount, and leave a minimum amount. The minimum amount you can cash in is usually £50 or £100, and the minimum amount you must leave varies between £100 and £1,000. There may be a maximum on the amount you can cash in – say 10 per cent of the value of your investment.

To make getting an income easier, bonds are often sold as a cluster or series of identical mini-policies so that you can cash in a whole policy, or several policies at a time, according to your needs. The tax rules are simpler, too, if you cash in a whole policy rather than part of one. Of course, cashing units to get an income will start eating into the value of your investment if the unit price increases at a lower rate than the rate at which you cash units.

Charges
The insurance company normally makes two charges:

- There is an initial charge of around 5 per cent of the amount you invest. This is usually included in the spread between the buying and selling prices.
- There is a regular charge deducted by the insurance company from the fund at regular intervals to cover the costs of managing the fund. This charge might add up to between 0.5 and 1.5 per cent of the value of the fund each year. Brokers charge between 0.75 per cent and 1 per cent on top of these charges for investment in a broker-managed fund.

However, check if (and by how much) charges can change once you have invested.

Tax

When you cash your bond, the gain you make is added to your investment income for the tax year. The gain is the amount you get (including any amounts you got earlier, on which you were not taxed at the time) less the amount you paid for the bond in the first place. You do not pay basic-rate tax on the gain but the insurance company will already have paid tax on the income and capital gains of the fund. You do, however, have to pay any higher-rate tax that is due, though your tax bill may be reduced by *top-slicing relief*. The tax rules are complicated (especially if you cash in only part of your bond), but they can be used to your advantage if you are careful when you cash your units in – see page 131.

Switching your investment between funds does not count as cashing in your bond for tax purposes, so does not affect your tax position at all.

The mortgage endowment saga

The performance of with-profits endowments linked to mortgages is of particular interest to millions of consumers. In the 1980s and 1990s the bulk of mortgages arranged were interest-only with an endowment policy attached to repay the capital sum at the end of the mortgage term – generally this term was 25 years. The proportion peaked in 1988 at 84 per cent, falling to 60 per cent in 1994.[1] The majority of endowment mortgages were with-profits – a particularly popular type was the low-cost/ low-start version where premiums started off at lower levels and increased over the years or premiums were priced at minimum required levels to be just enough to repay the mortgage and no more.

In many cases however, the investment growth rates used to set the premium levels have turned out to be over-optimistic. The effect of the unrealistic growth assumptions was to understate the level of monthly contribution needed to repay the capital at the end of the mortgage period, usually 25 years. This made the endowment mortgage more attractive and affordable than the repayment-type mortgage – the monthly payments were lower and there was the promise of a nice additional lump sum at the end of the period thrown in for good measure. It's not surprising that this type of endowment was so popular and outsold the repayment option, particularly among young people and those on low incomes.

It has become evident that for many endowment holders there is now a high risk that their investment will not grow sufficiently to repay the capital sum at the end of the mortgage. The FSA carried out a review of the sale of endowment mortgages. Around 11 million endowments linked to mortgages have been reassessed to establish whether these policies are on track to repay the mortgage. Policyholders are receiving letters which are colour-coded according to the perceived risk that the endowment will not be able to repay the mortgage sum outstanding. Red means that there is a high risk that there will be a shortfall, amber means medium risk, green means that the endowment is currently on track to repay the mortgage. According to latest estimates, around half of the endowments are at risk of not paying off the mortgage.

The result is that because of the inflated growth rates marketed by the life-

---

[1] OFT, Mortgage Repayment Methods, April 1995

insurance companies, these consumers are faced with substantial increases in monthly premiums to make up for the low investment growth rates, to ensure that the capital sum is repaid at the end of the mortgage term. In some cases, consumers are finding that their monthly premiums will have to be increased by 80 per cent to ensure the sum is repaid.

There is also evidence during the same period, of the misselling of endowment mortgages to consumers. Where consumers were not warned about the nature of the risk that an endowment mortgage brings (i.e that in certain circumstances it may not pay off the mortgage) or were recommended an endowment when it was not suitable for their personal circumstances, they could be entitled to redress from the company.

While the mortgage shortfall issue is undoubtedly very important, it is only half the picture. What has not been factored into the equation is the general risk endowment policyholders incurred because of the inherent structural faults resulting from low persistency rates and high surrender charges. Consumers' Association estimates that at least 40 per cent of consumers who took out a low-cost/ low-start with-profits endowment seven years ago would have surrendered their policy by now. As a result, the return they would have got would actually have been 2 per cent a year. This compares to a return of 3.3 per cent on a simple savings account (see chart overleaf).

Performance of endowments

Many people with mortgage endowments have lost out even after years of investment 'growth' - based on actual surrender values

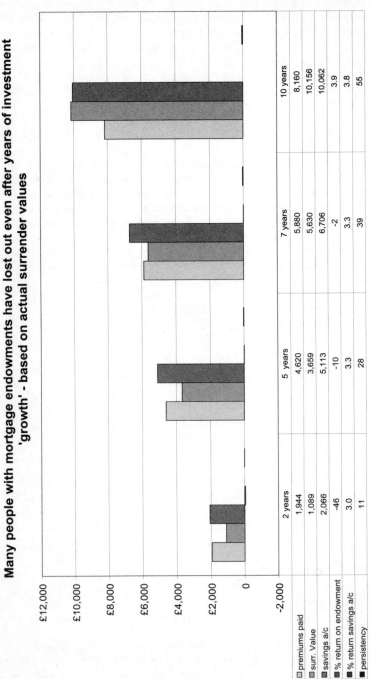

	2 years	5 years	7 years	10 years
premiums paid	1,944	4,620	5,880	8,160
surr. Value	1,089	3,659	5,630	10,156
savings a/c	2,066	5,113	6,706	10,062
% return on endowment	-46	-10	-2	3.9
% return savings a/c	3.0	3.3	3.3	3.8
persistency	11	28	39	55

Source: *Money Management*, December 1999, Consumers' Association calculations

Gilts

When the government needs to borrow to finance its expenditure, its principal method is to issue British Government Stock, also known as 'gilt-edged securites' or 'gilts'. Gilts form a large part of the investment market. Recent surpluses of revenue over expenditure has reduced the level of new gilts – down to £13.5 billion in 2001.

Gilts can prove to be good investments. In fact, although, over time, shares generally do much better, gilts actually outperformed them in 2000.

In the last couple of years we have experienced low inflation and low interest rates which look set to continue. Expectations for share growth have been lowered and it makes sense to look at other types of invesment, like gilts. Gilts are one of the safest forms of investment, second only to bank and building society savings accounts and National Savings.

Gilts suit four different types of people:

- those who want a regular (normally fixed) income and who are sure that they do not need their money back in a hurry
- those who want to invest for a specific time period, want a fixed return over that period and are not worried how much of the return comes as income or capital gain
- those who want to gamble that interest rates will fall (as gilt prices are then likely to rise, leading to capital growth)
- those who want to protect some of their money against inflation could choose index-linked gilts.

Conventional stocks

How they work

Most gilts pay a fixed amount of income each year and are *dated*, *convertible* or *undated*.

With stocks that are *dated*, the government promises to repay the stockholder a fixed sum at a fixed date (or within a fixed range of dates) in the future. With a few *convertible* stocks you can choose, usually once a year, to convert your stock to another offering a more attractive return. Once you have converted, you cannot change back. With *undated* stocks, no final date is specified and the government need never pay off its debt.

Like shares, stocks are bought and sold on the stock market. And, as with shares, the prices of stocks fluctuate – though not usually as widely as shares.

Getting to know the different stocks
Nominal value
Gilts are bought and sold in amounts which have a *nominal* (or face) value. For each £100 nominal of stock you hold, the government promises to pay you £100 in cash at an agreed time in the future – see 'Redemption date', below.

You can invest any amount of gilts and not just in multiples of £100. For example, you could invest £260 in a stock; if the current stock market price is £80 for each £100 nominal, you would get: 260 ÷ 80 = 3.25; 3.25 × £100 = £325 nominal of stock. In addition to interest on your loan, you have assured capital growth of £65 when the loan is redeemed.

Name
Each stock has a name, such as Exchequer, Treasury or War Loan. The name is of no particular significance to investors (although the latter has historical interest) but helps to distinguish one stock from another.

Coupon
The percentage immediately after the name of each stock is called the coupon – the before-tax income the stock pays out each year, expressed as a percentage of its nominal value. In the case of Treasury 8½% 2007, the stock pays out £8.50 for every £100 nominal. Interest on nearly all stocks is paid twice yearly in two equal instalments.

Redemption date
Following the name and the coupon is a year – 2007 in the example above. This is the date on which the government has promised to redeem the stock.

The date may be a range of years, for example Treasury 8% 2002–2006. In this case, the government (but not the investor) can choose in which year out of this range to redeem the stock. If the general level of interest rates remains higher than the coupon, the government is unlikely to redeem the stock before its last redemption date. In the case of convertible stocks you may be able to convert your stock into another with a later redemption date.

With a few stocks, the coupon is followed by a year and the words *or after*, for example 2010 *or after*. This means that the government can choose 2010 or any later year in which to redeem the stock. These, and a few other stocks which have no year quoted, are called *undated* and need never be redeemed: examples are War Loan 3½% or Consols 2½%. Unless interest rates in general fall below the level of the coupon, the government is unlikely to redeem these stocks.

The life of a stock
For practical trading reasons, stocks are generally split into four groups according to the time left until redemption. These are:

- **short-dated** if the stocks must be redeemed in the next 5 (or sometimes 7) years
- **medium-dated** if their latest redemption date is more than 5 (or 7), but not more than 15, years away
- **long-dated** if their latest redemption date is over 15 years away
- **undated** if no latest redemption date is given.

What makes stock prices change?

In general, changes in interest rates, inflation or the expectation of changes in the economy as a whole affect the prices of gilts. If interest rates are expected to rise, the price of stocks is likely to fall, and if interest rates are expected to fall, stock prices are likely to rise. Why is this?

Suppose you invest £100 in an undated gilt which pays out an income of £4 a year at a time when interest rates are 4 per cent. The yearly return is then 4 per cent.

But suppose interest rates rise. New investors could get a higher return on their money by investing elsewhere, so they hold off buying gilts like yours. This causes the price of gilts to fall until the yearly return it offers is comparable to the return investors could get elsewhere. For example, if interest rates double, the price of the undated stock paying out £4 a year may have to halve to £50, so that the yearly return it offers is 8 per cent. Conversely, if interest rates fall, the price of gilts is likely to rise.

In general, the shorter the remaining life of a gilt, the smaller the fluctuations in price and the more emphasis there is on interest rate changes rather than inflation rates. Take the example above of an undated gilt paying interest of £4 a year and halving in price from £100 to £50. Suppose this stock were instead a dated gilt that was due to end in a year's time, when the government would pay the holder £100. Unlike the undated stock, a dated stock would not halve in value to £50 when interest rates double. If it did, a new holder buying it at £50 would get back £100 in a year's time plus £4 in income – a return of around 108 per cent a year. So, with a dated stock that is about to be redeemed, the price needs to fall from £100 to a bit over £96 to give a total return of 8 per cent.

What makes interest rates change?

There is a whole host of reasons. For example, the Bank of England may increase interest rates to discourage people from borrowing or spending, in order to meet the inflation target set by the government. Or, as happened in early 2001, interest rates may be reduced by the Bank of England to stimulate the economy. Longer-term interest rates, such as those on long-dated gilts, are affected by what the markets expect longer-term inflation to be. The lower the expected rate of inflation, the lower the longer-term interest rates and vice versa.

The price you pay

The price of gilts is quoted per £100 nominal of stock. Buyers pay slightly more than the quoted price, sellers get less. As with shares, the difference between the two prices – the *spread* – varies according to the size of your transaction and how actively the particular stock is traded. Spreads tend to be larger with inactive stocks and small deals.

The price at which you buy or sell is adjusted for *accrued interest*.

Cum-dividend and ex-dividend

When you buy a gilt you generally buy it *cum-dividend*. This means that even if you have not held the stock for that long, you are entitled to a full half-year's interest when it next becomes due. So if you buy a stock five months before the interest payment date, the price is shown as, say, £122.12 + 30 days' accrued interest; this means you are paying for 30 days of interest to be included in the next dividend.

The quoted prices for gilts do not include accrued interest. This means that you have to pay more than the quoted price when you buy *cum-dividend*, less when you buy *ex-dividend*. The reverse is the case when you sell. Seven working days before the interest is due to be paid (ten working days for 3½% War Loan), the stock is declared *ex-dividend*. If you buy a stock ex-dividend, you are not entitled to the next interest payment. The quoted price for an ex-dividend stock has *xd* written after it.

The extra amount of *accrued interest* can be almost as much as half the coupon if you deal just before the stock goes ex-dividend. This makes dividend payment dates of critical importance when you buy or sell high-coupon stocks.

The return you get
Income

A stock's coupon tells you the before-tax income paid on each £100 nominal of stock. But paying £100 for each £100 nominal of stock is rare, so to work out the percentage income you get, do this sum:

coupon × 100 ÷ quoted price for each £100 nominal of stock.

This is known as the *interest yield* (or *running yield*). For example, you buy a gilt for £108.31, with a coupon of 6¼ (6.25) per cent.

$$6.25 \times 100 = 625: 625 \div 108.31 = 5.77$$

5.77 per cent is the interest yield, the rate of interest you get on your investment of £108.31.

Capital gain (or loss)

If you hold the stock until it is redeemed, you know you will be paid its nominal value, so you can work out the capital gain (or loss) you make. But, with undated stocks or stocks sold before redemption, you cannot know in advance what price you will get or when you will get it

The total return

With a dated stock, you can get some idea of the average yearly return on the stock if you hold it until it is redeemed by looking at what is known as the redemption yield. This takes account of both income paid out and the capital gain (or loss) you make on redemption. However, it does not take account of buying and selling costs and it assumes that the income paid out is reinvested at a rate of return equal to the redemption yield. For higher-coupon stocks this overstates the return you are likely to get in practice. Before-tax redemption yields are printed daily in the *Financial Times* and some other newspapers.

Working out after-tax redemption yields for any stock is not easy. This depends not only on whether you pay tax at 10, 20 or 40 per cent but also on how much of the return comes as taxable income and how much as tax-free capital gain.

Stocks vary widely in their redemption yields. As a general rule, when comparing stocks with about the same period of time left to run, higher-rate taxpayers tend to get the best after-tax redemption yields from relatively low-coupon stocks. By contrast, non-taxpayers get the best redemption yields from high-coupon stocks.

Gilt strips

Dated gilts give investors a stream of income payments and a capital payment at redemption. Some stocks can now be split up ('stripped') into components. This allows investors to buy the different components separately. Gilt strips are a flexible form of investment and can be used, for example, to design an income flow tailored to your needs.

Index-linked stocks

When the life of an index-linked stock comes to an end, the person then owning it is paid the nominal value of the stock increased in line with inflation over the lifetime of the stock.

All stocks also pay out income. Their coupon is usually 2 per cent or 2½ per cent depending on the stock; a few offer coupons over 4 per cent. This income is guaranteed to increase each year in line with inflation.

Will your investment keep pace with inflation?

Over the long term, the prices of gilts tend to rise roughly in line with inflation. If the price is £100, and the RPI goes up by 5 per cent a year, the price after a year might well be £105. But the price is also affected by people's views on the future rate of inflation and interest rates, and by the return they can get on other investments. The price of gilts with a longer life may well fluctuate more than the price of those with a short life.

Whether an index-linked gilt that you buy keeps pace with inflation depends on the price at which you buy (or sell) it and whether or not you hold it until redemption. Only if you bought £100 nominal value of stock for £100 when the stock was issued, and if you then kept it throughout the lifetime of the stock, can you be sure that the increase in capital would match the increase in inflation.

But suppose you had bought your £100 nominal value of stock for £90. As it is the £100 nominal value which is index-linked, your capital gain at the end of the stock's lifetime would be more than the rate of inflation. If you had bought at £110, your capital gain would be less.

If you want to buy stocks some time after they are first issued, compare the current market price with the nominal value adjusted for the increase in the RPI between the issue date and the time at which you want to buy. If the RPI has increased by 10 per cent, say, you should compare the market price with £110. If the price is higher, your capital gain at redemption is less than inflation; if lower, your capital gain is above inflation.

New issues of stocks

Large issues of stock are usually sold by auction carried out by the government's Debt Management Office. You choose the price at which you bid for the stock. The minimum bid is £1,000. If the stock is oversubscribed, only the highest bids are successful. However, private investors do not have to join the main auction. You can put in non-competitive bids, in which case you pay the *average* price of the issue.

Buying new stock direct from the Debt Management Office has the advantage that you pay no commission and there is no price spread (see above). New stocks are advertised in newspapers and you can also receive details of new issues direct – contact the Bank of England's Registrar's Department or go via the Internet (www.dmo.gov.uk).

How stocks are taxed

Although gilts are free of capital gains tax, you still have to pay income tax on the interest you receive.

Income from gilts is now paid gross, with the tax recovered through the self-assessment system. Gilts already held on the Bank of England Register on 6 April 1998 pay interest net of tax at 20 per cent – but you can request to switch to gross payments.

Remember that the price of gilts is the quoted price plus any accrued interest. Accrued interest is income and so subject to income tax rules.

The contract note you get when you buy or sell stock shows how much accrued interest is involved. How it is treated for income tax depends on whether you are a buyer or a seller:

- if you sell cum-dividend, you are taxed on the accrued interest included in the price
- if you sell ex-dividend, you get tax relief on the accrued interest deducted from the quoted price
- if you buy cum-dividend, you get tax relief on the accrued interest included in the price
- if you buy ex-dividend, you are taxed on the accrued interest deducted from the quoted price.

These rules may not affect you if the nominal value of all stocks to which accrued income applies is less than £5,000. For more details about how accrued interest is taxed, see Inland Revenue leaflet IR68 (available from tax offices and Tax Enquiry Centres).

Choosing a stock

Which stock to choose depends on what you want from your investment.

A high fixed income?
Go for a high-coupon stock; but note that if the price you pay is above the redemption value of £100 for non-index-linked stocks you may be sacrificing some of your capital to produce this income. Beware of choosing a stock that has a long time to go before it has to be redeemed. If you are forced to sell before then, you may lose heavily.

A known total return over a fixed period?
Go for a stock that lasts for the period you are interested in. Look out for one that gives the best after-tax redemption yield for someone in your tax position. In general, higher-rate taxpayers should go for a low-coupon stock, non-taxpayers for a high-coupon stock.

Want to gamble on interest rates falling?
Go for a stock with a long time to run, or for an undated stock, and choose one with a low coupon. But bear in mind that, if interest rates rise, you may lose heavily.

Protection against inflation?
Index-linked stocks might suit you. But remember you must buy stock at the right price and hold it until redemption to be sure that full index-linking is applied.

Where to get information and advice
Several newspapers give information each day about gilt prices; the most comprehensive is in the *Financial Times* and *The Times*.

To check after-tax redemption yields and to get advice on which stock would best suit your needs, contact a stockbroker, bank or a financial adviser. See Chapter 7.

How to buy and sell

You can buy and sell gilts through a stockbroker, high-street bank, some building societies, solicitors, accountants and independent financial advisers. You can also buy and sell by post through the Bank of England Brokerage Service (forms are available from post offices or by phoning 0800 818614). This service tends to be cheaper than other broking services for small parcels of stock. There is no charge for selling less than £5,000, and for buying up to £5,000 you pay 0.7 per cent and a minimum of £12.50.

Investing via a unit trust or open-ended investment company
Many unit trusts and open-ended investment companies specialise in gilts and other fixed-income investments.

Investing via such funds is generally more expensive than investing in stocks direct. The difference between the buying and selling prices of units can be as high as 5 per cent, and there is a yearly charge. For this extra cost you get professional management of a large portfolio of stocks, and the manager may be able to switch between stocks more actively than you could afford to do as a single investor.

From the income tax point of view, there is not a lot of difference between investing in a fund or investing direct. There is a difference with capital gains tax, however. Gilts are not liable for capital gains tax. Gains on unit trusts and open-ended investment companies, on the other hand, are liable, although the first £7,500 of your gains in the 2001–2 tax year are exempt.

Another problem with investing through funds is that you have to accept the range of stocks in which the trust chooses to invest. By investing directly, you can choose the particular stock that is best for your particular tax rate and investment needs.

 # Insurance-company bonds

Insurance companies regularly issue bonds which are suitable for lump-sum investments. You must invest for a fixed period (often four or five years, perhaps as much as ten years). In return, you normally get a fixed rate of interest for the period. Do not confuse these with National Savings Pensioners Bonds (see Chapter 13) which work (and are taxed) differently.

With an *income bond*, the return is paid out as regular income net of the basic rate of income tax (usually yearly, sometimes monthly). Some bonds may eat into your capital to provide the income, if investment performance is weak. With a *growth bond*, interest is left to accumulate and is paid out when the bond matures. If you die before then, the insurance company normally repays your original investment to your estate or nominated heirs plus, with some growth bonds, the return accumulated to date.

Alternatives to insurance bonds include National Savings Certificates, the various National Savings Bonds, bank and building society fixed-interest accounts. Rates for guaranteed income and growth bonds are always quoted net of basic-rate tax. When comparing the fixed rates for different investments, always look at the net (after-tax) return. See Chapters 12 and 13.

As with many products sold by insurance companies, do not invest in a bond if you may need to cash it in early. Some insurance companies do not allow you to do this, others may give you back less than you originally invested.

How bonds work
Bonds are normally available for only limited periods of time and the mechanics of newly-issued bonds change from time to time. These days, virtually all bonds are based on single-premium endowment policies. In the past some bonds were based on annuities (see Chapter 27) which are taxed differently. Before buying, check with the company how any bond is taxed – particularly if you are a higher-rate taxpayer.

Single-premium endowment bonds
Your investment buys a single-premium endowment policy with guaranteed bonuses. You can choose whether to have bonuses paid out as income or reinvested for growth (or you may be able to have part paid out, part reinvested). At the end of the term, you get back your original investment plus bonuses that you have not cashed in.

Series of single-premium endowment bonds
Your bond is divided up into a series of single-premium policies, one component to provide an income for each year of the term and one to return the original lump sum at the end of the investment term.

Tax
For basic-rate taxpayers tax has already been paid by the insurance company, so there is no tax to pay on either the income or the final payout. Non-taxpayers and starting-rate taxpayers however, cannot claim this tax back.

With a single endowment bond, you can take income of up to 5 per cent of the investment each year until the end of the bond's term without paying any tax. If income of more than 5 per cent is taken, a higher-rate taxpayer may have to pay some tax.

With a series of endowments, an endowment policy is cashed in every year to provide the income. The investor may have no tax to pay but the company may have paid some tax.

At the end of the term, unless you are a higher-rate taxpayer the proceeds from an endowment bond are free of tax.

How to choose a bond
For a list of companies which issue bonds and the various types, get a copy of the most recent issue of *Money Management** magazine. Bonds are often only available for a short period, so ask likely companies for details of their latest bonds.

Guaranteed equity bonds

Guaranteed equity bonds, also called guaranteed stock-market bonds, provide a guaranteed return linked to the general growth in share prices. So, for example, you might be offered 133 per cent of the growth in the FTSE 100 Share Index, with 100 per cent of your initial investment back if the FTSE 100 falls over the period of the bond. Beyond this common purpose, these bonds come in a myriad of different forms, which makes it particularly difficult to compare them. Broadly, they fall into three categories (with the tax treatment depending on the underyling investment in each case):

- **bonds based on building society accounts** are effectively high-interest building society accounts, with a fixed term and a predetermined interest rate expressed as a percentage of the growth in share prices
- **single-premium insurance bonds** may be based on endowment policies and have a fixed term of around five years. They may also be based on whole-life policies with no fixed term
- **unit trusts** work like a normal unit trust (and are not classed as bonds). You pay for a guarantee that ensures you get a minimum amount back (usually the money you invest) after a fixed period.

When guaranteed equity bonds first appeared, some were advertised and sold in a particularly misleading way: for example, the guaranteed return related purely to the growth in share prices, the income that shares also provide being conveniently forgotten. Industry regulators expressed their disapproval and practices have improved. Even so, proceed with caution. In particular, check the following:

- What exactly is guaranteed? Remember that the better the guarantee, the more the cost of providing it – particularly if interest rates are low. So, very broadly, if you go for a lower guarantee, the bond is more likely to beat it than if you go for a higher guarantee.
- How much would you get if you cashed in early? Some bonds guarantee the amount, others just pay the 'market value' of the bond.
- Do you have to take your money out at the end of the investment period? If you do not, you have more flexibility in case share prices are low at the end of the normal term.
- What are the charges? This depends on the underlying investment. So, for example, building society bond charges are rolled into their rate of return, while insurance bonds usually have an initial charge of around 5 per cent and an annual charge of, say, 1 per cent.

26 Corporate bonds, preference shares and convertibles

When companies listed on the stock exchange need additional funds – usually for investment in new products or equipment or to finance a takeover bid – they generally raise money in one of two ways. Either they issue more share capital, for example by offering shareholders a rights issue (see Chapter 20); or they decide to borrow money by issuing corporate bonds. Like gilts issued to finance government expenditure (see chapter 24), corporate bonds, or loan stocks, are simply borrowed money. Except in special circumstances, bond-holders have no voting rights in the company. Some bonds are secured by specific assets in the company, for example property; most are unsecured. Corporate loan stocks tend to offer higher rates of interest than gilts. This is because of the higher risk of default.

Many corporate bonds work in a similar way to gilts. They have a 'face' or 'nominal' value, a coupon (or interest rate) and a maturity date. The company issuing the bond agrees to pay interest at the coupon rate every year until maturity. For example, Newco Electronics 9% 2005 pays the bond-holder £9 a year for every £100 nominal until 2005. As with gilts, interest is usually paid in two equal payments a year.

Tax
Corporate bonds are taxed in the same way as gilts.

Debentures
Debentures, a kind of corporate bond, are always secured on specific assets of the company, so are safer than other corporate bonds. Even if the company goes into liquidation, you should expect to get your capital back. As a result, the yield tends to be lower.

Preference shares

Preference shares are not loans to a company and are not, therefore, technically corporate bonds. Like ordinary shares, they give you a stake in the ownership of a company, though voting rights may be restricted. They are taxed like ordinary shares and the dividend comes with a 10 per cent tax credit.

But from an investor's point of view preference shares are more like corporate bonds or debentures. They usually offer a fixed income, which is paid before any dividends to ordinary shareholders (hence 'preference' shares). If the company goes into liquidation, the preference shareholder gets paid before ordinary share-holders but after all loans have been repaid.

Preference shares behave in exactly the same way as corporate bonds. Some preference shares have a redemption date, others are irredeemable.

Convertibles

A convertible loan stock is a fixed-interest corporate bond that carries with it the right, on terms and conditions set out when the convertible is first issued, to convert into ordinary shares. The right (but not obligation) to convert a bond into shares is offered on a specific date (or within specific time periods) and at a specific share price. If the conversion rights are not exercised by the expiry date, the bond reverts to a conventional dated corporate bond.

There are two basic types of convertibles – convertible loan stocks and convertible preference shares. Unless the holder has decided to convert the bond to shares before the redemption date, convertible loan stocks are redeemed like other loan stocks. The same applies to most convertible preference shares.

Because a convertible bond can either become shares (if you choose) or stay as a bond, it is harder to work out whether or not they are better value than simple bonds or ordinary shares. For example, Newco Electronics 6.3% convertible preference shares have a nominal value of £1 each. You may exchange your holding for ordinary shares at any time between 1989 and 2015 at a rate of 14½ ordinary shares for every 100 preference shares held. If you do not exercise your conversion rights by 2015, your convertible preference shares will be redeemed at par (i.e. at the nominal value).

Assume in this case that the convertible preference share price is 109p and the ordinary share price 695p. So 100 nominal of preference shares would cost £109, whereas 14½ ordinary shares would cost £100.775 excluding share-dealing costs. To buy the convertibles and convert them straight away into ordinary shares is therefore an expensive way of buying the ordinary shares. The premium is £8.25 per 14½ ordinary shares or 8.19 per cent.

So, if you want a shareholding in Newco Electronics, buy the shares directly and, if you want a fixed-income bond, buy the convertible preference shares. As the share price in Newco rises, the conversion premium gets smaller and you might do better to convert to shares. However, before you do so, remember that you lose the fixed income that the convertible bond pays and get share dividends instead, which are likely to vary and may be much smaller.

Bulldog bonds and Eurosterling bonds

Bulldog bonds are loan stocks that are issued in sterling by foreign borrowers and traded on the London Stock Exchange. Eurosterling bonds are issued in sterling by both UK and foreign organisations. As with Eurobonds denominated in other currencies, Eurosterling bonds are traded offshore. The interest is paid gross but is liable for UK income tax; any gains are liable for capital gains tax. Bulldog and Eurosterling bonds are large-denomination bonds and are mainly used by professional investors.

Buying and selling bonds

As with shares, gilts and other stock-market investments, you can buy or sell corporate bonds, debentures, convertibles and other bonds through a stockbroker or financial adviser.

Corporate-bond funds

In addition to direct investment in corporate bonds, you can invest indirectly through a unit trust or open-ended investment company. Corporate-bond funds offer higher income yields than most share-based funds. Especially if you invest tax-free through an ISA (see pages 116–8), they may be particularly suitable for investors seeking income. Bonds tend to be less volatile than shares, so the risk of losing capital is generally lower. Conversely, the chances of making a capital gain are lower. But you can lose capital in corporate-bond funds. In particular, check out how a fund manages to offer a higher yield (income) than other, similar funds. Is it because it is investing in higher-risk corporate bonds, perhaps issued by companies that could be in trouble? Match that fact against your own attitude to risk before deciding to buy.

A bond fund cannot offer the same certainty of return as a single bond. If you buy a bond and hold it until maturity, you know exactly how much income and capital return you will receive, just as you do with conventional gilts (see Chapter 24). A bond fund does not mature at a fixed price and, as the fund manager buys and sells bonds within the fund, both the income and the capital value of your units vary.

 # Annuities

Annuities are a well-established form of lump-sum investment which pays a guaranteed income for the rest of your life. But the major drawback is that once you hand over your lump sum you cannot get it back.

You are most likely to come across annuities in connection with pensions because the tax rules say that if your pension contributions are used to build up a fund, most or all of it must be used to buy a pension annuity (also known as a 'compulsory purchase' annuity). This is the case if you have a personal or stakeholder pension, belong to an employer's money-purchase scheme or are topping up an employer's final-salary pension by making additional voluntary contributions (for more on pensions, see Chapters 16, 17 and 18). This chapter looks at the type of annuities that you can choose to buy yourself – called *purchased-life* annuities.

How annuities work

With any kind of annuity, you hand over your money to an insurance company in return for a guaranteed income. If you buy a 'single life' annuity, the income is paid until the 'annuitant' (i.e. the person to whom the income is paid) dies. In the case of an annuity arranged on a 'joint life, last survivor' basis, the income carries on being paid until both you and a second named person – usually, but not necessarily, a spouse – have died.

The income is determined by annuity rates at the time of purchase which in turn depend on the level of interest rates generally. Another factor affecting income is age: the older you are at the time you buy the annuity, the higher the income. Your gender is also a factor. A man gets a higher income than a woman of the same age. For example, in return for a lump sum of £10,000, a 70-year old woman could get a lifetime income of £913 (in June 2001) but a man would get £1,037. This difference arises because the woman is expected to live longer than the man, so the income has to be paid for longer.

While both pension and purchased-life annuities work in broadly the same way, purchase-life annuities differ from their compulsory counterparts in two important respects:

- the income from them is taxed much more favourably than the income from a pension annuity, all of which is subject to tax at your highest rate (see page 299)

- while you cannot get your lump sum back in *your* life time, by choosing 'capital protection' (see page 299) it is possible to ensure that when you die, what remains of your lump sum is repaid to your estate and so can be passed on to your heirs. This is not an option with pension annuities.

Is an annuity for you?

Whether or not an annuity proves to be a good investment in the long run depends on three unpredictable factors:

- **how long you live after buying it** – the longer you live, the better a buy the annuity becomes
- **what happens to interest rates** – and so annuity rates – after you have bought it. If they go up, you are left with a return on your investment which may be poor in comparison with other investments. But if interest rates fall, you end up with a bargain
- **the long-term effect of inflation on the buying power of your income** – if you choose an increasing annuity (see page 299), this is not a worry.

So you need to weigh these uncertainties against the one certainty that, once invested, you cannot get your lump sum back. According to annuity specialists, the Annuity Bureau*, purchased-life annuities are generally bought by people who want to maximise their retirement income and who are not concerned about leaving money after their death. Annuities can also be a useful way of providing for the costs of long-term care.

However, if you are under 70, investing in an annuity is not usually worth considering. Returns do not compare favourably with more conventional investments – although if you have serious health problems you can benefit from the enhanced rates offered by *impaired life* annuities.

Once you reach your 70s, however, the returns on annuities start to look quite

---

Types of annuity

There are three types of annuity:

- **temporary** where the lump sum buys a guaranteed income for a fixed number of years
- **deferred** where you pay a lump sum now and arrange for the income to start to be paid at a future date – in five years' time, for example. Deferred annuities are not very common these days and are usually used with retirement annuity contracts (see Chapter 19)
- **immediate** which is the type that this chapter deals with. As the name suggests, the guaranteed income starts to be paid shortly after the annuity has been purchased.

---

attractive compared with other sorts of investment – largely because of the tax treatment (see page 300).

Types of annuity

This chapter deals with *immediate* annuities. With these, the company starts paying you the income 'immediately'. There are also *deferred* annuities, where you pay a lump sum now and arrange for the income to start in the future (in five years' time, say). Deferred annuities form the basis of many personal pension plans. Immediate annuities come in various forms.

- **Level annuity** The income is the same each year. For a given outlay, this type will probably give you the largest income to start with – though, of course, inflation will erode its buying power over the years.
- **Increasing annuity** Income increases at regular intervals by an amount you decide on when buying the annuity.
- **Inflation-linked annuity** This gives an income that is linked to the Retail Prices Index. This type usually provides the lowest starting income.
- **Unit-linked annuity** This is offered by a few companies. Your income is linked to the performance of the fund (e.g. of property) and so goes up and down in amount.
- **With-profits annuity** The initial income is comparable to other types of annuities and each year extra bonuses are added depending on the profitability of the company. Their attraction lies in the prospects of high bonuses, although these are not guaranteed.
- **Single-life annuity** This ceases when the person who bought the annuity dies.
- **Joint-life, last-survivor annuity** This carries on until both the person buying the annuity and someone else, usually a wife or husband, are dead.
- **Impaired-life annuity** This pays a higher income than someone of your age and gender would normally get, because of serious health problems which reduce your life expectancy.

How much income?

As well as your age and gender, the income you get from an annuity also depends on the various options you choose. If you choose a *level annuity*, you will get the highest income. The income paid to you is fixed at the outset, never changes and ceases on death. You get a lower income if you choose:

- **capital protection** which means that if you die having received – in total gross income – less than the original amount invested, the balance is repaid as a lump sum to your estate
- a **guaranteed income** which is the alternative to capital protection and means that, even if you die before the fixed period comes to an end, the income is guaranteed to be paid for a fixed number of years. If you survive the period, you carry on getting the income until your death
- an **increasing income** which goes up each year either in line with inflation or by a fixed percentage
- to **provide an income** for someone else after your death by buying a joint-life annuity.

EXAMPLE

Jason is 75 and has a lump sum of £100,000 which he is considering investing in an annuity. If he goes for the simplest option of a level annuity he could get an income – which stops on his death – of £11,676. Including a five-year guarantee period would bring the income down to £11,148; a ten-year guarantee period would reduce it to £9,924. But the most expensive option – to protect his capital – would bring the income to £9,370. Since Jason is single and has no one he particularly wants to leave his money to, he chooses the level annuity.

The amount of income you get from an annuity is also affected by the company you buy from. This is largely because when pricing annuities, insurance companies take into account their own experience of how long past annuity customers have lived rather than using national average statistics. Companies whose customers have tended to live for a long time may offer lower rates than companies whose customers have tended to die relatively young. The difference between a low- and high-paying company can be as much as 25 per cent, so it makes sense to shop around for the best annuity rate by consulting an up-to-date copy of Money Management* magazine or Ceefax or by getting a specialist such as the Annuity Bureau* or Annuity Direct* to shop around on your behalf.

Tax treatment
Provided you are happy to part irrevocably with a lump sum, one of the main attractions of buying a purchased-life annuity is the favourable way in which the income is taxed. Unlike pension annuities, where all the income you get is subject to tax, with a purchased life annuity, only *part* of the income is taxed. This is because the tax system treats a proportion of the money paid to you as a return of some of the lump sum you invested – called the 'capital element'. This makes some of your income tax-free.

The amount of the tax-free part varies according to the type of annuity, your age and gender, the size of lump sum you invested and how often the income is paid. The older you are when you take out the annuity, the higher the capital element.

The taxable part of the income is taxed at 20 per cent and this is usually deducted from the income before you get it. Basic-rate taxpayers have no further tax to pay while higher-rate taxpayers have to pay an additional 20 per cent on the income element. Non-taxpayers can either reclaim all of the tax deducted or arrange for the income to be paid in full by completing form R89 available either from the company or a tax office. Those who pay tax at the starting rate of 10 per cent can reclaim half the tax deducted.

Alternatives to annuities

The main thing that distinguishes annuities from other sorts of investment is the lifetime guarantee – but it is a guarantee that has to be paid for by relinquishing all control over the lump sum you invest. If you are not comfortable with this, you should not invest in an annuity but should consider one of the following alternatives to boost your income. Note that, with the exception of guaranteed-income and single-premium investment bonds, all the investments mentioned below can be held in the tax-free wrapper of an Individual Savings Account (see pages 116–8).

Bank and building society deposit accounts allow you to increase your income by withdrawing the interest earned in a deposit account. Some accounts offer a monthly income option. Most deposit accounts have variable rates but you can also lock into fixed-rate accounts for up to five (or more) years. Fixed-rate accounts may appeal to people who want a stable income. They are especially worth considering at a time when the interest-rate cycle appears to be nearing a peak and when interest rates generally are expected to fall. You need to keep an ear on what the pundits are saying about the likely path of interest rates if you want to lock into a fixed rate at the top of the cycle, though experts and the general consensus can be wrong. Deposit accounts may offer a lower income than other forms of investment but appeal to people who do not want the risk that their capital will fall in value. For more on deposit accounts see Chapter 12.

National Savings investments are much the same as deposit accounts but are offered by the government as opposed to banks and building societies. There is a range of accounts, with both variable and fixed-rate options. Your capital is secure and cannot fall in value. The Pensioners Guaranteed Income Bond for those who are 60 or over pays a monthly income and allows you to lock into a fixed rate for two or five years. For more on National Savings, see Chapter 13.

Gilts are fixed-interest securities issued by the UK government, ideal for investors who want to increase income. If you buy gilts and hold them to their redemption date (the date when the government repays the money borrowed) you know exactly what return you will get. But if you sell them before the redemption date, remember that what you get back depends on the market value at the time. It could be more or less than you paid. Most gilts pay interest every six months. If you want to receive income more than twice a year, you can buy a number of different gilts with different interest-payment dates. For more on gilts, see Chapter 24.

Corporate bonds are fixed-interest investments similar to the gilts issued by the UK government but instead issued by companies. There is a risk that a company may get into difficulties and default on its obligations to pay interest or even the capital at the redemption date. (Since the government can always raise taxes to meet its obligations to holders of gilts, this risk is reckoned to be virtually non-existent with UK government gilts.)

Because of the extra risk, the interest rate (income) from corporate bonds is generally a little higher than from gilts. But investors need to take care. The higher the income, the higher the risk. The most common way to invest in corporate bonds is through a fund, such as a unit trust or open-ended investment company, which spreads the risk by investing in a range of bonds. The higher the rate a fund aims to achieve, the greater the risk that some of the bonds in the fund are issued by companies that could default. It is important to understand this risk before being tempted by an extra 1 per cent or so that one fund may be aiming to achieve. For more on corporate bonds, see Chapter 26.

Permanent interest-bearing shares (PIBS) are fixed-interest securities that are similar to corporate bonds. They are offered by building societies and ex-building societies that have converted to banks. They can offer a higher income than other fixed-interest securities but, unlike most gilts and corporate bonds, they have no redemption date. This means that the only way to get your capital back is to sell them on the stock market. What you get back may be more or less than you invested depending on the market value at the time you sell. You can invest in PIBS through a stockbroker or other share-dealing service. See Chapter 12.

Unit trust and open-ended investment company funds specialising in higher-yielding shares could be suitable for investors who are prepared to accept a lower income than can be found from fixed-interest investments. Investment funds adopt a range of different strategies. What are classified as equity income funds search out shares which pay good dividends, i.e. the dividend expressed as a percentage of the cost of buying the shares is relatively high.

Although the income is generally lower than with fixed-interest investments like gilts and corporate bonds, equity income funds offer the prospect of an income that rises each year as the companies in which the fund invests increase their dividends. For more on unit trust and open-ended investment company funds, see Chapter 21.

Unit trust and open-ended investment company funds specialising in higher-growth shares could be an alternative to funds specialising in higher-yielding shares (see above). Some funds concentrate on shares that are expected to grow in value at a greater rate than higher-yielding shares, while offering a relatively low dividend income.

Investing for growth may seem to be the opposite of what income investors want. But people who need spending money can cash in part of a growth investment. For example, you invest £10,000 in a fund that grows by 10 per cent over a year, i.e. by £1,000 to £11,000, and you want to protect the real value of your investment. During the year, inflation is 2.5 per cent. In this case, after one year you could cash in units to the value of £750 and keep the other £250 in the fund to meet inflation and grow further.

An advantage of this approach is that your £750 could be tax-free to the extent that it falls within the annual capital gains tax exemption – £7,500 in the 2001–2 tax year. This strategy might suit a tax-paying investor who has already used up the annual limit for investing in a tax-free ISA. The ISA can be used for higher-income investments and investments outside an ISA can be used for growth investments. For more on unit trust and open-ended investment companies, see Chapter 21.

Home income plans

If you do not have a cash lump sum to invest in an annuity (or other income-producing investment), one option, if you are over 70 and own your home outright, is to release the cash tied up in bricks and mortar to boost your income with a home income plan. There are two types:

- **mortgage-based schemes** where you get a loan based on the security of your home. The loan is used to buy an annuity from an insurance company. The interest rate and annuity rate are normally fixed at the time you take out the plan. You may be able to take part of the loan as a cash lump sum. While you live, you get the annuity income from which tax and interest on the loan have been deducted. When you die, the loan is repaid out of your estate (possibly by the sale of the home) before inheritance tax is worked out. If the house is occupied by two people (for example, husband and wife, or brother and sister) the annuity is arranged so that it continues for as long as either person is alive.
- **reversionary schemes** which involve selling all or part of your home. In exchange, you get an income for life – or, with some schemes, you simply get the cash to use as you please. While you or your spouse (or sibling or partner, for example) are alive, you retain the right to live in your home. You may also be able to move to another property. The company selling the plan makes its money by buying all or part of your house at a discounted price. The younger you are, the greater your life expectancy, so the greater the discount off your property's market value. In addition, the company benefits from any rise in the value of your home when it is sold after you die. However, if you sell only part of your house under such a scheme, the sale proceeds of the proportion you retain go to your estate.

If you get state benefits, such as income support, a home income plan could mean that you lose some or all of that benefit; so get advice from an independent financial adviser or welfare rights adviser before going ahead.

Investment trusts are, like unit trusts and open-ended investment companies, another form of investment fund. Some adopt a strategy that is aimed at maximising investment income. In addition, split-capital investment trusts divide investment returns to different classes of shareholder. For example, some shares entitle the holder to the returns from growth (i.e. the rise in value of the trust's investments) while other shares give the holders the income earned from dividends. The latter could be suitable for investors wanting to maximise income.

Split-capital trusts can divide investment returns in a variety of sometimes complicated ways and most would-be investors should get advice. Find out exactly how the trust and the income shares work and what the risks are. For more on investment trusts, see Chapter 22.

Direct investment in higher-yielding shares provides a riskier alternative to unit trust, investment trust and open-ended investment company funds (see above).

Instead of investing through a fund, you could invest directly in suitable shares – first getting advice from a stockbroker, if necessary. For more on investing in shares, see Chapter 20.

Guaranteed income bonds, sold by insurance companies, allow investors to lock into a fixed income for up to five or more years, with the return of their capital at the end of the period. For more on guaranteed income bonds, see Chapter 25.

Single-premium investment bonds, sold by insurance companies, offer a range of investment strategies. Some, such as distribution bonds, may be suitable for income-seeking investors. However, the sort of income-producing investments listed above are generally easier to understand in terms of how they work, their tax position and their flexibility. For more on single-premium investment bonds, see Chapter 23.

28 Property as an investment

Over the long term, buying property has proved to be a very good investment. And over the last 20 years, house prices have, on average, outpaced price inflation as measured by the Retail Prices Index (RPI) – see page 17. However, unlike other investments, if the property you have invested in is also your home, it usually generates no income – and unless you are prepared to sell you cannot realise your gains.

This is not the case if you buy property to let. On average, letting property yields an income of 5 per cent a year (after running costs but before income tax). You are also free to realise your capital at any time – although to have been a worthwhile investment, the property would have to have increased sufficiently in value to cover the substantial costs involved in buying and selling as well as any possible capital gains tax bill on your profit.

Is investing in property for you?

Although the income and potential gains compare favourably with other investments, investing in property is a high-risk and time-consuming form of investment. If you want the advantages without the responsibility of property maintenance, consider investing in a specialist property fund in a unit trust, OEIC or in an investment trust that invests in housing.

What type of property should you buy?

You need to decide which area of the letting market you want to target. In any region of the country there is, in practice, a minimum rental rate, so a one-bedroom flat at the bottom of the price range tends to provide a better return on your capital than a three-bedroom house, though it obviously depends on factors such as location. However, depending on the size of your property, your tenants will be different. A one-bedroom flat tends to be sought by young single people for short periods (although for legal reasons the minimum let is usually six months) and your flow of rent may be interrupted when tenants change. A family house may be rented by the same family for a few years – which tends to lower rents. You also need to decide whether you want to let the property furnished or unfurnished.

A holiday home is let on a weekly or monthly basis and (if fully let) provides the highest return. But you will need to consider the additional costs and responsibility of cleaning and laundry before new guests arrive and the length of season it is likely to be let.

Sorting out a mortgage

There are 'buy-to-let' mortgage schemes available to potential landlords. You usually need a deposit of at least 25 per cent of the value of the property. But before you can decide on the size of your mortgage you need to work out the figures carefully. You need to calculate your expected rental income against the cost of the mortgage and allow for all the overheads involved.

You have start-up costs when buying the property such as legal fees and stamp duty. There is no stamp duty on sales of up to £60,000. On sales over £60,000 and up to £250,000 it is payable at a rate of 1 per cent on the whole purchase price, including the first £60,000. On sales over £250,000 and up to £500,000 it is payable at a rate of 3 per cent on the whole price. On sales over £500,000 it is payable at a rate of 4 per cent on the whole price.

You also have ongoing maintenance costs. You should consider the worst-case scenario, i.e. for how long can you afford the property to be sitting empty between tenants? How do the figures add up if interest rates rise? Have you an emergency fund to replace the central heating boiler?

Should you use a rental agency?

Before you buy your property, it is important to research the existing rental market in your chosen area. Speak to a number of rental agencies to see what they offer and check the local papers to see how easy it is to advertise your property yourself. A competent rental agency should help you through the minefield of tenancy agreements and ensure that you draw up the appropriate agreement for your needs. If you decide not to use a letting agent, you need to consider how you will deal with awkward tenants or non-payment of the rent. Agents can manage the property on your behalf and simply send you the rent (net of their charges and maintenance costs). They can also advise you on the local rates for different properties and what aspects of the property will enhance or reduce the level of rent you can expect.

Tax

If rental income from letting property exceeds expenses incurred in earning it, you have to pay tax at your highest rate on the excess. You may also be liable for capital gains tax (see Chapter 10) when you come to sell the property. For more details of how rental income is taxed, ask your local tax office for leaflet IR150.

29 Ethical investments

For many people the only aim of an investment is to get as much return on their money as possible. However, more and more people are now concerned about the use to which the money they have invested is put. As a result, many financial services companies now offer specifically branded 'ethical' or 'socially responsible' investments. The first of these, the Stewardship ethical unit trust, was set up by Friends Provident in June 1984. The total amount currently invested in ethical trusts is £3.51 billion or just over three per cent of the value of all UK unit and investment trusts. However, this represents a growth of 30 per cent over the past 12 months, following a doubling in size the year before. The importances of ethical investments is reflected in the launch (at the time of writing) of a new stockmarket index, FTSE4Good, which tracks the performance of ethically responsible companies.

Financial services companies themselves may have a stated ethical approach to business, such as the Co-operative Bank or the Ecology Building Society. And there are investors who buy shares directly in companies who are demonstrating their ethical concerns by actively trying to influence the actions of directors.

Making your money work on a socially responsible basis has never been easier. Many of the financial products that most of us need during our lifetimes can be linked to an ethical fund. Personal pensions, mortgage endowments, unit trusts, life insurance, critical illness protection and general insurance can all be set up through funds that pursue ethical policies. Direct investments made in very large companies are unlikely to be totally 'clean', particularly if you have strongly held principles. Socially responsible investment does at least allow you to fit your financial decisions more closely to your personal views.

What is ethical investing?

In an ethical fund, ethical considerations influence the choice of investment. Ethical funds tend to be defined in positive terms, with investments only being made in certain sectors (recycling, for example, or community involvement). Some funds are specifically marketed as 'green' or 'environmental' funds. Ethical funds can also be defined in negative terms: your money is not invested in, say, arms manufacturers or companies involved in gambling or pornography.

Positive criteria
Investments are made by selecting companies involved in areas such as:

* conservation and recycling
* community involvement
* environmental protection
* ethical employment practices and equal opportunities
* pollution control
* public transport
* safety and the protection of human life

Negative criteria
Investments are avoided in companies linked with some or all of the following:

* alcohol production/promotion
* animal exploitation
* armaments and nuclear weapons
* biotechnology
* environmentally damaging practices or processes
* gambling
* nuclear power
* oppressive regimes
* poor employment practices
* pornography
* tobacco production/promotion

Note that some funds do not ban investment in any one of these areas completely. Rather they may set limits on the amount of revenue a company can derive from these activities.

People do not have identical ethical priorities. A fund describing itself as ethical may not meet your personal criteria, so make sure you ask for details of the investment strategy to see how well it matches up with your views. The majority of companies offering investments branded as ethical have their own Committee of Reference, which determines investment criteria and gives details in the annual report.

You may also now encounter ethical funds using 'best of sector' criteria. This more flexible approach means that entire sectors are not screened out, but rather that the fund manager chooses the most ethically correct companies in that industry. For example, your money may still be invested in oil companies, albeit 'good' ones – say, those who have a good record of cleaning up oil spills.

You, or your financial adviser, can find out about the practices of different companies through the Ethical Investment Research Service (EIRIS).* This organisation, a registered charity, was set up in 1983 to help people invest according to their principles. EIRIS has a list of ethical funds – mainly unit trusts – and a database of over 1,000 companies whose activities are measured against a wide range of ethical criteria. Both are accessible through the Internet.

Does ethical investment make a difference?

As the number of investors in ethical funds rises, the combined effect of such socially responsible investment may put pressure on companies to move away from solely maximising profits towards balancing profitability with wider social concerns. Furthermore, this rising public concern over company behaviour, say in their treatment of animals or the environment, may make companies less attractive as long-term investments.

The cost of ethics

Your money is no more at risk in a socially responsible investment. Financial institutions or financial advisers offering ethical investments are subject to the same levels of regulation as all other firms in the market. As with all investments, some ethical funds will perform better than others and the value of your investments can fall as well as rise. Consider your investment choices just as carefully as you would any other financial decision and, if in doubt, take professional financial advice.

Some people, however, are nervous of ethical investing, believing that the returns are worse than those from more mainstream funds, which do not place restrictions on the companies they invest in. Clearly it is true that restricting investment to a number of specific areas, or refusing to invest in companies involved in certain sectors, may give you or your financial adviser less room for manoeuvre. It is also worth recognising that, if your ethical criteria lead you to seek investments in organisations committed to, say, organic farming or sustainable energy, you may be directing your money to smaller companies. However, there is little evidence to suggest that ethical funds necessarily perform any worse than funds that do not screen their investments.

In fact, investors in ethical funds may create a virtuous circle. Companies that adopt an ethical or socially responsible commercial policy may find their brand becomes more popular in this more socially conscious age. This in turn boosts share prices leading to better returns for ethical investors.

Check how your preferred fund has fared over, say, the last year and five years, how it rates against other funds of the same type and against an index such as the FTSE All Share Index.

Charges on some ethical unit trusts are commonly pitched around 5 or 6 per cent. This can be higher than on a normal unscreened unit trust, reflecting the extra work entailed in assessing and monitoring the performance of chosen companies.

So, if you want to put your money where your principles are, choose carefully and make sure that you monitor your investment regularly.

Pension funds

In addition to the investment of your own individual savings or choice of a personal pension plan, money can be invested on your behalf through the pension scheme run by your employer. In the 1999 Department of Social Security consultation paper *A New Contract for Welfare: Partnership in pensions*, the government outlined its view that pension funds must consider how their funds are invested. New regulations effective from July 2000 require the trustees of company pension schemes to provide members with information on their ethical investment policy. If the trustees do not have an ethical stance, they must explain why not.

If you are a member of a company pension scheme, you can contact your scheme administrator or the trustees to see if the scheme has any ethical investment guidelines.

Financial institutions

As well as considering where your savings are invested, you may also wish to consider the institution you are banking with. Compared to the growing range of ethical unit trusts and pension funds, choice here is much more restricted.

The Co-operative Bank* has led the way, launching an ethical policy in 1992 and actively seeking to attract ethical depositors. The bank applies a wide range of ethical criteria, including refusing to accept as customers tobacco manufacturers and organisations involved in blood sports, animal fur production or factory farming methods. It also actively supports companies promoting Fair Trade. This policy has been a success for the Co-op but you need to decide if its policy fits with your own personal standards.

In a similar way, the Ecology Building Society* is concerned only with lending on ecologically sound properties. This might include organic farms, energy-efficient properties or small enterprises involved in, say, recycling or crafts. While saving into an account with the society works in the normal way, you can be sure that the Society lends only to promote an ecological way of life. A regular newsletter to savers gives details of where money has been loaned.

Triodos Bank* lends money only to projects that have environmental or social worth, such as organic farmers, people pioneering renewable energy sources, wholefood shops and housing associations. Like a high-street bank, it takes deposits and offers a current account facility.

Shareholder rights

Many people who buy shares directly in companies do so simply as an investment, hoping to make an income from the payment of dividends and a capital gain from the rising value of the shares. In this sense they are 'dormant' investors. However, shareholders are the legal owners of a company, so as an 'active' ethical investor you can try to influence its behaviour.

Shareholders have a wide range of rights, such as attending shareholders' meetings, proposing resolutions and voting on the appointment of the directors. The usual forum for shareholders to voice their concerns is the annual general meeting (AGM). All companies are required to hold an AGM, and all shareholders are entitled to attend, no matter how few shares they hold. It is here that anyone with an ethical stance can make their views known, either through a formal resolution, or through a question to the directors. By exerting pressure in this public way, shareholders with ethical concerns may be able to change the way the organisation operates.

The same applies to mutual organisations of which all borrowers and savers are members automatically.

How to get advice

If you want to make an ethical investment, you can research the products on offer and choose where to invest. Several organisations can help. The Ethical Investors Group (EIG)*, founded in 1989, is a campaigning body for socially responsible investment. It can provide information and advice about ethical aspects of the financial markets. The Pensions Investment Research Centre (PIRC)* acts for financial institutions that use ethical investment criteria and actively campaigns for institutions to exercise their rights as shareholders. The UK Social Investment Forum (UKSIF)* acts to promote and encourage the development and impact of socially responsible investment throughout the UK. The UKSIF runs regular seminars and publishes a newsletter.

However, when making a long-term financial decision, it is usually best to seek some professional advice. Although any authorised financial adviser can give advice on ethical investments, you may wish to approach a firm that specialises in this area. EIRIS can provide a list of independent financial advisers (IFAs) who claim expertise in ethical investing. You can also try the Ethical Investment Association (EIA)*, set up to promote ethical investment and representing a specialist group of IFAs. The EIA can also provide advice, information and screening services. Members are governed by a code of conduct, have regular meetings and conduct their own research. The EIA *Guide to Ethical Investments* includes a guide to charges, a comparative rating of individual funds in terms of their level of ethical screening and the top six ethical funds.

If you want further information, independent financial adviser Holden Meehan have produced a *Millennium Guide to Ethical and Environmental Investments,** which includes a questionnaire to establish an investor's level of ethical concern and general information on investments and funds, including ratings.

Ethical funds

Below is a list of funds that broadly adopt ethical criteria when investing in the stock market. They may not match up to your own criteria and it is up to you or your professional adviser to decide where to place your money.

Abbey Life Ethical Trust
Abtrust Ethical Fund
Acorn Ethical Unit Trust
Allchurches Amity Fund
CIS Environ Trust
Clerical Medical Evergreen Trust
Crédit Suisse Fellowship Trust

Commercial Union Environmental Trust
Eagle Star Environmental Opportunities Trust
Ethical Investors Group Cruelty Free Fund
Equitable Ethical Trust
Framlington Health Fund
Friends Provident Stewardship Fund
Henderson Touche Remnant Ethical Fund
Homeowners Green Chip Fund
Jupiter Ecology Fund
Merchant Investors Ethical Fund
National Provident Global Care
Scottish Equitable Ethical Unit Trust
Skandia Ethical Selection Fund
Sovereign Ethical Fund
TSB Environmental Investor Fund
The United Charities Ethical Trust

30 Alternative investments

The stock market has proved to be the best way to beat the effects of inflation over time. But it is worth remembering that there are alternatives to choose instead of the usual unit trusts, ISAs and shares. These may seem more interesting and exciting – but they often require specialist knowledge and, as different markets develop, are more risky. Crucially, they provide no income.

Some alternative investments have done pretty well compared to the return on an average savings account, but predictably stocks and shares have done the best by far. Alternative investments have almost the same risk as gambling. So, you should really think of them in the long-term and only use surplus cash you can afford to lose.

For example, gold bullion has the image of being the ultimate store of wealth. In reality returns are volatile and over the past two decades gold prices have plummeted. Since 1980 gold has lost about two thirds of its value – prices rose slightly between 1991 and 1996 and since then prices have fallen by about a third, helped in part by the UK government's decision to sell off some of the UK's gold reserves.

Which alternative investment to go for

In 1999 there was over £6 billion invested in alternative investments, with fine art and buy-to-let properties being the most popular. You can start investing in fine wine for around £200. Limited supply plus growing demand is what to look for in an alternative investment. Things like old stamps, Georgian silver and Roman coins are available in limited quantities; there is no way that more can be produced (forgeries apart). So, if more people want to own them, prices increase.

Limited supply, on its own, is not sufficient to make a good investment. For example, limited editions of books or prints which are produced in quantities of a few hundred or a few thousand are unlikely to prove good investments. People must want to buy them in the future.

Nor is a high level of demand enough to make a good investment. For example, many collectors snap up new issues of British stamps. But if several million are issued, it is unlikely they will ever become valuable. For the investor, only stamps in fairly short supply and popular with collectors are likely to gain significantly in value.

Should you put your money in alternative investments?

You should consider investing only part of your savings in this way – no more than 10 per cent, say – and certainly not your emergency fund or money you cannot afford to lose. Bear in mind that:

- because of the expenses of buying and selling, such as auctioneers' commissions or dealers' profit margins, you should really only consider alternative investments if you can invest long term (at least five years)
- money invested in this way will not give you a regular income, and you may have to pay for storage and insurance
- fashions in collecting change; what may have been an appreciating asset ten years ago may no longer be so today. It might be years before you see a profit – if, indeed, you ever do, and you may even lose your money
- you may find it hard to decide what price to ask when you sell, and, unless you sell at an auction, some haggling with buyers is likely to be involved. Going for a quick sale could mean you get a poor price
- alternative investments are not regulated as financial products and there is no ombudsman to go to if something goes wrong.

Alternative investments have one advantage that virtually all other types of investment lack: you can get pleasure out of finding and owning the things in which you invest. Indeed, if you do take an interest in them, you are more likely to invest successfully. Also, if your investments turn out to be unsuccessful, you at least have the consolation of owning an unusual stamp collection or a rock legend's guitar.

In this chapter we discuss a few of the wide range of alternative investments available. Bear in mind that these are included as examples only and we cannot guarantee that they will be profitable investments for you.

How should you invest?

You need to research your subject well before you part with any money, and ideally always invest in something that interests you for its own sake. Read up on the subject, join a relevant society, visit exhibitions, study auctioneers' catalogues, attend auctions – you can often visit the salerooms before the sale begins which gives you the opportunity to make your own estimates – and talk to experts. Make use of the resources of libraries and the Internet.

- Start small. Buy a few items and develop your knowledge before buying more. You can start investing in wine for just £200.
- Shop around. Prices vary and you should not be afraid to haggle. Use only respectable and established companies or dealers and remember to check going rates with experts.
- Watch out for 'get-rich-quick' schemes which are rarely genuine. Your motto should always be 'let the buyer beware'.
- Paying by credit card can give you extra rights if something goes wrong on purchases of between £100 and £30,000.
- Consider investing in things that are collected worldwide so that if UK demand falls, prices are not necessarily reduced.

- Aim for items in very good condition. In general, a couple of items in top condition are a far better investment than several tatty ones.

Ahead of the crowd?

If you invest in things that subsequently become popular with collectors, you can make more money. Do not expect to be right every time (or even most of the time) with this sort of speculation. If you are only in it for the money, and other speculators do catch on, you may need to be quick at spotting when a craze is reaching its height so that you sell before prices start tumbling.

Storage and insurance

Careful storage may be important for things like stamps, wine or paintings. Damp, sudden changes in temperature or the effects of sunlight can reduce (or even wipe out completely) the value of the items you collect.

You also need to insure your valuables against theft or fire. Typically, this might cost from £2 to £15 a year for each £1,000 of cover as part of a normal house contents policy (more if you live in a high-risk area). Cover for valuables varies, typically with a limit of £10,000 or a percentage of the total, often a third. Many house contents policies also offer cover against accidental damage as an optional extra for an additional charge.

Before you decide on a policy, check its terms carefully. There may be an unwelcome restriction, such as a low limit on the amount of cover for individual items. You might prefer to buy a special insurance policy for your collection. *The Which? Guide to Insurance* may help you with this.

If your collection is worth a lot of money (more than a few thousand pounds, say), the insurer is likely to insist on a safe, special locks and burglar alarms. It is also likely to ask for proof of your collection's value, so it is sensible to keep photographs of it, as well as a regularly updated professional valuation. A professional valuer (or a dealer) may charge perhaps 1.5 per cent of the valuation figure given for your collection. Remember to review the level of your insurance regularly.

Alternatively, you could store your collection in a bank's strongroom; insurance may be less if you do this. The bank makes a charge for storage – from £6 to £23.50 a year for an envelope, say, up to £50 a year or more for a bulky item. You may also have to pay an inspection charge of around £5 each time you need to remove your collection. You of course have to weigh up the aesthetic loss of not having your collection around you against the increased security. Some dealers also store and insure the things you buy from them; this may seem the simplest solution but ensure that ownership is clearly documented just in case the dealer goes bust.

What about tax?

Because there is usually no income from investing in physical items, there is usually no income tax to pay (unless the Inland Revenue decides you are carrying on a trade or business and taxes your profits as income).

You may have to pay capital gains tax if you sell your investment for more than you paid for it (less certain expenses). The exceptions to this are wine and racehorses, which are usually tax-free. But, normally, the first £7,500 a year of gains are tax-free (in 2001–2). You also have to pay income tax on any income

315

you get from renting out property. If you hold the asset for a number of years, you may benefit from the taper relief on chargeable gains introduced in 1998. Gains on chattels such as individual antiques, items of jewellery and other tangible moveable objects that you sell for a value of £6,000 or less (unless the items are part of a set with an overall value above £6,000) are also tax-free.

Alternative investments to consider

Wine
Laying down vintage wines has been highly profitable in the past. For example, a case of Châteaux Cheval Blanc 1947 worth £1,000 in 1980 was sold for £24,000 in 2000, and in 1995 a single bottle of Châteaux Margaux 1900 sold at auction for almost £7,000. Never invest more than you are prepared to lose or drink. Any profits you make are free of tax – unless the Inland Revenue believes you have gone into the wine trade.

Vintage wines have to be stored in carefully controlled conditions to maintain their quality and value. So, unless you have a cellar or a wine fridge, you have to pay storage costs to a wine merchant. This costs between £3 and £4 per case (12 bottles) per year, including insurance.

Not all wine produces a high investment. Research and expert help is vital and, as with all alternative investments, deal only with established and reputable companies.

Stamps
Apart from what they cost to use for postage, stamps are intrinsically worthless bits of paper. But they are avidly collected by many people all over the world, some of whom are prepared to pay large sums of money for stamps that are extremely rare or of historical interest.

Stamps which, in the past, have shown some of the largest increases in value have included examples (in fine condition) of rare nineteenth-century issues, sometimes called *classics*. In 1997, an extremely rare Swedish stamp sold for £1.4 million and in 2000 a collection put together by an ordinary collector fetched more than £250,000 at auction. In 1994, Far Eastern stamps, particularly those from Hong Kong, leapt in value as Hong Kong investors sought to put their money in tangibles before the return to Chinese rule.

If you want to invest seriously in stamps, you must know a lot about them – preferably as a hobby first – through studying catalogues and auction results, visiting dealers, joining a philatelic society. Small variations in printing and watermarks, and even the sheet from which the stamp has been torn, can affect the price dramatically. The condition of the stamp is also important. Stamps with printing errors (and, occasionally, forgeries) can be worth much more than ordinary stamps.

It is worth noting that, while collecting new issues and first day covers is an interesting hobby, it has not proved to be a good investment. This is because the market for stamps manufactured solely for the collector is artificial and interest quickly evaporates. Generally, prices raised at auction are more reliable than those quoted by dealers.

Limited editions

Many items are sold as limited editions, for example, silver or gold, plates, porcelain figures and prints. These are produced in one of two ways:

- The number to be sold is specified at the outset – say 500 or 5,000.
- The number sold is the number ordered or bought by a certain date. With this method the total number to be sold (important in evaluating scarcity) cannot be known until after you have agreed to buy.

With some limited editions, the limit mentioned in the advertisement may apply only to the UK; more may be sold in other countries, reducing value for the collectors.

Of course, the investment potential of limited editions depends not only on the number of items produced, but also on the demand for them from collectors. And with many editions, there is little hope of a big demand, even if only a few dozen were issued. Do not buy something just because it is a limited edition. Always choose something you like. You will enjoy owning it and, when you come to sell, potential buyers may as well.

With some limited editions you may find that it is not the limited nature of the item that makes it profitable but the intrinsic value of the material from which it is made. A set of commemorative silver ingots, say, may be worth more for their silver content as scrap when silver prices are high.

Memorabilia

If you are lucky, an interest in collecting memorabilia can produce a healthy investment return. Items such as autographs, programmes and posters can be worth large sums of money if the celebrity they are tied to becomes famous. However, fame is notoriously fickle and there is no guarantee that your prized set of Spice Girls autographs will be worth anything in the future.

Sporting, film and music memorabilia are among the most popular. Memorabilia do not have to be old to be worth something – a corset worn by Madonna was sold for over £11,000 in 2000. The critical factor is that it can be proved that the item is associated with a particular star, sporting team or movie.

The pop world still provides some of the most collectable items, with, rather macabrely, pieces closely linked with dead stars such as John Lennon, Jimmy Hendrix and Elvis Presley being especially valuable. A piano that had simply been played by John Lennon was sold for an incredible £1.45 million in 2000. In 1998 a guitar that had belonged to Jimmy Hendrix was sold at auction for £198,000. If you are beginning a collection now, items belonging to the late Freddie Mercury or Kurt Cobain may appreciate in the future.

The magic of the cinema has made items associated with it collectable. Again, if an actor or film-maker dies, the value of the associated items tends to increase. For example a dress worn by Judy Garland in *The Wizard of Oz* was sold for £200,000 in 1999 and in 2001 a film poster for the Boris Karloff film *The Mummy* was sold for a record price of over £80,000.

Sporting items are becoming increasingly attractive investments. Pre-nineteenth-century golf equipment, for instance, is very rare and a 1830 St Andrews feather-filled golf ball sold for more than £28,000 in 2000. Even clothing worn in historic games can be valuable: in 2000 the shirt worn by Geoff Hurst in the 1966 World Cup Final was sold for over £90,000.

As with almost any alternative investment, an interest in, and knowledge of, what you are buying stands you in good stead, and, no matter how popular or unpopular your 'stars' are, you always retain a stake in their history.

Horses
You do not have to be royalty to own a racehorse but do not expect to become rich from owning one either. You can buy a share in a racehorse for anything between £250 and £24,000 per year. With average prize money as low as £8,000, you are more likely to make a profit from the increase in the horse's value. Any profits you make are usually tax-free.

If you decide to join a syndicate, you need to choose carefully. As with all investments, do your research before you invest.

Buy-to-let
An increasingly popular form of investment is buying a second property to rent out. In 2001 there were about two thirds of a million properties bought as buy-to-let investments.

Any income you make from renting out the property will be subject to tax, less any letting expenses, as will any capital growth. For more detail, see Chapter 28.

Gold
For thousands of years, gold has been looked on as a store of wealth, and many people the world over believe that gold is a good asset to hold in times of political, financial or currency upheavals. If you are tempted to invest in gold, be prepared for a bumpy ride. Even daily fluctuations can be alarming, so gold is not suitable for the faint-hearted. In June 1999 gold prices had slumped to a 20-year low and prices remain low into 2000 and 2001.

Nowadays, you can buy and sell gold in any form. Here we look at buying gold coins (not to be confused with the rare coins that collectors go for) and gold bars. Other ways of investing include buying gold shares (for example the shares of companies that mine gold), buying units in a unit trust that specialises in gold shares and dealing in gold futures.

The main way of buying and selling coins and bullion is through banks, coin-dealers, jewellers and stockbrokers: note that you pay VAT unless your purchases come under a special scheme. Seek tax advice from a VAT expert. VAT is also not payable providing the gold stays offshore (Channel Islands, Isle of Man, for example). The bullion-dealing companies that make up the London Bullion Market Association do not normally deal with transactions for small amounts and the general public. Steer clear of jewellers, too, because they tend to have high mark-ups built into their prices. Note that if you invest via intermediaries such as stockbrokers, you have to pay commission on both buying and selling.

Bear in mind that the price at which a coin or bar is offered for sale is higher than its intrinsic value. On top of gold content you have to pay a *premium* for the cost of manufacture and distribution of the coins: 3.5 per cent is usual for a 1oz coin, 16 per cent for a new half sovereign. Premiums for particular coins fluctuate according to supply and demand. Note that bullion and foreign coins (but not post-1837 sovereigns and Britannias, the latest British gold coins) are liable for capital gains tax.

Few of us can afford to invest in gold bars in their standard sizes (400 troy ounces, around 12.5kg). Much smaller sizes are available, from 1 kg (costing around £6,200 in June 2001) down to a 5g 'wafer' (£31 in June 2001). Very small bars are not usually a sensible investment because the smaller the bar, the higher the premium.

Diamonds

Diamonds have always held a fascination for investors, but they are not a 'commodity' investment like gold or other precious metals. The price of rough and polished diamonds has kept up with inflation since the mid-1950s but has made no significant gain in real terms. The market is dominated by De Beers (it sells about 80 per cent of the world's uncut diamonds). The main interest of De Beers is to release new diamonds on to the market at a constant price.

There are two main ways of investing in diamonds: buying them over the counter or from a diamond investment company.

Buying and selling loose diamonds over the counter seems to make little financial sense. Even if you get good value when you buy (and you have no way of being certain about that), the dealer's mark-up, which can be as high as several hundred per cent, is likely to make diamonds a poor investment even over a ten-year period; and, particularly if you are looking for a sale on the spot, offers from jewellers are likely to be low. Diamonds are valued on the 'four Cs' – cut, colour, carat and clarity – and there are thousands of different categories of quality. Valuing diamonds is a matter of judgement and skill, probably beyond most high-street jewellers' competence.

With diamonds mounted in jewellery, you are unlikely to show a profit on *new* jewellery for a very long time. The investment market for *antique* jewellery is more like that for antique furniture or porcelain, say, than for loose diamonds. Putting antique diamond jewellery into an auction may be the best way to sell.

Information and sales

If you are on the trail of items such as vintage wine, antique furniture or fine art, it is worth contacting the major auction houses like Christie's,* Phillips* or Sotheby's.* You can also contact the Association of Art and Antique Dealers* or the British Antique Dealers Association.* The Wine and Spirit Association of Great Britain* can help if your interest is in vintage and non-vintage wine. If your investment capital is limited, check for antique and collectors' fairs under 'Collecting' in the 'Leisure' section of *Exchange & Mart* (available at newsagents). Local papers give information on auctions and house-clearance sales in your area.

Whatever you are looking to invest in, you are almost certain to find it at one of the many new Internet auction sites. Wines, rock memorabilia, antique furniture, jewellery, paintings and books can all be bought and sold online through sites such as eBay (*www.ebay.com*), QXL (*www.qxl.com*) and yahoo (*www.auctions.yahoo.com*). And these sites give a new meaning to 'alternative' investments: dinosaur bones, fighter aircraft and the Twin Towers from Wembley Stadium are just some of the items offered for Internet sale.

Online auctions work in much the same way as in a conventional auction house, with the web site acting as a link between buyers and sellers. Sellers register the goods they wish to sell, sometimes with a reserve price, and then buyers have a limited time, say a week, in which to bid. While it is estimated that some 20 million people worldwide have taken part in an Internet auction, be careful if you are considering buying online. Pay by credit card because of the extra protection this gives you and try to deal with reputable sites. Clearly the greatest drawback is that you cannot inspect the goods before you buy. So check the auctioneer's web site carefully before bidding, particularly the terms and conditions relating to defective or unsatisfactory goods. Even if you get the goods you want, arranging delivery and completing the paperwork (particularly for cross-border purchases) can be expensive and time-consuming.

Addresses and publications

Advertising Standards Agency (ASA)
2 Torrington Place
London WC1E 7HW
Tel: 020–7580 5555
Fax: 020–7631 3051
Email: inquiries@asa.org.uk
Web site: www.asa.org.uk
Written complaints only

The Annuity Bureau Ltd
The Tower
11 York Road
London SE1 7NX
Tel: 020–7902 2300
Fax: 020–7261 1888
Web site: www.annuity-bureau.co.uk

Annuity Direct
32 Scrutton Street
London EC2A 4RQ
Tel: 020–7684 5000
Fax: 020–7684 5001
Email: enquiry@annuitydirect.co.uk
Web site: www.annuitydirect.co.uk

Antique Collectors' Club
5 Church Street
Woodbridge
Suffolk IP12 1DS
Tel: (01394) 385501
Fax: (01394) 384434
Email: sales@antique-acc.com
Web site: www.antique-acc.com

Association of Chartered Certified Accountants (ACCA)
29 Lincoln's Inn Fields
London WC2A 3EE
Tel: 020–7242 6855 (general enquiries)
    020–7396 5900 (members)
Fax: 020–7831 8054 (general enquiries)
    020–7396 5959 (members)
Email: services.enquiries@accaglobal.com
Web site: www.accaglobal.com

Association of Independent Financial Advisers (AIFA)
Austin Friars House
2–6 Austin Friars
London EC2N 2HD
Tel: 020–7628 1287
Fax: 020–7628 1678
Email: info@aifa.net
Web site: www.aifa.net

Association of Investment Trust Companies (AITC)
Durrant House
8–13 Chiswell Street
London EC1Y 4YY
Tel: 020–7282 5555
Factsheet orderline: 020–7431 5222
Fax: 020–7282 5556
Email: info@aitc.co.uk
Web site: www.itsonline.co.uk

Association of Policy Market Makers (APMM)
Holywell Centre
1 Phipp Street
London EC2A 4PS
Tel: 020–7739 3949
Fax: 020–7613 2990
Email: enquiries@apmm.org
Web site: www.apmm.org

Association of Policy Traders (APT)
Skipton Chambers
12 Market Street
Bury BL9 0AJ
Tel: (08457) 191919 (local rates)
Other tel no: 0161–763 1919
Fax: 0161–797 1919
Email: polreg@cix.co.uk

Association of Private Client Investment Managers and Stockbrokers (APCIMS)
112 Middlesex Street
London E1 7HY
Tel: 020–7247 7080
Fax: 020–7377 0939
Email: info@apcims.co.uk
Web site: www.apcims.co.uk
Written enquiries preferred

Association of Unit Trust and Investment Funds (AUTIF)
65 Kingsway
London WC2B 6TD
Tel: 020–7831 0898
Recorded information request line:
020–8207 1361
Fax: 020–7831 9975
Email: autif@investmentfunds.org.uk
Web site: www.investmentfunds.org.uk

Bank of England
Publications and general enquiries
Tel: 020–7601 4012/4878
Email: enquiries@bankofengland.co.uk
Web site: www.bankofengland.co.uk

General enquiries about gilts
UK Debt Management Office
Cheapside House
138 Cheapside
London EC2V 6BB
Tel: 020–7862 6501

Information about buying and selling gilts
Bank of England Registrar's Department
Southgate House
Southgate Street
Gloucester GL1 1UW
Tel: (01452) 398080
Fax: (01452) 398098
Email:
admin@registrarsdept.demon.co.uk
Web site:
www.bankofengland.co.uk

Booklets and forms
Tel: (0800) 818614

Banking Ombudsman
See Office of the Banking Ombudsman

British Antique Dealers Association
20 Rutland Gate
London SW7 1BD
Tel: 020–7589 4128
Fax: 020–7581 9083
Email: enquiry@bada.demon.co.uk
Web site: www.bada.org

Building Societies Commission
Contact through the FSA

Office of the Building Societies Ombudsman
Contact through the Financial Ombudsman Service

Centre for Non Residents (CNR)
Fitzroy House
PO Box 46
Nottingham NG2 1BD
Tel: (0115) 974 2000
Fax: (0115) 974 1950
Web site: www.inlandrevenue.gov.uk/cnr/

Christie's
8 King Street
London SW1Y 6QT
Tel: 020–7839 9060
Fax: 020–7839 1611
Web site: www.christies.com

The Co-operative Bank
PO Box 101
1 Balloon Street
Manchester M60 4EP
Tel: 0161–832 3456
Fax: 0161–829 4475
Web site: www.co-operativebank.co.uk

Department of Social Security (DSSS)
as of June 2001 is now incorporated into the
Department of Work and Pensions (DWP).
At the time of writing, all detailed
information was still to be found at DSS web
site (*www.dss.gov.uk*)

The Ecology Building Society
18 Station Road
Cross Hills
Near Keighley BD20 5BR
Tel: (08456) 745566
Fax: (01535) 636166
Email: info@ecology.co.uk
Web site: www.ecology.co.uk

Ethical Investment Association (EIA)
Web site: www.ethicalinvestment.org.uk

Ethical Investment Research Service (EIRIS)
80–84 Bondway
London SW8 1SF
Tel: 020–7840 5700
Fax: 020–7735 5323
Email: ethics@eiris.org
Web site: www.eiris.org

Ethical Money Ltd
61a Friargate
Preston PR1 2AT
Tel: (0800) 0188557
Fax: (01772) 558525
Email: info@ethicalmoneyonline.com
Web site: www.ethicalmoneyonline.com

Ethical Investors Group
Greenfield House
Guiting Power
Cheltenham GL54 5TZ
Tel: (01451) 850777
Fax: (01451) 850705
Email: info@ethicalinvestors.co.uk
Web site: www.ethicalinvestors.co.uk

Financial Ombudsman Service
South Quay Plaza
183 Marsh Wall
London E14 9SR
Tel: 020–7964 1000
Fax: 020–7964 1001
Email: financial-ombudsman.org.uk
Web site: www.financial-
ombudsman.org.uk

Financial Services Authority
25 The North Colonnade
London E14 5HS
Tel: 020–7676 1000
Consumer Helpline Tel:
(0845) 606 1234
Fax: 020–7676 1099
Web site: www.fsa.gov.uk

Forestry Commission
231 Corstorphine Road
Edinburgh EH12 7AT
Tel: 0131–334 0303
Fax: 0131–334 4473
Email: enquiries@forestry.gsi.gov.uk
Web site: www.forestry.gsi.gov.uk

H. E. Foster & Cranfield
20 Britton Street
London EC1M 5TY
Tel: 020-7608 1941
Fax: 020-7608 1943
Email: admin@foster-and-cranfield.co.uk
Web site: www.foster-and-cranfield.co.uk

IFA Promotions Ltd
117 Farringdon Road
London EC1R 3BX
Tel: 0117-971 1177
Fax: 0117-972 4509
Email: contact@ifap.org.uk
Web site: www.unbiased.org.uk
For a list of independent financial advisers in your area

Independent Schools Information Service (ISIS)
Grosvenor Gardens House
35-37 Grosvenor Gardens
London SW1W 0BS
Tel: 020-7798 1500
Fax: 020-7798 1501
Email: national@isis.org.uk
Web site: www.isis.org.uk

Institute of Actuaries
Staple Inn Hall
High Holborn
London WC1V 7QJ
Tel: 020-7632 2100
Fax: 020-7632 2111
Web site: www.actuaries.org.uk

Institute of Chartered Accountants in England and Wales
PO Box 433
Chartered Accountants' Hall
Moorgate Place
London EC2P 2BJ
Tel: 020-7920 8100
Fax: 020-7920 0547
Web site: www.icaew.co.uk

Institute of Chartered Accountants in Ireland
Chartered Accountants' House
87-89 Pembroke Road
Ballsbridge
Dublin 4
Tel: 00 353 1637 7200
Fax: 00 353 1668 0842
Email: ca@icai.ie
Web site: www.icai.ie

Institute of Chartered Accountants of Scotland
CA House
21 Haymarket Yards
Edinburgh EH12 5BH
Tel: 0131-347 0100
Fax: 0131-347 0105
Email: icas@icas.org.uk
Web site: www.icas.org.uk

Institute of Financial Planning
Whitefriars Centre
Lewins Mead
Bristol BS1 2NT
Tel: 0117 9345 2470
Has a national register of fee-based financial planners

Insurance Directorate of the Department of Trade and Industry
Contact through the FSA

Insurance Ombudsman Bureau
Contact through the Financial Ombudsman Service
Email: enquiries@theiob.org.uk
Web site: www.theiob.org.uk

Investment Management Regulatory Organisation (IMRO)
Contact through the FSA
Web site: www.imro.co.uk

Investors Compensation Scheme (ICS)
7th Floor
Lloyds Chambers
1 Portsoken Street
London EC1 8BN
Tel: 020–7892 7300
Fax: 020–7892 7301
Web site: www.the-ics.org.uk

LAPADA (The Association of Art and Antique Dealers)
535 Kings Road
London SW10 0SZ
Tel: 020–7823 3511
Fax: 020–7823 3522
Email: lapada@lapada.co.uk
Web site: www.lapada.co.uk

Law Society of England and Wales
113 Chancery Lane
London WC2A 1PL
Tel: 020–7242 1222
Fax: 020–7831 0344
Call for relevant fax number
Web site: www.lawsociety.org.uk

Law Society of Northern Ireland
Law Society House
98 Victoria Street
Belfast BT1 3JZ
Tel: 028–9023 1614
Fax: 028–9023 2606
Emai: info@lawsoc-ni.org
Web site: www.lawsoc-ni.org

Law Society of Scotland
26 Drumsheugh Gardens
Edinburgh EH3 7YR
Tel: 0131–226 7411
Fax: 0131–225 2934
Email: lawscot@lawscot.org.uk
Web site: www.lawscot.org.uk

Money Management National Register of Independent Fee-based Advisers
c/o Matrix Data Ltd
FREEPOST 22 (SW1565)
London W1E 7EZ
Tel: (0870) 0131 925
Web site: www.moneywise.co.uk

National Savings
Sales Information Unit
Blackpool FY3 9YP
General enquiries: (0845) 645000 (calls charged at local rates)
For telephone purchases of premium bonds: (0500) 007007
Fax: (01253) 832025
Web site: www.nationalsavings.co.uk

National Savings ISA Investment Line
Tel: (08000) 921192

Office of the Pensions Advisory Service
11 Belgrave Road
London SW1V 1RB
Tel: 020–7233 8080
Fax: 020–7233 8016
Email: enquiries@opas.org.uk
Web site: www.opas.org.uk

Occupational Pensions Regulatory Authority (OPRA)
Invicta House
Trafalgar Place
Brighton
East Sussex BN1 4DW
Tel: (01273) 627600
Fax: (01273) 627 688
Email: helpdesk@opra.gov.uk
Web site: www.opra.gov.uk

Office of the Banking Ombudsman
Contact through the Financial Ombudsman Service
Email: banking.ombudsman@obo.org.uk
Web site: www.obo.org.uk

Office of the Investment Ombudsman
Contact through the Financial Ombudsman
Service

**Pensions Investment Research Consultants
Ltd (PIRC)**
4th Floor
Cityside
40 Adler Street
London E1 1EE
Tel: 020–7247 2323
Fax: 020–7247 2457
Web site: www.pirc.co.uk
Email: info@pirc.co.uk

Pensions Ombudsman
11 Belgrave Road
London SW1V 1RB
Tel: 020–7834 9144
Fax: 020–7821 0065
Web site: www.pensions-
ombudsman.org.uk
Email: enquiries@pensions-ombudsman.org.uk

Personal Investment Authority (PIA)
Contact through the PIA

**Personal Investment Authority (PIA)
Ombudsman**
Contact through the Financial Authority
Ombudsman

Phillips Fine Art Auctioneers
101 New Bond Street
London W1S 1SR
Tel: 020–7629 6602
Fax: 020–7629 8876
Web site: www.phillips-auctions.com

ProShare Investment Clubs (PIC)
Centurion House
24 Monument Street
London EC3R 8AQ
Information line: 020–7220 1750
Fax: 020–7220 1731
Web site: www.proshareclubs.co.uk

Securities and Futures Authority (SFA)
Contact through the Financial Services
Authority
Web site: www.sfa.org.uk

Society of Financial Advisers (SOFA)
20 Aldermanbury
London EC2V 7HY
Tel: 020–7417 4419
Fax: 020–7600 0766
Web site: www.sofa.org
Write for names and addresses of advisers.
For full contact details and search by subject
area, access web site

Sotheby's
34–35 New Bond Street
London W1A 2AA
Tel: 020–7293 5000
Fax: 020–7293 5989
Web site: www.sothebys.com

Triodos Bank
Brunel House
11 The Promenade
Clifton
Bristol BS8 3NN
Tel: 0117–973 9339
Freephone: (0500) 008720
Fax: 0117–973 9303
Email: mail@triodos.co.uk
Web site: www.triodos.co.uk

UK Social Investment Forum (UKSIF)
Holywell Centre
1 Phipp Street
London EC2A 4PS
Tel: 020–7749 4880
Fax: 020–7749 4881
Email: info@uksif.org
Web site: www.uksif.org

Unit Trust Information Service
Tel: 020–8207 1361
Information request line

Wine and Spirit Association of Great Britain
5 Kings House
1 Queen Street Place
London EC4R 1XX
Tel: 020–7248 5377
Fax: 020–7489 0322
Email: wsa@wsa.org.uk
Web site: www.wsa.org.uk

Publications

Inclusion in this list of publications in no way constitutes an endorsement by Consumers' Association or Which? except in relation to its own publications.

Croner CCH Group Ltd
145 London Road
Kingston-upon-Thames
Surrey KT2 6SR
Tel: 020–8547 3333
Fax: 020–8547 2637
Email: info@croner.cch.co.uk
Web site: www.croner.cch.co.uk

Financial Times Business:
Investors Chronicle/Money Management/
Pensions Management
Maple House
149 Tottenham Court Road
London W1P 9LL
Tel: 020–7896 2525
Fax: 020–7896 2099
Web site: www.ftbusiness.com
www.ftyourmoney.com

Moneyfacts
Moneyfacts House
66–70 Thorpe Road
Norwich
Norfolk NR1 1BJ
Tel: (01603) 476100
Fax: (01603) 476477
Email: enquiries@moneyfacts.co.uk
Web site: www.moneyfacts.co.uk

Money Observer
Subscription Enquiries
Garrard House
2–6 Homesdale Road
Bromley BR2 9WL
Tel: 020–8289 7960
Fax: 020–8402 8383
Web site: www.guardianunlimited.co.uk
Email: guardian@publishing-power.co.uk

Moneywise
Subscriptions Department
Readers Digest
11 Westferry Circus
Canary Wharf
London E14 4HB
Tel: (01858) 438895
Fax: (01858) 432164
Web site: www.Moneywise.co.uk

Planned Savings
33–39 Bowling Green Lane
London EC1R 0DA
Tel: 020–7505 8146
Fax: 020–7505 8186

What Investment
Charterhouse Communications Group Ltd
Arnold House
36–41 Holywell Lane
London EC2A 3SF
Tel: 020–7827 5454
Email: postmaster@charterhouse-communications.co.uk
Web site: www.themoneypages.com

Which? and Which? Books
FREEPOST
PO Box 44
Hertford X
SG14 1YB
Tel: (0800) 252100
Fax: (0800) 533053
Email: which@which.net
Web site: www.which.net

Index

The Which? Guide to Insurance

Insurance – the buying and selling of risk – is big business. Every year consumers spend billions of pounds on their policies. But how much of it do they really need and could they be paying less for any of it?

The Which? Guide to Insurance explains what to take into consideration before buying insurance so that you can avoid under- and over-insuring, and duplicating, and points out what to look for in the small print. It covers the range of policies from house contents and buildings to travel, health and car insurance. It also examines insurance, including life insurance, as an investment.

Using a no-nonsense, step-by-step approach, this guide shows you how to: work out how much insurance you need; buy the right insurance for your circumstances; cut the cost of your current insurance policies; make payments in the most cost-effective way; keep your insurance up to date; and complain if your claim is unreasonably rejected.

Sound, money-saving tips on what to insure and how, plus tried and tested advice on how to take on an insurance company and win, with case histories to illustrate, make this book a great investment for anyone who needs insurance.

Paperback   216 x 135mm   320 pages   £10.99

Available from bookshops, and by post from
Which?, Dept TAZM, Castlemead,
Gascoyne Way, Hertford X, SG14 1LH
or phone FREE on (0800) 252100
quoting Dept TAZM and your credit card details

The Which? Guide to Money

How can you cut the cost of your current account? How do you stop a cheque? Is it worth changing banks – and how do you go about it? What is the cheapest way to pay for things when you're abroad? What is the most cost-effective way to finance your child's education? *The Which? Guide to Money* answers these and many other questions to do with day-to-day spending.

It looks at the basic financial tools you will need throughout your life, such as current accounts, savings accounts and credit cards, and examines the options for: paying bills; renting or buying a home; financing holidays; buying a car; company cars; financial survival as a student; pensions; debt; what to do with a windfall.

Using handy calculators, case histories and tips, this no-nonsense guide will help you keep in control of your money at every stage of your financial life, from first bank account to retirement and beyond.

Paperback   216 x 135mm   448 pages   £9.99

Available from bookshops, and by post from
Which?, Dept TAZM, Castlemead,
Gascoyne Way, Hertford X, SG14 1LH
or phone FREE on (0800) 252100
quoting Dept TAZM and your credit card details

The Which? Guide to Pensions

State pensions are a foundation for your retirement income but will not, on their own, provide enough to fund a comfortable old age. But do the savings you've made so far through company pension schemes or other arrangements put you on track for the retirement you want? *The Which? Guide to Pensions* shows you how to assess the value of your retirement savings and fill the gaps in your retirement planning. It covers, in simple language, all the important issues, such as:

- how much you should save
- what the state will provide
- getting the best from an employer's scheme
- what new stakeholder plans will offer
- choosing the best personal plans
- alternatives to formal pension plans, such as ISAs
- boosting your pension
- pension choices when you change jobs
- aspects relevant to those facing redundancy or divorce
- pension planning in a family context
- tracing old pensions and claiming your pensions once you retire
- how retirement savings and pensions are treated for tax.

Clear explanations, charts, an extensive glossary and numerous examples unravel the mysteries to put you firmly in control of your future.

Paperback   216 x 135mm   336 pages   £9.99

Available from bookshops, and by post from
Which?, Dept TAZM, Castlemead,
Gascoyne Way, Hertford X, SG14 1LH
or phone FREE on (0800) 252100
quoting Dept TAZM and your credit card details

WHICH? BOOKS

The following titles were available as this book went to press.

General reference (legal, financial, practical, etc.)

Be Your Own Financial Adviser	432pp	£9.99
420 Legal Problems Solved	352pp	£9.99
150 Letters that Get Results	336pp	£9.99
What to Do When Someone Dies	176pp	£9.99
The Which? Computer Troubleshooter	192pp	£12.99
The Which? Guide to an Active Retirement	530pp	£12.99
The Which? Guide to Changing Careers	352pp	£10.99
The Which? Guide to Choosing a Career	336pp	£9.99
The Which? Guide to Choosing a School	336pp	£10.99
The Which? Guide to Computers	336pp	£10.99
The Which? Guide to Computers for Small Businesses	352pp	£10.99
The Which? Guide to Divorce	368pp	£10.99
The Which? Guide to Doing Your Own Conveyancing	208pp	£9.99
The Which? Guide to Domestic Help	208pp	£9.99
The Which? Guide to Employment	304pp	£10.99
The Which? Guide to Gambling	288pp	£9.99
The Which? Guide to Getting Married	224pp	£9.99
The Which? Guide to Giving and Inheriting	256pp	£9.99
The Which? Guide to Going Digital	272pp	£10.99
The Which? Guide to Home Safety and Security	198pp	£9.99
The Which? Guide to Insurance	320pp	£10.99
The Which? Guide to the Internet	320pp	£10.99
The Which? Guide to Money	448pp	£9.99
The Which? Guide to Pensions	336pp	£9.99
The Which? Guide to Renting and Letting	336pp	£10.99

The Which? Guide to Shares	288pp	£9.99
The Which? Guide to Shopping on the Internet	272pp	£10.99
The Which? Guide to Starting Your Own Business	288pp	£10.99
The Which? Guide to Working from Home	256pp	£9.99
Which? Way to Buy, Own and Sell a Flat	288pp	£10.99
Which? Way to Buy, Sell and Move House	320pp	£10.99
Which? Way to Clean It	256pp	£9.99
Which? Way to Drive Your Small Business	240pp	£10.99
Which? Way to Manage Your Time -- and Your Life	208pp	£9.99
Which? Way to Save and Invest	464pp	£14.99
Which? Way to Save Tax	320pp	£14.99
Wills and Probate	224pp	£10.99
Make Your Own Will	28pp	£10.99
Action Pack (A5 wallet with forms and 28-page book inside)		

Health

Understanding HRT and the Menopause	256pp	£9.99
The Which? Guide to Children's Health	288pp	£9.99
The Which? Guide to Complementary Medicine	270pp	£9.99
The Which? Guide to Managing Asthma	256pp	£9.99
The Which? Guide to Managing Back Trouble	160pp	£9.99
The Which? Guide to Managing Stress	252pp	£9.99
The Which? Guide to Men's Health	336pp	£9.99
The Which? Guide to Women's Health	448pp	£9.99
Which? Medicine	544pp	£12.99

Gardening

The Gardening Which? Guide to Growing Your Own Vegetables	224pp	£18.99

The Gardening Which? Guide to Patio and Container Plants	224pp	£17.99
The Gardening Which? Guide to Small Gardens	224pp	£12.99
The Gardening Which? Guide to Successful Perennials	224pp	£17.99
The Gardening Which? Guide to Successful Propagation	158pp	£12.99
The Gardening Which? Guide to Successful Pruning	240pp	£12.99
The Gardening Which? Guide to Successful Shrubs	224pp	£12.99

Do-it-yourself

The Which? Book of Do-It-Yourself	320pp	£14.99
The Which? Book of Plumbing and Central Heating	160pp	£13.99
The Which? Book of Wiring and Lighting	160pp	£16.99
Which? Way to Fix It	208pp	£12.99

Travel/leisure

The Good Bed and Breakfast Guide	640pp	£14.99
The Good Food Guide	736pp	£15.99
The Good Skiing and Snowboarding Guide	592pp	£15.99
The Good Walks Guide	320pp	£13.99
The Which? Guide to Country Pubs	576pp	£13.99
The Which? Guide to Pub Walks	256pp	£9.99
The Which? Guide to Scotland	528pp	£12.99
The Which? Guide to Tourist Attractions	544pp	£12.99
The Which? Guide to Weekend Breaks in Britain	528pp	£13.99
The Which? Hotel Guide	736pp	£15.99
The Which? Wine Guide	496pp	£14.99
Which? Holiday Destination	624pp	£12.99

Available from bookshops, and by post from:
Which?, Dept TAZM, Castlemead,
Gascoyne Way, Hertford X, SG14 1LH
or phone FREE on (0800) 252100
quoting Dept TAZM and your credit-card details